LIFE AS IS

LIFE AS IS

An Unorthodox Vision on Life of an
Expatriate from the Former USSR

Dr. Michael Kleenoff

Library of Congress Control Number:		2014908021
ISBN:	Hardcover	978-1-4990-1027-5
	Softcover	978-1-4990-1026-8
	eBook	978-1-4990-1028-2

Rev. date: 05/12/2014

To order additional copies of this book, contact:
Xlibris
1-888-795-4274
www.Xlibris.com
Orders@Xlibris.com
611833

CONTENTS

Introduction...9

Preface...13

BOOK ONE
PEOPLE AND GOD

PART ONE: IS GOD REALLY THERE?

CHAPTER 1:   Religion, Eternity, and God...25

CHAPTER 2:   Spirits, Souls, and the Universe 38

CHAPTER 3:   The Role of Scientists in the Generation
of Belief in God...49

CHAPTER 4:   Deciphering Signs of the Almighty.................................59

PART TWO: STUDYING THE HOLY BOOKS

CHAPTER 5:   Hinduism, Jainism, Buddhism, and Zoroastrianism.......71

CHAPTER 6:   The Bible and Judaism..94

CHAPTER 7:   Christianity as Religion...118

CHAPTER 8:   Islam—The Last Religious Stronghold.........................154

CHAPTER 9:   The Bahá'í Faith..173

PART THREE: STEPS OF EVOLUTION

CHAPTER 10: Reconsidering the Theory of Evolution 185

CHAPTER 11: Steps of Evolution with Genetics..................................222

CHAPTER 12: Steps of Evolution without Reference to Genetics 228

PART FOUR: BEHIND THE THEORY

CHAPTER 13: How Convincing Is the Big Bang?..................237
CHAPTER 14: Unidentified Massive Objects (UMOB)......................257
CHAPTER 15: The Strange Laws of Physics 264

Glossary 271
Afterword and General Conclusion 277

BOOK TWO
HUMAN NATURE

Preface...285

PART ONE: RECOGNIZING THE DIFFERENCE

CHAPTER 1: Mental versus Physical..................................291
CHAPTER 2: Classification 306
CHAPTER 3: Race and Humans...316

PART TWO: THE NETWORK OF SOCIETY

CHAPTER 4: Culture and Society.......................................331
CHAPTER 5: American Society...339
CHAPTER 6: Pro-Choice versus Pro-Life.............................355
CHAPTER 7: Animal Abuse and Sacrifice 359
CHAPTER 8: The Crowd and a Hero 361
CHAPTER 9: On Patriotism and Loyalty 364
CHAPTER 10: On the English Language..............................366
CHAPTER 11: Society and Its Morals.................................368
CHAPTER 12: Rearing Children..387
CHAPTER 13: Drug Users, Willpower,
            and the Power of Addiction 394

PART THREE: ETHNIC GROUPS AND SOCIETIES

CHAPTER 14: The Jewish Paradox..401
CHAPTER 15: Arab Muslims..426
CHAPTER 16: The Israeli-Arab Conflict...438
CHAPTER 17: The Real Russians...452
CHAPTER 18: The Blacks..468
CHAPTER 19: Hispanics in the United States of America....................487
CHAPTER 20: Non-African Blacks Outside of North America...........490

PART FOUR: SOME MORE FEATURES

CHAPTER 21: Few More Thoughts on Some Other
                    Dispositions of Humans..501
CHAPTER 22: Phenomenon of Death...509

Afterword and Final Conclusion...513
Acknowledgment 517
Glossary 519
Bibliography..529
Index 535

INTRODUCTION

Before I decided to write this book, I had to struggle with two main issues:

A. *Why people seek God?*

and

B. *What makes us dissimilar?*

These two questions, relatively unrelated, led me to write in fact two separate books. Yet when the topics were fathomed again and again, an evitable connection between the two became quite obvious.

By the time I was a child of about seven, I had learned that people are different. I struggled to understand what makes some people cruel, angry, and outright malignant. Could that be based on our cultural divergence, experience, and education, or could it be seated in our genes—a "gift" received at birth? I became curious about the ways in which a person's character is connected to the environment in which he or she grew up.

My perplexity was intensified by the fact that I was brought up as an atheist. In my country of birth, I was taught that "religion is the opiate of the people." Denial of religion was one of the main dictates of the Bolsheviks. There were to be no tsars and no god. Communism was the perfect substitute for both, meeting all the needs of all the people born within the limited borders under the unlimited power of the comrades. People were told how they must feel, think, and understand happiness; what they were allowed to possess; and how much they could keep of what they earned. They also learned that they should not pray anymore nor praise any God.

To complicate matters, I was born as a Jew. Never mind that my roots were sprouting from Indo-European ancestors. Real inheritance aside, I had to assume my parental lineage, and that fact was immediately imprinted on my government-issued birth certificate, where among main characteristics, such as the surname and the given name, the next and most important feature was the declaration of the nationality of the bearer. Thus, I was pronounced "Jew."

Jews were marked as such on the passports issued in the Union of Soviet Socialist Republics (USSR) as well. This mandatory document was something we had in common with all citizens, of course. The only difference was that being a Jew was not cool. The passport, the next obligatory document issued at age sixteen, had to be kept handy and shown in the event one needed to apply for a job, move to a new place of residence, rent an apartment, or enroll in a professional school or university. It was used in any and all official and semiofficial transactions, and it had one purpose: to tell an official in charge how to react toward the bearer of the document—99 percent out of all cases, based on his or her ethnic background.

So because I had no religion—as I was constantly reminded—I considered myself an atheist who happened to be Jewish by origin. I accepted both labels without grave thought to this issue.

When I came to the United States—a country of myriad religious beliefs—and became acquainted with people of a different upbringing, I gradually realized that I was not an atheist, because as an atheist I must completely deny the existence of any god. For me, that was nonsensical. Instinctively, I felt that God might exist, but I could not know that for certain.

Having a desire to rediscover my Jewishness, I began to study the Bible. I went a few times to a synagogue, and made the acquaintance of a number of fellow Jews. Unfortunately, I didn't develop a sense of belonging. This was not because I felt animosity toward the American Jews I met. On the contrary, I enjoyed talking to my new brethren, but that did not automatically stretch toward conformation of God's existence. And in my case specifically, it didn't extend toward the god of Jews.

Thus, I began to consider Christianity as possible more succinct direction towards embracing God. This time I went to a church and began to listen to the services of a preacher as well as tried to pay more attention to the televangelists on TV.

Yet my discovery of a new world didn't envelop me as new reality. I had a hard time accepting this unknown realm as truthful and without subtle premonition that people are guided to it by both their preacher on one side and the desire and willingness of the parishioners on the other.

Tragically, I began to appreciate a fact that I simply did not feel the need to affiliate with any of the religious groups here because they did not reflect my way of thinking. Apparently, the Soviet propaganda machine had fulfilled its purpose.

I came to the reluctant conclusion that I might be close to become an agnostic. In other words, while I had no proof of it, I was willing to consider the *possibility* that God existed. Paradoxically, that brought me to an awareness that the more I thought about it, the more I desired to either prove the existence of God or disprove it—by whatever evidence I would be able to gather for or against. With that in mind, I began writing this book, the substantial part of it devoted to that deepest of all questions: Does God really exist?

PREFACE

This book is unusual on many levels. It presents itself as being a religious advocacy of accepted traditions when it is not. It is strongly in support of recognizing the differences in people, and it is not in the boat of some promoters of conflation of all people. At the same time, this book is an attempt to show how people can not only tolerate each other but also live together without many conflicts. While this book is mostly presented not as written instructions, as can be encountered in some academic works, after reading it, one may have a fairly decent understanding of *who* we are and *how* we might continue to survive.

When I decided to write such a book, I very well recognized how improbable must be a writer (me), 33 years of whose were spent in the former Soviet Union far from being a writer, who had formal medical education totaling 13 years (accumulative result of which, was three medical Diplomas), and who devoted another 25 years treating hundreds of different people of many walks of life. To top it all, an American English became my second language, when I achieved quite mature age of legal and not very young adult.

My interest in and study of American history, therefore, was coming slowly and not as a priority in the light of demanding requirements on the subjects in the medical field.

Fortunately, owing my professional exposure to many Americans, and, none predicted, relocating from state to state, I managed to learn some curious features of people blended in an American society.

With regard to my interest in writing, it was always with me since the early age of eight, when I wrote my first novel and which, unfortunately, is now gone.

When I finally decided that I am ready to write this book, I approached the retirement age, surprisingly not feeling completely exhausted but mostly invigorated by the thought that ending my medical carrier opens literally an inconceivable opportunity for me.

I began to accumulate books, special literature, articles published on the Internet, and, of course, many English dictionaries. It was a slow yet not painful process which let me succinctly realize that I am as happy as those Americans who may pursue their goals without asking themselves would they be successful and would their achieved goal be financially rewarded. I also realized that the topic(s) I've chosen were not the easiest one(s). I had to consider the possibility that a reader might at first glance believe that this is one unwieldy and thus boring book not deserving much attention. Yet when I've read and reread it (not once or even twice, I might add), it didn't present itself to me as dull or as an unsophisticated book. True, the topics are hugely diverse, and while not too many people are normally interested in some of the subjects presented here, on the whole they should concern *everybody*. Having said that, I would recommend that the inquisitive reader conduct a small experimental reading on an article in which he/she might be interested. In case you find it reflective of your query, there also may be a chance that some other articles contain the answers to a question or two you might have.

While combining so many debatable matters, I was often on high alert that elucidation of each topic will undeniably be insufficient, as each demanded a substantial discussion. At the same time, I realized that not too many people would be able to swallow that much information at once. Having that in mind, I recognized that this is not a novel or a romantic book. It is not exactly a collection of monographs or a thesis or a schoolbook either. One might see it as a philosophical memoir without presenting it in an academic, standardized narrative. To make the raised questions in the book not only sound curious but also answerable by clear and substantiated answers, I had to consider concise and corollary approach.

Another peculiarity that came into existence while this book was written appeared as an inability to reproduce most details read and understood but with elapsed time vaguely remembered. I simply didn't have time to memorize and come into a firm possession of achieved knowledge. Thus, I often provided my own views seemingly without basing them on exegetical scholarship on the subject.

Developing an outline regarding possible existence of a supreme being, I noticed that topics not connected to the existence of God would frequently pop up. I came to appreciate that they needed to be addressed. For that reason, investigating each topic separately and without artificial pulling God in to it, I kept my mind on the potential role of God, many times questioning God's existence.

The first half of the book is mostly devoted to that particular theme, the possible reality of God. The curious thing, however, that came to me was that the god portrayed by people could not exist. Not in the form and shape in which people described God might be nor in any personal intervention people had been insisting on, as it was allegedly taking a place.

In addition to the long-surviving stories of "eyewitnesses" and the accumulated knowledge of people based on "historical facts," or those stories told by separate sects and religious schools, there were the doctrines and somewhat related holy books. The latter, especially the holy books, were an "official" authority on the topic, and that awareness alone required further investigation.

But as soon as I began to study this multitude of denominations, I became enveloped in the notion that most, if not, all major religions were dampened by significant flaws. I attempted to analyze why did I feel that, why those religious beliefs could not be acceptable by me. I tried to weigh why I perceived them as wrong and why their doctrines might be unacceptable to most nonbelievers. I tried to understand the reason why each newly created denomination had drifted apart from the rest while pursuing one visible goal: to appreciate one powerful God.

I have also devoted a few segments to the discussion of biological and genetic signs that could be argued as evidence for or against God. Given this approach, I couldn't avoid a discussion of evolution and the nature of the cosmos. Realizing the depth of knowledge that these last two topics would require, I in no way wish to mislead the reader to think I have a special background in physics and evolution. Having said that, I do not wish to give the wrong impression either, that I simply followed my logic and analysis without dissecting the main articles and works in each considered field.

Common wisdom might dictate that to write a book on the epistemology of the existence of God, one should be either a scientist or a theologian or both, suffice to say that I possess neither of these credentials, despite the fact that such subjects as are anatomy, biology, and genetics, were fairly easy recognizable to me. This, of course, had put me in quite a precarious position. First of all, how could one persuade the next fellow human to consider, become curious, and believe or be interested in hearing from someone unknown, someone who is not an accepted or recognized authority on a subject? How does one try to prove anything—especially of such magnitude as the actuality of God—without academic or scientific affiliation with any recognized school of thought in that field?

In this case, I felt it was a plus that I didn't have to cater to any scientific organization in order to win their approval. I didn't have to try to reach the "proper" conclusion as defined by any particular camp.

Of the presented historical facts, there were many I had to repeatedly analyze myself because I wanted to set forth an independent viewpoint rather than rephrase what had been previously written.

The first thing I did was to look among my personal acquaintances for those who—in my mind—seemed to have come upon answers to life's questions or at least seemed close to finding them. They were few, but their knowledge and advice about possible sources of information was immensely valuable to me.

As this no doubt was utterly inadequate, I began to study the Holy Bible, using it at first as a main source that allowed me to learn about the ancient Hebrews and the original Christians. To my surprise, I have learned that the god described in the Old Testament quite often interfered with humans, laying down laws and prescribing punishment for disobedience. Sometimes this god even recommended or participated in everyday tasks of humans. The god described by the Jewish sages was capricious, vindictive, jealous, and punitive—at least, by present-day standards.

The god that was presented in the New Testament, on the other hand, was often portrayed as soft and mild, almost always just, and not particularly vindictive. The Christian god came to be identified with Christ—Almighty Father to the Son of Man—and, later, as part of an indivisible Trinity.

Yet I also became increasingly aware that Christians for a long time were mostly uncertain who their god is. Their faith since its dawn was directed not to follow Jesus's teachings as much as to prove his divinity.

Reading the Qur'an, I realized that Muslims portrayed their god, Allah, as the only god who had ever existed. They assumed a rigorous task to prove that Allah, whose name is just the generic name for god, despite later incoming on the scene of religious history, is the God for all humanity. According to Islamic traditions, Allah—through the last Prophet Muhammad—gave his followers scriptures that could not and should not be added to or changed in any way. Among all the themes this god heeded, Allah was greatly concerned with justice.

After familiarizing myself with these three major religions, I encountered an unpleasant feeling that people, not god, place limitations, rules, and insurmountable obstacles prohibiting the other group to blend in to become one people for God.

The many gods of the Greeks were versatile and adventurous, joyful, and often had sexual intercourse with humans, giving their demigod children immortality and supernatural powers. There were also many different Egyptian gods and the Supreme Spirit of the Hindus, as well as the amorphous god of the Persian Zoroastrians— Ahura Mazda, the god of life and wisdom.

I also learned of the large number of internal variations within the Buddhist philosophy and, finally, of the recent development of the Bahá'í Faith, which sprang from the Muslim faith in much the same way that Christianity sprang from Judaism.

To reach a proper conclusion, I had to not only assay the descriptions of God of separate religions but also try to understand if these are actually different gods or if the same deity is described by different sectarian groups.

One powerful thing driven home to me during this process was that the world itself is quite old—billions of years old, according to contemporary science. Out of this recognition came a barrage of questions:

- Has this appreciation of God or gods influenced the events of humanity since its earliest days on earth or just for the last few thousand years? Has God or gods changed since man found them?
- What of the previously existing hominids whose distant history is vaguely mentioned in known records? Where did they go?
- What of other life-forms on the planet—the fish of the seas or the birds of the air or the long-gone creatures that inhabited the earth somewhere between sixty-five and five hundred million years ago? Who were their gods, if any?
- Are we kindred creatures or fundamentally different?
- Why did humans not appear for such a long time after other forms of life had appeared?
- Would we be able to understand each other if we were to meet?
- In what shape and form might we show in "another" life, if our body is destined to rot and dematerialize?
- If God does exist, what role does he play in the universe so vast and so little known to us?

As odd as some of these questions may seem, I had to pose these and similar questions in order to write this book about our past, our present, and the assumptions about our future life.

From time to time while writing this book, I made use of technical descriptions of events or processes. I did this with an eye to simplicity, although I went into detail in some cases, especially in chapters 4, 10, and 13, in order to clarify my thought processes. If these chapters are difficult to follow, it is not a *must* to read them to have a general idea of the themes presented. Only those who seek broader and more substantial knowledge may want to get into the intricate minutiae.

For the last one hundred or so years, science has made huge progress in defining multifold natural events in the world. Hundreds of occurrences that took place and that people happened to interpret according to their knowledge came about since the beginning of this world. Science, as a body of knowledge, is probably the most versatile of all the disciplines and subjects existing in the world. What is today accepted as dogma tomorrow might be completely disproved by new experiments, which scientists are not ashamed to acknowledge.

—

Yet in going through the endless various articles, I noticed that a hidden agenda lies behind each essay accepted by the establishment—a shadow of the particular standard that the scientific world would have to be able to approve. That discouraged me somewhat, especially when, in my mind, what was explained in such an article was not convincing enough to earn indisputable recognition. In order to find a proper and satisfying conclusion, I began to look for a number of disparate sources. There were countless that I recognized as proven, yet still were not always fully convincing.

This has forced me to seek my own truth, so instead of quietly agreeing with what was accepted dogma, seeking my own truth is what I did.

I wish to emphasize that if I ever veered away from established definitions of scientific, philosophical, or religious terminology, it was not done with malicious intent. I simply felt that those few descriptions with which I didn't agree were neither sufficient nor accurate.

In doing this, I did not plan to upset anyone, and I sometimes wondered if my bluntness would do more harm than good. My intent was to provide a healing balsamic potion, not a burning acid. Finding that balance, turned out to be the most difficult task in writing this book.

The second part of this work is mainly devoted to human beings, our nature, and our role in the society in which we live.

While we are all joined as one species, we are unique in a sense that no one person is an exact copy of any other. Any trait, no matter how similar it may seem, still manifests somewhat differently in each of us. This can inadvertently produce a misreading of a character or of motives for a particular behavior.

Once again, questions, as they became the norm for the style of this book, began to pile up anew.

- What motivates people?
- Why are we constantly preoccupied with finding a solution?
- Why does problem solving excite us?

As one can see, the tons of questions that were raised in this book were not necessarily the original ones as well as a number of historically existing answers. Nevertheless, I attempted to provide my own vision in the form of the answers that I came to and that not always coincided with those that exist today.

One more clarification that I believe will be appropriate in this preface: keep in mind that this book is written by an outsider. I have not intended to talk down to any group of people or purposely and with malicious intent use insulting language. The nontraditional narration that the reader will no doubt encounter must be appreciated based upon the knowledge that I am not an American writer. Those expressions or words that were used in a nonstandard manner were simply that and were not intended to offend.

The nonfiction genre demands great attention to detail. To thoroughly learn the structure of any particular society requires many corresponding circumstances and conditions, one of which is to be physically present in that society; the earlier in life this process begins, the better the results will be. It is one thing to understand, and it is another to absorb—or more precisely, to feel the network of the functioning body. One can see it, but only those who were born into the place and grew up in it may be able to "sense" it. Still, writing this book has filled my life with the joyful realization that there is no need to pretend, to unnecessarily hope for miracles, or to live in fear of an unavoidable end. With such an attitude on my side, any shadow of a doubt disappeared: I know I am doing the right thing in undertaking this process of self-discovery.

I hope I may inspire others to take a similar journey with me. With that in mind, let me humbly and with trepidation begin this chronicle.

BOOK ONE

PEOPLE AND GOD

PART ONE

IS GOD REALLY THERE?

CHAPTER 1

Religion, Eternity, and God

First of all, let me comment on why I will pose more questions than answers. This is quite natural, as we don't always know what we think we know. For example, history has shown many attempts to provide the correct answers to our existence and purpose. Yet digging into those subject matters, people came to realize that answers provided must often be reconsidered. To add to it, human design—however rigorous a process through which it went—has produced a complicated biological machine which in turn placed us in a constant state of ambiguity and doubt.

With regard to religion, one may ask such questions as

- Why do we need religion at all?
- What good or bad does it bestow?

We may also ask

- Are we foolish to desire to live forever?
- Can we sustain an eternity while possessing our rampant emotions?

Finally, we may ask such a profound question as

- Does God exist only in our imagination, or is his presence real?

These are not simple or easy questions to answer. In any event, our answers are ultimately connected to our beliefs—specifically, to those we call religious beliefs. For that reason, I feel that I should start by defining "religion."

According to the *American Heritage Dictionary*, religion is the "belief in and reverence for a supernatural power or powers, regarded as creating and governing the universe. A personal or institutionalized system grounded in such belief and worship."

According to the *Catholic Encyclopedia*, religion is the "voluntary subjection of oneself to God." And in *Webster's Third New International Dictionary*, "Religion is the personal commitment to and serving of God or a god with worshipful devotion, conduct in accord with divine commands esp. as found in accepted sacred or declared by authoritative teachers, a way of life recognized as incumbent on true believers, and typically the relating of oneself to an organized body of believers <ministers of~>."

The *Oxford English Dictionary* says the following: "Religion is an action or a conduct indicating a belief in, reverence for, and desire to please a divine ruling power."

These are but a few of the most popular and accepted definitions in the Western world of contemporary religions. There are, of course, many others, some of which I will speak of later in this book.

Religion has been transformed many times in the last ten thousand years or so. As far as we know, at the dawn of history gods were often portrayed in animal forms that from our modern point of view, connects them more to the mythic than to the real. One could say that our understanding of that past view of deity suffers from a lack of relevant evidence and knowledge, as we don't find enough archaeological or historical documentation to draw ready conclusions about the nature of animal deities. We cannot always tell, for example, whether the animals themselves were worshipped as gods or whether they were merely symbolic of certain gods because of perceived qualities.

There are many unknowns as well in what exactly motivated people to believe in forces of nature, as one cannot categorically declare that it was connected to simply human ignorance.

In that regard, we can point to one of the major organized religions in Japan today—Shinto—in which gods are shown mostly as *kami*, which means spirits that inanimate elements of nature possess. This religion of the Japanese people is actually a guide to the system of beliefs and traditions that the people of Japan follow in life.

To generalize at this point, one might say that it is hard to determine if religion came about because of a natural fear of the unknown, the mystical respect human beings developed for creatures, a growing desire to live forever, some other motives, or a combination thereof. The scriptural record, of course, tells us that it was God who spoke first—that he communicated with us through his emissaries (among other means) and that religion is our response to that communication.

Originating from the Latin word *religio* (to bind together), religion has focused on providing meaning for our existence on earth. That may be the most powerful tool religion possesses and the reason why it absorbs billions into its ranks. Part of this search for meaning involves the idea that God loves us, and therefore a proper response is to love him in return. Many religious denominations stress that this love of God for man is unconditional without immediate elucidation of what that means.

In exploring the question: "Why does God want us to love him?" I considered a number of unusual answers. Here, let me remind you that being from a formerly communist country, I had not experienced religion as people outside that carefully manufactured culture may have experienced it.

I grew up amid Marxist teachings, which posited that religion is a tool for keeping people subdued, obedient, and submissive. Marxism didn't acknowledge that people *voluntarily* accept the tenets of faith or love for God. It did not explore the idea that people might feel joy in realizing their connection with God and his powers. It directed us through calculated propaganda into "proper" thinking, i.e., that we would be happy if we did not believe in God. It taught us to derive our beliefs about happiness and our joy in life without any yearning for some supreme Unknown. Yet we had been constantly molded to reach an indisputable paradise named communism.

Therefore, to a nonbeliever like me, this all-embracing kind of love flowing between mankind and an invisible, unidentified, and unimaginable power did not induce me in to any assurance whatsoever. I, naturally, ended up with questions: Why would God need my love? Why would he need to be appreciated? Why would he even care if we

—

loved him or not? What difference could that make to God whatever or whoever he is?

I would not argue the point that it is quite possible that if we learn how to love God, it might simultaneously teach us to love each other and therefore help us to become more engaged in reciprocal relationships. But that would mean that religious advocates had been preoccupied with a hidden agenda. An immediate question that would come up then was would such teachings be effective if the object of our love was not God but some inanimate thing that had no connection to our hope for eternal life? Is immortality of some sort the ultimate reward of religion?

Religion also teaches us that we were created in God's image. That would mean that humans had formed an image of God much earlier than one might realize. That would also suggest that God must love us if he made us according to his form (whatever one construes that to mean). Did he need to have billions of tiny gods? Could God literally have the physical shape and form as we do? Can he afford such powerful emotions as love? And why did he make us anyway?

With such questions in mind, let me begin to play devil's advocate.

I have a picture in my head of the staggering number of people on this planet—a number that has increased with most centuries since the beginning of our species. According to some sources, only fifty years from now, the human population will number roughly ten billion people. This figure would not be an exaggeration despite the possibility of catastrophic wars or pandemic killer diseases and famine and, consequently, death from hunger. Avoiding those, we would have end up with even larger numbers.

Thus, highlighting the earth's overpopulation might sound mighty reasonable as there is no way that such huge number of people could be sustained. Shouldn't God have foreseen that sort of an inconvenience? Even if we were recycled (reincarnated)—in which case, we might not be growing in similarly corresponding numbers of souls—it would hardly accomplish anyone's desire to save humans. Also comes to mind is the question, why do we believe that we are coming back? Would fallen leaves from a tree come back to life at any point in the future? Would a myriad of withered flowers return again? Would now gone wild or domesticated animals come back too?

These kinds of questions might be too vague to consider at once, so I will revisit them from time to time in the course of this book.

—

But the question pertaining to why God would accumulate our souls or our bodies seems legitimate to me. We live on earth, we die on earth, and yet for one reason or another we wish to be accepted someplace else.

Can that sort of a wish be justified?

In an attempt to answer some of the questions raised here, let's start with a description of what (or who) is God.

I'll begin this discussion by confessing that I myself do not have a clear and precise answer. I've come to the conclusion that through my analysis I am very close to the "truth." But that's about it. After reading this book in its entirety, one may definitely appreciate the vision I have. Yet at this point, it would be more appropriate for me to disagree with some of the most prevalent ideas about what God is than to agree with them, especially after reading such pronouncements as "And you will seek Me and find *Me,* when you search for Me with all your heart" (Jeremiah 29:13, 14a NKJV 1982).

Scripture is one attempt to give evidence that God is here with us. Another avenue of search is to find indirect signs of God, if such exist. Those signs might be literally endless if we consider the complexity of observed events, interrelated systems, entities, and objects found not only in our galaxy but in the universe as a whole. Most of them obviously belong to the realm of physics where theories are built upon extrapolating what we do not know from what we *do* know or *think* we know.

In consideration of how the indirect signs might be connected to an unknown yet perfect designer we call God, we need to go into detail, and this will be the topic of the following chapters. The main problem that arises is, of course, that there is not one universally accepted definition of God. People from different societies, diverse cultures, philosophers, scientists, and theologians all have something to bring to the discussion, ascribing to God distinct conceptions they accept as dogma or fact.

It is also quite possible that, because of human limitations, we are destined never to find out what God might actually be or how he operates. We are limited in our ability to know and to study even the material things that are readily available to us, let alone something immaterial—something that may not even be the same sort of being that we are or bound by the laws by which we are bound. At best,

—

we can only make assumptions, hypothesize, or theorize based on scientific or not-so-scientific methods.

So let's see why the existing descriptions of God are quite naturally perceived as illogical and naïve among civilized minds in the contemporary world.

In Western theology, we derive our knowledge mainly from holy books, such as the Old and New Testaments of the Bible and the Qur'an. Without being afraid of repeating many points said before me, I will not simply say that these sources of knowledge are controversial, but there is no other way to speak about these books than to show how incongruent so-called facts and events were presented in those books. To begin, I must say that when any of these sources were compiled and handed down orally and then finally written, people "knew" that the earth was the center of the universe, in spite of an idea that had existed since the time of Aristarchus (an ancient Greek astronomer and mathematician, ca. 310-230 BCE) that the earth revolves about the sun. But until Nicolaus Copernicus—a Polish priest and astronomer—that idea was not widely considered in the Western world.

The assumption that we were at the center of the universe, which informed our sense of importance, was based on a false premise. We suddenly learned that we were not the center of anything. Our galaxy, the Milky Way, contains billions of stars. Our sun was but one, and our planet turned out to be a minuscule one of many. To add to this picture, galaxies like ours are common—they can be counted on a scale of billions as well—four hundred billion according to the latest count.

So our earth—that playfully titled "third rock from the sun"—is a tiny, almost invisible planet, smaller than a pebble in the vastness of the cosmos. In that vastness, can one picture a God—though omnipotent, omniscient, and so forth—who would live on or near earth and watch each and every creature every hour of every day, year after year, millennia after millennia, as well as consciously handle all the existing laws and structures of the universe without overextending himself?

Just picture yourself in an airplane for a moment. How many structures, small details below can one see? Now imagine people in these structures. Or as another example, picture a huge crowd of people gathering in squares, stadiums marching in for different events. Can one, after visualizing the expressions of their faces, also know what thoughts will appear in their heads and predict the expected further moves? Would God allow himself to be busy with distinguishing the people, happening events, people's thoughts and motives, along with consideration of the movements of the planets, galaxies, and other cosmic structures?

If not, how about a god who is watching and protecting and judging each of us constantly, without any ability to relax, because this kind of job demands no slackening whatsoever?

That particular type of god, in order to rule us, would have to be preoccupied with every millisecond of our plans. Isn't it a ridiculously childish desire even to be considered briefly? Forget about the United States of America. Think globally. Think of continents and countries. Think of Australian aborigines and indigenous people in different places. Think of the seven or so billion people in the world. That's a lot of people of whom to keep track.

But, of course, if God is the ruler of the universe, then it doesn't end there. Think of the fish in the seas and of fauna and flora. Think of the other stars and planets. Think of possible life in other galaxies. Think of spirit and of the other matter beyond our solar system.

Aren't we exaggerating our importance on the cosmic scale?

Behind that postulate lie so many different theories and assumptions. Where does God stay or live? Does he have a place he calls home? Does he need one? Does he exist as a Great Spirit? Can he function in a physical world as a spirit? Does he need the brain or another apparatus of thought to function in a spiritual way? How can he influence the stars, the cosmos, or us? How can he set the temperature of a star? Can God be stretched to be here and there and everywhere at the same time? Can he conversely be a person?

So let's once again refresh the definition of God:

- The supreme or ultimate reality
- The incorporeal, divine Principal ruling over all as eternal Spirit
- The indescribable, uncreated, self-existent, eternal source of all reality and being
- The Creator, Preserver, and Destroyer of all that is

—

- One member of a divine Trinity that is almighty and all knowing
- Intelligence that is, in some way, beyond the things it has created, even as it supports them, and whose essential quality is love
- Divine educator, parent, friend, and lover

Some even say that God speaks to them constantly. Others insist that God points out his path in most secretive ways and only the one who listens will hear him and understand. Still others argue that we need to accept our belief in God because it is common sense to do so.

It is also quite possible that we are limited in our ability not only to know and to study the material things that are readily available to us—we are definitely deprived to understand something immaterial—something that may not even be the same sort of being that we are or bound by the laws by which we are bound. At best, we can only make assumptions, hypothesize, or theorize based on scientific or not-so-scientific methods.

THE TWO CAMPS

Given our seemingly disparate nature, it is no wonder that many of us see the situation as black or white. That creates the conditions when people find themselves in diametrically opposed camps. One belongs to a creationists' camp; another accepts Darwin's theory of evolution, denying the role of any special designer. Not surprisingly, representatives from both sides have firm beliefs in their correctness, yet there are inherent deficiencies in the logic of both groups. Neither theologians nor scientists have so far provided any real proof that would point to indisputable facts that would end these arguments once and for all. Not surprisingly, both teams believe they are right, and this belief is satisfactory to them.

Why they think they are right is its own story, stemming from faith, persuasion, hubris, or what have you. I'll touch on the possible thought processes of specific groups of people in the second part of this book. For now, I'd like to repeatedly ask that same deep and much-asked question: What might God be?

—

To no one's surprise there are many arguments *against* the belief in God. These generally fall into three major categories:

Empirical arguments: These are directed toward an inconsistency of facts relating to the interaction of God with humans, including those narrated in the scriptures.

Selective arguments: These are based upon the reasons why God could not be what humans desire him to be in their constantly changing concepts of society. These are the type of arguments my communist teachers used to explain why there was no reason for the universe to have a god.

Subjective arguments: These are based on a subjective denial of the existence of God—i.e., personal reasons for not believing in a particular version of God.

My experience, or lack thereof, with the "God concept" nevertheless filled me with even more questions:

- How do we know what God wants us to do?
- Did he design us to become his puppets or slaves?
- Why would we believe that God protects us in particular situations?
- Why do natural disasters—disasters unrelated to human behavior or activity—strike without warning?
- Why are human beings—especially children—stricken with terminal illness?
- Why are we confronted with mass deaths, not connected to the behavior of people, but striking like pandemic disease?

These were not just the questions that may simply hang out in the air. I attempted to answer them in order to understand the possible presence and role of God. At times, I felt some of them were satisfactorily resolved, while some eluded resolution.

In any event, the following is my attempt to answer what I felt I knew.

RECOGNIZING THE ORIGIN
OF CONTEMPORARY RELIGIONS

Our knowledge of what we should do in regard to requests from God comes largely from our religious leaders. Can we trust them? Shall

—

33

we quietly and calmly agree with them and not question their sincerity, through fear of blasphemy? Shall we take it on faith that we should trust the authority of those who may promise paradise and the continuation of life after death, or should we rather ask from where they derive their authority and demand proof that such authority even exists?

Let's take the dawn of Christianity for example. One of the earlier organized groups of Christians was the Ebionites. This name was thought by Origen to originate from the Hebrew word *evyon* (poor).

Ebionites were Jewish Christians who believed that Jesus was the Messiah and adopted Son of God. For that reason, the Ebionites were also called Adoptionists. The claim that Jesus was the adopted Son of God was derived from the words of Psalm 2:7, which the author of the books of Acts and of Hebrews links to the appearance of Jesus: "I will declare the decree: The Lord has said to Me, 'You are My son, Today I have begotten You'" (Psalms 2:7, NKJV)

While other groups continued to observe Jewish law in addition to their new messianic beliefs, the Ebionites were the first distinct group that imposed that observance on converts. The Apostle Paul speaks of this "circumcision group" in his letter to the Galatians, noting that James feared them. He comments in the letter, "For in Christ Jesus neither circumcision availeth any thing, nor uncircumcision; but faith which worketh by love." (Galatians 5:6, NIV).

The church fathers came to view this group as heretical because of its insistence that Jewish laws must be obeyed even by non-Jewish converts. Thus the two terms "heresy" and "orthodoxy," meaning, respectively, "a choice" and the "right belief," had appeared. The orthodox group eventually became dominant, and a number of other groups of that period, whose teachings deviated from orthodox doctrine, were branded as heretics, having made the "wrong choice." It should be noted that a contrasting heresy is *antinomianism*, which is almost an opposite view from the Ebionite emphasis on observance. Antinomian belief holds that the true believer is completely *above* religious laws and need not practice obedience to any of them.

The irony of this, of course, is that Christians on both sides believed that their chosen religious group was organized and managed in such a way as to give the world (or at least the community of believers) light, hope, and a road to the future. They believed this faith would protect them from the chilling effect of facing their ultimate demise.

The need of the Christian community—or any other community with varied patterns of belief—seemed to require the rise of a priesthood to decide whose beliefs were acceptable, along with centralized worship in churches, synagogues, and mosques.

Many modern religious bodies also advocate providing moral codes to the societies of which they are a part. This too raises a question: Do these codes depend on the accepted norms of the particular society, or do they reflect a global way of thinking and an appreciation of the above-mentioned reasons that orthodoxies arise?

According to whom you survey, there are at least twelve classical religions in the world that are considered historically important: Hinduism, Buddhism, Confucianism, Jainism, Taoism, Sikhism, Shinto, Zoroastrianism, Christianity, Judaism, and Islam, with the latest addition to that list, the Bahá'í Faith.

With all these religions and many smaller denominations and sects, one might wonder what drives people to create a new and separate religion rather than accept an existing one. What brings people to one group or another? Do separate religions carry different or similar messages? Is it a good thing that we have so many separate religions?

There is no simple answer to all of these questions, since people have different cultures, desires, understandings, and so on. Also, new religions arise in different ways, independently or through schism or reform. It may be that our human nature produces the need to find religions that are more "fitting" to our cultural and personal desires and needs. There is no question that because of the tremendous diversity in demography, culture, and societies, people find many different ways to interpret the meaning of their lives.

On the other hand, we also have those who don't believe in an outside force at all, finding it unnatural and artificial. Atheists, agnostics, other secular nonbelievers perceive religion as superstition. When people refer to miracles, say they've seen ghosts, and claim divine intervention by a supernatural power from time to time, all this suggests that humans quite easily fall into the trap of spiritualism. Mystery that promises to provide us with many answers, strangely enough, offers a source of calming relief that opposes the knowledge of our unavoidable demise. And because such task might be achieved fairly easy, we're happily falling for it. Here, we find such mysteries as near-death experiences, paranormal activities, hunted

—

houses, astrological readings and predictions, as well as many other experiences humanity armed itself with for thousands of years.

Besides, isn't a fact of being alive a miracle of its own by any standard?

Thus comes the Bible. This book, without real surprise, sells much better than any other existing book. Why is that? Why an old book with no sophisticated literary ability sells century after century in no question increasing numbers among different believers? And I am sure in nonbelievers as well.

In my mind, the success story winds down to these two obvious and fairly simple reasons: (a) we humans are dazzled by unexplained mysteries that are plenty in these books, and (b) we hope to be rewarded by true revelations of our remotely hidden future.

With that in mind, it is impossible to distinguish which experiences of humanity is truthful and which is not, and we have no choice but to rely on common sense that it is in itself an unreliable thing to do.

Simply put, we do not know anything for certain. Therefore, we accept that some people possess telepathic ability and others can predict our future. To deny that would necessarily mean we must be sure, but we aren't.

A prominent contemporary proponent of atheism, Richard Dawkins, in his book *The God Delusion,* named a whole chapter "Why There Almost Certainly Is No God." Did he put that "almost" there just in case? Did Dawkins—while not denying his atheism—decide to give God some leeway in case he were to suddenly provide proof of his existence?

One might even ask what causes some nonbelievers to not only reject the promise of faith but also to vigorously fight it as if it were their enemy, what drives atheists to such strong disbelief despite the promise of spiritual rewards and if not paradise, then hope for afterlife. The threat of punishment does not scare them either but looks like it fuels them with even more vigor. Why is that?

In an attempt to understand, one might consider such references of atheists as Richard Dawkins or Sam Harris or the late Christopher Hitchens, who tirelessly insist that only science could provide that necessary tool that may explain many "mysterious" events the theists are using God in their rebuttal in almost all the cases. Uneducated, common, and fearful people often fall in such trap not trying to fathom the conundrum as to what God might be with the only "helping" hand stretched from their religious advocates. But when atheists show how science may redirect people into the right track, it provides the release of not many but enough people that were blinded by faith.

So far, enough said, and while one will be ruminating on all those questions, seeking for possible answers, I'd like to consider a new topic: the immaterial world.

CHAPTER 2

Spirits, Souls, and the Universe

- What do we know about spirits and souls? Could they be real?
- Can we equate a soul with the term "mind," or is a soul a different entity?
- What is the soul's role and function in the human and in humanity?
- Does it exist separately from a body while still connected to it?
- Could it be immortal?

Such questions have always occupied the mind of civilized man. If they could be answered empirically—or at least satisfactorily for all—they would not be asked again and again. But as this is not the case, these questions still kindle acute interest among different people and societies.

First, I'd like to look at some of the existing answers to such query. Then I would like to offer you a somewhat different set of ideas.

One of the oldest known sources that referred to the action of the mind or soul was the *Rig-Veda*, an ancient collection of sacred Sanskrit hymns. It considered the soul as created breath (*atman*) at the beginning of time and imprisoned in an earthly body at birth. Thus, according to Hinduism—arguably the oldest revealed religion in existence—the ultimate goal of the atman (described by the Indian avatar Krishna in the Bhagavad Gita as the "spirit of God in man") is to be liberated from material existence and to merge with the Universal Spirit in oneness, a condition known as *moksha*.

The set of views taught later by Zarathustra (also known as Zoroaster)—the ancient Persian prophet and founder of the Zoroastrian faith—includes a description of the relationship between body and mind. Zoroaster taught that the Divine Wisdom (Ahura Mazda) gave spiritual guidance to our mind and soul. He also taught doctrines that have been equated with heaven and hell and spoke of the future resurrection of the soul that in later Zoroastrian documents became equated with bodily resurrection.

In Greece, during the time of Homer, the soul was considered to be a substance that existed on its own. Epicurus, who was an atomist, believed that the soul—which he defined as an unknown substance that is responsible for sense perception—consists of mysterious atoms held together by the body. I find this theory particularly interesting and will enlarge on this point later.

At the dawn of the philosophical approach to life, philosophers like Plato and Aristotle attempted to explain the function of the brain, its processes, and the connection to the outer divine world. For Plato, the nonphysical soul existed beyond the material body and would continue on its own after the material body died. Aristotle—Plato's student at the time—had a different opinion. He believed a soul was like a body but was not the material thing and that when the body died, so would the soul.

Saint Thomas Aquinas (thirteen century CE)—a Dominican philosopher and theologian from Italy—suggested the Trinitarian aspects of the soul. He theorized that a form, an intellect, and a soul were the three parts of the same singular individual. This was closer to Aristotle's approach than to Plato's. However, Aquinas's teaching differed in the Trinitarian notion that all three human aspects could only be physically manifested through the body while a soul's substance could exist independently of the body.

Then René Descartes—a French mathematician and philosopher of the seventeenth century—suggested that the pineal gland (the unpaired physical structure in the brain) is the seat of the soul. For the last few centuries, that organ has been ascribed numerous functions. These include serving as a vestigial third eye in reptiles and birds, as an organ dedicated to staving off infection. It later turned out to produce the pigment-enhancing hormone melatonin and found to play a regulatory role in sexual and reproductive functions.

—

In the eighteenth century, Leonhard Euler and others theorized that the *corpus callosum* (the structure in the brain that connects the cerebral hemispheres) was the site of the soul.

Between now and then, there has been much thought about the soul's role and its physical location (if indeed there is one). Not surprisingly, there were many suggestions among religious adherents as well. The main branches of Christianity hold the view that the soul, which is an entity independent from a body, will be judged by God, and those who have not repented of their sins will go to hell while those who were true believers will inherit eternal life along with eternal fellowship with God. The Catholic Church holds that the body will reunite with the soul at the time of Resurrection. This has become an official doctrine for many Christian denominations. Some Protestants do not accept it, however, and teach that only the immaterial soul goes to heaven (variously defined), leaving the body behind. This is based on Christ's assertion that "no one can enter the kingdom of God unless they are born of water and the Spirit." It also is confirmed by Paul's affirmation that "flesh and blood cannot inherit the kingdom of God." This doctrine extrapolates on the idea that if God is spirit and we are created in his image, then we must also be spiritual beings.

Today the general approach of many believers is that a soul—being independent of a bodily entity—can be characterized as an intangible, energetic, immortal, and powerful faculty. Many would agree that the soul is a mysterious power that cannot be empirically identified. Perhaps it is chemically produced through evolution, though in the scientific world it might not be called a soul, but rather "mind" or "consciousness." It could also be a mythological product of the powerful human imagination, reinforced by centuries of belief. Yet neither one of these ideas adequately explains how our ability to comprehend our world as we do was produced in or bestowed upon us.

Thus our understanding of the soul is still unclear, whether that understanding stems from theological or secular thought. And for these reasons, I feel that another attempt to weigh in on it is justifiable, possibly with new definitions and clarification. What I am about to offer here might seem revolutionary to some readers, as it necessitates the replacement of currently accepted beliefs in both theological and secular circles.

—

First, let's reconstruct the understanding of the human body. A body is the physical framework for all the organs, systems, hormones, and enzymes found in it. Each and every one of these substances is made of atoms. In order to function, a human body needs twenty-four so-called essential atoms out of ninety-two naturally found on earth and that produce substances through different combinations.

The main building blocks of our bodies are cells. All living things consist of cells. Each cell is made up of proteins, lipids, sugars, and water. Yet the chemical structure of these substances is always the same. They are always represented by a combination of atoms: nitrogen (N), oxygen (O), hydrogen (H), and carbon (C) acting as the main atoms, and some have, in addition, sulfur (S) and phosphorus (P), and a few others. The only difference is in the proportion and structural combination of these elements needed for different parts of a body.

All these elements are found in abundance in our surroundings. The six elements previously mentioned are not only the main particles needed to build up a cell; they are also pivotal ingredients for transferring hereditary traits. The systems and organs of the body are interconnected and act like programs in computers. Unlike computers, they rely on their interdependence to work.

Bodily interconnections are called *receptors* and *synapses*. The Greek word *synapsis* (as a singular structure versus many synapses) means "junction." The human brain has a tremendous number of such junctions. As an example, one cubic millimeter of an adult brain contains ten trillion synapses. The special chemical that sends messages through the synapses is called a "neurotransmitter," and it is recyclable. When the receptors or the synapses are damaged or underdeveloped, connections they provide begin to malfunction. In the case of severe damage or deficiency in vitally important organs and systems, the body refuses to perform and becomes handicapped or dies. So in order to work properly, the body needs to have good connections between sound anatomical structures and elements.

Hormones and enzymes help provide better conduit—and thus higher performance—for healthy, intact structures. All the connections in the body are facilitated by chemical reactions that occur as long as the body continues to function and produce cells.

—

My hypothesis is that the mechanical interconnection of the chemicals with the healthy bodily structures gives rise to a complicated formation, which I call a spirit.

Why did I term this organization a spirit and not a soul?

For one thing, people have gotten used to the term "soul" being connected to something divine. People also use both terms interchangeably. That contributes to confusion, because it leads to the use of the words "spirit" and "soul" without real distinction.

Second, a spirit is not just a regular bonded substance, but it is also a special one produced by and connected to both a body and a soul. This description allows me to emphasize the difference between a spirit and a soul.

Third, since a spirit is always connected to a body, it becomes a necessary part of the living organism.

Schematically, it works like this: When all the materials are in place—the body with its sound anatomical structures and the chemicals that are bonded to them create a spirit that, if properly assembled, gives rise to a finished product—a soul. Soul is always nonmaterial and always is produced as a result of the proper combination of sound anatomical structures with a specific set of chemicals.

This is like the light produced by an electrical circuit. To produce that finished product—light—one needs to properly assemble the accessories, wires, switches, and bulb and to introduce an electrical current. This electrical current can be generated by different sources, such as wind, water, or a man-made gas-powered generator. In the case of humans, the body parts are the accessories and wires, with the brain as the bulb.

This combination is a platform through which runs a spirit (an electrical current) and which produces a soul.

All accounted, the most substantial difference between the light expressed through the bulb and the human soul expressed through the body and spirit is that we know where the energy for the light originates. In the case of the soul, we don't.

In other words, one cannot precisely point why human body "translates" consumed products into energy enough to be transformed into a soul.

This is where God comes in.

To reiterate: a soul somehow comes into existence as the result of the combination of a body and the chemically bonded set of atoms that produce a spirit. By this hypothesis, one may conclude that all living organisms that have bodies also have spirits and souls. How those souls manifest theoretically depends upon which anatomical structures are present in a particular body along with the numbers and qualities of receptors and synapses, as well as the orderly numbers and qualities of genes. In other words, just as different elements found on earth are structured differently despite containing the same particles, each organism displays different qualities and abilities in its behavior.

This is a superficial and somewhat simplistic description of a soul; obviously, it must be understood in a more involved and detailed study than that. I will try to convey my point by comparing humans to our closest relatives—common chimpanzees and bonobos. That we are closely related is today an accepted fact in the scientific community.

To make this statement less controversial for those who may find it so, let us consider the difference between a bonobo and a human being. There are theories to the effect that humans and chimpanzees split from one common ancestor millions of years ago. The evidence of this is that we have close to 99.9 percent of the same genetic material as bonobos in our DNA. While we have the same "wiring," very close anatomical structures, and closely related genes, we are light-years apart in many other aspects.

Why this is the case is a field of great interest for evolutionary geneticists. According to Andrew G. Clark of Cornell University, "We found hundreds of genes showing a pattern of sequence change consistent with adaptive evolution occurring in human ancestors" (cited on the Emptysuit blog).

It is also confirmed that—despite a close relationship between humans and chimps—we underwent different mutations in selected genes. A human has twenty-three pairs of chromosomes while a chimpanzee has twenty-four. Some chromosomes are of different sizes and show evidence of being "remodeled," meaning that these genes are not in the same order in the human and chimpanzee. Why that is remains a mystery.

In addition to different sequencing of these genes, adaptation is also shown by a difference in the way humans and chimps metabolize amino acids and digest proteins. Clark speculates that this latter function could have begun to change when early humans began to eat meat. As chimpanzees are also omnivores and are known to eat meat, this is open to argument.

Besides the genetic differences, there are anatomical and morphological differences as well. These undoubtedly influenced the different ways the two species adapted to the environment, including the ability to walk, the use of the senses, and, finally, comprehension of the physical and intellectual world.

Yet human beings and chimpanzees are different species. We cannot interbreed and produce fertile offspring, even though there has been some speculation that early members of the two species interbred. The differences between humans and chimps—including the contrast between bipedal and quadrupedal movement and the drastically different environments in which the two species developed—are also effective blocks to interspecies compatibility.

Coming back to the concept of a soul, one may say that even though no agreement exists as to what it is and which species may or may not possess it, it manifests itself only in living organisms of higher taxonomy—in other words, organisms that display qualities we connect to the term "mind."

Out of this arises a very important possibility that a soul is not an independent entity, but rather that the soul appears as the result of a bond between the structures of a healthy body and "properly" bonded chemicals. It is also possible that a soul arises as the result of a certain quality and quantity of existing receptors and synapses along with a number of hormones, enzymes, and genes. I believe a soul manifests itself according to its combined physical ingredients.

And here comes a tricky question: how can a body—along with a spirit—produce an entity that possesses the qualities of mind, intellect, or soul? I don't pretend for a moment that I have an answer to that question. I merely wish to emphasize here that all the parts of each functioning human system were provided to us by an unknown entity or impetus with specific and precise qualities that cannot be measured by contemporary scientific methods. How can a soul come to life through anatomical structures connected to a handful of atoms? Would that require the presence of a higher intelligence with the capacity to produce such a distinctive entity? Or is it a result of the

—

"natural" ability of atoms to possess such qualities when combined in a certain way?

I believe that each of us must decide on our own what the soul is. I will try to conduct an analysis of what a soul might or might not be, but at this juncture, let me make a generalization about the term "soul": most people who believe in the soul think it is divine in nature and is given to us through unexplainable mystery.

A soul is unique in the sense that it can be both subjective and objective. One can look at objective events but must still be subjective in making one's decisions about what those events mean. That is how an understanding of *self* appears. The self, while it is somewhat subordinate feature of the soul, I hypothesize, these are one and the same, with self acting internally and soul being that which manifests itself externally through our intellect or mind.

Because this book is not a scientific treatise, I will not investigate the faculty of self much further. For those who desire deeper exploration of these themes, there are plenty of sources in neurological, psychological, philosophical, and related documentation.

The only summation I'd like to make for now is that someone produced "live" atoms that in specific combinations might and do act as sentient organisms.

Now I'd like to return to my customary method of compiling sets of questions for consideration, combination of which succinctly shows how immature our comprehension of meaning of a soul is. Let me start from what bothers me the most about the concept of the soul as I have seen it expressed in some mainstream religious doctrines.

- Why would a soul—an immaterial, divine, and eternal faculty—descend into a material, feeble, and limited body?
- Why would it remain with an imperfect structure, which so easily becomes injured or diseased?
- How and where are souls born?
- Are they ready made to descend into or attach to a new body?
- What decides which body they will occupy?
- Why do they always start with a newly born body and never leave it until the organism dies?
- What makes them remain "loyal" even if they enter the body of someone who, for instance, becomes a criminal?

—

- Do they have a distinct character or personality or possibly even a human shape?
- Does this character coincide with a character of the physical person or is it separate from it?
- Is the soul somehow connected in its manifestation to a physical development of a body?
- What happens to the soul of a sick person, a mentally ill person, or a person who has lost his or her memory?
- If a soul is so powerful that it doesn't expire with the body, why can't it stay in the body so the person can go on? Why it cannot heal the sick?
- In reincarnation, must a "used" soul readjust itself to accommodate a new body?
- Do souls bring old "baggage" with them into a new life, or are their past lives forgotten forever?
- Does a soul retain any and/or all the senses a human being possesses?
- What is the relationship between a soul and a body: is it incarnation, reflection, or attachment?
- How strong is this connection of the soul to the body?
- If, as expected by some religious denominations, the body will be resurrected, what will happen to the deceased if the body it occupied was completely destroyed to the condition of dust?
- How can the soul of a deceased person be recognized by other souls? Do souls distinguish among themselves?
- Do souls travel in the whole universe or they are destined to stick to the galaxy of their birth?
- By which attributes are these entities identified after they leave the body?
- Why would the Highest Spirit of the universe wish to reconnect with any human soul, whatever its quality?

I'm going to stop here, although surely there are many more such questions that could be asked. Besides, you're probably more confused now than you were before I began my strange sermon. But remember, I said right from the beginning that I don't know who or what God is, if he exists. I also said that it is much easier for me to point out what seems odd than to struggle toward the "correct" answer.

—

With that in mind, I come to the conclusion that science and religion—though from different perspectives—may lead us to nonanswers. We try. We hope. And yet we might never discover the answers we seek. Human beings can and do exaggerate, imagine things, cultivate different hopes and wishes, meditate and dream, entertain suggestions, and ponder diverse conclusions. Each of these human capacities, if sufficiently developed, might produce a colorful and distinctive philosophical realm.

Having these attributes in our arsenal makes us unique, vibrant, and full of desires, with which we struggle for most of our lives. With time, they may wear us down, and finally we might tire of them and long for a quiet life without the emotional drama. When that doesn't happen, we might become unstable, irritable, irrational, and unsatisfied with our existence. Or we might tire up to the point that we wish to expire.

At that time, we might decide that we want out, that it is time for us to leave. But we do not want to go away forever, and so a vicious cycle evolves. If we try to visualize ourselves back in our childhood or in our youth, we realize that we cannot go back. What we are left with is not clear. Perhaps we have lost our self-esteem. We are no longer full of energy, and if we are privileged to live for roughly one hundred years, we may realize that we could not continue like this for another century or more. Eventually we may come to the conclusion that we have exhausted our existence and that our biological clock has run down. Such as this, we are not designed to live forever, in spite of what we might hope from reading the Bible . . . or science fiction and fantasy.

In this created picture, can one imagine an emotional god who is involved with each and every one of us, who is able not only to solve our problems, but who also has shepherded the human world since time immemorial and who will continue to do so without any sign of weariness? Can such a god exist? Can such a god last?

When our cycle is complete, we may start to realize that we cannot afford to go on. The saying "your time is up"—though cruel—is true for all, eventually. And so we accept our demise as unavoidable. Given a choice, most would choose to live on. But because we cannot, we maintain the hope that we will live on in some other form and place. This conviction provides us with some relief during the very short journey that has been allotted to us by an invisible hand here on earth.

—

We didn't invent ourselves, though it might have been better if we had. And maybe we would make ourselves much more versatile and more practical, were we given a chance.

With this flow of doubts about the role of our eternal soul and overall its existence, let me speak a few words of another human invention—a place of eternal torture simply called hell. First off, I wish to emphasize how cruel from a Christian view point it must be to send someone's soul for eternal torture without granting such soul leisure to repent and to be rehabilitated. Is it a Christian way to never forgive and punish someone with everlasting eternity? Why then even offer such cruelty, prohibiting God to reduce, alleviate, or withdraw his punishment? Would that be not a hellish decision on the side of God? Now assuming it is still unfortunate reality that God has taken long ago, and he does not "feel" like removing it to teach humans to be compliant with his rules, what part of human might be condemned to suffering? A soul cannot feel, as it is devoid of a nervous system. In fact, it has none of any systems human beings have. How then might it be explicated in human terms? What part of a soul would express pain, suffering, humiliation, and so on? And even if it could, is it possible that a soul somehow must be responsible for a corrupted and sinful body? Why then and by who was it offered, such an incredulous nonsense as the existence of hell?

As the only logical answer that must follow, it looks like that it was human invention. Under which particular circumstance, in what exact time this invention came about, really does not matter much. And as the majority of cases, with time, it was allowed to grow in almost permissible reality, with a sizeable number of people believing in it close to 100 percent. The others who we call doubters would not express their firm belief as their nature would demand it, and yet another group who we usually call cynics and sometimes scientists would deny it as absolute impossibility that is not connected to the real world.

CHAPTER 3

The Role of Scientists in the Generation of Belief in God

I raise this question because of the general approach of the scientific world toward the obvious and subtle laws of the universe. While scientists recognize the existence of these laws, they do not discuss the premise of how did they come about. Beginning as recently as the last century, scientists James Watson and Francis Crick declared that they had found the "secret of life." This event began with the decipherment of the structure of DNA in 1953 and continued with the decoding of the genome in the 1990s, which introduced the possibility of solving many genetically determined diseases by the end of the century.

Besides giving the impression that the secret of life was a secret no more, these scientists took an improbably sunny view of their ability to accomplish miracles. They essentially declared that if anyone still believed in a God, the scientist's approach to problem solving indicated that God either did not exist or that the word *god* might be applied to scientists themselves.

This raised another question: Do people always act rationally when they are equipped with a certain amount of knowledge and persuasive power? Persuasion usually comes as a result of the interpretation of data, and we all know how unreliable both data and human interpretation can be.

There is a huge difference between the recognition of a process and the understanding of how that process began. Mere recognition of it does not offer the understanding of how the task has been foreseen and contemplated. What preparation had to be done, what materials used, and where did such materials come from? Thus, whether presently accepted laws were introduced to the cosmic system through the cognition of a Creator, or via mere coincidence, remains a subject of debate among researchers and scientists.

The way science works, however, is based on an outlined pattern. Scientists propose a theory and then try to conduct a repeatable experiment that confirms their findings. Then they either accept it or dismiss it—which will depend on the results of an experiment. If the theory is accepted as valid, it becomes knowable to the masses. At that point, scientists move to another task, and we nonscientists begin to apply their discoveries to our lives.

Nevertheless, most scientists know their limitations. The discovery or confirmation of existing laws (which are theoretical in nature) can't happen without some basic knowledge. Yet the more science discovers about our past and present or offers predictions about our future, the more rational human beings consciously consider what role a Creator might have played, if he indeed exists. In that regard, it is somewhat puzzling that among scientists one can come across those who claim that they are Christians and that their faith does not interfere with their work as scientists.

This claim is absolutely irresponsible for many reasons, not only because such claim would be inconceivable. A human body, with its corrupted organs and systems, cannot be compatible with either a great spirit of God or the greatness of God who will try to reduce itself to such unremarkable construction as human body is. Whatever humans understand of God incarnated, incompatibility must be obvious as well as tremendously impractical. All those attributes that humans gifted God with such as omniscience, omnipotence, etc., would not conform at a skeleton, brain, or other human physical and mental limitations. Even if God, for some illogical reason, decided to do it anyway, the human body would expire (and more likely explode) rather immediately, not being able to withstand stress.

And with such definite thoughts, some people want to believe in our unique and special creation, while others try to prove that we are

—

neither unique nor created. Each relies on their own viewpoints in deciphering the world we share. But so far there is no one who can prove or disprove the existence of God to the satisfaction of everyone.

That is why when someone comes along with an agenda that tips toward either pole, we do well to make sure that rational thinking is still in place and that eloquence does not blind us to the truth.

Thus I wish to bring to the discussion some curious suggestions made by Richard Dawkins, author of *The God Delusion*. From that book, I chose to analyze two chapters: "Arguments for God's Existence" and "Why There Almost Certainly Is No God." I chose these two chapters because I believe them to be representative of the ideas and observations on which Dawkins bases most of his arguments. These topics demand the objective eye of an agnostic, and I bravely consider myself one. Therefore, I will not propose to argue as someone who is in opposition or in agreement, but as someone seeking the truth.

Right from the start, Dawkins chooses not to play fair. He begins chapter 3 of his book with a reference to Thomas Aquinas's "proofs" (quotation marks are his) for the existence of God. Dawkins's intention is to expose "vacuous" attempts at proving God's existence provided by a theological giant. (Aquinas, it should be noted, lived in the thirteenth century CE.) Dawkins insists that Aquinas's three arguments really represent the same argument expressed in three different ways.

Somehow it seems not to have occurred to Dawkins that the redundancy of which he accuses Aquinas was the way a man who lived four centuries before the formulation of Newton's laws of gravitation and motion could prove his point. Such a task might be perceived by a contemporary man—equipped with the laws of nature discovered since that time—as ordinary. Simply put, Aquinas did not have the tools at his disposal that we have now.

In none of his three arguments, Dawkins posits, is Aquinas able to prove anything. But this is a dubious claim. Let's take, for instance, Dawkins's rebuttal, in which he writes:

> *The five "proofs" asserted by Thomas Aquinas don't prove anything, and are easily—though I hesitate to say so, given his eminence—exposed as "vacuous." . . . Even if we allow*

the dubious luxury of arbitrarily conjuring up a terminator to an infinite regress and giving it a name, simply because we need one, there is absolutely no reason to endow that terminator with any of the properties normally ascribed to God: omnipotence, omniscience, goodness, creativity of design. (The God Delusion, 77)

He further writes:

Incidentally, it has not escaped the notice of logicians that omniscience and omnipotence are mutually incompatible. If God is omniscient, he must already know how he is going to intervene to change the course of history using his omnipotence. But that means he can't change his mind about his intervention, which means he is not omnipotent. (ibid., 77-78)

Let me respectfully disagree with such a conclusion, as the presumed activity of God might differ from its reality and might be erroneously perceived by even a contemporary human being as something it is not. What if God, being omniscient and omnipotent, did not plan to change anything? What if his grand plan is simply a process leading to a goal or goals? What if only when God achieves his goals—without correcting the process—does he come to a decision about what to do next to reach any further goal?

This critique is followed by one on "The Theological Argument, or Argument from Design" given by Aquinas. *The God Delusion* reads as follows:

Things in the world, especially living things, look as though they have been designed. Nothing that we know looks designed unless it is designed. Therefore there must be a designer and we call him God. (79)

"The argument from design," continues Dawkins, "is the only one still in regular use today, and it still sounds like the ultimate knockdown argument."

—

To disprove Aquinas, Dawkins invokes Charles Darwin's "unexpected and devastating" reasoning that "blew a popular belief out of the water," with reference to evolution by natural selection.

We will return to the topic of evolution in a later chapter. For now, let me present to you how Dawkins solves the problem of our complicated nervous systems by referring to natural selection as if it were a magic wand or even, God forbid, an unseen Creator. That is, he gives natural selection the attributes of God. In *The God Delusion*, we read:

> *Evolution by natural selection produces an excellent simulacrum of design, mounting prodigious heights of complexity and elegance. And among these eminences of pseudo-design are nervous systems which—among their more modest accomplishments—manifest goal-seeking behavior that, even in a tiny insect, resembles a sophisticated heat-seeking missile more than a simple arrow on target.*
> (79)

Is it merely an impression—created by admirable eloquence of speech—that the problem of our seemingly intelligent design has been simply and elegantly solved by invoking natural selection instead of God? Has Dawkins really offered a mechanism whereby the nervous system became so powerful and sophisticated? Does the nervous system—or other adaptive mechanisms existing in the world—pursue a coherent goal? Does it answer the demands of natural selection by actively seeking self-improvement? And if that is so, then has not natural selection been awarded powerful, godlike attributes?

From this simplified solution, a not-so-simple question arises: Why does natural selection not produce regressive patterns or even chaotic ones if not in preponderance then as often as it produces improvements? Does it undergo a thoughtful process of its selection criteria before "making" a decision? What if natural selection produced such grave conditions that organisms in their majority would not be able to adapt to in order to continue progress?

Reading *The God Delusion* chapter after chapter, I could not dismiss my unpleasant surprise that such a remarkable figure as

—

Dawkins had decided to use rather cheap and superficial arguments in trying to prove his points. In attempting to show how silly his opponents are for arguing the existence of God, he finds questionable sources such as those collected on the Godless Geeks website (see bibliography). The following arguments from the website are found on page 85 of Dawkins' book:

> *36.* Argument from Incomplete Devastation: *1) A plane crashed killing 143 passengers and crew. 2) But one child survived with only third-degree burns. 3) Therefore God exists.*
>
> *40.* Argument from Post-Death Experience: *1) Person X died an atheist. 2) He now realizes his mistake. 3) Therefore God exists.*

Whether Dawkins uses these weak (and somewhat irrelevant) arguments in all seriousness or simply because he does not wish to answer real opposition to his conclusions, I am ambivalent about his philosophy. Dawkins seems to believe that he is correct and does not need cogent arguments.

His criticism in "The argument from beauty" portion ends with the illogical conclusion that there is no linkage between great art and the existence of God or "it is not spelled out by its (religious) proponents" (*The God Delusion*, 86-87).

In saying that the religious Michelangelo might have produced a no less inspirational painting on the ceiling of a museum of science had he received commissions equal to those he received from the church for the Sistine Chapel, Dawkins reduces the talent of that great painter to commercialism by proposing that the artist derived no inspiration from his faith. Certainly he could argue that a nonbeliever of equal talent might create an equally magnificent work for the ceiling of a museum of science, but the artist would not be Michelangelo and that inspiration would not be the same.

In "The argument from personal experience" on the same page, Dawkins gives the following example:

> *Many people believe in God because they believe they have seen a vision of him—or of an angel or a virgin in*

—

blue—with their own eyes. Or he speaks to them inside their heads. This argument from personal experience is the most convincing to those who claim to have had one. But it is the least convincing to anyone else, and anyone knowledgeable about psychology.

He continues:

You say you experienced God directly? Well, some people have experienced a pink elephant, but that probably does not impress you. Peter Sutcliffe, the Yorkshire Ripper, distinctly heard the voice of Jesus telling him to kill women, and he was locked up for life . . . Individuals in asylums think they are Napoleon or Charlie Chaplin, or that the entire world is conspiring against them, or that they can broadcast their thoughts into other people's heads. (Ibid. 88)

I didn't have to comment after reading such an "explanation" concerning the existence or nonexistence of God. I could have said, "How ridiculously superficial and irrelevant these 'proofs' are." I could even suppose that everybody must have noticed the ill-assorted mixture of unrelated samples Dawkins adduces.

Or could I?

Would readers view the Yorkshire Ripper, the ancient conspiracy theorist, and benign schizophrenics as representative of the same class of psychosis? Would they assume all claimants to divine revelation to be of that identical type?

Rather than rely on my assumptions about what people would or would not construe from Dawkins's examples, I decided to try to connect the dots myself.

I ask: Do these samples prove that God does not exist and that if you think he does, you are mentally ill?

Further, can we suppose that God would reveal himself by simply showing up some place one day so everybody could see him (in some form) and say, "See, here he is," and that if he did this, we would all recognize him?

Perhaps Dawkins will not accept anything less than an in-your-face proof from God that he exists, but I suppose that must remain

—

between Dawkins and God. Who knows, maybe Dawkins needs to forge a covenant with God as the Jewish patriarchs did in ages past. Something along the lines of "Show yourself to me in a way that I must accept, and I will believe in you."

In any event, I wish that people of Dawkins's obvious intelligence would not attempt to prove a point of which they are uncertain themselves.

In chapter 4 of *The God Delusion*, Dawkins takes on quite a different role. As a clever manipulator of words in the portion titled "Irreducible Complexity," Dawkins begins a skillful sermon:

> *It is impossible to exaggerate the magnitude of the problem that Darwin and Wallace solved. I could mention the anatomy, cellular structure, biochemistry and behavior of literally any living organism by example. But the most striking feats of apparent design are those picked out—for obvious reasons—by creationist authors, and it is with gentle irony that I derive mine from a creationist book, 'Life—How Did It Get Here?'* (119)

Then Dawkins refers to two examples from the creationist book, which was published by the Watchtower Society (Jehovah's Witnesses). One is *Euplectella aspergillum*, which has glassy fibers attaching a sponged skeleton to the ocean floor and which produces silica from seawater. The other is the *Aristolochia trilobata*, an unusually beautiful frugal plant that can be grown almost anywhere as long as the temperature does not drop below thirty degrees Fahrenheit. In both cases, the creationist author emphasizes that such intricate and beautiful construction would be improbable as the result of random chance but rather hints at a design and Designer.

"The Watchtower authors," says Dawkins, "lose no time in adding their own punch line in that chance is not the likely designer." This is a conclusion with which Dawkins and "all sane biologists would agree." He adds that "the candidate solutions to the riddle of improbability are not, as is falsely implied, design and chance. They are design and natural selection" (ibid., 119-120).

Dawkins next proceeds to tell us, "Design is not a real solution either." Now we can watch how skillfully the author plays with the

—

words in a carefully constructed context. "The intricate elegance of the flower moves Watchtower to ask, 'did all of this happen by chance? Or did it happen by intelligent design?'"

Dawkins responds:

> *Once again, no, of course it didn't happen by chance. Once again, intelligent design is not the proper alternative to chance. Natural selection is not only a parsimonious, plausible and elegant solution; it is the only workable alternative to chance that has ever been suggested.* (ibid., 120)

The dexterity with which Dawkins navigates these waters is almost unnoticeable. First it was an agreement: chance is not a solution, but intelligent design and natural selection are. Yet it is not an *intelligent* design either, but rather one of natural (unguided) selection. After that comes, almost naturally, a consolidation of thought:

> *Intelligent design suffers from exactly the same objection as chance. It is simply not a plausible solution to the riddle of statistical improbability. And the higher improbability, the more implausible intelligent design becomes. Seen clearly, intelligent design will turn out to be a redoubling of the problem.* (ibid., 120)

Just like that. Not even an attempt to explain why natural selection is the most appropriate choice. Take it or leave it, period.

After that, Dawkins tackles the problem of the alleged Designer. He writes:

> *The designer himself raises the bigger problem of his own origin. Any entity capable of intelligently designing something as improbable as a Dutchman's Pipe (Aristolochia trilobata) would have to be even more improbable than a Dutchman's Pipe.*

Is that conclusion not the weakest one yet? If God is improbable because he must be designed by an even more sophisticated designer, then we must ask: whence came this process of natural selection that is driving the evolution of everything—including the universe itself? After all, does it not, by Dawkins's logic, have to be a process more sophisticated than the many biological processes it has spawned?

Among scientists exists an understanding that they are trying to find the solution to a jigsaw puzzle without having the instructions. The ability to see a puzzle and to attempt to solve it implies that such a puzzle already existed whether we saw it or not. We also have to theorize that the necessary items, objects, and ingredients we find for the solution of that puzzle were somehow also provided. Our ability to bring those parts together in an attempt to connect them makes us only navigators who are equipped with limited knowledge and capacity.

Does that make us gods?

I'd like to emphasize that my ambivalence about Dawkins does not come from any disagreement with his stance regarding God, angels, hallucinations, and dreams; they all are legitimate grounds for objection—or at least for questioning. My reason for arguing with Dawkins has to do with his *methods* and not his *viewpoint*, as it is simply unbelievable how simplistically he tries to prove his points.

I wish to say once again: science does not consider the question of God's existence, but human beings do. And science is a collective social activity of human beings.

CHAPTER 4

Deciphering Signs of the Almighty

Saying that the world we live in is complicated at any level will not surprise anyone. Humanity has reached the point of understanding a number of facets of life; we grasp the function of a variety of different chemicals, we have begun to decode heredity, and we have figured out a process of evolutionary steps in developing organisms. We also can now explain a number of the laws managing the universe.

Yet despite all these achievements, we cannot say for certain who or what set these miraculous laws in motion, who or what originated live organisms, and why only humans—another miracle—are increasingly able to decipher them. If we look at these processes carefully, we might also agree that there is no clear and simple explanation presented so far, either from scientific or from theological points of view.

To understand something complex, one must start with some knowledge about how this complexity came about. When subatomic particles came together, they produced atoms with different qualities than those subatomic particles possess. When molecules came into existence after different atoms joined with each other, they acquired new qualities distinct from these original atoms they were made from. We could say the same thing about the appearance of thought, emotions, and senses after molecules and atoms, which possess none of these characteristics, joined in the human organism.

So while science searches for the laws of the universe via observation and reproducible experimentation—using the acquired knowledge of physics, chemistry, biology, and other disciplines—it is trying to decipher only what presently exists in the observable, physical world.

Theologians, on the other hand, plays a somewhat unfair game, not only by claiming communication with a Supreme Being, but also by suggesting that if science cannot explain all things, then God must have done it.

But again, the only thing we are lacking is a working description of that powerful entity we call God. Certainly, many of the attributes of God are described in scripture: his benevolence, his wisdom, his all-embracing love. The question is how do we know these things about God? What is the nature of the revelations claimed throughout the ages by such figures as Krishna, Buddha, Moses, Christ, Muhammad, and Bahá'u'lláh? As of now, there is no clear-cut winner in this contest of who has given us the most accurate description of God. But, being human, we want a decisive champion to whom we can give the prize.

The issue becomes even more complicated because some theologians and scientists claim that there is no real conflict between faith and science, that the so-called rift between the two is exaggerated or misinterpreted. Meanwhile, other people in both camps warn of the danger of either party trespassing into the other's territory. Hence, it looks like we have no choice but to look at how different groups approach the exploration of the origin of life.

Before scientists began to explore this question, they had to struggle with another fundamental issue: "What is life?" Very soon they recognized that while trying to distinguish between living and nonliving systems, they might easily fall into a trap of false dichotomy. Tackling the issue yielded many different variants; the best they could come up with was a theory of gradual sequential steps through which life most likely arose. Scientists concluded that chemical reactions among the simple organic molecules produced complicated structures that slowly evolved to become self-replicating molecules with different degrees of complexity. This assumed process was referred to as the "bottom-up approach."

It is now widely accepted that life originated on earth between 3.8 and four billion years ago. Such a declaration conflicts as much with the claim of Scientologists that mankind is at least sixty *trillion* years old as it does with the fundamentalist Christian assertion that it is somewhere in the order of six thousand years.

—

The modern view of the majority of scientists tells us that when the earth was about four billion years old, its hostile, red-hot surface was racked by volcanic eruptions and constantly bombarded by meteorites and comets from outer space. Then everything began slowly to cool. These dates are supported by authorities such as University of California, Los Angeles (UCLA) paleontologist J. William Schopf, who in 1993 announced the discovery of a fossil from Australia in which several cells were found, preserved for approximately 3.5 billion years. This—and the results of geophysical investigations conducted by a Danish mining company that found graphite carbon deposits in 3.8 billion year old rock in western Greenland—would indicate that very early models of life appeared in many places at once.

Whether life on earth developed from elements in the deep layers of its crust or as a result of falling meteorites remains an enigma. On the other hand, to accept a theory about the evolutionary development of self-replicating molecules we need to posit that these molecules must have possessed or acquired a brain like faculty as well as rational thinking processes in order to progress in their assumed task. To me, this seems quite a stretch.

To explore this subject further, let us start with a cell. There is nothing simple about a "simple cell." All living things are made up of them, but the structure of the cell is such that even one cell is sufficient for some living things to function (e.g., bacteria or protists). Humans, who are made of a bundle of cells with different functions, will be the subject of our discussion here.

Our cells are called *eukaryotes*. That term means that the tiny, complex structures of each cell are contained within membranes. Each cell contains a well-defined nucleus—the "brain" of a cell. On average, the size of a cell is one-thousandth of a millimeter—which is very, very small, indeed. To visualize this, bear in mind that a human hair is ten times the diameter of a cell. Yet within this tiny structure are very important units called *organelles*. These are burdened with many precise and complicated tasks and thus make a cell a sort of factory with many different functions.

For instance, a nucleus collects and contains the genetic information defining the genotype of an individual. So-called "Golgi bodies" package chemicals that will be removed from a cell after their use. *Lysosomes* are another organelle containing enzymes that

—

61

facilitate digestion. *Mitochondria* are the organelles that extract the energy necessary for practically all the functions of a cell from the nutrients that it takes in. *Cytoplasm*, a gel-like substance that dissolves sugars, salts, and other electrolytes, provides a watery environment full of nutrients in the cell. Many chemicals that find their way into a cell are water-soluble. Those that cannot be dissolved are suspended in the water as solid particles to later undergo a chemical reaction.

The reason I am explaining all this is because nobody knows how and why the body gathered all these different types of organelles into one cell. It remains an unsolved mystery how these organelles assumed such precise tasks, in addition to producing different types of cells.

To further examine how complicated their role is, let's consider the red blood cells, *erythrocytes*. One of their major functions is to transfer oxygen from the lungs to the tissues of the body. This function is accomplished on the shoulders of a protein called *hemoglobin*. In order for red blood cells to transport oxygen, hemoglobin must exist inside the cells. Why? What caused this complex relationship to occur?

The body can adjust to the needs of its environment, but that ability alone indicates a directed selection of what is needed for its proper function. In other words, a system would have to process the knowledge of what material an organism needed to survive, which would require direction or thought. Without such direction, it would be more natural for a body and its inclusions to behave in a more chaotic, random way.

Besides transporting hemoglobin, red blood cells accomplish another no-less-important task: with the help of an enzyme called *carbonic anhydrase*, they catalyze the chemical reaction between carbon dioxide and water. This reaction accomplishes the safe removal of enormous quantities of poisonous carbon dioxide in the form of the bicarbonate ion. The question, of course, is what brought that specific enzyme into the red cell and not another?

Without getting further into the details of these processes, one might come to the conclusion that blood flows in different parts of a body through vessels of different diameters because the body knows that oxygen is needed for tissue maintenance and function. In some places, the vessels are so tiny that red blood cells have to be squeezed

—

in order to get through. They could "choose" not to go through, but they don't. They rely instead on their special membranes and seem to know they will therefore not be crushed while squeezing through the capillaries.

I wish to add here one small but quite significant detail: the average lifespan of red blood cells is 120 days. When they die, the blood supply would be diminished without a means of replenishing them. In adults, that job falls to the bone marrow, where red cells are produced. In childhood, the sources of red blood cells are the liver, the spleen, and the bone marrow. Whether one classes these processes as mutational changes, adaptation, or natural selection, it does not really give a clear explanation of this phenomenon.

I previously mentioned that all organisms in the world consist of cells. These cells, in order to function, need nutrients in the form of proteins, sugars, and fats. The cells require that food be consumed and wastes removed. This process is called *homeostasis*, and it is conducted through a cell membrane.

The cell membrane that separates the cell's contents from the outer environment is a unique structure in itself. It is composed of a bilayer of lipids that have *hydrophilic* (water loving) heads and *hydrophobic* (water avoiding) tails. The heads face the outward boundaries of the membrane, and the tails face the inside of the structure. The area where the tails meet inside the membrane chemically repels water. This arrangement allows the membrane to be selectively permeable—meaning that it lets through only select substances—such as hydrophobic molecules. The traffic is directed by transmembrane protein complexes.

Now we also have to keep in mind that all these proteins, carbohydrates, lipids, enzymes, bones, systems, and organs are made of hydrogen, nitrogen, oxygen, carbon, sulfur, and phosphorus (H, N, O, C, S, and P on the periodic table) and just a handful more atoms that—through some agency—play a complicated and precise role in this strangely organized world.

To support a theory of evolutionary bottom-up cell development, we have to agree that all these atoms—in order to form self-replicating, complex structures—had to have one general goal in mind. That is, they had to know whether they were to end up as human beings or other specialized living organisms.

Even to suggest this opens the possibility, of course, that natural selection acts selectively and is goal-oriented—which seems ridiculous. Nevertheless, scientists continue to consider seriously such a theory. One can imagine why. The human body contains approximately one hundred trillion cells. Not only did these cells find each other and "agree" on what sort of life-form they were supposed to be, they gathered in discrete but interdependent groups to form particular organs, such as the liver, pancreas, lungs, heart, and kidneys. Then they adapted to purposefully produce the most sophisticated creature on earth so far: us.

Is it rational to believe that all these things came together coincidentally and randomly or that they gathered one day and decided that their assembly was enough to function as, say, the liver, with all the complex functions it has had to assume and, in addition, to provide the necessary connections to the rest of the cells in the body? What (or maybe *who*) was the messenger that informed the heart of its important duties? And while we are questioning what caused these organs to exist at all, why not two hearts instead of two kidneys? They would enhance one's ability to survive, wouldn't they?

With the major systems of the human body—nervous, respiratory, digestive, and others—we can only wonder how natural selection might have played a major role in making simple, chemical, independent reactions much more complicated so that they would be able to work together for the survival of our bodies.

At this point, I would like to remind you how microscopically small that factory called a cell is. In spite of its size, the cell, like everything else on earth, follows some definite rules, one of which is entropy—that is, wear and tear. It cannot last forever. It lives, it exhausts itself, and it dies. We are fortunate that it somehow learned to replicate itself by dividing so the collective life of the body could go on.

Would this process repeatedly and methodically happen through natural selection alone? Would cells always make another proper cell and nothing else that might jeopardize the future organism or send it into a complete chaos?

To study this metaphorically, imagine that someone decided to build a house. Where would he start? First of all, he would need to have a clear vision of what he wanted to make. Then he would need to make a blueprint of the design he envisioned. He would acquire all the materials and tools to build the house. And finally he would apply his knowledge and skill to construct it.

To go through all these rigorous processes, there must be intelligence present with a clear vision and goals, and that intelligence must be complex enough to comprehend the construction of the house. Perhaps it is even an intelligence of irreducible complexity. Would that be a God acting through natural selection, or would it be natural selection acting as God?

We know that our genes, besides controlling the functions of cells, give us hereditary traits from our parents. This knowledge is predicated on the ability of scientists to read DNA. DNA is a skeleton or scaffolding for a gene—i.e., it is a framework designed to hold the genes. We compare DNA with a spiral staircase because DNA is a helix—it has two parallel, spiraling sides equipped to hold transverse treads. These treads are called *nucleotides* and are always composed of three substances: a five-carbon sugar called *pentose*, a phosphate group, and a *nucleobase* (commonly referred to as simply a base), such as adenine, guanine, cytosine, and thymine (A, G, C, and T). Pentose and the phosphate group are part of the treads of the DNA staircase-looking structure.

The bases are held inside the staircase. They are not allowed to move out of the framework to see the world but instead are held in a strict order with hydrogen bonds in two—and three-bonded connections. The space between the spiral rails of the staircase is constructed in such a manner that the number of bonded connections and the size of the bases are specified in order to fit within it. If you try to squeeze more of these nucleotides or change their number inside the structure of DNA, it will destroy the whole gene.

Who specified this arrangement and how?

To transfer features from parents to their progeny, one needs to move that information from one place to another. In the case of humans, it happens via a process called *mitosis* or *meiosis* in cells. Broadly speaking, when a cell divides, it replicates its contents and distributes its components equally between two so-called daughter cells. The nucleus is an absolutely astonishing feature of the cell. It contains large numbers of DNA molecules that are the structural frames for the genes. These molecules of DNA, joined together, are

—

called *chromosomes*. Humans always have forty-six chromosomes in each cell, with each parent transmitting half of that number. In other words, the forty-six chromosomes in a newly conceived human are supplied in two sets of twenty-three base pairs, from the male and female parents. Each chromosome contains one hundred to one thousand genes. Therefore, in each such cell, the number of genes varies, but it is usually between thirty thousand and eighty thousand.

It's hard enough to imagine that number of components in one tiny cell, let alone comprehend how the simple combination of base pairs can influence the heredity of a species. How indeed did the genetic system take on a regulatory form, determining when cells needed to divide and form new cells? Questions like this remain a deep mystery, and scientists, while not able to answer them either philosophically or scientifically, continue to pursue other answers.

Another puzzle for the scientific world: What triggered sexual reproduction? What evolutionary advantage is there to requiring two not interchangeable, parental entities?

If we try to trace the reproductive ability of male/female organs, we will be able to see how intricate and complicated these functions are. But let's begin with the structure of a human *spermatozoon*. A spermatozoon—which at the age of sixty-four days is ready to fertilize an egg—is composed of a head, a body, and a tail.

The head contains the nucleus around which is situated a thick cap (the *acrosome*) that contains the Golgi apparatus. The Golgi apparatus is comprised of enzymes that digest the proteins the sperm encounters on its way to an egg. These enzymes are needed to clear the way to the ovum so the sperm will be able to fertilize it. But *spermatozoa* (sperm), swimming toward the ovum, must distinguish what is a barrier that should be eliminated and what is not.

The energy and speed with which a spermatozoon moves are supplied by *adenosine triphosphate* (ATP) that is synthesized in the mitochondria found in the body—the segment of tail directly behind the head. These spermatozoa, after being formed, are stored in the testes, reaching an average number of up to 120 million each day. They remain fertile for at least one month. There are multiple, local, inhibitory substances, hormones, and enzymes found in the different parts of the body that regulate how long *spermatogenesis* (the ability

–

to generate sperm) will last and determine the vigor and quantity of the sperm that can be maintained.

What produced awareness for the spermatozoon of the existence of vagina at some location? What gave this spermatozoon the need to join in reaction with unknown substance?

The chemical environment within the female vagina also plays a role in the directed movement of sperm. There are many more factors that play a role in the process of fertilization.

Suffice it to say that those who try to explain even this single regular process in the body by referring to natural selection, mutations, or adaptation must at least acknowledge that invoking natural selection doesn't begin to explain these phenomena—at least, not in any sense that fits neatly with the scientific method.

Another set of questions: Why does a sexual attraction exist between the male and female of the species? What produces desire, passion, and sexual arousal? I think the answers to these questions at this point may be more philosophical than physiological, and I hope to address them in a second volume.

For now I'd like to sum up the foregoing ideas: Everything mentioned above—DNA, genes, and chromosomes—is, in fact, constructed from only six simple atoms: carbon, hydrogen, nitrogen, oxygen, phosphorus, and sulfur. These simple atoms, in different combinations, manage to form a gamut of substances. Our bodies depend on those substances, and they are proportionately provided in the form of proteins, carbohydrates, and lipids.

Proteins represent the framework that physically supports our systems. Sometimes it is considered the main ingredient in a body.

Proteins also survive the longest in the environment, which is why scientists have been able to unearth bones that are millions of years old. Of the numerous proteins found naturally in our environment, we need the amino acids that are the building blocks of proteins. And of the existing amino acids, our bodies need only twenty specific amino acids for survival.

How can the human body know what specific amino acids it needs? Why is it so choosy? What suggested to the human body and the components that direct its development—or for that matter, any other kind of body—that it must be fed exactly these combinations and not others? And, finally, how can these six atoms, found everywhere in the world, produce such complicated organisms with so many complicated functions?

At this point theologians again appear in life of the scientists, voicing their stand on life's origins, on God, and on related religious beliefs. Sacred books such as the Vedas, the Bible, the Qur'an, and others suggest that if we study them, we might obtain some of the necessary answers.

To see if such statements hold any truth, I suggest we look at some of the claims of these books.

PART TWO

STUDYING
THE HOLY BOOKS

CHAPTER 5

Hinduism, Jainism, Buddhism, and Zoroastrianism

HINDUISM

Hinduism is considered by many to be simultaneously both a philosophy and a religion. It is sometimes called "Sanatana Dharma," which could be translated as "everlasting truth." It is believed by some to be the oldest and most profound philosophy in the world. It is also the third largest religion in existence, counting more than one billion adherents.

The origination of this religion is ascribed to the people of the Indus River Valley, who are presently known to us as Hindus. Some scholars believe the Hindu culture arose from the mix of two ancient civilizations, Indus and Aryan that go back at least 4,500 years. Around that time, the Aryans invaded the lands belonging to the people of the Indus River Valley and conquered them. Eventually these two advanced cultures coalesced, forming a single civilization with a common dominant faith: Hinduism.

Scholars infer that Aryans created the sacred hymns of the *Rig-Veda*, the oldest of the Vedas. Unfortunately, the original Indus people did not leave many artifacts. It is known, however, that they lived in at least two major cities: Harappa (hence Harappan culture) and Mohenjo-daro. The latter became a significant urban center of the original Hindu civilization.

Because it began as one of the oldest, Hindu religion at its dawn had worshiped many gods.

In researching Sanskrit literature, scriptures, and archaeological excavations, one may conclude that the Indus people believed in sacred signs of nature, the winds, the storms, the sun, and especially the presence of the fresh, pure, and useful water and fire. They held certain animals to be sacred to—or symbolic of—particular deities or aspects of deity. The cow, for example, which is emblematic of both the earth and Lord Shiva, is respected (though not worshipped) as a sacred animal. This is a possible source of the expressions "holy cow" and "sacred cow."

Hindus do not claim any single founder or any single book that exclusively shaped their faith. Hindus believe that God reveals himself through a series of avatars, which are literally those who descended into human forms. Such were Lord Krishna, Rama, and Manu. The latter is revered in the Hindu culture as the "father of mankind."

According to Hindu tradition, the doctrines of Hinduism began to accumulate around 2500-2000 BCE. At that time, local people began collecting philosophical and religious knowledge that they claim was revealed directly from heaven and therefore was considered divine in nature. It eventually turned into the two Indian epics, the larger one the *Mahabharata* and the other the *Ramayana*.

To set a context for the roots of this religion, one must realize that Hindu society in its formative period, in contrast to many Middle Eastern cultures, was relatively isolated and did not feel much influence from the outside world. Despite or possible because of this, India has experienced the rise of many different philosophical schools—including materialistic, agnostic, and atheistic—that have questioned the authority of religion and challenged the traditional methods of knowledge, weakening long-held conceptions of truth and faith. Yet through it all, Hinduism has remained, in its multifaceted manifestation, the dominant religious tradition.

Accordingly, a system of great complexity arose over time, with a complicated caste system, competing ideas about life, death, and the afterlife, and at times dominant priesthood, the Brahmins. The priesthood, however, was generally tolerant of the way people preferred to worship the gods; it allowed religious debate without enforcing one rigid faith or set of beliefs upon all.

It is of great interest that came to us as a spiritual work disclosing the Hindu philosophy and faith, an excerpt from the *Mahabharata* called *the Bhagavad Gita*. In it the incarnated god Krishna enlightens his best friend and the warrior Arjuna how to fight and win not only on the battlefield but in one's own soul.

Revealing the many truths Krishna teaches Arjuna and the reader many aspects of life, cosmic connections, and, of course, gods.

One of the most revered avatars in Hinduism, Krishna does not diminish other gods, yet does not hide his own identity either, commenting:

> *Those who love the gods go to the gods; but those who love me come to me. The unwise think J am that form of my lower nature which is seen by mortal eyes; they know not my higher nature, imperishable and supreme.* (Bhagavad Gita 7:23-24)

Later, Arjuna exclaims: "I see in thee all the gods, o my God: and the infinity of the beings of thy creation." (ibid. 11:15)

Krishna may have styled those who loved the gods as "unwise," but he did not deny them the right to be unwise. In the Bhagavad Gita, he also reveals certain truths regarding the qualities of the universe and the human being. He speaks about the idea of *dehin*, (the occupier of *deha*), that is, the occupier of the body, which is the soul. This is a term Krishna uses in the second chapter of the Bhagavad Gita, where he is teaching Arjuna that his soul (dehin) is eternal and will take up a new existence after the death of the present body. This has been interpreted variously as meaning that the soul gets a new physical human body (or even transmigrates to another life-form) or that it takes up some other existence. This is complicated by the teaching that there are different kinds of bodies, such as the *dharma-deha* (spiritual body), the *linga-deha* (subtle body), and the *karma-deha*, (action body). Whether this means a body acquired through the action of the soul, or the body in which one may act in the physical world, is open to debate.

In chapter 8 of the Bhagavad Gita, Krishna uses another term for the eternal component in human beings, atman, which he defines as "the spirit of God in man." This idea of an eternal soul that is in some way created in the image of God is a prevalent idea in most religions. In Hinduism this has been extrapolated to mean that human beings should view any material wishes as transient and ephemeral. The only real treasure the human being is to value is his soul, because at the end of its life cycle(s) it will be connected to the Highest Spirit of the universe. Based on this idea, humans should worry about their actions in everyday life only as those actions might help or hinder them in their journey toward enlightenment and the highest bond with the Divine.

The relative freedom that Hindu people had practiced, naturally led to the appearance of many schools of religious philosophy and thought. Around the sixth century BCE, it coincided with an explosion of subcultures in Hindu society. New philosophies propagated in the societal net, with such notables as Carvaka and Buddhism.

The Carvakas got their name from the foremost proponent of this philosophy, which came into existence before the birth of the Buddha. Disputing the established spiritual philosophy of the time, they largely denied the existence of God, the soul (atman), and life after death, thus expressing mainly atheistic views and opinions. Along with Carvaka, a number of less prominent schools appeared. Such were Mimamsa, Samkhya, and others, some of which, though less strict, still denied the existence of God.

However, in spite of the existence of many different sects and doctrines, Hindu culture was mainly influenced by the belief in one supreme cosmic Spirit, an uncreated creator that pervaded and ruled the universe.

> *Who verily knows and who can here declare it, whence it was born and whence comes this creation? The gods are later than this world's production. Who knows then whence it came first into being? He, the first origin of this creation, whether he formed it or did not form it, Whose eye controls this world in highest heaven, he verily knows it.* (Rig-Veda, Hymn CXXIX, "Creation")

With many different currents in society, it was a natural consequence that some religious texts became more influential than others. Such were the Vedas. The original Vedas were passed orally from generation to generation and were preserved with the help of a specifically developed technique called mnemonics.

The Vedas (knowledge) are the compiled sacred texts that became the scriptures of ancient Hinduism. They are assembled in four major parts, starting with four Samhitas (collections), which are considered to be the main Vedic texts. The first and oldest among them, as I noted, is the *Rig-Veda* (to praise knowledge). The *Rig-Veda* includes more than one thousand hymns in praise of the Hindu gods. It is accepted by most scholars that the *Rig-Veda* was compiled as a text around 1500-1000 BCE.

The second Veda, Yajur Veda, teaches the believer how to perform sacrifices, while the third, the Sama Veda, is devoted to chanting. The last of these canonical works is the Atharva Veda. It contains the incantations and spells or prayers used for physical and spiritual healing. It also teaches how one can be protected from demons.

The Vedic Sanskrit corpus also consists of the Brahmanas. These are prose texts that discuss in detail the performance and meaning of Vedic sacrificial rituals. The third division of the Vedas is the Aranyakas. Aranyakas were compiled by reclusive *yogis* (devotees) who lived and meditated in the forests. These texts do not give instruction on ritual but rather delve into the spiritual meaning of ritual.

The fourth part of the Vedas, the Upanishads or *Vedanta* (the end of the Vedas), is an anthology of collected spiritual knowledge. The first known Upanishads were compiled between 800 and 400 BCE and are composed of 112 treatises. This theological anthology was compiled over more than two millennia, with the last verses written down as late as the fifteenth century CE.

The final revised version of the Vedas was published in 1973-1976. It was extended to 1,800 pages with the inclusion of the Vedangas, the auxiliary disciplines that help devotees study and understand the Vedas.

In India today, there exist many philosophies that take different approaches to the Vedas. Those Indian sects that accept the Vedas as their scriptures are considered orthodox. Traditions (specifically Buddhism and Jainism) that do not accept the Vedas as authoritative documents are considered to be heterodox.

—

According to Hindu belief, the ancient people to whom the Vedas were originally revealed were the *rishis*. Rishis were the seers who became prominent some three thousand years ago. They claimed to receive divine revelations via higher consciousness.

Today, the Vedas are among the oldest religious documents in existence that form the basis of a currently practiced religion. They represent an amazing collection of scientific and spiritual knowledge. To help teach the core doctrines of the Vedas, sages popularized them in the form of epics, the *Mahabharata* as we already discussed and the second one is the *Ramayana*. The hero of the *Ramayana* is the Lord Rama. Both though, according to Hindu belief, are the avatars of the god Vishnu, a member of the Hindu "trinity," which includes also Brahma and Shiva.

The *Ramayana* is the story of Prince Rama, who comes to earth to teach humankind how to live a virtuous life. As in any life story, there are evil forces with which Prince Rama has to struggle. But eventually good, noble forces win over what is perceived as evil, and Rama ascends to the throne rightfully belonging to him. While this epic story involves many characters, humankind may learn many good lessons of morality versus immorality, nobility versus evil.

The majority of Hindus recognize Hinduism as a monotheistic religion. They consider the avatars to be the human manifestations of one god—a cosmic Spirit with three aspects: Brahma (the Creator), Vishnu (the Preserver), and Shiva (the Destroyer). Thus the three aspects together represent the eternal cycle of birth, existence, and death, which is one of the main themes of Hindu theology. There are also Hindu schools that revere Christ and Buddha as avatars of the Supreme Spirit. Hindus also believe in many celestial entities, called *devas*.

Though it is considered a single faith, Hinduism embraces varying religious doctrines. As a philosophy, its tolerance of other religions comes from the belief that the truth is one no matter what one calls it. The basic doctrines of Hindu belief include moral duties, obligations, actions, the operation of the law of *karma*—which is a spiritual manifestation of the physical law of cause and effect—and the eventual goal of each righteous Hindu to attain moksha.

According to Hindu philosophy, all living beings are divine, and those who are evil in their deeds or thought are simply ignorant and lack knowledge of their spiritual reality. This is succinctly reflected in the philosophy of *Yoga* (union). The Yogic philosophy is based on physical, psychological, and ethical progress of a man's soul. It holds that if an individual wants to realize the meaning of his existence, he must develop as a whole being in a way that will connect him to the transcendent world.

Thus the main teaching of Yoga is a mastery of the mind. Not in the sense that the mind should be the master of a man, but in the sense that the soul must become the master of the mind. "They say that the senses are great," says Krishna. "But greater than the senses is the mind. Greater than the mind is *Buddhi*, reason; and greater than reason is He—the Spirit in man and in all." (Bhagavad Gita 3:42)

When man achieves this mastery, he achieves the state of Yoga, of union with the divine.

Now with this very short and abbreviated excurse into Hinduism, I would like to conduct some critical analysis of a number of claims for which Hinduism is known.

—CONCEPT 1—

Some Hindu thinkers claim that because God is everywhere, around us and within us, it would be a truthful statement to claim that "we are God."

—RESPONSE 1—

Even if we accept the notion that God is everywhere, it does not mean that we are, in any literal sense, God. This is true whether God made us the way we are, or whether it is only our desire that this be so. A robot that is programmed to perform human tasks does not become human in capacity no matter how close to human norms we program its behavior to be.

—CONCEPT 2—

Many schools of Hinduism believe in reincarnation, the physical rebirth of the soul (atman) in a new body. The atman is immortal and, according to these schools of thought, lives endless cycles in numerous human or animal forms. Although the Vedas don't speak of rebirth but rather of re-death, Krishna speaks of rebirth in the Bhagavad Gita. In verse 2:22 he says, "Just as a man discards worn out clothes and puts on new clothes, the soul discards worn out bodies and wears new ones." As previously noted, however, this idea is complicated by the theorized existence of different types of bodies, some distinctly nonphysical.

In Hindu philosophy, the process of transmigration goes approximately like this: When the creative process begins, a soul (dehin) comes to an individual and hides behind the created personality (*maya*). There is also a concept of the mind that includes the subtle body (linga-deha) and an outer personality (ego). Ego is represented by the body. At the end cycle of one's life, the body and the mind return to the earth. The soul survives. It goes into a series of bodies and, at the end of its innumerable cycles, a soul either ascends to heaven, where it is united with Brahman, or descends to hell, the realm of Yama, the Lord of Death.

Depending on the accumulated amount of bad or good actions (karma), the soul stays in those places for as long as it needs to expiate the bad karma. After that, it comes back to the earth to be born again as a new and distinct individual dehin.

—RESPONSE 2—

When taking up its new body, a soul (atman) brings leftover baggage from its previous lives. Yet if the soul is immortal—which means it does not have a beginning or end—why would it be burdened with the accumulated deeds of past lives? Why does it have to be responsible for one's mortal deeds? Does it have to feel remorse for human's bad deeds?

As far as a newborn baby is concerned, it has done nothing from which it can learn or for which it can feel remorse. The deeds from its previous life might as well have been committed by someone else. In that sense, in that it does not remember its past lives, a soul is purged each time it begins a new cycle. If God is just, shouldn't its slate be wiped as clean as its memory each time it descends to a new life?

The alleged purpose of reincarnation is the education of the soul. In this context, the theory is not logical. If someone cannot learn from what he cannot remember, then how feasible should reincarnation be? Besides, if we are to believe the Vedas' and Gita's words about the Creator's justice and love, how can we imagine that this Creator would force the atman to participate in a process of birth and death without any memory of what it is supposed to be making restitution for? Based on this analysis, one might easily conclude that this process of reincarnation is pure fantasy invented by humans thirsty to last forever.

While reincarnation was definitely an invention of Hinduism, it was somewhat surprising to me that this philosophy, though alien to the minds of devotees from many other religions, has in recent decades been attracting many believers other than Hindus. These new believers speak of memories of past lives and of many physical places they "remember" but have never visited during their present lifetimes. Not investigating such a way of thinking with contentious analysis, people allow themselves to be pulled in by mythical beliefs, whether that makes them feel more accomplished or not.

There are a few other conspicuous theories that exist, the most notable being the theory of transmigration. This theory supports the idea that the souls of humans may occupy the bodies of animals as well as plants as punishment for sins committed in previous lives. Here, again, there is no logic in bringing suffering onto an animal that had not participated in human misdeeds. Besides, does this consequence make sense when animals don't possess the human intellect that would enable them to make choices about their behavior? A human may choose to be savage or benign. Indeed savagery, in a human, is an evil. In a wolf, which has no choice, it may be considered a virtue. This also calls into question the justice of a god who would send a soul to earth in a body that allows it no capacity for learning human virtue.

The ultimate goal of this process is to achieve a condition called moksha, that is, the liberation of the soul from the cycle of death and rebirth. Every Hindu strives to achieve that condition, and in that regard I will speak a little later while presenting the philosophy of Buddhism.

—CONCEPT 3—

Hindus believe the deeds and actions of a person, whether good or bad, always have consequences. In Indian religion, this process of action and consequence is called the law of karma. Hindus believe that karma is the result of causation, with or without the involvement of a Supreme Being.

Karma literally means "action," but it also refers to the accumulated consequences of action. In the Bhagavad Gita, Krishna speaks of three types of human actions: karma, actions that elevate the soul; *vikarma*, actions that degrade the soul; and *akarma*, actions that are neutral because they create neither good nor bad consequences. Thus we talk of "good karma" and "bad karma," which are stored up and which determine, along with our free will, the course of our destinies.

The law of karma deals then with the accountability of the individual soul, and it rests on each soul's capacity to make choices while in human form.

—RESPONSE 3—

By the law of karma, as it is generally understood, a man is the product of his choices and present or past deeds, whether committed in his current life or in past lives. Because of a frequent pairing of the concepts of reincarnation and karma, the two are quite often erroneously used interchangeably or assumed to be inseparable. In this context, the most prevalent explanation of both is as such: The dehin survives a bodily death and, based on its karma, is reborn as a living being to continue its journey until the end of the cycle of birth and death.

Given that, let's consider a couple of hypothetical situations. First, let's assume that a man buys stocks in various companies, but the moment he buys them, their value decreases. No matter what business he is transacting, no matter how high the value of the stocks appear to be before his purchase, and no matter how analytical he is and how many variants he has calculated, he always loses money. He comes to believe that his bad luck in the stock market is his karma—either from bad things he's done in his present life or in a previous existence.

If these deeds were done in this life, and he remembers them, he might be persuaded to change his behavior, but what is he to do if the vikarma (bad karma) is from a previous life that he cannot recall? What good is punishment for behavior or attitudes that one cannot remember? He might assume his vikarma has something to do with money or perhaps greed, but he will never be certain of this and so what attitude or behavior should he change? What is he to learn?

Another example: A child is born with a terminal disease. If the child is the product of parents who were drug addicts, then the causal progression can be seen, but if it is the result of the parents' karma for other evils that did not affect them physically, why should the innocent child be punished? Why would an innocent child be punished anyway? If the disease is the vikarma for sins committed by this soul in a previous life, how is the child, who has no memory of these sins, expected to feel regret or remorse? Why then must this child suffer for what it cannot remember? What just God would require its suffering?

In my opinion, suffering is not adequately explained by the law of karma combined with the doctrine of reincarnation. In this form, it seems not so much a law of causation as an explanation for the inexplicable. We *imagine* that we have explained why there is suffering in the world. I believe I am justified in suggesting that perhaps this process is just that: a product of the limited human imagination.

The *American Heritage Dictionary* defines *imagination* as "the power of the mind to form a mental image or concept of something that is not real or present." I include this definition here because I believe it explains everything in the above-mentioned examples. We ask why and then use imagination to answer.

Not being able to fathom the mechanics of many phenomena, such as our ability to think and experience emotions, the birth and death of our bodies, and the complicated laws of the universe, we are taken by a desire to find out whether these phenomena are real or not. That desire has given birth to science. It has also given birth to fanciful explanations when rational answers fail to come easily.

To conclude, Hinduism is a philosophical aggregate of ideas that at some point became religious expression of Hindu people. Despite many (over a billion) followers, there is no one scriptural doctrine accepted by all Hindus. That, nevertheless, does not change the basic belief of these people in dharma (ethics and duties), samsara (rebirth), karma (right action), and moksha (liberation of the soul).

JAINISM

Whether the founder of Jainism was Rishabhadeva, the first Tirthankara or Parsvanatha, the twenty-third Tirthankara, is not really important. Jainism is considered one of the most ancient traditions in India. It began as an ascetic sect with a number of aspects similar to Hinduism, such as belief in karma and moksha, or *nirvana*. Practicing vegetarianism, followers of Jainism propagated the principles of truthfulness, nonviolence, detachment from worldly pleasures, chastity, and reaching a condition of total freedom from the cycles of birth and death.

The twenty-fourth Tirthankara, the Lord Mahavira, was a contemporary of Gautama Buddha. A great teacher, Mahavira travelled to the deepest corners of India with his ascetic message of how to attain the internal beauty and liberation of the soul. Not a founder but a reformer of an already-existing faith, Mahavira was successful in obliterating the conception of God as the Creator. He denounced the worship of gods while encouraging prayers to enlightened and liberated souls, saluting the Tirthankaras—the saints of the world.

Whether a historical fact or by sheer coincidence, the early life of Mahavira reminds me of that of Gautama Buddha, though the two taught sometimes-opposing doctrines. Born in a princely family, Mahavira married and had a daughter, only to abandon his family to become an ascetic after the death of his parents. He wandered from place to place for twelve years, subjecting himself to rigid austerity, and became enlightened while sitting under a Sal tree one day. He fell ill and died at age seventy-two around 468 BCE, according to most historical accounts. After the death of Mahavira, Jainism did not undergo many drastic changes, though it developed a few schisms.

The followers of Hinduism largely dismissed the teacher and teachings of Jainism as delusional, while many acknowledged that Buddha, like Krishna, was an avatar of Vishnu.

Jainism lately became known as a religion of nonviolence, with its followers close to four million people. Practicing Jainism followers

–

are rigorously in pursuit of ascetic self-control approach to life with a goal to reach final liberation from bodily and human mischief.

BUDDHISM

Siddhartha Gautama—also known as the Gautama Buddha—was a spiritual teacher in the ancient Indian subcontinent, circa 534-483 BCE. He was born to a royal family in what is today Nepal and lived as a prince of the Sakya tribe until he realized the emptiness of his royal style of life when contrasted to the suffering of most humans. Through his father, King Suddhodana, he inherited a luxurious existence and faced a future as the head of his clan. But at age twenty-nine, after a sudden encounter with the suffering and evils of the world, Siddhartha abandoned his inheritance, left his wife and son (both of whom later became his disciples), and dedicated his life to the study of how to overcome suffering. The methods of his learning were unbelievably rigorous. Yet despite such severe methods, the prince could not realize his goal.

According to Bukkyo Dendo Kyokal,

> *after six years in the forest he gave up the practice of asceticism. He went bathing in the river and accepted a bowl of milk from a maiden who lived in the neighboring village. He was still weak, but at the risk of losing his life he attempted yet another period of meditation, saying to himself, "Blood may become exhausted, flesh may decay, bones may fall apart, but I will never leave this place until I find the way to Enlightenment." It was an intense and incomparable struggle for him. He was desperate and filled with confusing thoughts, dark shadows overhung his spirits, and he was beleaguered by all the lures of the devils. Carefully and patiently he examined them one by one and rejected them all. It was hard struggle indeed, making his blood run thin, his flesh fall away, and his bones crack.*
>
> *But when morning star appeared in the eastern sky, the struggle was over and the Prince's mind was as clear and*

—

*bright as the breaking day. He had, at last, found the path
to Enlightenment.*

Siddhartha became known as the *Buddha* (enlightened, i.e.,
awakened to the truth or Dharma) after obtaining spiritual understanding
(enlightenment) at the age of thirty-five, when he became known as
"The Perfectly Self-Awakened One," the Samyaksambuddha (Pali:
Sammasambuddha). He began his journey to learn how to resist
the attacks of temptations, evils of life (demons), how not to suffer
from pains or disease, and how to meet death. He sought these things
first through meditation, self-mortification, and extreme asceticism
such was as taught by Mahavira. The Buddha proclaimed a life of
moderation, nonviolence, and compassion known in Buddhism as the
Middle Way. His philosophy was fairly simple: To find the way to joy,
look no further than your true self. In essence, Buddha renewed the
core teaching of the Vedas and the Bhagavad Gita.

At the time, the majority of Indians followed Vedantic Hinduism.
They believed in ritual, a strict caste system, and the holiness and power
of their rich and elite priesthood, the Brahmins. Buddha questioned
the Brahmins' authority, claiming that he, not they, knew the path to
God. Contrary to their emphasis on ritual, Buddha advocated reliance
on individual experience and suggested using plain language, leading
a simple life, and attempting to discover spirituality directly, on one's
own, by following the teaching of the Buddhas (among whom he
included Krishna). In striving to provide guidance and inspiration for
life, he taught how to become compassionate, loving, and respectful
through right meditation. Far from being elitist, his teachings were
directed to people from all walks of life.

Some of his teachings are quite strange to the mind of the
westerner, and I wish to discuss those in an attempt to shed some
light on them. Buddha taught the need for detachment from self or
ego. In some modern Buddhist teaching, such as Zen Buddhism, this
is expressed in a denial of the atman and, by extension, of God. In
Mahayana Buddhism, one of the oldest of the two major divisions
within the faith, and in the more recent Dhammakaya Movement from
Thailand, the atman is rather defined as the Buddha nature in each
human being (contracted with Krishna's statement that the atman is
the spirit of God in man).

–

For Zen Buddhists, there is no transmigration of souls and, therefore, no actual reincarnation. Rather there is the spiritual rebirth of a human being. Our life, at some point, allows us to achieve liberation from all selfish attachments. That state of mind is called *nirvana* in Buddhism. In Mahayana Buddhism, nirvana is associated with the discovery within one's self or the Buddha nature (atman).

The teachings of Buddha are summarized in the Four Noble Truths. According to Buddha, they are:

The Noble Truth of suffering

The Noble Truth of the origin of suffering

The Noble Truth of the cessation of suffering

The Noble Truth of the Way leading to the cessation of suffering.

(Buddha, Digha Nikaya, Sutra 16)

The Noble Eightfold Path is the principal teaching of how to achieve self-awakening. It includes:

- Right View
- Right Intention
- Right Speech
- Right Action
- Right Livelihood
- Right Effort
- Right Mindfulness
- Right Concentration

In Buddhist philosophy, the three main sources of pain are:

Impermanence: Everything is changing; therefore humans suffer pain because of their attachments to things that will inevitably change.

There is no separate self: Meaning that the concept of self, or "I," is a construct of the human mind rather than a reality. This is reminiscent of Krishna's statement that

—

When one sees eternity in things that pass away and infinity in finite things, then one has pure knowledge. But if one merely sees the diversity of things then one has impure knowledge. And if one selfishly sees a thing as if it were everything, independent of the ONE and the many, then one is in the darkness of ignorance.(Bhagavad Gita 18:20-22)

Discontent: This concept, drawn from the Sanskrit word *dukkha*, has nuanced meaning that is not necessarily negative. The idea, as interpreted by some scholars, is that the individual is dissatisfied or discontent with existence and seeks change. This is ironic since change is also a cause of suffering.

Among other major philosophical tenets, Buddhism also advocates complete detachment from everything material, every thirst a person can experience during his lifetime. It teaches that everything we desire brings us suffering, so to not suffer means to move beyond our desires. Buddhism calls this achievement an absolute truth (nirvana). Because all things around us have a beginning and an end, nothing material can be ultimately satisfying.

As long as our minds must interact with the phenomenal world, achieving nirvana is the only way to be released from suffering. This sounds very similar to the Hindu idea of moksha, but in Zen Buddhism, for example, since there is no unchanging soul, there is nothing eternal that can be released from suffering. The human reality (whether you call it atman or not) develops and changes just like everything else.

In Buddhism, as in Hinduism, the karma means "doing" or "action" and is intimately connected to mental intent. In much Buddhist doctrine, however, it is not used with the connection to a cosmological influence from heaven or God. Inasmuch as everyone is responsible for his or her own actions—with karma as the immediate result—karma in Buddhism is more clearly a theory of cause and effect, though the connection to deeds done in past lives does still exist in some Buddhist doctrines.

One can see in Buddhism an acknowledgement of the negative effects of outside influences. Even though we think we're immune to them, outside forces always exist in any human culture, as well as in our physical environment. These outside forces quite often have a negative impact on us: they distress and disturb us, and they can make us physically ill. Those forces cannot be easily overcome no matter how vigorously we resist them. In addition, it seems we are preprogrammed to suffer. However, I strongly disagree with Buddha's teachings on how we are to fight our emotions, and I will say a few words about this at the end of this article.

Buddha also stated that a person should accept someone's teaching only if one's own experience verifies it and if it is praised by the wise:

> *Do not go upon what has been acquired by repeated hearing; nor upon tradition; nor upon rumor; nor upon what is in a scripture; nor upon surmise; nor upon an axiom; nor upon specious reasoning; nor upon a bias towards a notion that has been pondered over; nor upon another's seeming ability; nor upon the consideration, 'The monk is our teacher.' Kalamas, when you yourselves know: 'These things are good; these things are not blamable; these things are praised by the wise; undertaken and observed, these things lead to benefit and happiness,' enter on and abide in them.* (Kalama Sutra, verse 10)

Now this may lead some to ask, if someone applies his own experience as verification, then why does he need a teacher? Let's consider the plight of a child with a talent for music. She possesses a strong sense of rhythm, relative pitch, and melody; she has a charming voice. This child might also wish to become a professional vocalist. Does she need a teacher? After all, she possesses natural talent. She knows how to sing—isn't that enough?

Most people would agree that it is not, not if the child wishes to learn the full extent of her abilities or perhaps to know music theory. Wise parents would send this child to a music teacher so she could learn the principles of melody and harmony and the control of her voice.

Certainly, there will be many times—especially early in the course of her lessons—that the child must submit to the teacher's instruction without question. She may wonder why she must sing scales for hours on end, but presumably she will stop wondering when the rigorous exercise results in the strengthening of her voice.

But before they choose a music teacher, presumably the parents would ask to see credentials, perhaps meet other pupils to see if this teacher's methods worked well, or solicit opinions of the teacher's methods from other trusted experts. They might, for example, determine if the teacher treated his pupils with respect. This highly pragmatic model is what Buddha seems to be proposing for spiritual guidance as well.

The teachings of Buddha propose five basic tenets: not to kill, not to lie, not to steal, not to drink (alcohol), and finally to be morally pure. All this, when practiced, might lead to nirvana, which Buddha leaves somewhat undefined. Of it, he comments that:

> And as all things originate from one Essence, so they are developing according to one law, and they are destined to one aim which is Nirvana. Nirvana comes to thee ... when thou understandest thoroughly and livest according to that understanding, that all things are of one Essence and that there is but one law. (Sanskrit Dhammapada)

His philosophy—as construed by some sects of Buddhism—seems not to conform to the basic teachings of religion, since they interpret it as having denied the existence of both God and soul. Yet by reaching enlightenment, Buddha claimed, one would acquire supernatural (that is, spiritual) powers that would help him in all experiences of life. Indeed, one of the important branches of Buddhism—Mahayana—sees the Buddha as the Supreme Reality cloaked in the human form. This is part of the philosophy of the Three Bodies: the Essential Body (the impersonal ultimate reality), the Bliss Body (the personal, but disembodied spirit of Buddha), and the Transformation Body (the appearance of the Buddha as a human teacher).

Does God exist in Buddha's philosophy? This depends on whom you talk to and what references they cite. The great Pali collection of Buddhist writings portrays Buddha as an atheist, possibly because of his disputes with the Brahmin priests of Hinduism. Other sources argue against this interpretation and indicate that Buddha viewed himself as being one in a long line of related avatars or Buddhas sent from the world of Brahman as this passage from the Digha Nikaya suggests:

—

The Tathagata knows the straight path that leads to union with Brahma. He knows it as one who entered the world of Brahma and has been born in it. There can be no doubt in the Tathagata. (1.235)

The teachings of Buddha were and are accepted by many with open arms because he showed us how to struggle with our own ills. On a large scale, he taught how to overpower what is found in us that produces suffering. In other words, he taught us to be strong and to always control our emotions. If—and only if—one could achieve these conditions one would be able to achieve peace with oneself and thus attain nirvana.

At this point I wish to express my views on some teachings of Buddha. First of all I personally see nothing wrong with being bombarded with the problems aimed at us, owing to which we learn how to navigate through and to achieve our goals. While everything is in constant change (including us), we learn how to adjust to the new conditions. That makes us stronger. That makes us wiser. That makes us able to help others. That makes us alive.

While Buddhism teaches that people need to learn how to rid themselves of sufferings, denying themselves any attachments, these attempts necessarily lead to sufferings. We are born with emotions. They overwhelm us. They make us suffer. Yet in the meantime our emotions make us *feel* life, and getting rid of them might only produce an emotionless creature that inadvertently will speed up one's eventual expiration.

On that note I'd like to pose here a series of questions:

- Given the doctrine that we have no soul and that there is no God that provides us with it, what explains our peculiar human consciousness?
- What develops this consciousness and our sense of interrelatedness with each other and the world?
- How can we explain the origin of our emotions if no souls exist?
- Even though contemporary scientific theories espouse a bottom-up chain of chemical reactions, how can anyone explain the symphony of existing laws of humanity, nature, and the cosmos in purely chemical terms?

As these questions are not original and are from time to time repeated in the pages of this book, I do not plan to answer them here. The reason I ask them is to once again call for conducting an analysis of our existence, especially as sentient creatures in this world.

As to the incarnated God, such as the avatars, messengers, or the manifestations of God—no matter how similarly they speak, they simply might be the brightest representatives of a particular stock of people, seeking the meaning of life. Thus while God may indeed exist in any shape and form, it does not follow he would necessarily choose to become human being to be understood and accepted.

ZOROASTRIANISM

Founded sometime before the sixth century BCE in Persia (Iran), Zoroastrianism was a substantially practiced religion among pre-Islamic Iranian people. This powerful and widely known teaching shares concepts and tenets with other religions, including Judaism, Christianity, Islam, Hinduism, Buddhism, and Sikhism. Some scholars believe Zoroastrianism was the first to teach of heaven and hell, the resurrection of the deceased, and the everlasting life of the reunited soul and body.

Zoroastrianism is the original religion of millions of Shi'a and Sunni Muslims and Iranian Bahá'ís. The followers of this faith believe in one powerful, beneficent god, Ahura Mazda (Wise Lord), uncreated Creator, a transcendental god who holds the whole universe in order, keeping chaos at bay. Zoroastrians named their religion Mazdayasna, which in the Avestan language is a combination of two words: god (*Mazda*) and worship or devotion (*yasna*). So it is literally and simply the devotion to God. They also give the meaning of their religion as "good religion."

Zoroastrians believe in the spiritual powers of nature, especially water and fire. Water symbolizes the source of wisdom, while fire is the medium through which wisdom is achieved. Both water and fire are considered agents of purity, and Zoroastrians, while worshipping neither fire nor water, often pray in the presence of fire.

Zoroastrian doctrine acknowledges both good and evil in the thoughts of each human being. The term for good is *spenta mainyu*, which implies progressive, expansive (good) mind or thoughts. The term for evil is *agra mainyu* or backward (bad) mind or thoughts.

These two forces—the productive and the destructive or regressive—have been personified in various ways, usually as Ahura Mazda and Ahriman. While Zoroastrianism is strictly monotheistic, a later offshoot called Zurvanism casts Ahriman (or Agra Mainyu) as an evil being who is the twin of Ahura Mazda. Both are sons of Zurvan, the god of time. This dualism is considered a heresy by mainstream Zoroastrianism, as expressed in a text thought to have been written after the fall of the Sassanian Empire and the impact of Islam on Zoroastrian belief.

> *The Creator (Ahura Mazda) is all goodness, and the Destroyer is the accursed Destructive Spirit who is all wickedness and full of death, a liar and a deceiver.* (*The Book of Counsel of Zartusht* verses 13, 14)

Zoroastrian doctrine also clearly distinguishes between the life of the soul (*jan*), which will be freed upon death, and that of the body, which will be dissolved. The whole of Zoroastrian doctrine centers on the belief in the benevolence of God and the purification of the soul. It holds that man will destroy himself and all around him if he follows evil in thoughts, words, and deeds.

A symbol of the Zoroastrian religion, *Faravahar* (the winged disk), was adopted by the Pahlavi dynasty to represent the spirit of the Iranian people sent to the material world to fight evil.

The central scripture of Zoroastrianism, called the Zend Avesta, is a collection of sacred texts, the most ancient of which are the Gathas. They were mostly destroyed by the conquering forces of Alexander the Great. Thus only a fraction of the texts have survived. It is believed that the Avesta was compiled over a period of several hundred years and had originally been a collection of orally transmitted verses. The paraphrases from the lost Avesta texts were later written in such sacred literature as Pahlavi texts that became known to the western world only in the eighteenth century CE.

Zoroaster (Zarathustra or Zartusht), who is believed to have lived around 1200 BCE, created the original seventeen hymns devoted to Ahura Mazda that became the main portion of the Gathas (the

—

centerpiece of inspiration to Zoroastrians). According to the Avesta, Zoroaster taught three essential ethical principles: *Humata, Hukhta, and Huvarshta*, that is, good thought, good speech, and good action.

Zoroastrianism was established as a state religion in the time *of Darius* (died 486 BCE) until the Arab Muslims defeated the Sassanids and brought Islam to Persia. Some Zoroastrians held out against Islam for another three centuries, but eventually most of their countrymen accepted Islam. Since the mid-1800s, many Zoroastrians have become members of the Bahá'í Faith, but there is still a small Zoroastrian community in Iran.

The prophet Zoroaster was born into a polytheistic religion in Bronze Age Iran. Though he was a priest, Zoroaster rejected polytheism, rituals such as the sacrifice of animals, and the oppression by the elite class of ordinary people. He advocated equality for all the people irrespective of religion, race, or gender. Eventually, his religion acquired a tremendous respect among millions of Iranian people who enthusiastically accepted it as belief in one universal god.

According to Zoroastrian tradition—as in Hinduism—each human being is expected to participate in the battle between good and evil in the material world. Zoroastrians believe that in the final days evil will be vanquished, after which God will judge the world and (in later forms of the faith) resurrect the dead.

Many ideas reflected in Zoroastrianism are shared or adopted by religions such as Judaism, Christianity, and others. Concepts such as heaven and hell, a savior (Messiah), a virgin birth, and a judgment of souls are common themes. Some scholars believe they trace their conception back to Zoroastrianism; others maintain that all these faiths have a common source.

Today, the Zoroastrian community, though still present in a few countries (such as Persia, India, and Pakistan, is on the verge of complete obliteration. This trend mainly arises from the faith's reluctance to accept converts, the increase of interfaith marriages, and a growing number of believers who have converted to other religions. There are, in my opinion, intangible reasons as well, such as a refusal to teach their heritage to their young people and the disbelief of some that their religion attaches anything meaningful to life. These things promote an accelerated loss of identity for these people.

One example of such dwindling is the Parsi community in India. The Parsis emigrated from Iran about ten centuries ago. While Parsi history tells of a mass exodus of these people fleeing persecution by the Umayyad Muslims, recent scholarship suggests that the emigration began earlier due to economic pressures and took place over a longer period of time than previously thought. During their tenure in Northern India, the Parsis lost their familial ties in Greater Iran, as well as their original language, social customs, and history.

Once in India, they occupied themselves with agriculture, changing the jungle territory they populated into fruitful gardens, thus enjoying comparative prosperity. But in the year 1315, when the Hindu government was overthrown, they were forced to leave their houses and lands again, moving to another part of Gujarat. In spite of political disturbance, they were welcomed by the new king as they showed loyalty and gratitude to the rulers of the country.

Though the Parsis grew to prominence in different fields over the centuries, their community decreased dramatically for a variety of reasons, some of which I suggested above. Whether this trend can be related to religious impurity or is due to the low birth rate among members of the community, it remains an unfortunate statistical fact: The Parsi population has decreased substantially. With this reduction of the community comes a reduction in of its importance (or even acknowledgment) in the rest of the world. The Parsis of India face the same fate as other marginalized ethnic groups.

CHAPTER 6

The Bible and Judaism

Before I provide my analysis of whether what is written in the Bible is true or not, I suggest we start with the facts connecting us to the so-called prehistoric period. There are at least three sources that might be used in order to decipher human history. One is archaeological, the second is scriptural/historical, and the third is biological/anthropological (that is, the theory of evolution). All three have their own merit and so should be substantially discussed, but as I reasoned in the beginning of this book, it does not prove possible to ponder on any of the raised subjects in a forum such as this. For that ground alone, I must stay within strict limitations and turn to much fewer authorities and examples that one normally would, hopefully supplying enough material to prove my points.

Using archaeological findings and scientific dating methods, scientists have concluded that human beings emerged roughly two and a half million years ago, branching from the hominid tree from an ancestor we held in common with the great apes.

A hominid skull dated six to seven million years ago was unearthed in the southern Sahara by French paleoanthropologists Michel Brunet and Patrick Vignaud. A research team headed by Tim White discovered in 1992 in the Middle Awash River valley of Ethiopia, a fossil dated to 4.4 million years showing seventeen fragments of the hominid genus. They named this *Ardipithecus ramidus* (Ardi for short). There have been a few more findings of such fossils in other parts of Africa as well, placing the appearance of hominids roughly in that same time bracket. Obviously this conflicts with the 5,770 or so years that literal biblical reckoning affords us since the time of creation.

Right there, we might stop investigating the possible flaws of the Hebrew Bible since there is clearly a discrepancy between the scientific timeline and the one some theologians have drawn from the biblical narrative. But let's assume that the creation of the world began the way it was described in the Hebrew Bible—literally—and that the timeline extrapolated from the "begets" (the ancestral lists of patriarchs and their offspring) is really representative of the history of the biblical people.

Genesis 1:1 starts with these words: "In the beginning God created the heavens and the earth." With such a firm statement, the Bible begins its long, barely apologetic narration. While I don't plan or wish to tediously analyze every sentence and word in it, I do want to warn the reader: You are about to enter an almost sarcastic criticism that is rooted not in any malicious intent but arises out of necessity to produce a credible analysis by an indifferent author's point of view. Those who do not want dip into that kind of polemic may definitely skip this and other religious topics.

In the meantime I will proceed to ask: Does the word "heaven" imply the whole universe or only the visible sky? Or does it mean something other than either of those more obvious terms? By "heaven" does the author of Genesis perhaps mean a spiritual realm? Or, yet again, are both the visible and invisible heavens (at least not visible from earth) meant?

If the answer is the latter, then one has to assume that both the visible and invisible heavens were also created at that time, for to believe that this applies to just the visible heaven and the piece of rock we call the earth and not the remaining 99.999 percent of the objects in the universe, seems limiting.

Reading further, we find this doubtful statement "And God said, Let there be light: and there was light" (Genesis 1:3 KJV). Given this, it would be reasonable for the original readers of the text to conclude that the Bible speaks precisely and only about our visible skies because the only light then known was our own sun.

Now the way the narration of the first six days in Genesis goes, though it sounds as if God's work was both discerned and appreciated

—

by someone, such as the author, this cannot have been the case. One can infer that God at some point (about 13.7 billion years after his creation of the universe) revealed what he did to a human agent, perhaps as he communicated his commandments to Moses, though, perhaps because of human capacity, not *how* he did it.

We further learn in Genesis 2:2 that "And on the seventh day God ended His work which He had done, and He rested on the seventh day from all His work which He had done" (KJV). I will assume that the fact that God rested means he got tired. Would that also mean that God possesses some of the same attributes as flesh and blood beings have (i.e., muscles that can grow weary)? That begs the further question as to whether God would have needed more rest if his tasks had been even more labor intensive, such as making other planets?

After the description of God's cosmic accomplishments, next comes the story of the Garden of Eden. Genesis 2:9 reads, "And out of the ground the Lord God made every tree grow that is pleasant to the sight and good for food. The tree of life was also in the midst of the garden, and the tree of the knowledge of good and evil" (NKJV). Genesis 2:15-17 reads, "Then the Lord God took the man and put him in the Garden of Eden to tend and keep it. And the Lord God commanded the man, saying, 'Of every tree of the garden you may freely eat; but of the tree of the knowledge of good and evil you shall not eat, for in the day that you eat of it you shall surely die'" (NKJV).

And here rises the first real dilemma, as I see it. Why would the Almighty want to place a tree near his ultimate creation—man—and immediately warn him of the danger in approaching and eating from it?

The answers provided so far by the religious apologists, such as that God prohibits man to eat from the "tree of knowledge" to keep him out of sin and that man should not only love the one who created him but also trust and that man cannot know God's way of thinking and thus shouldn't make assumptions, in fact, all those recommendations dodge the question why the tree was placed there.

If that tree of knowledge was so prohibitive to man's well-being, wouldn't it be more appropriate not to place it there at all? Who, besides man, could have used it? Who, besides man, could have appreciated it? Therefore, to plant such a tree in the Garden of Eden wouldn't be a wise idea. Must we conclude then that God is not wise? Or that he is a trickster god?

—

Must not have God foreseen that the just-created-by-him man does not have any experience and cannot be expected to know life and the obstacles it produces and, therefore, would not possess any wisdom on how to survive?

Such way of thinking also brings another point, that we are confronted with a need to understand God's attributes. We see him getting tired or displaying a short fuse from time to time, just as a man might. Does God really possess these human failings? Is it possible that he could be weary and impatient, that he could accumulate frustration and stress? How can he, if he is supposed to last forever?

A possible moral of the story, as the narrator presents it, could be that God wanted to warn people that knowledge carries both good and bad consequences. If a man lives without knowledge of good and evil, he will be always blissfully ignorant of the fact that he is mortal and will "surely die," for example. Was that the real message from God?

In addition, given the knowledge to discern good from evil, man suddenly becomes accountable for his choices and is no longer free to indulge his animal appetites without thought to the consequences. Further, the minute man begins to know *something*, he begins to experience dissatisfaction. He begins to search and struggle for improvement in his life, and the more he knows, the more he realizes that to achieve complete satisfaction is impossible, no matter what he does.

On the other hand, if he remains ignorant, man would surely stop striving toward progress, and his life would stagnate into an endless eddy of feeding himself in order not to die and reproducing to continue his species. What is human life if it is reducible to no more than what any animal might experience? I will return to this question in more detail later, in the second part of this book.

For now, let me move on to the creation of woman. Here I'm assuming that, as fundamentalist believers avow, Adam did exist as the first man in creation. Wouldn't the removal of even one rib from his body have produced some kind of damage to his thoracic skeleton? After all, the count of the ribs would be shortened to eleven after the surgery instead of the normal twelve in our symmetrical body. Did God mean to make Adam imperfect? Why would God need Adam's rib to produce a woman anyway? Couldn't he have created her in the same way he created Adam?

—

Theologians posit that by this, God meant to show man's and woman's interdependency and oneness, but some have taken it further, noting the significance of this particular bone's location. It is not from Adam's head, so woman is not his superior. It is not from his foot, so she is not his inferior. It is from near his heart and under his arm where she might be loved and protected. In doing this, interestingly, these theologians assign the creation story a symbology and metaphorical value which begs the question of why they take any of it literally.

Another seeming inconsistency is the placement of a subtle, elusive, and cunning beast in that garden along with the innocent humans. This might be interpreted as yet another gross provocation on God's part, especially as he lets it use Eve as an instrument of seduction. Wouldn't it be much simpler and more appropriate for God to eliminate the serpent before it did so much damage that God would have to punish Adam and Eve and all the rest of humanity?

Again, the *metaphorical* value of this is that the new humans are being offered a choice of voices to listen to. And again, if it is agreed upon that the value is metaphorical, then why do some insist that it is also literal?

Accorded a literal interpretation, the ordinary reader might start to feel that neither God nor the life he has given man are fair, at least not as described in the Hebrew Bible. God is vengeful instead of just. His creations, Adam and Eve, are tested and punished from the moment of their appearance on earth. They are not even warned not to listen to the snake; for all they know, everything in God's creation is—like them—good and innocent.

Yet they are driven from Eden, and God places a cherubim and a "flaming sword" at the entrance of the Garden of Eden "to guard the way to the tree of life" (Genesis 3:24 NKJV). And this is just the beginning.

The children of Adam and Eve, Cain and Abel, are not treated equally, in spite of each showing respect to the Lord in his own way. God likes Abel's offering from his flock, but he does not respect Cain's offering from his crops. The Bible doesn't explain why this is, but God tells Cain, "If you do well, will you not be accepted? And if you do not do well, sin lies at the door. And its desire is for you, but you should rule over it" (Genesis 4:7 NKJV).

Such mistreatment enrages Cain, apparently, and he kills Abel. Out of four people, which if we believe the fundamentalist's interpretation

—

of Genesis there were only four people on the planet, still this heinous act is allowed to happen.

Almost immediately Cain is punished for this act. He is banished from the land of his birth to be a lonely and restless wanderer till the end of his days. Moreover, there will be no merciful end to his suffering. Cain begs for mercy:

> *"My punishment is greater than I can bear! Surely You have driven me out this day from the face of the ground; I shall be hidden from Your face; I shall be a fugitive and a vagabond on the Earth, and it will happen that anyone who finds me will kill me." And the Lord said to him, "Therefore, whoever kills Cain, vengeance shall be taken on him sevenfold." And the Lord set a mark on Cain, lest anyone finding him should kill him. Then Cain went out from the presence of the Lord and dwelt in the land of Nod on the east of Eden.* (Genesis 4:13-17 NKJV)

Was Cain's punishment too severe? Was it too lenient? Certainly, God's marking Cain so others would not kill him might be a small mercy, but he would be separated from both his kindred and his God until he died.

Reading this saga further, we surprisingly learn that the Bible does not tell us about the appearance of the woman Cain married. We are not told whether they were married prior to his murder of Abel or after that dreadful act. One nevertheless must assume that either she was an unidentified sister of Cain or that other people also had been created and not mentioned in the Bible. In any event, Cain married this unknown woman, who then bore him a son they called Enoch. There was yet another woman for Cain's son to marry as well, which, since his family had been exiled from Adam's household, one must assume came from somewhere else. But, if we are to interpret Genesis literally as saying that Adam and Eve were the first and only humans on earth, how is that possible?

I should note at this juncture that the traditional Jewish interpretation of Genesis is that it is a *symbolic* history of the Jewish people, not the literal history of life, the universe, and everything else. Whether one decides to agree with this interpretation of the Jewish sages or not is clearly up to each individual who has been familiarized with this and hundreds of other stories.

I am not going to speculate on the longevity of each member of Adam's family either, who lived for hundreds of years, according to the chronology of generations from Adam to Noah. It might be easier to enumerate the necessary names without muddling them with a date stamp. That has been a subject of study for other interpreters, who have arrived at the age of our planet based on the supposed length of biblical lifespan. Instead, I'm going to fast-forward to Noah. Genesis 6:7 reads:

> So the Lord said, "I will destroy man whom I have created from the face of the Earth, both man and beast, creeping thing and birds of the air, for I am sorry that I have made them." (NKJV)

He regretted everyone but Noah, whom the Bible tells us "But Noah found grace in the eyes of the Lord" (Genesis 6:8). It is Noah God chooses to save, along with his family, and he offers him the instructions for making an ark, which is a great vessel in which the faithful can escape the coming *cataclysm*. Genesis 6:15 reads "And this is how you shall make it: The length of the ark shall be three hundred *cubits*, its width fifty cubits, and its height thirty cubits" (NKJV).

Despite the fact that Noah found grace in the eyes of the Lord, I have at least three objections to God's decision.

What did the other living creatures do to make God regret making them?

Why did God make the decision that all the relatives of Noah deserved to be saved? Were they all as virtuous as Noah? Were there really no other righteous humans around? Or is it possible that Noah just needed help to build his huge ark? Or might he have been too grief-stricken if God hadn't saved his wife and sons and grandchildren?

Having knowledge of genetics and mutation (as we do now) as well as divine foresight, didn't God realize that Noah's descendants would become as wicked and wrathful as the contemporaries of Noah, no matter how good and just Noah might have been in God's eyes?

There are practical questions as well, of course:

How could every species on earth (even then) fit into such a small boat?

What did they eat—especially the *carnivores*—either on the ark or once they stepped off it onto a land scrubbed free of any kind of life?

What about fish? Did they survive the flood because they could live and swim in the water? God doesn't mention them. But there are salt and freshwater fishes, and most of those cannot survive in both environments, yet they are able to survive in water.

What about plant life? Shouldn't it all be destroyed after forty days of inundation with salt water? Wouldn't that damage the atmosphere and reduce amount of oxygen, for instance?

I could go on, but instead of giving you further variations on what's wrong with a literal interpretation of the Genesis account, let's look instead at the world in which the story arose.

In the southern region of Mesopotamia during the time of the later Genesis chronicles there were an advanced civilization, the Sumerians. Their land was even mentioned in the book of Genesis (10:10) along with their king, Nimrod, son of Cush, son of Ham, son of Noah. According to Genesis 10:10, "the beginning of his kingdom was Babel, Erech, Accad, and Calneh, in the land of Shinar" (the biblical name of Sumer).

Not only are the Sumerians thought to have developed the first writing system (circa 3000 BCE), but they also constructed one of the earliest known temples to their god Enki. The famous *ziggurats* belonged to them. They achieved not a few technological breakthroughs in terms of long-lasting dwellings. They were inventors of an advanced *hexadecimal* mathematical system and an astronomical calendar. They used petroleum products extensively in many fields of construction and business, even in medicine. But the most remarkable events that reached our times, in my mind, were the events in *The Epic of Gilgamesh*.

As we now know, the stories of the Great Flood, of paradise of Eden, of the serpent, and of the creation of man were also described by the Sumerians, who were either the originators of them or who also borrowed them from an even earlier source unknown to us. Which is correct is hard to say, but the Sumerians who lived as a distinct culture one thousand years *earlier* than the Hebrews are apparently the

—

original source of the information that the book of Genesis relates. If the Jewish Bible was trying to hint that the Sumerians could possibly be the ancestors of the ancient Hebrews, it is certainly not so as by now it has definitely been proven that Sumerians were not Semites.

At the same time, one cannot deny that there have been archaeological findings confirming the historical accounts of a great regional flood and the existence of Mesopotamian cities like Ur, Hazor, and Megiddo. Whether they point to a civilization that was founded by the Hebrews or whether they point to a civilization founded by other people is something that some are still trying to discover. My concern is with the claim of the Hebrew Bible that its chroniclers discovered those events and that only a small handful of people survived the Flood.

Despite the fact that a civilization older than the Jews chronicles this watery cataclysm, according to the Bible Noah and his family were the only humans saved. Noah's three sons, Shem, Ham, and Japheth, are alleged to be the progenitors of all the nations existing on earth today.

The next great event in human history—if the Bible record is to be taken as the exclusive record—is the epic of the Tower of Babylon (Gate of God). Genesis 11:1 tells us: "Now the whole Earth had one language and one speech" (NKJV). It is hard to imagine how this posed a threat to God's well-being or authority, yet the Bible describes the Lord God saying:

> *And the Lord said, "Indeed the people are one and they all*
> *have one language, and this is what they begin to do; now*
> *nothing that they propose to do will be withheld from them.*
> *Come, let Us go down and there confuse their language,*
> *that they may not understand one another's speech."*
> (Genesis 11:6-7 NKJV)

One might ask why the common knowledge of one language in a relatively small community would be a problem for anyone, especially God. One might also ask who God is talking to when he says, "Come, let *Us* go down," as the concept of the Trinity is not always a common understanding.

Moreover, the fear of unity that forced God to scatter people all over the earth arguably produced the estrangement and animosity that humans exhibit toward strangers today. What did God intend to accomplish by his decision? Or perhaps the more apt question is, what did the authors of Genesis *believe* he intended to accomplish? Why did they imagine he would be disturbed by a unified humanity? Would the latest tenets of Bahá'í Faith to unite humanity be an impediment to God's decision or simply contrary to what Hebrew sages refer to in the Bible?

In view of this episode, how are we to understand all of those passages of scripture in which God reminds us that we are destined for unity—notably in the prophetic book of Isaiah?

A reasonable alternative interpretation of the narrative would be that the compilers of the Bible had no other reasonable explanation for the existence of separate ethnic Semitic groups in that region. After all, if they all came from the same post deluge family not all that long ago, then why did they speak different languages?

At this point, I will stop to analyze some early statements in the Bible and proceed to how this book possibly came to be.

POSSIBLE ORIGIN OF THE BIBLE

The English word *bible* comes from the Greek *biblion*, which means "scroll" or a "book." It is also believed that this word can be traced to an ancient Mediterranean city-port Gebal (*Byblos* in Greek) from which the Egyptian papyrus was exported to Greece. This Phoenician city was the place where a library with many papyrus scrolls was found. But whatever the source, the word *bible* literary means paper or scroll.

The Hebrew Bible is considered to be a sacred book. It is in fact the first religious book that ancient Hebrews produced, out of which grew such important religions as Judaism, Christianity, and Islam. The contemporary Bible consists of sixty-six books (or more, depending upon the sectarian audience) that cover a variety of religious and historical territory. The Old Testament consists of forty-nine books and the New Testament of twenty-seven books, the latter of which makes up the specifically Christian scriptures.

In addition to viewing different books within the Bible differently, the groups that hold it in common also have different views about what that sacredness entails. While some groups hold that the Bible *is* the inerrant, infallible word of God from start to finish, others maintain that it is a record that *contains* the word of God (where a distinct prophetic voice is speaking, for example) but also acknowledge its many human authors and interpretations.

The holy book of the Jewish faith is really a collection of books called variously: the Jewish Bible, the *Tanakh*, the Hebrew Bible, and among non-Jewish scholars, the Old Testament. The Jewish word *Tanakh* is an acronym for the parts that make up its whole: the *Torah* (the *Pentateuch* or Law), the *Nevim* (Prophets), and the *Ketuvim* (Writings).

For the sake of simplicity, from this point on I will use the term Hebrew Bible. This must not be construed, though, as giving a priority to this particular religious group. I simply felt that this title would be more appropriate to distinguish between the Jewish Bible and the Old and New Testaments. This makes my point well: it is through rabbinical interpretation of scripture that the religion we know as Judaism appeared. Judaism—as it is practiced today—has developed a vast amount of tradition and literature (the *Mishnah, Gemara, Talmud, Midrash,* and the mystical *Zohar)* that speak to the necessity of helping the Jewish people follow accepted practices.

There are a number of different sectarian groups and belief systems within Judaism due to the different levels of acceptance of the texts and the different interpretations of Jewish law arising from rabbinical discourses.

The substance of Judaism, however, is not challenged by any of these groups. The covenant (contract) between God and the Jewish people has remained the same. According to Judaism, it is an agreement in which God commanded that as long as his "chosen people" followed his guidance, he would take care of them.

Judaism does not have a central authority. Instead, many rabbis and scholars interpret the Jewish laws and texts differently. These variations allow many different interpretations and beliefs to exist within Judaism. Hence Judaism, as most religions in today's world, relies for authority on both scripture and ecclesiastics.

Judaism requires the observance of most of the laws found in the Torah, particularly in the fifth book, Deuteronomy. This book contains

—

the most treasured of the Jewish laws, the Ten Commandments, or Decalogue, where it is repeated after its first mention in Exodus.

Traditional Rabbinic Judaism claims that the Hebrew Bible was compiled through the divine revelation of God and appeared in the form of the oral and written Torah. Karaite Jews challenged that claim, insisting that only the written Torah was revealed at the top of Mount Horeb through Moses who was called there by God. The Conservative Jews, while not challenging Orthodox Judaism, recommended a more open interpretation of the Jewish laws. And finally, Reformist Jews substituted progressive guidelines for the restrictions required by Jewish law.

All in all, the Torah or Pentateuch consists of five books. The word Torah implies instructions that are not limited to laws or liturgical prescriptions for religious services. According to Orthodox rabbis, God gave the Torah to Moses and it was passed down through the generations to different Jewish groups and, at length, formally written on parchment by specially trained scribes.

The *Talmud*, a secondary scripture to the Torah, states that the Hebrew Bible was compiled for the most part in 450 BCE. Yet many modern scholars do not accept this date and are inclined to consider the canonization of the books between 200 BCE and 200 CE. Whenever the Bible might have appeared, Moses, who, according to some sources supposedly received divine revelations from God at Mount Sinai (Mount Horeb) in about 1400 BCE, by any calculation had the Bible a millennia apart from the canonization of the Bible.

The fathers of traditional Rabbinic Judaism were the Pharisees. They were one of four major schools of thought that grew into the contemporary traditional rabbinical schools. The Pharisees were supported by the common people and considered themselves democratic representatives of Jewish law. Another school, the Sadducees, who were associated with the elite aristocrats, represented their major theological opposition.

I bring up these two religious parties for a couple reasons. One is that the Pharisees interpreted some parts of the Torah literally and other parts liberally. The Sadducees, on the other hand, maintained that the entire Torah had to be accepted literally as a divine gift of God to the Hebrews. The Sadducees did not believe in resurrection or an afterlife, nor did they support the existence of an oral Torah.

—

They maintained that only the written document had been spiritually delivered by God. The Pharisees—and later rabbis of that school of thought—believed in the oral Torah and insisted that the text of the Torah must undergo interpretation and analysis. This led to the creation of the Talmud.

Unfortunately, the Sadducees, who were intimately connected to the Temple, disappeared after the destruction of the Second Temple by the Romans, as they had no more ability to practice their religion officially. The Pharisees were gone too but only in name, as they became the Orthodox rabbis that began the Rabbinic (teaching) Era of Judaism.

There are, of course, different sectarian groups within Judaism with diverse understandings about Jewish law and the role of the rabbinical schools in shaping doctrine. And those groups are sometimes at odds with and even hostile toward each other. One assumes they also read the history of Judaism as offered by the Hebrew Bible in diverse ways.

Notwithstanding this rift, many Jews seem to believe that the laws depicted in the Bible have always existed without change or addition since the time of Moses, and they therefore follow them faithfully. As one can see from the discussion here, however, such could not be necessarily the case.

At this point, let me consider who the original Hebrews were, God's so-called chosen people, those whom the Bible describes so thoroughly.

GOD'S CHOSEN PEOPLE

According to the Torah, a small family of people who lived in the ancient land of Mesopotamia (Ur) one day decided to move out of that land and to go to a land called Canaan. Located in contemporary Iraq, Ur was known as a place of advanced culture and opulence and the decision to move out by this particular family isn't emphasized in the Torah.

And Terah took Abram his son, and Lot the son of Haran his son's son, and Sarai his daughter-in-law, his son Abram's

wife; and they went forth with them from Ur of the Chaldees,
to go into the land of Canaan. (Genesis 11:31 KJV)

Whatever reasons Terah had for removing his family from Ur Kasdim (usually rendered in English as Ur of the Chaldees), he and his household went north and not south, where Canaan was located. Here the family stayed until Terah's death. After the death of his father, Abram allegedly encountered God, who instructed him to leave this household—which was now in Haran (contemporary Turkey)—and move south to the land of Canaan. The Bible does not explain why Canaan must become the place for these people, just that it must. In any event, with little overt consideration and instead simply following God's strong recommendation, Abram, his wife, and his nephew, without further delay, proceeded to move to Canaan.

The land of Canaan nevertheless had its own people. Perhaps God didn't see any problem with Abram and his family relocating there, and it's possible the Canaanites had no problem with it either. The land at that time was ample, and this family began to adjust in their new environment rather quickly.

Only ten years after Abram's family relocated to Canaan, a famine fell on the land. Without much explanation, the Bible tells us that Abram took his household to the neighboring country of Egypt, where crops were still abundant. It was quite as if borders didn't matter at that time. Egypt, a country of opulence and prosperity, had no problem with allowing other people from the neighboring countries to join their communities.

While the journey itself was not a complicated one, we further read that Abram nevertheless feared the Egyptians, that they "might covet his wife, Sarai," who is described as "a fair woman to look upon," and kill him because of her. He therefore presented her as his sister (which was partially true). Abram's worst fears materialized; because of Sarai's beauty, the *pharaoh* wished to marry her. He gave Abram a great number of animals and even servants, presumably as a bride price. And here, according to the Bible, God refused to accept such an expedient and "plagued Pharaoh and his house with great plagues" (Genesis 12:17 KJV).

When the pharaoh found out that Abram had lied to him, he ordered him and his family to leave the country. Still, in a noble

—

gesture the pharaoh allowed Abram to take all their flocks, herds, and tents with them: "And Abram went up out of Egypt, he, and his wife, and all that he had, and Lot with him, into the south" (Genesis 13:1 KJV). Abram and his wife returned to Canaan, while Lot went to live in what is now Jordan. Here is a description of that split as narrated in the Bible: "And the land was not able to bear them, that they might dwell together: for their substance was great, so that they could not dwell together" (Genesis 13:6 KJV). While it is possible that the land of Canaan was not enough to maintain the overgrown livestock of Abraham and Lot, it is hard to believe that only ten years later, the *paraphernalia* of these two people exceeded their ability to sojourn.

Here I would like to mention that if one reads the Hebrew Bible without consulting sources that describe and interpret the events in it, such as was just described, for instance, one cannot easily extract meaning from many of them on one's own. One anecdote has it that Moses, after his death, was granted the privilege to visit the contemporary rabbinical schools as an invisible spirit. After listening to the students discussing the Torah, he realized he didn't understand a word they were saying.

The Hebrews did not exist as a separate group before Terah and Abram (later called Abraham), in 2000-1800 BCE. Terah and his first wife had three sons, one of whom was Abram, the other two were Nahor and Haran. Nahor married his niece Milkah (his brother Haran's daughter). Haran's son, Lot, was a nephew of Abram.

Abram/Abraham marries Sarai/Sarah, who was actually his half sister and a daughter of Terah and his second wife. Isaac, a son of Abraham and Sarah, later married his niece Rebecca. From their marriage came twin sons: Esau and Jacob. Esau was in fact the firstborn and therefore had the right to inherit all the privileges that were practiced in Hebrew families. But Rebecca tricked her dim-sighted husband into giving the rights of the firstborn son to the second born, thus violating Jewish tradition. As a result, Jacob became the father of the Israelite nation.

Reading the Biblical account further, we learn that three generations later, Abram's grandson, Jacob—himself a father of twelve sons—again experienced famine in the land of Canaan. But this time, instead of immediately relocating his family, he sent his sons to Egypt to seek grain. While there, they discovered their lost brother,

Joseph, whom they had sold earlier in to slavery out of jealousy of the close relationship between Joseph and their father. They didn't expect to find Joseph in that country, let alone to find that he was quite successful and had become the pharaoh's foremost advisor—granted the title "Father of the Pharaoh"—and had stewardship over the entire country. To their further surprise, when they might have expected vengeance, instead they were received with forgiveness, and Jacob was reunited with his lost son. This was the beginning of the Twelve Tribes of Israel (literally a tribe for each of Jacob's sons) and of the Hebrews' sojourn in Egypt.

In the meantime, the brothers liked their new country so much that they decided to stay there indefinitely in an area called Goshen. Here the Hebrew population began to grow and multiply, but in time another pharaoh who didn't know Joseph became fearful of their numbers and turned them into slaves.

Though Jacob's twelve sons are progenitors of the Hebrew tribes, they were born of four different women. Two were Jacob's legitimate wives and two were concubines. According to Kabbalah, the matriarchal souls that were both divine and royal belonged to the wives of Jacob, Rachel and Leah, and not to Bilhah and Zilpah, his handmaids. Therefore, generations of Israelites who descended from Bilhah and Zilpah are not noble, according to the teachings of Kabbalah. Are they even Hebrews?

Jacob and Leah's daughter Dinah had her own children, of course, but there is no account given of her descendants. Jacob had more daughters, but neither their names nor their children are mentioned in Hebrew scripture. The Biblical narration at last settles the question: only the twelve sons of *Jacob* are Israelites. The descendants of the firstborn son of Isaac, Esau—the Amalekites and Midianites (for whom an alternate genesis is also given)—are not only excluded from the straight lineage of Hebrew descendants, they are treated as enemies who deserve to be wiped out. Another genealogical branch, the children of Lot, is also delineated from the Hebrews. Though in this case it makes a little more sense for the Hebrews not to acknowledge their blood relatives as Lot fathered his two sons, Moab and Ammon, by having sex with his own daughters.

At any rate, what is lacking is some indication as to who are really numbered among God's chosen people and why. If behavior is an issue, the people God seems to favor are no more virtuous than those he has them destroy.

What does it all mean? Are we really meant to take it all literally? Or would it be more appropriate to follow the suggestion of rabbinical sages and accept some parts of the Bible literally and other liberally? Or must we simply see the Bible as a literary work collectively compiled by different narrators?

In any event, as the Bible starts with the first book of Moses, let me say a few words about this famous and deeply venerated Jewish prophet. The story goes that Moses belonged to the Levite tribe of Israel. His parents, at the time of his birth, lived in slavery in Egypt. The pharaoh had instructed the soldiers of his army to kill all newborn Hebrew babies by drowning them in the River Nile, because the Hebrews were multiplying at a speed exceeding the native Egyptians. When Moses' mother set her young child adrift on the river in an attempt to avoid an order of the pharaoh, the pharaoh's daughter, bathing near the shore, found the bulrush craft with the baby in it and saved him.

Of course, she would have known of the instructions given by her father, and it is highly suspicious that she disobeyed them in order to save a Hebrew child. It is also strange that she decided to save this particular child and none of the others that were killed and not guilty of any crime. The facts of this story are also arguable, especially when one recalls that such events are said to have happened to King Sargon of Akkad in the twenty-third century BCE that in no way were connected to the description in the Hebrew Bible.

It must be said here that this is not the only discrepancy in the Bible that I would like to mention, but there are many more similarly powerful stories, some of which, especially the most conspicuous ones, I will discuss.

One such story that I find peculiar is the narration in the Bible of the episode when the relatively young but quite mature Moses kills an Egyptian soldier while protecting a Hebrew slave.

Question: Why did Moses slay an Egyptian soldier on behalf of a Hebrew slave? Moses could not possibly affiliate emotionally with the Hebrews as he was brought up as Egyptian royalty. Even if one perceived this man as noble and just, how could it translate into aggression and the murder of his fellow citizen?

—

In the meantime, one must acknowledge that Moses is the most enigmatic figure in the Hebrew Bible. While he is God's appointee as a leader of the Hebrew tribes and one who was destined to mold them into a distinguished people, it is puzzling that this man was chosen to become a prophet for Jewish people.

The Hebrew Bible, as it is accepted, was originally written in both the Hebrew and Aramaic languages. Aramaic as a language predates Hebrew, yet the books of the Tanakh that relay the oldest histories and the laws are in Hebrew. If they existed previously in Aramaic, we no longer have those texts.

The questions I compiled and that were bothersome for me are as follows:

What language did Moses speak when he supposedly wrote the five books of the Bible? Was it the common language of the Egyptians, Aramaic, or was it Hebrew? He was born in Egypt, reared by the daughter of the Egyptian royal family of the pharaoh, and while in his late thirties married a Midianite woman. None of these facts show us how did he have knowledge of and especially the ability to write Aramaic or Hebrew. When he left Egypt, he might have spoken a few languages, as was normal for Egyptians, but where did he learn how to write in Hebrew? He spent about forty years in a family of Midianite priests after he married, before he took supposedly the Hebrews out of bondage. Midianites definitely didn't speak Hebrew at home, as Midianites were Cushites. The Cushites' ancestors were Abraham and Keturah (Abraham's Egyptian concubine). So according to Jewish law, Midianites were not Hebrews.

Why did God Almighty choose Moses? Moses, from his first encounter with God, was reluctant to become a leader of the Jewish people. In his brief communication with God, Moses cites a number of things that disqualify him for the job of prophet and redeemer: "Who am I that I should go to Pharaoh, and that I should bring the children of Israel out of Egypt?" (Exodus 3:11 NKJV) He later said, "O my Lord, I am not eloquent, neither before nor since You have spoken to Your servant; but I am slow of speech and slow of tongue" (Exodus 4:10 NKJV). God himself had to persuade this appointee to accept such a brave and dangerous role.

Why did Moses choose to hide from the pharaoh's revenge among the Midianites? True, Midianites were not the Egyptians. But they

—

were also not exactly of the Hebrew race. Moses could have chosen to go farther into Canaan, for example, after God spoke to him. And, finally, why out of all the Hebrews living in Egypt, including generations of Moses' lineage, did he turn to the least respected ones, as Midianites were?

Moses' marriage to the daughter of a Midianite priest is another story inadequately explained. Moses might have fallen in love with the young and beautiful daughter of a Midianite priest, of course. But after being married to her for many years and having fathered two children with that woman, it seems bizarre that Moses, as the Bible describes it, orders Israelite soldiers to set on fire all the cities of the Midianites and slay every Midianite male child and every woman. This happens when a plague afflicted the Israelite army, obliterating the majority of Hebrew soldiers. Moses attributes the evil to the Midianites. Why? There are no descriptions in the Bible of Moses disrespecting his father-in-law, his father-in-law's blood relatives, and finally his own family. One can only wonder what provoked God to assign Moses such a horrific task, as we also read that this decision came from God.

At first, when I began to read the Bible, I did so without consulting modern interpretations and scholarly articles. As a result, I continued to generate the questions for which I felt compelled to find answers. They were many, but the most important in my mind were these: Why would an all-loving God not only see people selectively but make and keep promises to a chosen people while eliminating others for various failings? Indeed, by what standard may we understand the god of Hebrews as all-loving or just?

Why—according to the sermon of Moses—did God see some people as his followers and others as foes, demanding not only to "cast them out," but also to destroy their altars and break down their images and burn with fire?

What prompted God to smite all non-Hebrew people, including women and children, in order to give their houses and the land and vineyards and olive trees to Hebrews attempting to occupy the land that non-Hebrews already inhabited?

Why did God forgive the apparently unforeseen idolatry that the children of Israel displayed during Moses' temporary absence on Mount Sinai?

I was also puzzled by the transformation of Moses from a timid stutterer into a forceful, courageous prophet of Jehovah. First portrayed as remote, Moses later in the story becomes compassionate, father-like figure, devoted to the Hebrews' cause and trying to persuade God himself not to punish the Hebrews when they are disobedient, but to continue to take care of them.

In Deuteronomy 9:26-28 he prays:

'O Lord God, do not destroy Your people and Your inheritance whom You have redeemed through Your greatness, whom You have brought out of Egypt with a mighty hand. Remember Your servants, Abraham, Isaac, and Jacob; do not look on the stubbornness of this people, or on their wickedness or their sin, lest the land from which You brought us should say, "Because the Lord was not able to bring them to the land which He promised them, and because He hated them, He has brought them out to kill them in the wilderness." (NKJV)

The question arises: Was this transformation real, or did the Bible authors simply decide that Moses needed to be more decisive and authoritarian than he actually was?

As he leads them out of Egypt, Moses tells the Israelites, "Then it shall be, if you by any means forget the Lord your God, and follow other gods, and serve them and worship them, I testify against you this day that you shall surely perish" (Deuteronomy 8:19 NKJV). This sounds more like a threat than a promise. And it is repeated:

Then the Lord said to me, 'Arise, begin your journey before the people, that they may go in and possess the land which I swore to their fathers to give them.' And now, Israel, what does the Lord your God require of you, but to fear the Lord your God, to walk in all His ways and to love Him, to serve the Lord your God with all your heart and with all your soul, and to keep the commandments of the Lord and His statutes which I command you today for your good? (Deuteronomy 10:11-13 NKJV)

—

Serving other gods was emphasized throughout the Bible as one of the worst crimes that one could commit. This is especially stark in the last passages of Deuteronomy. Damnation comes to its apogee in this part of the book. Assuredly the worship of the idols common among the Hebrew's neighbors often required human sacrifice and other practices that we would find quite barbaric, but could the injection of this level of fear have been necessary?

A particularly peculiar event occurs when Moses returns from Mount Horeb (Mount Sinai) with the Ten Commandments. He learns from God that the Hebrews have made themselves a golden calf to worship, with the permission of his brother, Aaron. Their argument to Aaron was, "Make us gods that shall go before us; as for this Moses, the man who brought us out of the land of Egypt, we do not know what has become of him" (Exodus 32:23 NKJV). Aaron was Moses' older brother and the progenitor of the priest class (Levites). In the act of allowing the Hebrews to create an idol for praying purposes, he showed himself to be less than balanced when it came to the spiritual support of the Jewish people.

As a result of this disobedience, God made clear to Aaron and their sister Miriam that Moses was not merely a seer or visionary, but something else altogether.

> If there is a prophet among you,
> I, the Lord, make Myself known to him in a vision;
> I speak to him in a dream.
> Not so with My servant Moses;
> He is faithful in all My house.
> I speak with him face to face,
> Even plainly, and not in dark sayings;
> And he sees the form of the Lord.
> Why then were you not afraid
> To speak against My servant Moses?

> (Numbers 12:6-8 NKJV)

Yet despite this act, God forgives Aaron, and after Aaron's death God allows the Levites to represent the Hebrews in rituals and to interpret law. This is strangely inconsistent. This forgiving God punishes those who do not belong to his chosen people (who therefore can have no idea, one assumes, of what behavior he expects), but lets the sins of his chosen people go unpunished.

In any event, whomever these people were who went to live in Canaan, they were present in that land until the Roman Empire finally exiled them in 135 CE.

And with that I would like to say a few words about the final dispersion of the Jews from the Canaan land. After the Hebrews were crushed by the Roman military machine, this land acquired a new name, Palestine. Whether justifiably or not, the name Palestine would remain until the present day.

With the destruction of the second temple in Jerusalem in 70 CE, following the Roman-Jewish war, the Jews were scattered around the vast Roman Empire, no longer an organized group. This caused Jewish scholars in about 90 CE to gather in Jamnia, a Judean town west of Jerusalem, with one goal in mind: maintaining their Jewish identity.

Though held exclusively by a relatively small group (most sources quote a figure of around fifteen million adherents to Judaism), it would only be fair to call the Jewish religion a forefather of Christianity, Islam, and the Bahá'í Faith, which easily constitute two-thirds of the religious population in the world today. (This can also be said of Zoroastrianism, which stands in the confluence between two great streams of religious tradition, the Vedic and Abrahamic.)

The Bible has been published and translated more times than any other religious book in the history of publishing. Taken literally, it is claimed by sectarian groups within the larger domains of Judaism, Christianity, and Islam to record the whole history of the world from the beginning to an indeterminate future.

Scholars, pseudoscholars, and those who are just curious about historical artifacts regardless of the religious texts they are reading draw diverse conclusions from these texts. Emphasis and meaning varies from group to group, different aspects of faith are exaggerated or underplayed, and interpretations run the gamut from metaphorical to literal.

If the narrative so far is not sufficient to reveal the Hebrew authors' conflicting ideas about God, one need only look at some other examples.

In this connection, I would like to mention the Kabbalah. Kabbalah is a form of religious mysticism that claims that—beyond human myth and divine allegory—the Hebrew Bible has hidden meanings. According to some sources, we are asked to believe that Kabbalah has been openly practiced since the tenth century BCE. The religious leaders (the Sanhedrin) were—as it is explained in various Jewish religious sources—forced to make their teachings secretive out of fear that non-Jewish invaders of their developing country might misuse them.

In the thirteenth century CE, the Zohar (Radiance) became the major literary work of Jewish mystical thought and the main source for the contemplation of Kabbalah. In modern times, the teaching of the Kabbalah method no longer requires being secretive, but that does not mean it is any easier to understand. It teaches that every Hebrew word and number—even the diacritical marks by which they are pronounced—are the vehicles of hidden messages. Thus the concepts of Kabbalah remain hidden and poorly understood by lay people.

This movement postulates that God is unknowable and that he is neither material nor spiritual but the creator of both material and spiritual realities. His contact with humans comes from the divine emanations (*sefirot*), only part of which can be properly received by human minds; hence the mystery.

I have a somewhat different take on this mysticism: I believe it's possible that Kabbalah is a method purposely introduced by Hebrew sages to confuse ordinary people. It places itself above scientific knowledge, shamelessly declaring its comprehension of the transcendent spiritual world. Bombastic rhetoric and intricately tangled words of vague meaning are common in this so-called teaching. I conclude that it is purposely esoteric as its adherents have a vested interest in it remaining cryptic.

I am not going to discuss all the innovations and interpretations introduced by the rabbinical sages during their long history, but they include such things as the lighting of the Menorah on Hanukah, the canonization of the Tanakh, and a belief in Judgment Day.

Here is the important point: By whatever means the leading party introduced additions or revisions to the existing laws, they were assumed by believers to have the authority to do so, for the new rules became indisputable and were habitually followed by certain groups.

—

As human nature is designed, our trustworthiness in the authority combined with our tendency to act idly leads most of the time to our inability to see facts separately from exaggerations and lies.

It is not my intent to tell anyone what to believe. I have simply tried to analyze the history of the Jewish people as the Hebrew Bible tells it. I skipped quite a few inconsistencies and incredible stories, all of which made me realize that the Hebrews were not always portrayed as a noble people, even in their own scriptures. I do not think, however, that they are purposely shown as grotesque or deceitful. For one thing, what we human beings consider virtuous changes from age to age. They do not always coincide, and it is dangerous to judge ancient societies that existed under harsh conditions by today's standards.

To say a few positive words, it needs to be acknowledged that the Hebrews were one of the early promoters of monotheism, a belief in a single god. They offered an idea of a covenant between a people and God and conceived of this covenant as a special, filial relationship. Further, they ritualized it so it would be remembered from generation to generation. They created many new observances, prayers, and rituals based on their religious principles to remind them to be just, loyal, and kind.

Moreover, they were among the few cultures to tell the life story of an entire people in the pages of their religious text, a feat similar to the primary ancient texts of Hinduism's Vedas.

As much as the Jews struggled with their concepts of self, community, "other," and God, their history offers us a case study in the growth of a cultural group from infancy to maturity.

CHAPTER 7

Christianity as Religion

Christianity as a word came to be used by the followers of Jesus Christ. The word Christian therefore is reflective of the founder of this faith, Jesus the Christ. Today, many related denominations call themselves Christians, and because there is great emphasis placed on the name Jesus Christ, a look at the etymology of both words might be of some interest. Jesus is an English transliteration of the Latinized pronunciation of the Hebrew name *Yahshua* or *Jehoshua* (in which the letter *j* is pronounced more like a *y*). The Greek transliteration of this name became Iesous and the Latin *Iesus* was manipulated into the English version, in which the letter *j* is pronounced like a soft *g*. Therefore the name has become Jesus. In Slavic, it is *Isus*; in Arabic and Hindi, *Issa*.

Christ, on the other hand, is not a proper name, but a title indicating "anointed one" or *Messiah* (Hebrew *Mashiah*, Tiberian *Masiah*). The Greek version of that word was *Christakos*, which was Latinized to *Kristos*. In English, this became *Christ*.

The adherents of the faith began to apply the name Christian to themselves, with the original apostles applying this title some twenty years after Jesus' death. As these apostles were true and loyal followers of the teachings of Jesus, this was somewhat justified. But rather soon, however, the main motif of the first promoters of new belief became connected to the resurrection of Christ. Paul, who was the most visible advocate of it, actually built his theory on that same

–

118

theme—resurrection with an attempt to apply it to all the believers. In the contemporary world, roughly two billion plus people with many cultural, demographic, and sectarian differences have assumed the name Christian without referring to themselves as the "anointed ones" yet accepting that promising consequence of being allowed in this esoteric group that will necessarily lead to another life through death and resurrection.

With such a rigor displayed by those who consider themselves Christians, it must be an absolutely adequate attempt on my side to conduct a critical analysis of the most visible tenets of Christianity as a whole and specifically of Jesus Christ, who he might have been indeed a Son of God and a savior, incarnated God himself, or just a man with a number of remarkable abilities?

Being born, as we learn from the Bible and other sources of the process that he was, this man underwent quite drastic evolutionary changes depicted through the recorded humanity history, today a little over two thousand years ago. Originally, somewhat unruly, with mostly rebellious ideas but nevertheless a man, Jesus gradually was transformed in the minds of his followers in becoming something larger than life, shedding the unnecessary for his believers' regular features of human while acquiring the credentials of God.

Yet those doubtful stories that became an edifice for the doctrine of Christianity, nonetheless, still the stories hard to swallow by non-Christians, mainly the transformation of Jesus the man into Jesus part of Trinity and God himself. And with this comes a tally of questions: Would that be possible that Almighty God allowed himself to transform into a developing fetus in a womb of a brittle young woman who would be able to withstand all the physical burdens a body of a young pregnant woman might be subjected to? Not only such a decision on behalf of God would be immature and irresponsible, but it would also be downright dangerous from any perspective. Would God trust an unremarkable developing female body all his might and be certain that that would not be too much of a burden for such a body? Would God consciously agree to reduce himself to an embryo that would slowly develop in a uterus for the long nine months? Who would he trust to take care and manage all the events, structures, and the laws of the universe while he must've stayed in the uterus of a teenage girl? How thoughtful such a decision might have been,

—

provided that was a decision of an all-powerful god. On another point, didn't God have enough knowledge of the cruel, revengeful, and unpredictable nature of a man and, therefore, subjected himself and his mother to undue risks that might very well terminate if not his existence then the life of his young mother? Most of us are aware of a story from the Bible of the action of Herod after he learned of the coming future Messiah.

Now up to his mother—if Jesus, accepted today as an incarnated god and acting as a man while present on earth, might have had a mother, who had given birth to him, then wouldn't such a way of thinking lead to Mary actually becoming the most powerful woman and a mother of God Almighty who must be an uncreated power in whole universe?

The main literature accepted within the Christian religious community as a whole is a compilation of scriptural texts referred to as the New Testament. Today's Bible consists of two volumes: the Old Testament, which is based on the original book used by the Hebrews under the name Tanakh, and the New Testament, the specifically Christian part of the Bible.

Many Christians understand the teachings in the New Testament to be the words of God. Yet only a small number of them seem conscious of the fact that before the New Testament was canonized as a collection of twenty-seven books written by different authors, there were many other writings that were considered but that did not make it into the canon. During the early development of Christianity, at least forty gospels, along with hundreds of letters (known as epistles) appeared among various faith groups.

The reason for this was quite natural: there were numerous unrelated groups that accepted Christianity as their religion. These Christian communities were taught by whichever apostles reached them with the message. They had their own versions of Christ's teachings, which led to long-lasting (sometimes over a century), rigorous debates about which books were worthy to be accepted as representing Christ's intent.

Yet the logical approach must have been as such—if the Bible reflects the true words of God, no matter when and under which circumstance the authenticated documents were found, they had to

—

be included in the holy book without consideration and approval of local authority.

Gospels, epistles, and other literature that were not included in the canonical New Testament were labeled as *apocryphal*, which literally means "hidden" and was often taken to mean heretical. In this category fell the book of Revelation (which was later reconsidered), the Shepherd of Hermas, and the Acts of Paul. On the other hand, in that period, there were many books that were falsely presented as authentic. These were written either by unknown authors or by those who falsely claimed to be known apostles. Such literature was labeled as pseudepigraphical (meaning that they were written under a false name) and counted as heretical.

Some gospels did not get into the New Testament simply because they were discovered in later times. These, for example, were the Gospel of Peter, the Gospel of Philip, the Gospel of Mary Magdalene, and Apocryphal Acts.

Among noncanonical books, there were those that were claimed to have been written by Jesus's contemporaries but that were not known at the earlier time. For instance, the Coptic Gospel of Thomas, discovered in the Nag Hammadi Library in Egypt in December 1945, is alleged to have been written by Judas Didymus Thomas, who was among the original twelve disciples. He presumably collected 114 sayings of Jesus Christ while witnessing the events in the life of the historical Jesus. Jesus died around the year 30 CE, or thereabouts, at the age of thirty-three to thirty-four. According to some sources, the Gospel of Thomas was written between 110 and 120 CE (or so most scholars believe), which means that, even if Thomas was significantly younger than Jesus, he would have been around one hundred years old when he wrote it. This is not impossible, but it is improbable.

It has been noted that both *Didymus* and *Thomas* mean "twin," and indeed Thomas is often referred to as "Thomas the Twin." The Syrian Christians believed that Judas Didymus Thomas was the twin brother of Jesus. The Gnostic Christians called Thomas "Didymus, the Twin Brother of Jesus," and some people have taken this in confusion that he was Jesus' twin rather than merely *a* twin. However, since Jesus quite often called his disciples "brothers," the Gnostic phrase, for want of punctuation, could also be read as "Thomas the Twin, Brother of

—

Jesus." In any event, the relationship is not established fact but rather speculation based on Thomas's title and the Gnostic commentary.

From my perspective, it is not that important. What intrigues me is the idea that it took Thomas such a long time to write down the words of Christ. Not only did he wait for an unreasonable period of time to write what Jesus had said, he also could not possibly have remembered when, how, and why those words were told. Yet it happened with most of the expressions of Jesus, and no one claimed to write them down while Jesus was speaking.

In brief, despite the fact that most of the books in the New Testament were written in the first century CE, it took another three hundred years to declare them as canonical. There were challenges involved in determining the authenticity of these writings, as I've alluded to above. Scholars still debate the veracity of some of these texts, their historical contexts, and their ages, despite their acceptance by the Council of Nicaea in 325 CE.

The argument for authenticity becomes even more fraught if we take into consideration that Jesus preached in Aramaic and that we possess only translations in Greek and Latin. It is hard to know how closely translators followed the original texts, especially because they were presented as *logia* (utterances) without a narrative description when they were found.

Another important element in the description of Christianity as a religion is that from the start Christians were not a monolithic group of people ethnically or demographically. The various groups of Christians that arose early in the history of the faith were sometimes diametrically opposed in their outlooks. These independent groups not only disagreed about doctrine but also harbored animosity toward each other, possibly because of their varied ethnic and cultural backgrounds.

Such, for example, were the Christian Ebionites (mentioned earlier in the preface of this book), whose adherents came only from among the Jews. In order to be accepted in that Christian sect, the adherents had to be circumcised and be observant of the laws of Moses. This conflicted, of course, with the creeds of the one of the four early centers of the Christian community, the Coptic congregation in Alexandria, which was founded in 42 CE by the Apostle Mark (Marcus). The Coptic Christians held that baptism and the Eucharist (memorial of the Last Supper) were the symbols of the Christian covenant and that circumcision was no longer necessary.

At the opposite extreme were such groups as the Marcionites, who came into being in the middle of the second century. This group rejected everything remotely Jewish in their understanding of the teachings of Jesus. Labeled heretics by the other Christian communities, they claimed that Ebionites were themselves heretics who had nothing to do with Jesus.

Among the more mystical groups were the Gnostics. They claimed that the god of the Hebrews was a wrathful god who created an evil material world and that Jesus could not be the son of this god, but rather had been begotten by a different spiritual and true god.

What becomes interesting from my point of view is that all Christian denominations since the Ebionites began to move toward disapproval of the Hebrew faith and eventually dissociated themselves from the Jews while shamelessly accepting the origination of the Christian faith with Jesus, unquestionably the son of a Jewish mother. It is also worth noting that all the New Testament authors, with the possible exception of the writer of Acts of the Apostles, were Hebrews. Remember that at the dawn of the Christian religion, the sacred text of the early believers was the Hebrew Bible. These texts were translated into Greek and Latin and acquired a new name, the Old Testament.

Many people think that the Old Testament is not only patriarchal but obsolete, and that it is kept within the same covers as the New Testament more out of respect than anything else. That is a misconception, which, I believe, becomes increasingly clearer the more one knows about Christianity.

As one can see, there was a lot of confusion from the very beginning of this new faith.

Over time, many different writings emerged, some of which were considered to have been influenced by apostolic teachings or by authors who had personal relationships with some of the apostles. The advocates of these teachings became known as the Apostolic Fathers and were represented by such figures as Clement of Rome, Ignatius of Antioch, and Polycarp of Smyrna.

The Church Fathers finally endorsed a particular form of orthodoxy, which was the precursor of contemporary Orthodox

—

and Catholic doctrines. They were in opposition to the previously mentioned religious groups that sat at the extreme fringes of belief.

Eventually all these previous movements fell under the umbrella of lost forms of Christianity, not only because their varying beliefs were forgotten, but because they practiced Christianity before the Church Fathers settled on what was and what not orthodox scripture was.

Accepted texts were called the New Testament and have been in use ever since among Christians of most denominations with some variations and with a variety of translations.

Most Christian theology differs from that of other religions in that it stresses the uniqueness of the person of Jesus Christ in addition—to one degree or another—to applying his teachings and the interpretive work of his disciples. In spite of this, believers in the first three centuries of the Christian era (up until the Council of Nicaea) held a wide variety of understandings about who Jesus Christ really was. Some claimed that Jesus was a human being with a divine nature, others that he was completely divine and not at all human. Still others believed that he was a part of a trinity (defined as one god in three persons) and therefore—some claimed—was God himself.

We will discuss these conjectures later on. For now I'd like to continue to sort out why Christians have accumulated so many denominations over the centuries according to a number of sources upward of thirty thousand by a recent count.

A HOUSE DIVIDED

The existing schools of thought had to eventually decide what distinguished their beliefs from others, and inevitably, an orthodoxy was established so they could confirm what was true faith versus what was not.

The first serious conflict among Christian theologians arose between Saint Athanasius, the bishop of Alexandria, Egypt, and a Christian elder, Arius, whose teaching about the Trinity (God the Father, God the Son, and God the Holy Spirit) emphasized the Father's primacy over the Son. That fight ended in the destruction of all the writings of Arius. Following the order of Emperor Constantine, all of

Arius's books were burned and condemned, yet the Arian controversy continued to exist until after the First Council of Constantinople in 381.

After the First Council of Nicaea, called by Emperor Constantine the Great in 325 CE, the major differences of Christian doctrines were successfully resolved, resulting in the Nicene Creed. The first uniform and orthodox doctrines of Christendom were established. And yet even the canonized New Testament continued to support a variety of dissimilar beliefs. Those were attributed to many different authors who had written at different times, for different groups of people, under different circumstances.

In spite of all these confusions, Jesus Christ remained the main figure in the newly established religion. He was a son of Mary, secretly (or divinely) begotten, and no member of suddenly engendered faith ever doubted his true assignment—to become the redeemer of humanity.

Accordingly, an assumption of Christian believers that they will be resurrected, either as physical bodies or as souls, must involve their misunderstanding why Jesus had corresponded to such proposition and they were not. First, Jesus was resurrected, according to the New Testament, as the begotten son of God. Second, his suffering was planned by God to redeem humanity. Third, nowhere in the Bible there is a promise by God to accept any other soul but Jesus's. Why then the contemporary as well as earlier Christians feel that their sins would not be only forgiven but also rewarded in life after death? It remains somewhat obscure.

As to Jesus's birth and short life, no matter which sources one uses details are scarce and subject to much conjecture. However, as we do know of the birth and life of Jesus Christ from sources like the Bible, the New Testament apocrypha, the Gospel of Thomas, the Gospel of Peter, and other available sources, we have no choice but to use them for our exegesis. This would seem to be enough material to speculate on the subject and make a more or less educated summation.

Let us begin by investigating the precursory circumstance under which the Christian religion was born. A study of Judaism directs us to the first discovery of the Dead Sea Scrolls at Qumran in 1947, an archaeological site on the West Bank. From these scrolls we learned about the Essenes. The Essenes were also mentioned in works of

—

such authorities as philosopher Philo of Alexandria, Pliny the Elder (a geographer and a writer), and Titus Flavius Josephus, a Jewish historian and author of the *Antiquities of the Jews*, among other works.

The Essenes were one of the four most prominent Jewish sects, the more powerful ones being the Pharisees and the Sadducees. The Essenes were not a large group of people (numbering only about four thousand) and lived in secluded areas circa 150 BCE to 70 CE. They inhabited the desert northwest of the Dead Sea, away from the major cities.

Many of the writings found in the Qumran Scrolls describe a codex of the Essenes that is similar in content to the teachings of Jesus and early Christianity. Because they were practicing their religion for almost two hundred years before the time of Christ, the Church tried very hard to suppress knowledge about this sect.

One of the most recognizable traditions of the Essenes was the use of a daily ritual bath, required to symbolize purity. This bath, called *mikvah*, is still practiced by Jews today. Among Christians, it acquired the term *baptism* (the Greek word for "to wash" or "to immerse in water")—no longer a daily event—and is the main symbol of ritual purification that occasions the acceptance of belief in Jesus Christ. Their writings also describe a ritual that is very similar to the Christian communion or Eucharist.

The Essenes were ascetics, living communally and accepting poverty as the righteous way of life. They also believed in the resurrection of the physical body and were concerned with eschatology, that is, the final destiny of humanity.

This recognizable group of religious Jewish people had abandoned Jerusalem in protest of the existing laws and the ways in which religious life was conducted in the Temple. They thought of themselves as the only truthful and righteous people in the eyes of God, and that belief influenced their code of morals, their culture, and their behavior. They believed that God would send a Messiah (or a "Teacher of Righteousness" as they called him) whose teachings were about the nature of penance, love for one's neighbor, and many other virtues. Whether by some coincidence or not, these are the same themes found in the New Testament. (The Teacher of Righteousness or Righteous One is also a title of the Buddha, in other words, the Tathagata.) And like Jesus in the New Testament, their Teacher of Righteousness would be condemned and put to death.

—

If the early Christians remind us much of the Essenes, the latter were gone by 70 CE, when the Romans destroyed the Second Temple.

Jesus, as is accepted by most theologians, was born four to six years before the Common Era, but it is not chronological exactness that is my concern here. Rather, I am interested in the description of the birth, life, and the acts of this man.

THE MAN JESUS AND THE APOSTLE PAUL

The principal sources of information about the life of Jesus are the surviving Christian texts, the earliest being attributed to Saul of Tarsus (Saint Paul), dated approximately 50 CE, and the Synoptic and Apocryphal Gospels, written circa 60-90 CE and up to the middle of the second century. These books, especially the Synoptic Gospels, are ascribed to different authors, some of whom claimed to have witnessed the life of Jesus personally and others—like Luke—who acknowledged that they had collected their knowledge from other sources. None of these gospels, of course, are definitely written by the named authors.

There is also the fifth book in the New Testament, the Acts of the Apostles, the authorship of which is traditionally ascribed to Luke the Evangelist. This title for the work has been in use since the late second century CE. While the authorship of Acts remains a subject of debate among scholars even today, it is generally accepted that Luke wrote this book using the Gospel of Mark and possibly the Hebrew Gospel as his main sources. Some sources suggest that Luke was a companion of Jesus, but more traditional scholars believe that Luke could not have been an eyewitness of Jesus' ministry. Luke himself says of his eponymous narrative:

> *Many have undertaken to draw up an account of the things that have been fulfilled among us, just as they were handed down to us by those who from the first were eyewitnesses and servants of the word. With this in mind, since I myself have carefully investigated everything from the beginning, I too decided to write an orderly account for you, most excellent Theophilus, so that you may know the certainty of the things you have been taught.* (Luke 1:1-4 NIV 1984)

—

127

In any event, whoever wrote Acts, for one reason or another devoted almost half of that book to the life and deeds of Saint Paul. Nevertheless, some scholars believe that the author most likely did not know about Paul's letters, as there are none mentioned in Acts. It is of some interest to me that a number of descriptions of Paul's acts do not coincide with Paul's own account of the events found in his Epistles. The authenticity of the described events, therefore, is hard to prove.

Because Paul's writings are the most abundant in the New Testament, let me start with the epistles of Paul, also known as Saul of Tarsus. Paul was born about the same time as Jesus. He was a Hellenic Jew, meaning he was raised in the Greek culture still present in the newly expanded Roman Empire. He was of the Hebrew tribe of Benjamin and thought of himself as quintessentially Jewish.

He was a Pharisee by religious affiliation. The Pharisees, incidentally, were strong believers in life after death and in the resurrection of the dead. Paul was a devotee of this philosophy, and, being a deeply religious man, he made it his mission to persecute those who were in opposition to it or who had different interpretations of the laws God gave to Moses. This included, by his own admission, the followers of Jesus Christ. Indeed he is said to have been present at the stoning of the disciple Stephen.

Stephen was a loyal supporter of the teachings of Jesus. When Jews belonging to the Synagogue of the Freedmen (as those hailing from Asia, Cilicia, and Egypt were called) spread rumors that Stephen had claimed Jesus would destroy the Temple and abolish the teachings of Moses, Paul was the first among those who sought his death. With fanatical zeal, he solicited and obtained the approval of the Sanhedrin to actively persecute the Nazarenes (the name given to the followers of Jesus and those who worked to spread his teachings).

The persecution in which Paul engaged is described in the Acts of the Apostles in the New Testament. Paul was rigorous and relentless in his work, so it is no surprise that it took a lot of courage and time for Jesus' followers to trust this man when he came to them after his conversion, claiming to believe as they did.

Paul's conversion to Christianity, by his own account, was sudden and unexpected. It took place while he was on the road to Damascus. At that time, Paul said, he experienced a vision of the martyred Christ, a revelation that blinded him for a short period of time. A voice, clearly identifying itself as the voice of Jesus Christ, demanded to know why Paul continued his persecution.

So deeply was this religious man affected by this event that, in his ardor, he jumped from one extreme to another. At the age of approximately forty, he accepted Christianity as the true faith, abruptly transforming himself into a fearless apostle of this new belief. He accepted unreservedly and with all his heart that this Jesus, who had revealed himself on the road to Damascus, was the Righteous One the martyred Stephen had proclaimed.

Whether or not Paul's vision was real, I find it hard to believe that Jesus would encourage Paul to become an advocate of his faith, especially since Jesus, by that time, was gone. Why not use his persuasive power while he was still alive? Why go for the most virulent and stubborn representative of a sect for which Jesus had no trust whatsoever? It is well documented in the Gospels that Jesus did not trust the Pharisees, calling them hypocrites and vipers. Did Jesus change his mind after his resurrection? The sequence of events related in the Bible did not make this clear at all.

Paul spends some time trying to comprehend what his new role should be. As an advocate of the new religious doctrine, he stirs up many followers of the Jewish religion, who did not and could not see Jesus of Nazareth in the role of Messiah. No wonder then that a crowd of agitated people tries to kill Paul the first chance they get. Despite this hostility, Paul is persistent in pursuit of his new role, actively traveling through different regions with the clear goal of converting as many Gentiles as possible to this new faith.

I must emphasize here that Paul, without a doubt, saw the distinction between "the Father, who is in Heaven," in the words of the Lord's Prayer, and Jesus. Accordingly, in his letter to the Romans, we read Paul's attempts to make this distinction clear for his audience.

To all who are in Rome, beloved of God, called to be saints: Grace to you and peace from God our Father and the Lord Jesus Christ. First, I thank my God through Jesus Christ for you all, that your faith is spoken of throughout the whole world. For God is my witness, whom I serve with my spirit in the gospel of His Son, that without ceasing I make mention of you always in my prayers. (Romans 1:7-9 NKJV)

—

Paul's transformation is precipitous, and, even as he evangelizes, he is seeking the true meaning of his beliefs and establishing himself in his new role: advocate of the teachings of Jesus, the Righteous One, and the anointed Son of God. He is as rigorous in his devotion and his apostolic work as he was previously in his persecution of his new fellow believers. He is sometimes harsh in judgment—not just of his fellow men, but of himself. "As it is written: 'There is none righteous, no, not one,' Paul writes in Romans 3:10 (NKJV). And he does not consider himself any exception to this.

In spite of the fact that he never met Jesus in person, Paul becomes one of the most energetic advocates of Jesus' teachings. From his conversion, the main task Paul imposes on himself is to spread faith in the one and only god. His mission is to educate the pagans who believe in many gods, whom he wants to make aware of this one truth. Yet at no time did Paul seem confused about the role of Almighty God, his original god, the God of Hebrews. He distinguishes this from the role of the Son of God, Jesus Christ.

Most of the details of Paul's work come to us through his letters, the Epistles, seven of which are considered by scholars to be authentic. As to the other six, scholars are less certain who wrote them. Placing the question of authenticity aside, let us examine some of these letters, starting with Paul's letter to the Romans.

In this first letter, Paul clearly links the God of the Jews with Jesus by referring to "God our father, and the Lord Jesus Christ" (Romans 1:7 NKJV). In ancient times, the word "lord" was used interchangeably with different applications, ranging from a name given to a husband or, as in case of Jesus Christ, to express someone's authority. It is sometimes used interchangeably with teacher or rabbi. In 1 Corinthians 8:5-6 Paul says:

> *For even if there are so-called gods, whether in heaven or on earth (as there are many gods and many lords), yet for us there is one God, the Father, of whom are all things, and we for Him; and one Lord Jesus Christ, through whom are all things, and through whom we live.* (NKJV)

In his letter to Romans, Paul explains the role of Jesus, whom he now calls the Son of God: "Through Him we have received grace and

—

apostleship for obedience to the faith among all nations for His name" (Romans 1:5 NKJV). Paul's mission is quite clearly described in Romans 1:9-10: "For God is my witness, whom I serve with my spirit in the gospel of His Son, that without ceasing I make mention of you always in my prayers, making request if, by some means, now at last I may find a way in the will of God to come to you" (NKJV). Paul's stand is unambiguous and frequently offers menacing verdicts reminiscent of the Old Testament and presented as instructions received from God. In Romans 1:18-19, we find: "For the wrath of God is revealed from heaven against all ungodliness and unrighteousness of men, who suppress the truth in unrighteousness, because what may be known of God is manifest in them, for God has shown it to them."

In Romans 1:29-31, he expresses his disgust and despair for people who are

> *filled with all unrighteousness, sexual immorality, wickedness, covetousness, maliciousness; full of envy, murder, strife, deceit, evil-mindedness; they are whisperers, backbiters, haters of God, violent, proud, boasters, inventors of evil things, disobedient to parents, undiscerning, untrustworthy, unloving, unforgiving, unmerciful.* (NKJV)

In Romans 5:8, Paul writes, "But God demonstrates His own love toward us, in that while we were still sinners, Christ died for us" (NKJV). With this argument, Paul expresses his belief that people had to learn the grave lesson that came with the death of the Son of God. Therefore, he concludes that the death of Christ will ultimately result in reconciliation among all enemies, even as prophesied in the Torah. The world will one day be just, sinners will no more sin but live righteous lives, because, as he exclaims, "But the free gift is not like the offense. For if by the one man's offense many died, much more the grace of God and the gift by the grace of the one Man, Jesus Christ, abounded to many" (Romans 5:15 NKJV). Such a vision was based on Paul's own persuasion that the love sacrifice Christ represented would heal the iniquities of the world. His writings indicate he expected that to happen in his lifetime.

How much of Paul's wishful thinking that peace would soon come to earth has actually been fulfilled? My answer, not surprisingly,

–

would be very little, if any. In the last two millennia, territorial, tribal, and religious wars; hostility among neighboring nations; and the annihilation of one people by another have relentlessly continued.

Another theological argument offered by Paul was that "For we know that the law is spiritual, but I am carnal, sold under sin" (Romans 7:14 NKJV). He goes on to say: "For I know that in me (that is, in my flesh) nothing good dwells; for to will is present with me, but how to perform what is good I do not find" (Romans 7:18 NKJV). With this remark, Paul expresses his belief that the desires of our bodies cannot be clean and without sin.

He enlarges on this in his first letter to the Corinthian congregation: "For as in Adam all die, even so in Christ all shall be made alive" (1 Corinthians 15:22 NKJV). In other words, only by accepting and following the words of Christ can we overcome our desires for the things that destroy us.

At this juncture, I'd like to introduce two more important and related phenomena brought up throughout Paul's letters: baptism and resurrection.

BAPTISM AND RESURRECTION

When Paul refers to the sinful nature of the flesh, he compares it to a corruptible being that is subject to death. But when he mentions the spirit, it is portrayed as the glorified source of eternal life. Paul proceeds to explain that our corrupt desires are the enemy of God, as they cause us to sin.

A number of different conclusions might be drawn from his teachings. One might suppose that only the death of the corruptible body can release the divine spirit that is eternal and worthy of God. Mainstream theology, however, interprets Paul as saying that the desires of the flesh can only be overcome through observation of the teachings of Christ and that the spiritual strength necessary to that enterprise comes through a firm and passionate belief in Christ himself. When this happens, the believer is said to be reborn or "quickened" or brought to life in the spirit, while the old, purely physical nature is said to die.

In Romans 6:3-4, Paul speaks of the symbolic meaning of baptism:

—

Or do you not know that as many of us as were baptized into Christ Jesus were baptized into His death? Therefore we were buried with Him through baptism into death, that just as Christ was raised from the dead by the glory of the Father, even so we also should walk in newness of life. (NKJV)

And here is my real first problem with a literal understanding of Paul's words. Why are we to believe that those who follow Jesus, after being baptized, must be raised from the dead? Even if we accept that Jesus Christ, being something rather more than just human, was literally, physically raised from death after his crucifixion, what has persuaded generations of Christians that Paul is saying that the baptized must first *physically* die to then be *physically* resurrected?

In other words, why must there be a resurrection, especially a physical resurrection, given Jesus' distinction between physical and spiritual life, especially in John 6:63: "It is the Spirit who gives life; the flesh profits nothing. The words that I speak to you are spirit, and they are life" (NKJV). Why, given Paul's assertion "that flesh and blood cannot inherit the kingdom of God" (1 Corinthians 15:50 NKJV), do so many Christians believe in a physical resurrection of the material body?

This belief that God will raise all the dead who led righteous lives to an eternal physical existence in some heavenly dwelling not only seems hopelessly childish, it also hints at an extreme attachment to the physical, a condition from which Jesus Christ labored and suffered to save believers.

It is in regard to salvation that I would like to pose another question: Why would God create us in a form that is inherently corruptible and sinful and then leave us powerless to do anything about it? How could it be our fault?

According to Paul and the Christian doctrine to which his writings have led, we come to earth in our physical bodies with no choice but to conduct our lives the way we do. Whether you blame Adam and Eve or Satan for this state of affairs, no one since the dawn of human consciousness asked for it. Yet we have a conscience that feels guilt, and thus we make ourselves even more miserable. And this is in addition to the other problems that come in such abundance.

—

Could the question of why are we corruptible be yet one more piece in the intricate puzzle provided to us by God that we need to solve?

I would also ask why, if God knew that human beings must always be sinful, he would send his Son to us in the same corruptible body? Perhaps the answer to this is also in Corinthians. Here Paul holds up Christ as an example; because Christ has conquered death, we may also conquer it.

Here is my dilemma with this in relation to the concept of Christ as God incarnate. If, as some theologians teach, Jesus was Almighty God, then it is hard to credit that the physical suffering of a mere human body would have had much effect on the omnipotent Lord of Creation. Certainly he did not actually die. He came to earth for a brief thirty-three years, performed his tasks, and then returned to heaven.

Then was it all for show? If it was, what of Paul's confidence?

> *If Christ is preached that He has been raised from the dead how, do some among you say that there is no resurrection of the dead?* (1 Corinthians 15:12 NKJV)

Again I ask, in what way are we to understand Christ's sacrifice?

Suffice it to say that many different denominations today understand this key concept of Christian faith differently. Yet the point remains that God has, at least according to the Torah, been so unhappy with his creation that he has regretted it more than once. And prophetic utterances indicate that the future of mankind is to be at least as sordid as its past. Wouldn't it be a naïve move on God's part then to imagine that Christ's sacrifice would magically make sinful and corruptible humans pure and incorruptible? Why not develop a new breed of human instead that would not travel down a sinful path?

In 2 Corinthians 5:1-4, Paul suggests that when

> *our earthly house, this tent, is destroyed, we have a building from God, a house not made with hands, eternal in the heavens. For in this we groan, earnestly desiring to be clothed with our habitation which is from heaven, if indeed, having been clothed, we shall not be found naked. For we who are in this tent groan, being burdened, not because we*

want to be unclothed, but further clothed, that mortality
may be swallowed up by life.

According to Professor Phillip Cary's course on the history of Christian theology, what Paul is addressing in this letter to the church at Corinth was the Christian view of the end time when all true believers will leave these physical "tents" and take up residence in heavenly dwellings. Paul's words then, combined with prophetic and highly metaphorical utterances in the Revelation of Saint John, have led to the belief in a massive resurrection of physical bodies at the second coming of Christ.

> *Now this I say, brethren, that flesh and blood cannot*
> *inherit the kingdom of God; nor does corruption inherit*
> *incorruption. Behold, I tell you a mystery: We shall not all*
> *sleep, but we shall all be changed—in a moment, in the*
> *twinkling of an eye, at the last trumpet. For the trumpet will*
> *sound, and the dead will be raised incorruptible, and we*
> *shall be changed.* (1 Corinthians 15:50-52 NKJV)

To what is Paul referring? Does he mean that our spiritual body (what is sometimes translated as our "celestial body" or "glorified body") will not be a body of flesh and blood but will take some other form that will then go to its heavenly dwelling? Or is this new form, itself, the heavenly dwelling of which he speaks?

This theme of resurrection (whether spiritual or physical) is repeated in some form in nearly all known religions, undoubtedly expressing the desire of humans to last, if not forever, at least for a good long time.

Another theological idea that can be traced to Paul's letters is his insistence on justification by faith, which is derived from the belief that Gentiles do not need to be circumcised or to become Jews in order to convert to Christianity. That doctrine alone has contributed to some major splits in Christianity, beginning with the early Christian sects such as, for instance, the Marcionites were. The schism arises around the relative importance of the elements of faith, grace, and works in Christian belief and in the process of salvation, with different churches falling at different points along the continuum.

It is ironic that the Church Fathers found themselves on both sides of Paul's religious quest for faith. When he believed he was the emissary of the Hebrew God, Jehovah, they received his hatred and vitriol. Once he believed he was the emissary of the Christian God of the same name, they received his love and instruction.

Thus I must pose a question: Did the Church Fathers accept Paul's teachings out of necessity?

What is interesting to me about this transition in Paul's life was that it did not change Paul's character insofar as the zeal with which he prosecuted his assumed duties. His religious orientation had changed; his level of activity did not.

Surrendering to this heavenly power caused sweeping and difficult changes in Paul's worldview. His concept of what was the only true religion, his judgment of people, his discrimination of what was pure and sinful, all were abruptly transformed with the acceptance this new (or resurrected) faith. He now acquired a new outlook on life and a renewed purpose of his beliefs. He was changed "in the twinkling of an eye."

He acquired a new credence in this man who had called himself the Son of God, a man taken by many as a fool and an impostor, a man who was crucified without dignity or respect, a man who seemed, except to a very few at the time, to have died in ignominious defeat. And in the service of this man, Paul began to expiate the guilt of his prior existence, a theme that rises again and again in his writings.

To further expand on the topic, the apostles, the first followers of Jesus Christ, had started to spread the teachings of Jesus, pursuing the main task in trying to convert as many people as possible. Still, it would seem self-explanatory that they encountered opposition from the Jewish orthodoxy, such as the Sadducees and the representatives of the Sanhedrin, and also from lay people who did not recognize Jesus as Messiah. This small band of devoted people, the apostles, were warned more than once not to spoil the minds of the Hebrews by referring to Jesus Christ as the Son of God. But with Peter and John in the vanguard, the apostles did not listen to these warnings; they faithfully communicated to people what they taught and, most importantly, believed in the righteousness of their mission.

So strong was the belief of these apostles that in spite of the real danger (eventually most of them were put in prison), and they realized

—

that they might be killed, they continued to insist that Jesus was the Son of God, the Messiah prophesied in Daniel, blissfully asserting that God would protect them in their ministry. Eventually, all of the apostles suffered, and many, including Peter, died as martyrs to the cause of Christ. Yet despite this tragic finale, the message of Christ continued to spread, and one must wonder why.

THE GOSPEL RECORD

Paul, of course, was not the only contributor to Christian doctrine. Other contributors to our understanding of Jesus's life included the Gospel writers—Matthew, Mark, Luke, and John. As I mentioned, these Gospels are written in such a manner that to prove who wrote them is impossible. Nevertheless, it is accepted by the believers that those were written by four individuals named Matthew, Mark, Luke, and John. Whether or not they were the originators of the Gospels, from my standing, is not important, as we are not considering the authorship but rather the truthfulness, or lack thereof, of these documents.

The New Testament begins with the Gospel of Matthew, even though the Gospel of Mark (founder of the Christian church at Alexandria and later acquiring the name of Coptic Christian Church) is believed to have been written earlier. (Some sources give that primacy to the Gospel of John.) But since the New Testament starts with the Gospel of Matthew, I will begin there.

The Gospel of Matthew starts with the following words: "The book of the genealogy of Jesus Christ, the Son of David, the Son of Abraham" (Matthew 1:1 NKJV). Then follows a chronological listing of Jesus' genealogy: "Abraham begot Isaac, Isaac begot Jacob, and Jacob begot Judah and his brothers" (Matthew 1:2 NKJV), altogether forty-two generations. Thus we read in Matthew 1:16, "And Jacob begot Joseph the husband of Mary, of whom was born Jesus who is called Christ" (NKJV).

And with that, I see the first problematic claim made by Matthew, as Joseph could not be the biological father of Jesus. "After His mother Mary was betrothed to Joseph, before they came together, she was found with child of the Holy Spirit" (Matthew 1:18 NKJV).

–

Now, if Joseph was not the biological father of Jesus, what makes Jesus the descendant of the mentioned above lineage of David?

The contemporary advocates of Christianity insist that Mary was herself a descendant of that lineage. If that is so, she is the first woman introduced in the genealogical tree according to the chronology of the Bible.

Second, as we read in Matthew 1:19-21:

> *Then Joseph her husband, being a just man, and not wanting to make her a public example, was minded to put her away secretly. But while he thought about these things, behold, an angel of the Lord appeared to him in a dream, saying, "Joseph, son of David, do not be afraid to take to you Mary your wife, for that which is conceived in her is of the Holy Spirit. And she will bring forth a Son, and you shall call His name Jesus, for He will save His people from their sins.* (NKJV)

Without any unduly sarcasm, but more with sadness, I read these words promising a coming savior, whose coming turned into historically the longest persecution of a whole ethnic group of innocent people. With all due respect to the angel sent by God announcing the news, I also can't even imagine what Joseph must have thought and felt about such announcement. Even if Joseph was a very religious man, he most likely would be overwhelmed when his wife (as well as an angel), tells him that she is pregnant through the agency of the Holy Spirit—the same Shekinah that was said to flash forth from the Ark of the Covenant and hover over the Tabernacle in the desert—and, further, that their future son is going "to save His people from their sins." In other words, he would be a Messiah.

Because of the prophecies in the Torah, the expectation of a Messiah was high at that time, and there were, according to the Gospels and other historical records, many would-be messiahs wandering the hills around Jerusalem. To be told that your child was the one in such an unusual and unanswerable way should have bewildered Joseph, to suggest the least.

The beliefs about Mary are nearly as varied as those about her son. Mary is presented as having not only conceived Jesus while a virgin, which is medically still somewhat possible, but is believed by the Catholic Church to have been perpetually a virgin during and after his birth. This is despite the fact that the Bible mentions his having siblings. (Although the Catholic Church explains that these were actually cousins.)

The Catholic doctrines on Mary claim that Jesus was born in such a way that his mother's integrity was maintained. Further, in 1854, the church formalized the dogma of Mary's Immaculate Conception, thus moving the stain of original sin further away from Jesus. These doctrines seem to have been reasoned from the doctrinal imperative of believing that Mary was perpetually virginal rather than to have been drawn from scripture.

The Catholic Church, whether intentionally or not, also raises the disturbing point that God made seriously questionable decision by picking a young teenage girl who would bring to the world the future Messiah. While the Gospels don't say anything about Mary's age, the *Catholic Encyclopedia* notes that she could have been as young as thirteen. Based on the fact that a Jewish woman was considered marriageable at the age of twelve, this postulate does not sound that awful. But to me, it seems quite strange that God made his decision by choosing such a young girl to provide an optimum solution for a whole nation and, as it turned out, for the majority of mankind. I am also not convinced that this poor girl's husband (who, according to some apocryphal sources, was ninety years old) would quietly accept such a naive notion as his child-wife being pregnant by the Holy Spirit.

King Herod's massacre of Jewish boy babies (referred to in religious documents as the "Slaughter of the Innocents") is the event that seems to have been borrowed from the Old Testament. In the Old Testament, the pharaoh ordered the slaughter of every Jewish male newborn to keep the population of able-bodied Jews in check. In the New Testament, Herod allegedly tried to foil Zoroastrian and Jewish prophecy and put Jesus' life in jeopardy by directing the killing of all newborn Jewish boys.

In any event, this portrayal of Herod is recorded only in the biblical book of Matthew and is corroborated by no other historical source, even within the Gospel record. It is, however, on par with other recorded atrocities committed by Herod Antipas, and Christian sources suggest

—

this is enough to suppose it was a real event. In Matthew, the author notes that the massacre fulfilled a prophecy: "Then was fulfilled what was spoken by Jeremiah the prophet, saying: 'A voice was heard in Ramah, Lamentation, weeping, and great mourning, Rachel weeping for her children, Refusing to be comforted, Because they are no more'" (Matthew 2:17-18 NKJV).

This practice of citing such an event in the life of Jesus Christ as a fulfillment of prophecy is a common one among New Testament writers. But, in context, this particular prophecy is part of a passage about the Jews being returned to Israel after their long captivity in Babylon. What it has to do with the birth of Jesus is unclear.

In any event, if one is to believe that the birth of Jesus meant the divine arrival of the Christ, which would coincide with the demise of many innocent babies, seems quite cruel to me, especially as foreseen by God.

Another thought in the Bible—the idea that Jesus was sent to save the Jewish people from their sins, as described by the narrator of Matthew—it seems fully naïve to me in the sense that it puts Jesus in direct conflict with the Pharisees, Sadducees, and Sanhedrin. Take, for example, the statement he makes when the Pharisees criticize him for having his disciples gather grain on the Sabbath. He reminds them that it is less than what King David did when his men were hungry on the Sabbath; David went into the Holy Place and offered his men the consecrated bread. Christ concludes, "'The Sabbath was made for man, and not man for the Sabbath'" (Mark 2:27 NKJV).

Jesus' statement about the purpose of the Sabbath would probably not have bothered the Pharisees much; they understood that the laws of God were created to serve and preserve man. But clearly his claiming to be Lord of the Sabbath—with the authority to change the law and even to forgive sins—angers them a great deal.

Indeed, Jesus shows little respect for the Pharisees' authority. In fact, he displays a decided preference for the company of people those same Pharisees viewed with contempt: tax collectors, prostitutes, and the poor and disenfranchised. When the Pharisees call him to account for this behavior, Jesus says, "'Those who are well have no need of a physician, but those who are sick. I did not come to call the righteous, but sinners, to repentance'" (Mark 2:17 NKJV). In that regard, it is quite curious that the contemporary Christianity insists that Jesus upon his return will punish sinners and nonbelievers.

Another strange inconsistency, at least in my mind, is that while Jesus teaches tolerance and kindness for the poor and sick, he is despairing of the rich. When a wealthy young man fails to choose following Jesus over his wealth, the Gospels tell us that:

> *Then Jesus looked around and said to His disciples, "How hard it is for those who have riches to enter the kingdom of God!" And the disciples were astonished at His words. But Jesus answered again and said to them, "Children, how hard it is for those who trust in riches to enter the kingdom of God! It is easier for a camel to go through the eye of a needle than for a rich man to enter the kingdom of God."*
> (Mark 10: 23-25 NKJV)

Why would such a separation of people be justifiable? Do rich people, in the eyes of Jesus and consequently God, deserve to be punished only because they, in their lifespan, achieved riches? Why must those people, who were able to make it in terms of success, be punished? Could that be true love coming from God who should have embraced all people? This is less an appeal to an Essene's asceticism, according to some scholars, than a principle of socialism; the idea being that Jesus advocated that the wealthy learn to detach themselves from their wealth and sacrifice it willingly for the benefit of the giver and recipient alike.

It is known that this kind of teaching is found in the teachings of Buddha as well. But in today's world, it is strangely reminiscent of the contemporary socialist ideas, is it not? It doesn't matter if you are able. What matters is that you *must* give it away to those who weren't and aren't able, with emphasis on a word "must."

The warning about the dangers of attachment to wealth is repeated not only by Jesus but by the Apostle Paul:

> *"No servant can serve two masters; for either he will hate the one and love the other, or else he will be loyal to the one and despise the other. You cannot serve God and mammon." Now the Pharisees, who were lovers of money, also heard all these things, and they derided Him.* (Luke 16:13-14 NKJV)

—

For the love of money is a root of all kinds of evil, for which some have strayed from the faith in their greediness, and pierced themselves through with many sorrows. (1 Timothy 6:10 NKJV)

So this problem of mankind could be solved altogether with the elimination of currency? Must this course of Christ's teaching be accepted by humanity as a sound one?

As for those who, like the Pharisees, fail to accept his teachings, Jesus instructs his disciples not to waste energy arguing with them. We read in Mark 6:11: "And whoever will not receive you nor hear you, when you depart from there, shake off the dust under your feet as a testimony against them" (NKJV). In the meantime, Jesus says of his ministry that he came not to abolish the law, but to fulfill it. Here he apparently draws a sharp distinction between the law of God and Moses and the wisdom of the fathers. I find it ironic that such a flouter of old authority (which he likens to old wineskins) should establish a new authority. There seem to be two sides to Jesus Christ: the kind, loving upholder of the rights of the downtrodden, and the witty, shrewd, rebellious, disrespectful dissenter from accepted tradition for those who became rich or well-to-do.

When Christ gathers his disciples at the mountain and begins to teach them how to be righteous and obey the Ten Commandments, it is truly remarkable to read, "Blessed are the poor in spirit . . . Blessed are they that are mourn . . . Blessed are the merciful . . . Blessed are the peacemakers . . . Blessed are the meek . . ." With regard to the many other teachings of Jesus, such as offering the kingdom of heaven to the poor, to the meek, to the hungered, to the righteous, and to the sinners, he, along with blessing all of them, surprisingly, not in divine but in human terms, points at those who will not get God's blessings. Those are the "other" group of people, whom he does not accept or does not want to teach or does not forgive for any proposed or not proposed sins, they are condemned for God's wrath once and for all. Is he a divider?

From now on, one can find not-so-wise lines of separation among people teaching them selectively and not necessarily wisely. And these are not the only bothersome deficiencies of human judgmental approach.

—

At the beginning of the book of Matthew, we read how Jesus gathered the first followers of his journey. "And Jesus walking by the sea of Galilee, saw two brethren, Simon called Peter, and Andrew his brother, casting a net into the sea: for they were fishers. And he saith unto them, Follow me, and I will make you fishers of men. And they straightway left their nets, and followed him" (Matthew 4:18-20).

This marvelous decision made by the two brothers should be the least commendable for anyone who tries to use a common sense. Why would these busy and responsible people trust a stranger up to the pointless and gullible abandoning their lifestyle? Why the other not related ten young adults would throw away everything they treasured and immediately become not concerned with their success in future life?

It might be justified only under one circumstance—these people knew beforehand who Jesus was. But did they?

Matthew also enumerates many other teachings of Christ. Are all those teachings noble and divine in nature? Just consider such saying as "Beware of false prophets, which come to you in sheep's clothing, but inwardly, they are ravening wolves." Who Jesus is referring to? Does he warn that people are generally surrounded by crooks and shady dealers? His teachings are often simplistic in nature and should be seen as black and white without providing many attributes and conditional motivations of a man in any given particular situation. Sometimes he exaggerates the existing words of wisdom, making his own conclusion, be those correct or not.

We read, "If your right eye causes you to sin, pluck it out and cast it from you; for it is more profitable for you that one of your members perish, than for your whole body to be cast into hell. And if your right hand causes you to sin, cut it off and cast it from you; for it is more profitable for you that one member perish, than for your whole body to be cast into hell" (Mathew 5:29-30 NKJV).

Does Jesus deny or is he not familiar with the "control center" in the brain managing our actions and deeds?

When one reads the words "You shall not commit adultery," one realizes that Jesus surpasses the Old Testament law: "But I say to you that whoever looks at a woman to lust for her has already committed adultery with her in his heart" (Matthew 5:28 NKJV). Can such chastity be only justified among those who were prepared for the

—

143

monastery and not for life in the real world? It is almost impossible to not have those feelings of attraction that will deny the very nature of our existence, would it not?

I do not know what to make of such teachings of Christ as for instance, "But I tell you not to resist an evil person. But whoever slaps you on your right cheek, turn the other to him also." Or this one, "If anyone wants to sue you and take away your tunic, let him have your cloak also" (Mathew 5:39-40).

Is the American society, according to these standards, transformed into more litigious society with very little Christian mentality or becoming irreligious in that sense altogether?

One could read further, "And when you pray, you shall not be like hypocrites. (Pharisees?) For they love to pray standing in the synagogues and on the corners of the streets, that they may be seen by men . . ." Is this kind of admonishing what was completely justified, or could such a behavior of the believers be interpreted also as a desire to involve more people in the belief and trust in God?

Without trying to reproduce the whole text from this Gospel, I can truthfully remark that, along with positive messages that are definitely might be found in the book, the reader can easily see that well over half of the Gospel text devoted to the obedience, complete trust to the good will of the almighty, and lack of self-initiation on the side of the reader or the listener who were exposed to the Bible.

Now let's take a look at other gospels.

The Gospel of Mark happens to be the shortest and is also arguably the earliest Gospel. It is almost entirely devoted to unfathomable stories from the life and actions of Jesus Christ. Yet while it makes claims that Jesus possessed an unusual power to heal the sick, it reminds me of the Old Testament narrative about the prophet Elijah, who lived in the ninth century BCE. The Israelite prophet Elijah is said to have raised the dead, brought fire from the sky, and predicted the future. He is also said to have been taken up to heaven while still alive.

When I looked into the similarities, I found that the prophet Malachi indicated that Elijah would return at some auspicious future date. Malachi 4:5 reads, "Behold, I will send you Elijah the prophet before the coming of the great and dreadful day of the Lord" (NKJV).

Because of this prophecy, Jesus was identified with Elijah by his Jewish audience, who related it to their Messianic expectations. Matthew 16:13-14 tells us: "When Jesus came into the region of Caesarea Philippi, He asked his disciples, saying, 'Who do men say that I, the Son of Man, am?' So they said, 'Some say John the Baptist, some Elijah, and others Jeremiah or one of the prophets'" (NKJV). But Jesus had already denied being the return of Elijah. In Matthew 11:14, he points to John the Baptist, saying of him, "'And if you are willing to receive it, he is Elijah who is to come'" (NKJV). Clearly this connection is an appeal to the Jewish sense of prophecy.

As the Gospel of Mark presented, the reader (me) cannot escape the feeling that we are faced with wonders of a magical, if not mysterious, height. Jesus had no problem treating lepers or lying-in-bed paralytics or raising the dead. He had no problem "commanding the unclean spirits to obey him." It did not concern him what caused the problem. He would not even bother ask, just proceeded to miraculously heal the sick. And for some reason, he did not do it in an orderly fashion. He even warned people who he helped not to talk about his powers. "And He strictly warned him (a leper) and sent him away at once, and said to him, 'See that you say nothing to anyone . . .'" (Mark 1:43-44).

But why? If Jesus was preoccupied with helping people as the miracle worker, why was he against attracting much attention to himself? That is absolutely incongruent to me. If he is what he says he is, then why would he stay away from much attention?

It is also difficult to understand why would he curb his natural abilities. Was he afraid of reprisals? He possessed rare powers, no doubt, plus he was able to forgive sins. Why would he do it randomly?

Another puzzle comes with Jesus's specific and indiscriminate desire to help the tax collectors. These people were known as those Jews who collected taxes from fellow Jews for the Roman Empire. Of course, they were the sinners as probably the rest of most people are. But this particular group of people was making living by charging an extra amount for their own benefit and was often considered the traitors, who became wealthy at the expense of their own brethren. Was such consideration of this layer of people who had to be forgiven not coincidental with the rest of wealthy class of "the money-hungry sinners"? Why separate? Why distinguish then? Why this class of people had to be helped without questioning their conduct but not

—

those who got rich through the other means not mentioned in the Bible and not necessarily the corrupt way?

Why would Jesus disturb the old traditions of his people in such provocative, rebellious way instead of trying to persuade the Pharisees and other elites to go along with his teaching? As he himself says, "And if a house be divided against itself, that house cannot stand" (Mark 3:25).

Was Jesus a divider then?

There are, of course, many positive descriptions of Jesus's teachings, such as love of one's neighbor and parents and, of course, love of God. But those don't jump into your eyes and ears as something unusual or extraordinary.

Thus, we try to see what else would point to Jesus as a Son of God. And again, I had no choice but to separate a desire of people to find an idol, who will pull them through a jungle of life-forest and a good-natured man who had no other reason but to help those who suffered, along with his philosophical, as we say it now, but more like humanistic discourse.

Of course, as Jesus's parables and teachings described by this Gospel are plenty, there is nothing controversial or unusual in his behavior and the behavior of the people who followed Jesus. What stands out in my mind, though, is the powerful desire of contemporary people, equipped with tremendous load of contemporary knowledge of exact science, to not only try to interpret described events of the past as something divinely magical, instead of analyzing them logically, but also apply those far-fetched events without credulous justification into the contemporary world.

The Gospel of Luke, which as Luke himself explains, is the result of his having "taken in hand to set in order a narrative of those things which have been fulfilled among us" (Luke 1:1 NKJV). Overall, it reminds the reader of the Gospels of Mark and Matthew. Yet Luke introduces a few unoriginal utterances. Hence, we read in chapter 1 verse 5 of Luke's gospel, "There was in the days of Herod, the king of Judea, a certain priest named Zacharias, of the division of Abijah. His wife was of the daughters of Aaron, and her name was Elizabeth" (NKJV). Then Luke explains that Elizabeth became pregnant in spite of her old age, and God sent Gabriel to deliver the good news to her that she would have a very special child. This narrative is suspiciously reminiscent of the story of Sarah and Abraham, as it echoes the case of ninety-year-old Sarah, who would have given birth to Isaac long after menopause. In both cases, an angel makes the announcement and a miracle is required for the conception to take place.

Six months later, her cousin Mary got a similar blessing. In both cases, these women were provided in advance with the names for their unborn children: John and Jehoshua.

Then all themes are more or less repeated as in previous Gospels, and one shall wonder how much do people need of miracles.

Whether those are unexplained cures of the ill or magic rising of the dead or presumed events, such as, for instance, suggested resurrection, all subject matter lead to the relentless desire of men to live forever. Is such desire enough? Is promise to good-hearted obedient man a road to eternity justifiable? How much credence would be in these promises have they related to scientific proof or even simple explanation of event not related to immortality, afterlife, or what have you?

The last of the four canonical gospels is the Gospel of John. The Gospels of Mark, Matthew, and Luke are called synoptic because each is a synopsis of exactly the same events in Jesus' short ministry. However, the Gospel of John places the events not only in a different order, but also tells them from a different point of view. Whoever wrote this gospel, whether a disciple of Jesus or some unknown author, the gospel claims that Jesus is the Son of God, and Jesus himself quite often claims it. While he performs miracles, Jesus predicts his own time on earth, and he speaks as prophet and philosopher.

Again, miracles play a major role in the accounts the author gives us in the first few chapters. Why? Perhaps because human beings, as well as most of the other creatures, are mostly dependent on physical "signs and wonders." Thus diminishing the needs of words of wisdom, humans are more in tune with miracles to prove the point.

But Jesus, besides presenting himself as miracle worker, also behaves as a rebel who accuses the Pharisees and the high priest of lies and hypocrisy. He accuses them and their forebears of misleading the Jewish people, saying that they "do what you have seen with your father" (John 8:38 NKJV). When they protest that "Abraham is our father" (John 8:39 NKJV), Jesus tells them, "If you were Abraham's

—

children, you would do the works of Abraham" (John 8:39 NKJV). When his audience takes him literally and protests that they are not illegitimate children, Jesus tells them, "If God were your Father, you would love Me, for I proceeded forth and came from God; nor have I come of Myself, but He sent Me. Why do you not understand My speech?" (John 8: 42-43 NKJV). Jesus also gives this fiery speech:

> You are of your father the devil, and the desires of your father you want to do. He was a murderer from the beginning, and does not stand in the truth, because there is no truth in him. When he speaks a lie, he speaks from his own resources, for he is a liar and the father of it. But because I tell the truth, you do not believe Me. Which of you convicts Me of sin? And if I tell the truth, why do you not believe Me? He who is of God hears God's words; therefore you do not hear, because you are not of God. (John 8:44-47 NKJV)

I cannot prove that the Jewish religious loyalists interpreted such a declaration as dangerous and blasphemous, but it would have been natural for them to accept the words of any man presenting himself as the Son of God as a rude dismissal of their beliefs, would it not?

After hearing someone who talks this way, it would be quite a normal reaction, in my opinion, for people to ask Jesus, "'Are You greater than our father Abraham, who is dead? And the prophets are dead. Who do You make Yourself out to be?'" (John 8:53 NKJV). No wonder people who were not fond of Jesus' preaching tried to kill him.

In conclusion, it is safe to say that all four Gospels have blemishes from either a religious or historical point of view. True, they were written by lay people and not by professional writers. And with that, I have no argument. My concern is that while these narrators were depicting acts of Jesus as unique, they were actually not that unique and described in the Old Testament as previously having place. Another historical facts, that had been described as unique for Christianity for the most part had been borrowed from many Jewish customs and were just assumed by the Christians. Yet many Christians seem to believe they are uniquely theirs.

For example, there were exactly as many disciples surrounding Christ as there were Israelite tribes? Why? The meaning of twelve sons of Jacob and twelve tribes of Israelites is obvious. What is the meaning of twelve apostles?

Why did the Christian church end up with the priests, belief in paradise, and the need for mediators between God and men, in almost exactly the same manner as Jewish Bible would have it?

I would not object such resemblance, be it that the New Testament is a continuation of the Old Testament. But as it turned eventually out, it is not.

Christianity might insist on connection to Judean traditions, but it does more out of convenience than anything else. There are many more commonalities and parallels that could be picked up here. But that is not my goal.

Now, while I was provoked by the conduct of Jesus, starting from the time he began to act as if he were superhuman, I was continuously puzzled by his desire to cure the sick. If God the Father wished people to be healed, you'd think he could do it himself. He would not need Jesus Christ to appear for such a short period of time and cure a limited number of people. And if that healing was not the goal of God, then why was Jesus burdened with the assignment? Was that a way of proving his divine powers? Or was he so sensitive to the plight of his fellow men that he decided to cure some of them? Assuming the latter was the case, why wouldn't he heal everyone he met? Wouldn't it be more humane to ask God the Father to let all sufferers shed their sicknesses and return to health?

Nevertheless, if Jesus' speeches, recommendations, and ability to cure people are historical facts, can we not come to the proper conclusion that he was only repeating the many deeds ascribed to the prophet Elijah, who was a human being and not a son of God? Viewed in that light, wasn't Jesus merely a miracle worker with the superior qualities of a spectacular magician and nothing more? So to call Jesus Christ the Son of Man or the Son of God because the Bible claims he performed miracles is neither reasonable nor justified. Yet is it not because of these physical miracles believers viewed him as divine? Or is there perhaps some other reason?

Let's take a look at the life of Jesus of Nazareth, a man called by many as the Lord Jesus Christ. Most of Jesus' adult life coincides with the second and third decades of the first century CE. At that time, the Jews were a distinct religious group who worshiped the Creator of the universe, the one God they called *Yahweh* (YHWH), *Jehovah*, or *Adonai* (Lord). The majority of the people who surrounded the Hebrews were pagans; they were polytheistic, not monotheistic.

Even though the Hebrews were a small community and worshipped one god, they were divided into at least three prominent religious groups with different tenets of faith. Jesus represented yet another religious view, distinct from these major groups. His sermons, as we see in the Gospels, were not always benevolent:

Do not think that I came to bring peace on earth. I did not come to bring peace but a sword. For I have come to 'set a man against his father, a daughter against her mother, and a daughter-in-law against her mother-in-law;' and 'a man's enemies will be those of his own household.' (Matthew 10:34-36 NKJV)

In the above passage, Jesus is quoting the Old Testament prophet Micah, who is describing the sad state of affairs that will exist "the day God visits you" (Micah 7:4 NIV). Certainly, this accurately describes what might occur in a household if one of its members strayed from the Jewish faith to belief that Jesus of Nazareth was the Christ.

Jesus goes on to make this meaning clear. Verse 37 of Matthew reads, "He who loves father or mother more than Me is not worthy of Me. And he who loves son or daughter more than Me is not worthy of Me" (NASB). If such a proclamation were heard by people who did not see Jesus as the Messiah—or even worse, wouldn't welcome him if they *did* see him that way—what kind of reaction could this elicit besides frustration and enmity?

Jesus announces his mission early in his ministry in the synagogue in Nazareth. He states it by reading from the book of Isaiah:

> The Spirit of the Lord is upon Me,
> Because He has anointed Me
> To preach the gospel to the poor;
> He has sent Me to heal the brokenhearted,
> To proclaim liberty to the captives
> And recovery of sight to the blind,
> To set at liberty those who are oppressed;
> To proclaim the acceptable year of the Lord.

(Luke 4: 18-19 NKJV)

In Matthew 1:21 we are told that "He will save His people from their sins." This too is a reminiscent of an Old Testament prophecy, as it seems. For example, in the prophetic book of Ezekiel we read that:

> *And I will make them one nation in the land, on the mountains of Israel; and one king shall be king over them all; they shall no longer be two nations, nor shall they ever be divided into two kingdoms again. They shall not defile themselves anymore with their idols, nor with their detestable things, nor with any of their transgressions; but I will deliver them from all their dwelling places in which they have sinned, and will cleanse them. Then they shall be My people, and I will be their God. David My servant shall be king over them, and they shall all have one shepherd; they shall also walk in My judgments and observe My statutes, and do them.* (37:22-24 NKJV)

It is very close to what Jesus was proclaiming. Again, I do not deny any good deeds Jesus had accomplished, and I am certainly in no position to claim that Jesus was a fraud. But how much humanity benefited from his teaching?

Certainly millions have found Jesus' teachings liberating and elevating, but Christianity has, over the centuries, not been united. It has produced and continues to produce ever more denominations, many of which are hostile to each other, considering themselves to be true and all others false.

The problem is manifold when one considers Christianity's interaction with diverse peoples and cultures. When one speaks of Christians, one cannot refer to a single body of believers, for there are a vast number of different doctrines and interpretations of spiritual and material values covered by that name. Right from the start, organized Christianity went in so many directions that one group often denied another its validity. Ebionites, Marcionites, proto-orthodox, hetero-orthodox, Gnostics—these were only a handful of the religious sects that appeared in the first few centuries of Christianity, many to be labeled as heretical.

I cannot attribute this multitude of groups solely to an inability to understand the Christian doctrine uniformly. It is almost impossible

—

for me myself to make sense of the first suggestions of who Jesus Christ was.

But I increasingly believe that Jesus was not a god nor the Son of God and that he definitely could not be a part of the Trinity—another invented divine substance of convenience and justification.

Today, many historian scholars believe that Jesus was a charismatic leader who, in a short period of time, organized a new religious movement, revealing God's will and apocalypse.

In his teachings, he appeared as a rebel to the two major Jewish sects, whom he rebuked for their legalism, greed, and intolerance. He called the Pharisees hypocrites, and he mistrusted the sincerity of the Sadducees and the high priest. He was a populist, curing mainly the poor, and helping people who had sinned. He warned of the dangers of material wealth and taught that people must be willing to lose their life's accumulations as he claimed those things would keep them from the kingdom of God. Jesus taught that God prized meekness, humility, and love. He exhorted his followers to turn the other cheek, to pray even for their enemies, and to treat others as they would like to be treated.

When God some unknown time ago for some unknown reason had made a decision to create the universe, he must have had some vision of earth as the place where all his major deeds would take place. He probably thought it through carefully enough, when he chose the earth out of billions of other places to create life. He must have thought it through thoroughly when he finally finished his creation with human beings. Even while the first protagonists of his creation were the primitive replica of a future human sapience, he had to know that people would end up sophisticated and resourceful.

Still, it is hard to understand what motivated God when he, relatively recently in terms of the history of earth, decided that only the Jews, of the many people on earth, were making sense of his immediate tasks. And consequently, why did God then decide to better people through a very strange method and to teach them a lesson by throwing his only son to be crudely tormented, so that people would repent forever? True, Jesus' suffering made people aware of their sins. But only a handful of people were sympathetic with Jesus' ordeal at the time. It took another three hundred years of persecution, agony, and misery of the believers before new generations of accepting people came to live on earth. Did God plan to kill even more people before they will accept a new faith? Without a doubt, the more time that elapsed, the more people believed in the teachings of Christ. But most definitely not all people. Besides, in all versions of common sense, should the acceptance of the new faith have to bring more human suffering before the end to any suffering of people? While Jesus had taught people of God's word, shouldn't people have to become noble, righteous, and accepting?

In reality, the opposite happened. History shows that only two thousand years later, people became less united, more aggressive, and more belligerent. They now feel even more distant, filled with more animosity toward each other, along with more devilishly sophisticated wars. They progressed tremendously in the annihilation of their own kind. While discarding some very few sins, people explored others. And the Jews. They have always been a highly embattled ethnic group. Was that intent of God when he sent his beloved Son to save people from their own sins?

Was that the reason that God sent another prophet by the name of Muhammad? Christians don't think so. Jews do not believe so. Even atheist and agnostics didn't budge to reconsider their stances.

But before I proceed to make any conclusion, let me continue to speak on other religions and faiths.

CHAPTER 8

Islam—The Last Religious Stronghold

Before I begin discussing Islam, its holy book, the *Qur'an*, the life and work of the Prophet Muhammad, and some of the related topics, I wish to mention that it is not my intention to argue for or against the veracity of specific historical points cited in scholarly articles about when the first written works of the faith appeared or were accepted as canon. For me, this is not of critical importance for one simple reason: Time and again, history has demonstrated that chroniclers and historians are never objective enough to rely on facts. Reality may be objective, but observers of reality are not. What becomes history is an interpretive art form, not a science.

That Islam has found its roots sprouted from the Arab people no one doubts. It engendered in Mecca (Makkah), a city in the southern part of the Arabian Peninsula, connected to a story of the life of a man by the name of Muhammad. The faith acquired the specific word, Islam, and the people who follow it began to call themselves Muslims.

With that in mind, let me give you my own vision what Islam is for humanity in general sense.

Islam, possibly because it is a younger and therefore a more recent faith, claims that the Qur'an supersedes the Hebrew Bible and the New Testament as a vehicle of revelation. If that is the case, then it would mean one of two things: Either the Qur'an used some revelations from earlier faiths, or God decided to reveal more information this time than he had delivered previously. The trend of teaching Islam as a new, lately revealed religion, seems an emphasis of its advocates that corrupts and perverts the two previous faiths—Judaism and Christianity.

Despite such a conclusion, in analyzing Islam as a religion, I tried to examine it without more comparison to Judaism and Christianity than I felt was necessary. I tried to use a common sense in an attempt to discuss known facts, be those benevolently or belligerently perceived by humanity. I also wish to assure the reader that I didn't feel more bias toward the religion of Islam compared to my description of Christianity and Judaism, trying not to be influenced by the latest tendency of the majority of the Western world to portray this religious body as aggressors or terrorists or outcasts. Instead, I used my usual set of questions as a means of possible correctly understanding Muslim theology with an emphasis on the most obvious and prevalent in my mind discrepancies and unconformities. Thus, the following became first in my line of inquiries:

- What made the principle advocates of Islam accept and promote it?
- Why did God—omnipotent and omniscient—again choose another group of people, instead of sticking to the Hebrews or Christians to continue his teachings?
- Did the birth of Islam accomplish its task of unifying other faiths and religions as it promised to do?
- Did this faith spread through the calls for military action, or did it expand by the word and persuasion alone?
- Why is there a continuous rift between the major two factions, Shi'a and Sunni?
- Why does this faith produce violent fringe extremists?

In my attempt to answer these questions, I decided to start from the remote past of the people in that region, hoping to achieve a better understanding of what made them end up with the Muslim faith. Soon, I realized that I had to deal with the lack of established facts about who were in fact the people inhabiting the Arabian Peninsula. Even today, there is no clear documentation to whom those ancient tribes belonged to ethnically and even if they interrelated at all.

In my quest of how the original Muslims turned out to be such a powerful force that in a fairly short time, they had spread throughout most parts of the world, I had to analyze not only their message but their methods as well. I had to apply my knowledge of human nature in order to distinguish between Sunnis, Shi'as, and other Muslim groups around the world. These all were not easy tasks to solve, but I tackled them in both parts of my book, hoping to answer the raised questions.

The history of pre-Islamic Arabia is little known for many reasons. For one, the archaeological findings in the Arabian Peninsula are sparse. The most ancient sources known at present on which one can rely on are those that come from such cities as Petra, where the nomadic Nabateans settled, along with Edomites, leaving grand, carved temples and buildings to document their existence.

Were the Nabateans the original Arab people? No one knows for certain, as these people didn't leave any surviving artifacts besides the edifices in the city of Petra itself. Many sources indicate that the Nabateans appeared along with such Semitic tribes as the Moabites, Ammonites, and Arameans. According to the biblical stories, the Nabateans were the direct descendants of Abraham or the members of his family.

We learn from Arab traditions that the Semitic-speaking people of the Arabian Peninsula originated from the Qahtani tribe. Qahtan, who himself is a semi legendary figure, claimed his descent from the Yemenites. Whether the Nabatean people were assimilated into the Qahtani culture and gradually became part of it is not known.

It is generally accepted that most of the people we call Arabs began to migrate from the Arabian Peninsula to neighboring regions. Yet by the time Islam was established, there were no clear roots connecting the Arabs to the ancients. The only definitive connection of the Arabs to the ancient peoples of the region comes from the Bible. And even though taking the Bible as a reliable authentic source is not a scholarly prudent thing to do, we learn that Abraham was a Hebrew and that he fathered Ishmael with an Egyptian woman named Hagar. Would that reference properly suggest the beginning of Arabs?

Ancient Egypt was located geographically at the crossroads of several major cultures and engaged in trade with its neighbors. It experienced a number of long-lasting invasions by groups whose conquest left significant marks on the development and ethnicity of its people. The history of Egypt tells us that the country experienced significant cultural ups and downs for at least four thousand years before the Common Era. Could one say for certain then that the ancient Egyptians and Arabs were the same people? There have been numerous attempts to extract DNA from ancient Egyptian remains, but even today there is no mutually accepted evidence that might identify who the ancient Egyptians were.

General consensus among ethnologists is that they were most likely of Eurasian (60 percent), African (30 percent), and Mediterranean basin (the remaining 10 percent) descent. The main sources of that information are the hieroglyphic writings on the walls of temples, pyramids, and tombs. Would that be enough to say that Arabs descended from this lineage?

To follow the Bible stories further, we learn that Ishmael married an Egyptian woman and that he had twelve sons who later became tribal princes. Contemporary Islamic traditions consider Ishmael to be the ancestor of the Arab people—I have occasionally heard the term "Arabized Arabs" applied to such lineage.

In the Bible, the Ishmaelites (descendants of Ishmael) are also alternatively called the Midianites. Since Moses' wife was a Midianite, that would mean that Moses' sons, Gershom and Eliezer, were only half Hebrew. According to Jewish tradition, the mother is the determining vehicle in establishing the genealogical connection to the family. That would make the sons of Moses more Arab than Jew if the Midianites would fit such definition.

There are many accounts such as these in the stories of pre-Islamic culture. But in spite of ample of new sources that exist today, none sheds enough light to trace such important part of peoples history as of that region.

With that in mind, I realized that to do justice to the pre-Islamic world, a single chapter in this book might not be adequate. I do not wish to diminish the colorful history of the pre-Islamic world, and I don't want to mislead a reader either. Therefore, for those who wish to learn more on the topic, I suggest turning to the numerous sources existing today. I also promise that more clarification follows in the second part of this book. That being said, let us now turn to the Muslim faith itself.

First the conclusion I came to was that the Muslims, declaring their new faith, had no other choice but to rely on the Hebrew Bible as well as the New Testament for its justification in existence. In other words, this faith became a continuation of the two previously found religions, Judaism and Christianity. Whether Allah is a god for the explicitly Arab people or Almighty for the people of the world is not a significant problem in my mind. This is why.

The word "Islam" has multiple meanings, one of which is translated as "returning the people to God." The word also implies to accept, to surrender, to worship, and to submit to God.

As the contemporary religious world is clearly dominated by the two large bodies of followers, Christianity and Islam, it is no surprise that from both camps different interpretations of the two religions exist.

At this juncture, I'd like to use as a reference a book by Shaykh Fadhlalla Haeri, *The Elements of Islam*. This scholar has written many comprehensive and respected books on religious topics. Whether he is always or even mostly objective in making analysis of his religion, I offer the curious reader to decide on his own. My task was more to the point—to describe the author's approach to the topic in that particular book and attempt to analyze it.

In the first chapter, titled "The Rise of Islam," Shaykh Haeri explains how Islam became "the most complete system for awakening people to the highest spiritual state." He states, "While Adam and all the Prophets were Prophets of Islam, the collective prophetic consciousness reached its completion with Muhammad." If one wonders what made this scholar present Islam as a religion for all people, it is self-explanatory: Islam simply means submission to God, and all believers, regardless of their creed, submit to God. Therefore, such a statement becomes substantiated and valid.

But there is more to it than that, for Haeri writes:

> *The Qur'an says: "We make no distinction between any of the Messengers and Prophets [i.e. in the eyes of God]" (3:84). All the Prophets of Islam shared between them the knowledge of God but advocated different outer rules . . . The optimum outer bounds and basic laws of conduct were thus universalized for all human beings and for all time by the last of the Prophets, Muhammad. The rise of Islam in the revelation of the Qur'an and the prophetic conduct*

[called Sunnah] superseded all previously revealed laws
for they are appropriate to every age and society. (The
Elements of Islam, 6)

This explanation leads to the conclusion that Islam in its most recent form is the only source of a new revelation for all human beings desiring to believe in God. This is clearly the author's intent, for he prefaces his book by saying, "Islam is the culmination of all the faiths emanating from the Fertile Crescent." Then the author notes that:

Most Western writers on Islam and Muslims are alien to
the path of Islam . . . If a writer is alien to the Islamic
transformative process then it follows that most of his
observations and commentary on Islam or on Muslim
behavior and culture will be generally superficial despite
appearing to reflect depth in their analysis. (The Elements
of Islam, 2)

I respectfully decline these suggestions and wish to give my opinion concerning Islam, God, and the history of the original Muslims.

In Arabic, God's name is *Allah*. Some scholars believe that this name comes from a combination of two words: *Al* and *Illah*. *Illah* in Arabic means "God," and *Al* is a definite article; hence, "The God." The first Jewish scholars who translated the name of God from the Torah into the Arabic language used the name Allah as well. The Hebrews' generic plural word for God is *Elohim*, which is from the Aramaic *elah* and Hebrew *eloah*. All three names are believed to come from the cognate proto-Semitic languages of the region.

Today, about 1.6 billion people claim to be Muslims, the majority of whom are not Arabs, contrary to popular belief. Muslims live all over the world, including countries in Asia, Africa, Europe, the Americas, and the Middle East. Islam is quite a strict religion, yet its many followers claim that it offers them a spiritual resort of relief, hope, and purpose. According to some sources, on average, 90 percent of Muslims believe that Islam is their mental, traditional, and everyday guidance compare to 54 percent of Christian Americans and even fewer Europeans who similarly rely on their faith.

Statistics says a lot. Muslims are those people who unshakably (90 percent!) believe that whatever the Qur'an says, offers, or dictates must be taken literally. While such approach might be considered commendable, it also reflects a small and often dangerous part of human nature. I say this because rigorously following religious instructions usually limits an individual into an independent thinking as well as inflexibly points to one's normative behavior.

The Muslim way of life (the Sunnah) is guided by the Qur'an, *Hadiths* (sayings of the Prophet recorded by individuals believed to have heard them), and the various traditions that have arisen from Muslim schools of thought and law. Yet while neither Hadiths nor traditions are considered as binding as the words of the Qur'an, the majority of Muslims find it less problematic to follow them. Hadiths, in fact, contains those words of the Prophet that were noted by his companions and by a chain of transmitted narrations that were conveyed from one generation to the next. Such consideration makes it more appropriate to comply with recommendations of Hadith. Still because Hadiths were originally oral traditions collected up to over one hundred years after the death of the Prophet, many utterances ascribed to Muhammad cannot be authenticated.

And yet Muslims, and specifically Arab Muslims, do not question, doubt, or argue the validity of the introduced sayings of the Prophet. The question is, when and how all those words were introduced? The same is true in regards to the writing of the Qur'an. When Muhammad died in 632 CE, his expressions and words had already been collected in several different versions of the Qur'an that existed in tribal dialects. Later, during the rule of Uthman, one version was chosen to become the authoritative Qur'an. This was not an easy task, as two groups arose in the years following Muhammad's passing: Those who followed his first cousin and son-in-law, Ali, whom he had verbally appointed his successor, and those who believed—as did the Prophet's father-in-law, Abu Bakr—that Ali was too young to be the temporal leader and that Muhammad intended him to be the spiritual leader only. Abu Bakr was elected to be the first caliph of the group that called itself the Sunni (those who follow the Sunnah, or Way of the Prophet), while Ali's followers were called Shias, also meaning "followers," but not the way the Sunni implied. The difference lay in understanding that Shias, while they were, in fact, the followers of the

Prophet Muhammad, believed in the appointment of the successor on the basis of blood relation to the Prophet.

The fight between these two groups of followers was not so much for prestige and a usurpation of power as for trying to prove who represented the Muslim faith better. Still, this first sign of disagreement pointed toward an unchanged quality of man's nature—the tendency to fight for one's own vision of truth.

With the assassination of Uthman, the third caliph, in 656 CE, a civil war erupted. Muhammad's son-in-law, Ali, was pressed to succeed him. Yet his position as a leader of Muslims didn't last long. Ali himself was assassinated in 661, an act that precipitated a second civil war. This led to the rise of Muawiyah, the first caliph of the Umayyad Dynasty. Muhaviyyih's rule is remarkable in part for his attempt in the year 666 to change the Islamic point of adoration (which Muslims face when they pray) from Mecca to his political capital, Damascus. From this point forward, the gulf between Shias and Sunnis grew. This antagonism was compounded by the killing of the Imam Husayn (the Prophet's grandson) at the Battle of Karbala by forces loyal to Umayyads.

When the Abbasids seized the caliphate in 758, Muslims were faced with having to reconcile a number of contradicting traditions. By this time, the various written and oral Hadiths were collected and reviewed. A hierarchy of authenticity was established and controversial sayings that could not be traced to an individual companion of the Prophet were removed as not authentic. By the end of the eighth century, the Muslim world had a total of eight volumes of written Hadiths which informed the way of the Prophet, upon which Muslims wished to pattern their own lives.

Each year during the holy month of Ramadan, which celebrates the beginning of the New Year and the revelation of the Qur'an, millions of Muslims make the pilgrimage to Mecca, touching the Black Stone of the Kaaba ("House of God") as an expression of devotion to Allah.

Muslims view the Qur'an as the "Mother Book" revealed to Muhammad via the angel Gabriel (Gibriel in Arabic) over a period of twenty-three years. Thus the Qur'an is considered to have been dictated by God through his angel in increments and in response to different circumstances. It has been criticized, especially by Westerners, for its use of repetition and seeming lack of logic and

—

cohesiveness. Such criticisms invite study, certainly, but it should be noted that there are challenges to translating Arabic into other languages that have resulted in verses that differ widely in tone from translation to translation. The Muslim point of view is simply that the text was dictated by God, and therefore each person must make his best effort to understand it. To complicate the matter, majority of Arab scholars insists that those who are not Arabs and specifically those who did not read the text in original tongue cannot and should not raise their opinion of the meaning of the words in the Qur'an. For that reason alone, I am not going to have a discussion on the validity of the written verses in this holy book. My approach to it must, therefore, come from a different angle. For example, I personally find it highly suspicious that revelations from God stopped with Muhammad's death. This raises a number of questions, given the Muslim claim that Muhammad is the final prophet from God for all time.

1. Why did God allow his final prophet to die of poisoning at the relatively young age of sixty-three? Did Muhammad finish his work? Did he become useless? Would ending the life of the last prophet be considered a prudent decision at the time?
2. Why, after the death of Muhammad, did animosity erupt between what would become the Sunnis and Shias as different groups? Couldn't God envision such a possibility and teach Muhammad how to prevent the rift?
3. Why did God not secure peace and understanding among all the people before taking the life of his last prophet?
4. And finally, why would the omniscient God decide to abandon a partially educated humanity for the rest of its life on earth?

Studying the Muslim religion, I realized that there were more troublesome issues. Some arose from the tenets of Islam, some of which were not as clear as they could have been, while others were simply illogical and required better explanation. I began to look for those tenets that were available. I did not try to analyze everything I came across but devoted my attention to the particular aspects that I felt were important to me because of their high visibility, such as for instance the Arabs' claims about the location of the Dome of the Rock, the establishment of Islam as a religion, the separation of

–

Muslims into two major factions, and a variety of subsects or schools (such as the Shaykhi and Sufi schools), as well as the historical role of Abraham and his son Ishmael in regards to the relationship with Arabs.

Let me start with the Dome of the Rock. According to Islamic tradition, the Dome of the Rock was erected at the place from which, as Islamic scholars continuously maintain as a true story, the Prophet Muhammad ascended to heaven to meet Allah. Muhammad, accompanied by the archangel Gabriel, is said to have ascended from this spot to meet Allah in the "seventh heaven," where he received God's revelation. According to the same tradition, Muhammad attended God, alongside Abraham, Moses, and Jesus. Perhaps this was intended to show that these prior prophets did not view Muhammad as competition. Or perhaps by suggesting that communal, Muslim sages tried to show the monolith of all three major religions. It is hard to say.

Nevertheless, most scholars of different than Muslim faith opine that Muhammad's visit to the Temple Mount took place in a dream rather than in the material sense, especially after reaffirming the fact that Muhammad, at the time of his claimed ascension, physically had been residing at Masjid al-Haram, which is the same as Mecca. As this explanation sounds more reasonable to me, I am ready to accept it as solid and truthful. Besides, it doesn't seem a strong argument, in my mind, that this event, whether connected to a material ascension or to a dream, would make a place any more sacred than it had been previously.

According to the Hebrew Bible, "The Holy House"—or the First Temple, as contemporary Westerners know it—was built by King Solomon on the Temple Mount in Jerusalem during his reign (circa 970-930 BCE). This is the same spot on which the Dome of the Rock was established over one thousand six hundred years later. The First Temple was built to house the Ark of the Covenant, which, according to the Hebrew Bible, was a sacred container of the tablets received by Moses with the Ten Commandments written on them. It is also the place—again, according to the Hebrew Bible—where Abraham prepared to sacrifice his son Isaac.

The First Temple stood for 375 years—in Jewish belief—acting as a place of God's presence. It was destroyed in 586 BCE by the

—

Babylonians during their invasion of Israel but was erected again by Jews returning from exile in 538 BCE.

The Second Temple served as a sacred shrine until circa 70 CE when it was destroyed again, this time by Roman troops under General Titus. The Jews tried to build the Third Temple but failed for various reasons, although they never abandoned their hope of rebuilding this holy place.

When the spread of Islam led to the conquest of Jerusalem in 638 CE, the Muslim Caliph Umar gave an order to build a small mosque for Muslim worshipers on the Temple Mount. About fifty years later, the Umayyad Caliph Abd al-Malik built a spectacular and imposing structure next to it: the Dome of the Rock, erected upon exactly the same spot where the two Jewish temples had previously stood. The Dome of the Rock was finished between 687 and 691 CE and has been a religious shrine of the Muslim faith ever since.

The question I have is that while the Arab Muslims insist they are exhorted by Muhammad to respect the Hebrews, why did they place their sacred edifice over the exact location where the most sacred Jewish shrine was twice demolished? Wouldn't it have been a more respectful and proper gesture to offer to rebuild the third Jewish temple there or at least a combined Jewish-Muslim sacred place, if the Jews would have agreed? While this had not been the case, scholars, religious scientists, and philosophers began to seek the answers that might still be logically applied in this case.

Some Muslims, however, claim that the building the Dome of the Rock was a political attempt to discourage the pilgrimage of Muslims to Mecca, the capital of Arabia at the time. In other words, the Dome of the Rock was set up as a rival to the Kaaba that was blessed by Muhammad. Whether it is true or not is hard to authenticate, as it is not written in historical documents.

Nevertheless, whatever caused this event, while the first Muslims who came to power were tolerant of Christianity and Judaism, allowing pilgrims of both religions to visit the Holy City and awarding Jews and Christians important positions in society and government, the *Encyclopedia Judaica*, among other sources, notes that an aberration in this behavior occurred during the latter part of the reign of al-Hakim (around 1012). The caliph began a campaign to humiliate and limit the rights of non-Muslims, culminating in the destruction of synagogues

—

and churches, including, according to Christian sources, the Church of the Holy Sepulchre. Eventually al-Hakim also prohibited Jews and Christians from visiting the Holy City on pilgrimage.

This prohibition famously set off the Crusades under Pope Urban II. Ironically, when al-Zahir succeeded al-Hakim in 1020, tolerance was restored to earlier levels, but the Crusading army was already on its way. According to Jewish sources, the economic environment was very favorable, especially for Jews, while Christians and Jews both filled government posts as high as regional governor and vizier.

The Crusades successfully—and bloodily—overpowered the Muslim regime, massacring Jewish and Muslim civilians by the hundreds. They converted the Dome of the Rock into a Christian shrine, renaming it the Temple of the Lord. Christian rule lasted in the area for only ninety years, but during that time both Jews and Muslims were barred from making pilgrimage to the sacred city.

Between the twelfth and nineteenth centuries, different religious groups controlled Jerusalem. For example, in 1187 Saladin (Salāh al-Dīn Yūsuf ibn Ayyūb) retook Jerusalem with little bloodshed, struck a treaty to let the Frankish civilians leave, and invited the Jews to return to the city. Later this Muslim leader had a change of heart and entered into a pact with Richard Lion heart, leader of the Third Crusade that left Jerusalem in the hands of the Muslims but allowed for Christian pilgrims to visit their holy places. The Jews again were placed at the fringes of this mixed Muslim-Christian society. In spite of this, Jews, who had been steadily shuffled back and forth since their first dispersion by the Romans, in fact never completely abandoned their hope of returning someday to the place they would be able again to call home. In the meantime, the Dome of the Rock remained a point of pilgrimage for Muslims only.

When, finally, in 1948, the modern state of Israel was founded, the Jews began to return to this land en masse as to their restored home. At the present, however, the Jews are not allowed to come to that previously sacred place of the Jews, the Jewish temple, as there the Muslim's Dome of the Rock sits instead, restricting Jewish prayers to the outer Wailing Wall.

It is, in my mind, an unfortunate fact that the Palestinian Arabs and Israelis could not find common ground in sharing the Palestinian land according to the British Mandate. After different sporadic

—

confrontations between the two peoples, the war of 1967 erupted. I will speak on this matter in more detail in the second part of this book.

History has repeated itself. First, the Jews claimed the role of originators of mankind's chronicle by appearing with their own god, who allegedly awarded them previously occupied lands and gave them permission to eliminate the occupants. Their prophet Moses, as it is accepted among the contemporary interpreters of the Bible, said to have the final message from God until Judgment Day. Next, the Christians claimed that Jesus Christ received the final message from God, until Judgment Day. And finally, the Muslims appeared with their prophet, insisting that only Muslims have embraced the full truth of Allah's most recent message, that this *really* was the last message this time.

Does the behavior of these different peoples trying to separate themselves from the rest of the world (and from each other) on religious grounds explain why God seemingly cannot make up his mind and decide which religious group must be given the priority? Or is that behavior, of seeking superiority over others, simply demonstrates a common human failing? Does God, as the Muslims suggest, want all of us to recognize that these three faiths are really one faith? Or is he concerned with people's intolerance of each other and inability to embrace a different religion, and therefore such must be the consequence of human insensitivity?

I'd like to turn now to the descriptions of how Allah communicated with Muhammad. As I mentioned earlier, Muhammad received revelations over a period of twenty-three years. Muhammad was forty when he received his first revelation while meditating in a cave on Mount Hira. The message from God came through the archangel Gabriel, who insisted that Muhammad should read the verses of the Qur'an. Muhammad (who was illiterate, by his own admission) protested that he could *not* read. Gabriel made the demand three times, and three times Muhammad protested that he could not read. Whether Muhammad suddenly and miraculously learned how to read or whether he had some education from one of his literate relations is unknown.

There is, of course, a third possibility—that all these claims were simply made-up thoughts of a man deeply impounded in his imaginary world. How much meditation differs from a mental image of something that is not real indeed?

As we learn from the Qur'an, Muhammad was offered to read. But read from what? On what were the *Suras* (chapters of the Qur'an) written? Arab traditions insist that the words of God were written on different materials, even pieces of cloth. Were these deliveries of messages well thought of by the Almighty? For what reason were the verses of the Qur'an given in gradual increments over twenty-three years? That's a lot of time to bother sending an angel. No wonder the messages had no consequential logic and were often repeated. Another question that arises with these visits of Gabriel is no less legitimate—how were the material substances delivered? Were they written in advance or God directed Gabriel to write them on an appropriate material and, thus, Gabriel had to memorize them to make sure they would be delivered in precise logic and meaning and not to be controversial in case they were recited before? Nobody but Muhammad encountered Gabriel, and the only person who received these revelations from God was Muhammad himself. Did he contact Gabriel as humans contact each other in our physical realm, or was it some kind of more subtle and unusual interrelation? Did Muhammad have to memorize all the messages from Gabriel in the exact delivered form, as Muslim clerics insist, and was the angel patiently waiting until Muhammad got it right? Then another question comes to mind—how quickly did Muhammad reveal each collected message? Was Muhammad able to deliver them without placing his own thoughts and words in the dictation he gave to his scribes, or did he actually bring with him those physically written verses?

My presumed sarcasm does not come from the desire to diminish and ridicule the procedure but merely from disbelief in such contact with a supernatural being.

After his first meeting with Gabriel, the new prophet was filled with great anxiety; he came home and asked his wife, Khadijah, whether he was in his right mind and not inventing things. Khadijah assured him that, knowing what she did of Muhammad's character, she did not believe Allah would allow him to be misled. It's arguable that such faith in her husband confirmed that he had experienced a meeting with something divine. And such good qualities as Muhammad possessed (gentleness, humility, etc.), while not normally praised in a man of that period, don't necessarily make that man a prophet. Of course, one may argue the point on how many people have repeated conversations with the angel Gabriel or with God?

Nevertheless, eventually, Muhammad accepted his role as the Prophet of Allah, and we are left to analyze whether those events are possible revelations from God or whether they are the strong imagination of one deeply resourceful and fancifully visionary man.

So what we learn from it is that this impetuous force that enveloped the mind of this simple man was so powerful that it never left this man for the rest of his life.

The self-proclaimed mission of the Prophet Muhammad was to restore worship of the one true God, as taught by the prophets Abraham, Moses, and Jesus.

Why did God designate yet another spokesman, another messenger of his laws? One possible answer would be that the previous messengers, due to the vagaries of human nature, were forgotten or needed to be updated as the world continued to change. But why it had to be a new faith? Were the Jews and the Christians not trustworthy any longer? Is that a routine approach of God to humans? Was Muhammad, along with the Arab people, to become that new reliable source of always fallible human qualities?

If so, can we assume, as Muslims do, that Muhammad is the last messenger?

If such is the case, what can one say about the more recent and newer messengers who announce themselves as, for instance, Bahá'u'lláh (prophet of the Bahá'í Faith) did a little more than 150 years ago?

I asked, at the beginning of this chapter, why history keeps repeating itself in that the teachings of each new prophet are met with outright hostility, especially from the leaders of the prophet's own tribe, in Muhammad's case, the Quraysh. Muhammad's grandfather was an influential leader of this tribe in Mecca. The Kaaba—the point of adoration—was under his care for many years. One of Muhammad's uncles, Abu Lahab, insisted that Muhammad had to stop preaching Islam as directed revelations from God; the other uncle, Abu Talib, tried to persuade Muhammad to abandon his message altogether.

Still Muhammad insisted that he had accepted his role as messenger of God. He continued preaching the new faith trying to persuade as many people as he could. Muhammad's zeal was reminiscent of the apostle Paul's as he spread his new faith among the pagans.

But while the resentment of Muhammad's opposition grew greater, he was still able to win a few believers to his cause. When

—

the persecution became unbearable for most Muslims (they were fewer than ninety at the time), the Prophet advised them, in the fifth year of his mission, to immigrate to Abyssinia (modern Ethiopia). Eighty people, not counting small children, went to that country. They only returned when they were promised safety, which was stipulated under the condition that neither Muhammad nor his followers would continue to spread the idea of Islam.

The Quraysh tribal leaders took this as a truce and lifted a ban they had implemented. The ban had lasted for three long years, severing all contacts between the general population and the Prophet's family.

So what can be summed up at this point from the point of view of any unbiased thinker? These followed below the first three conclusions are barely different than those mentioned in two preceded Islam religions:

- The God of Islam is the same one true God invoked before by the previous monotheistic religions.
- The revelation was heralded by the same Angel Gabriel as in the Torah and in the New Testament Gospel of Luke.
- The essential message is the same: an unquestioning reverence for and obedience to God.

The only obvious change that underlined the new religion of Islam was the new messenger, the Prophet Muhammad, who is chosen to restore the worship of the one God. This quiet, good-mannered, trustworthy, and most likely righteous man, for one reason or another, almost immediately fully accepted a role of a leader able to connect his people to God, who should be one and the only God.

The ascendance of Muhammad to the prophetic stage was also marked by the gradual reshaping of his character and behavior. At the beginning of establishing the Islamic faith, Muhammad struggled with the Quraysh tribe, with only few people on his side. This resulted in a truce and a hands-off attitude on the Muslim side. Muhammad reluctantly proclaimed, "To you be your Way, and to me mine" (Qur'an 109). But as soon as Muhammad was convinced that people began to accept his faith, he changed his tactics from quiet diplomacy to greater aggression, though, for him, it might have been a gradual transition from a doubtful and fearful man to a man of power, authority, and military might.

—

An interesting piece of history comes with Muhammad's exhorting the Jews and Christians to view Islam as the culmination of their own faith. Is this a peaceful offer or a callous insult? Jews and Christians alike were satisfied with their religions. Why would they even think of converting to this new faith? Muhammad specified that those who did not convert were still to be viewed as brothers of the Muslims, and he gave instructions that they were to be protected and aided when in need. But did this promise last?

True, when the Jews of Yathrib (Medina) first accepted Muhammad and signed a treaty of allegiance, they were given full citizenship, equal to that of Arab Muslims. However, according to Islamic scholar and Qur'an translator of Marmaduke Pickthall (himself a Christian convert to Islam), when they later decided to throw in their lot with the enemies of Islam (such as the powerful Quraysh tribe was) and tried to kill Muhammad and wipe out his followers, the Jewish tribes found themselves at war with the Muslims.

In this regard, another interesting narration comes from the historical document, such as, for instance, written by Scottish historian William Montgomery Watt, describing the Battle of Khaybar in 629 CE. After familiarizing oneself with the details of that battle, one can find the new features of a growing new leader and military warrior as Muhammad gradually became. At first, those who fell under the Muslim rule but did not accept Islam as their own religion were treated fairly as long as they paid the tribute and didn't rebel against the new regime. Dhimmi, as these non-Muslim communities were called, were allowed to practice their own religion and follow their accepted communal autonomy. Yet when the Jews rejected Muhammad as a prophet, mainly on the merit that he was non-Jew, and when local Jewish tribes took a side with the Quraysh tribe fighting Muhammad, as for instance they fought him at Badr, they were expelled from Medina.

Not diminishing previous descriptions of Muhammad as warm, loving, friendly, and considerate, I find that it would only be fair to describe Muhammad as a man of conviction, of moderate aggression, as well as displaying quality of fierce fighter who would not yield until becoming victorious.

First, he decided to go in to battle with his main enemy, the Quraysh tribe.

Starting from the year 624 CE till December of 630, Muslim fighters found themselves in a number of battles with Quraysh, at the end conquering their most important religious stronghold, the city of Mecca, along with house of prayer, Kaaba. On his visit to this sanctuary, Muhammad gave an order to destroy all the idols of gods the people of the Quraysh tribe were praying to. With that move, Muhammad boldly announced that "there should be no God but Allah."

After winning such an important fight, Muhammad was already ill yet began preparation for another even more expansive battle, the battle against the Roman Empire.

By this time, Muhammad realized that the more people come to his side, the more successful he'll be.

The politics of expansion, however, did not come to Islamic Muslims immediately and in full force. Not at least until the death of a prophet after which it grew swiftly. And with that, the tactics of the Muslim fighters began to change as well. Many historians, though, point at different and somewhat alien Muslim tactics practiced specifically among Christians. This new experience would strongly influence the treatment of the enemy whenever victorious are Muslims.

According to Shaykh Haeri, it was during the Crusades that the nature of Muslim warfare changed radically. With the Crusaders the Muslims were faced with an enemy that played by different rules. These Christians, the Muslims quickly learned, had no rules pertaining to such things as the treatment of prisoners of war and civilians. They would slaughter surrendering armies and massacre civilian populations without hesitation. This contributed to changing the nature of jihad and the way in which Islam was spread. Despite the Prophet's teaching that there was no compulsion in religion, some Muslim generals retaliated viciously against the enemy, spreading Islam by force when needed.

In conclusion, let me say this: Islam has found its place in the hearts of close to 1.7 billion people in different parts of the world. Does that mean that the rest of humanity should join this faith as well? Do people have the right to pursue their religious beliefs along different paths, or must they come together to pursue the same goal of finding a true and meaningful God, the one and only God for all?

I will speak more on that topic in this and the second part of this book.

CHAPTER 9

The Bahá'í Faith

I'd like to move now to the last prominent representative in the line of allegedly divine messengers that have appeared to humankind. I am referring to a prophet from Persia called *Bahá'u'lláh* (a title meaning "the Glory of God"). Born into the family of a prominent Persian dignitary as Mírzá Husayn-`Alí Núrí, he took the name Bahá'u'lláh in 1848 while presiding over the gathering of eighty-one members of the Báb'í Faith at the village of Badasht.

Husayn-`Alí Núrí not only took a new name himself, but he also gave new names to members of the gathering, notably the poetess of Qazvin, Zarin-Taj, whom he renamed *Tahirih* (Pure One) and Mullá Muhammad 'Alí-i-Bárfurúshi, to whom he gave the title *Quddus* (Most Holy).

The predecessor of Bahá'u'lláh—another Persian citizen and the founder of the Báb'í Faith—was born on October 20, 1819, in Shiraz as Siyyid Mirza 'Ali-Muhammad. In 1844, he took the name the *Báb* (Gate).

The Báb claimed to be the initiator of a new prophetic cycle, and the Promised One of Islam. He declared that his mission was to alert people to the imminent appearance of the Messenger of God ("Him Whom God Would Make Manifest") awaited by all the peoples of the world of whatever faith. This outrageous claim infuriated Muslim clergy, who, along with the Persian government, persecuted and eventually massacred the Báb and around twenty thousand of his

—

followers and imprisoned many more, including Bahá'u'lláh. The Báb himself was executed publicly by a firing squad on July 9, 1850, in a barracks square in Tabriz.

That didn't stop a new movement, though, and the Bahá'í Faith was born.

The ills of man, as we know them, were not magically solved by the previous messengers from God. Hence the coming of yet another prophet with a mission to save humanity was not surprising; people continued to expect a messiah who would bring to their gradually maturing societies new (or renewed) divine revelations.

In 1863, while in exile in Baghdad, Bahá'u'lláh, after proclaiming himself to be the one prophesied by the Báb, announced that his main mission was to unify the entire human race. The Bahá'í Faith, as distinct from the Báb'í Faith, dates from this time. Since then it has spread to more than 250 countries and, according to Christian sources, is the second most-widely-spread faith next to Christianity. There are roughly seven to eight million followers at present.

Bahá'u'lláh began his teaching with the proclamation that the succession of divine teachers, among whom were Moses, Zoroaster, Christ, and Muhammad, reflected a single historic plan of God educating humanity about its spiritual reality. His teachings, beginning with the independent investigation of reality, were all aimed at unity. At the core was the teaching that there was one God, one faith, and one human family.

Bahá'u'lláh, who received his summons from the Báb in a letter delivered by the Báb's first disciple, Mullah Husayn, made an attempt in the summer of 1848 to visit the Báb in Azerbaijan, where he was imprisoned. The two, however, never met face to face, though they did correspond with each other until the execution of the Báb in 1850. In fact, the Báb's last earthly task was to send his pens, pen case, and seal to Bahá'u'lláh along with a document bearing a calligraphy of the name Bahá in the shape of a five-pointed star.

Soon after this, Bahá'u'lláh was imprisoned for four months in the Siyah-Chal, also known as the Black Pit of Tehran. This imprisonment began a forty-year period of exile that ended in the prison of the city of Akká across the bay from Haifa, Israel.

Bahá'u'lláh's leadership of the Báb'í community was not unchallenged. The Báb had verbally placed Bahá'u'lláh's half

–

brother, Mirza Yahya, in charge until such time as the next Messenger revealed himself. Yahya made a number of attempts to get rid of his half brother even after April 1863, when Bahá'u'lláh told his close companions that he was the one the Báb had foretold.

It is curious that this announcement meant different things to different people. Allegedly, to the Shi'a Muslims, the Báb had been the return of the Twelfth Imam who it was said had disappeared centuries earlier. Meanwhile Bahá'u'lláh was associated with the martyred Imam Husayn who was killed by Umayyad forces at Karbala. To Sunnis, the prophecies were somewhat different. The Báb was Elijah, and Bahá'u'lláh was the return of Christ, whom Muhammad referred to as *Ruh'u'lláh* (Spirit of God).

Persia (Iran and Iraq) had once enjoyed magnificent glory, high achievements, and prosperity. But in Bahá'u'lláh's time it had descended into a deep decline of corruption and fanaticism. What made someone appear at this particular time as the divinely inspired "He Whom God Shall Make Manifest" and declare himself as the "Manifestation of God" for the age?

It is true that those among us who have innate talent are given chances to succeed. But few of us have the endurance to pursue a goal no matter what life throws at us. We cannot simply achieve it by acquiring education, which was something Bahá'u'lláh did not have. Yet even without a formal education, Bahá'u'lláh's combined inspiration, endurance, and beliefs placed him in the rare ranks of those people we call leaders.

He possessed an unusually elevated sense of right and wrong. Given the ills of the country in which he lived, including the mistreatment of women, the lack of aspiration by people with any level of education, religious and political corruption, the torture of those who displeased officials, and an atmosphere that generally treated liberal ideas as satanic—it was no wonder that a man with the wits to point out the road to recovery would be seen either as an idealistic fool, a mystic genius, a subversive rebel, or a madman.

Because of his ideas on how to improve society and his seemingly bizarre concern about arms control and international relations, it was quite understandable that such a person was accepted by some as being divinely inspired—another Prophet of God—and by others as a dangerous agitator who must be constrained.

—

Following the many teachings of Bahá'u'lláh, one can trace two major tenets throughout the numerous volumes of his work; one is the unconditional love of God, and the other is the unity of mankind. The rest of Bahá'u'lláh's principles and laws, such as the equality of women and men, the abolition of racism, the pursuit of world peace, and the universal need for education, are all related to the first two. There are social laws as well, of course, for Bahá'u'lláh was not blind to the diversity of humankind. There are laws and exhortations covering marriage and family life, individuals' personal conduct, and implementing the laws of society.

Let us try to dissect the major tenets of his teachings, starting with the nature of God. All religious doctrines insist that God is beyond our comprehension. Yet right from the start we are provided conflicting messages—at least, in my opinion. If God is beyond our comprehension, then I see no need to try to figure him out. Yet Bahá'u'lláh insists that God created all humanity "to know Him and to love Him":

> *Having created the world and all that liveth and moveth therein, He, through the direct operation of His unconstrained and sovereign Will, chose to confer upon man the unique distinction and capacity to know Him and to love Him—a capacity that must needs be regarded as the generating impulse and the primary purpose underlying the whole of creation . . . . Upon the inmost reality of each and every created thing He hath shed the light of one of His names, and made it a recipient of the glory of one of His attributes. Upon the reality of man, however, He hath focused the radiance of all of His names and attributes, and made it a mirror of His own Self. Alone of all created things man hath been singled out for so great a favor, so enduring a bounty. (Gleanings from the Writings of Baha'u'llah XXVII)*

But how is man to know God? The Bible tells us, "The heavens declare the glory of God; And the firmament shows His handiwork" (Psalms 19:1 NKJV). Muhammad says the same thing: "He is God, the Creator, the Evolver, the Bestower of Forms (or Colors). To Him

—

belong the Most Beautiful Names: whatever is in the heavens and on Earth, doth declare His Praises and Glory: and He is the Exalted in Might, the Wise" (Qur'an, Sura 59:22-24). Bahá'u'lláh agrees:

> *Whatever is in the heavens and whatever is on the Earth is a direct evidence of the revelation within it of the attributes and names of God, inasmuch as within every atom are enshrined the signs that bear eloquent testimony to the revelation of that Most Great Light . . . . To a supreme degree is this true of man, who, among all created things, hath been invested with the robe of such gifts, and hath been singled out for the glory of such distinction. For in him are potentially revealed all the attributes and names of God to a degree that no other created being hath excelled or surpassed . . . . Even as He hath revealed: "We will surely show them Our signs in the world and within themselves." . . . In this connection, He Who is the eternal King—may the souls of all that dwell within the mystic Tabernacle be a sacrifice unto Him—hath spoken: "He hath known God who hath known himself." (Gleanings from the Writings of Baha'u'llah, XC)*

But how does even looking within our human selves tell us everything about God? Indeed, is the knowledge of God the only knowledge we need?

This raises another Bahá'í tenet: the independent investigation of truth and reality. This in turn would suggest something of the Bahá'í attitude toward science. In fact, the Bahá'í scriptures tell us that science and religion are the two wings of one bird. The bird cannot achieve flight without both. They further tell us that religion and science must be in harmony with each other.

> *Between scientists and the followers of religion there has always been controversy and strife for the reason that the latter have proclaimed religion superior in authority to science and considered scientific announcement opposed to the teachings of religion. Bahá'u'lláh declared that religion is in complete harmony with science and reason. If religious*

—

> *belief and doctrine is at variance with reason, it proceeds*
> *from the limited mind of man and not from God; therefore,*
> *it is unworthy of belief and not deserving of attention;*
> *the heart finds no rest in it, and real faith is impossible.*
> *How can man believe that which he knows to be opposed*
> *to reason? . . . Reason is the first faculty of man, and the*
> *religion of God is in harmony with it.* (Abdu'l-Bahá, 231)

So is the message of Bahá'u'lláh that if we want to succeed as human beings we must study religion scientifically and gain as much knowledge as possible?

To accept the necessity of knowledge as a prerequisite in Bahá'u'lláh's teaching, let us now consider the second tenet of this prophet; that is, our need for unity: "So powerful is the light of unity that it can illuminate the whole world," wrote Bahá'u'lláh (*Gleanings from the Writings of Bahá'u'lláh*, CXXXII) in expressing a core principal of his faith. He pleaded for the oneness of humankind, one human race, unity of spiritual and social development, and one religion. Rather than leaving the organization of his own religion entirely to posterity, he established an administrative order with bodies called Houses of Justice at local, national, and global levels. The political life of the planet, he wrote, must also be organized, growing out of "an all-embracing assemblage of men" that the world's leaders must attend and consider the needs of the world they had inherited.

Let us analyze these recommendations of unity starting from the administration of the Bahá'í Faith. The idea of a divine pattern for its continuous administration was expressed in a tangible covenant between Bahá'u'lláh and his followers that was intended to safeguard the unity of his Faith. The covenant, along with interpretive authority and responsibility for the care of the believers, was assigned via his will and testament to his oldest son, Abdu'l-Bahá. Abdu'l-Bahá laid the foundations of the first national Houses of Justice (currently referred to as Spiritual Assemblies) and designated his grandson, Shoghi Effendi, as Guardian of the Bahá'í Faith in his written testament. Shoghi Effendi, along with a group of Bahá'ís called the Hands of the Cause of God, began working toward the foundation of the first Universal House of Justice, which was elected in 1963 on the 100th anniversary of Bahá'u'lláh's proclamation of his mission.

–

Surprisingly, few of the followers, with the exception of some family members and their allies and one of the Hands, resisted such unprecedented developments in the religion. These moves to ensure the covenant were obviously critical to a faith that hoped to unite the entire world.

As to other Bahá'í suggestions for international unity, it is my opinion that, although the ideas are beautiful, none of them can be accomplished. That reasoning will be explained in later chapters.

But let me turn to the idea of what Bahá'ís refer to as the "progressive revelation" of religion as expressed in these words of Abdu'l-Bahá:

> Religion . . . must be living, vitalized, moving and progressive. If it be . . . non-progressive . . . it is dead. The divine institutes are evolutionary; therefore the revelation of them must be progressive and continuous . . . . Sciences of former ages and philosophies of the past are useless today . . . . Ancient laws and archaic ethical systems will not meet the requirements of modern conditions . . . . In view of this, shall blind imitations of ancestral forms and theological interpretations continue to guide . . . the spiritual development of humanity today? Shall man, gifted with the power of reason, unthinkingly adhere to dogma . . . which will not bear the analysis of reason . . . ? (Foundations of World Unity, 83)

According to Bahá'í theology, all the Messengers who came to earth arrived with one goal in mind: to rediscover and firmly establish the one truth that would educate and draw human souls together. But if we set that contention aside and view the various religions as being in competition rather than in cooperation with each other, I must ask: If God wished us to know him and appreciate this need for unity, why would then he hide it from the majority of humanity? Wouldn't that inclination and one of the main attributes of a man—the need to compete—shake the most important part of foundation for survival of humankind? If a man to become indifferent to success, shouldn't such attitude make him not only dull but stagnate a progress and therefore destroy civilization per se?

—

As we already considered it previously somewhere in this book, wouldn't our natural inadequacies as humans lead to a massive amount of bodies and/or souls that God for some reason would wish to accumulate? Then why in the world would God want to collect us either as resurrected bodies or as freed souls? Why would he want to gather so many malignancies, iniquities, ills, depravities, and other similar vices to him? And here I'm not even speaking of possibly sentient beings elsewhere in the universe.

It is no secret that much of humankind is ignorant, self-indulgent, hostile, jealous, and filled with animosity. Many of us find bringing harm to our fellow human beings to be enjoyable. These tendencies exist in people of every culture. The proclamations of the Messengers, such as disavowing the pursuit of unnecessary wealth and caring for less fortunate people, contradict the laws of nature.

I will discuss this tenet in more detail later in the book. But here I wish to conclude that competition is a main driver of humans, animals, and other developing creatures; by competing we survive, improve, and progress. This process has been termed *evolution*.

The Prophets or Messiahs—including Manu, Zoroaster, Moses, Jesus, Buddha, Muhammad, and Bahá'u'lláh—I believe were foolishly good in nature, unable to see us as we really are, what we were programmed to be by nature. They didn't see that we have no choice but are forced to fight to survive. Their desire to improve the world made them both noble and naïve.

If God needed or wanted us all to be perfect, he would not create the blind and sick, the less fortunate, and the poor. He would not produce predators and prey, and he would not make us struggle between the desire to be good and the desire for survival.

In light of such descriptions of our misery, I must also conclude that when these so-called messengers show up from time to time among us, each claiming that he has the solution for how to change the world, we might believe them but only to a point. This point is where one must separate the desire to do good from the desire to believe the prophet's claims.

Yes, the messengers influence our emotions, and they do draw like-minded people to them and even cause transformation of a sort. Yet I believe these men come, not because God sends them, but because they possess brilliant intellectual minds. They are on the frontiers of the societies in which they are living and find that to keep quiet is no longer possible, that the ills of society must be corrected, else we will rush into chaos that will destroy humanity.

Why do they claim they are the messengers of God? The question is relevant but, as yet, unanswerable.

My last word in this long, frustrated polemic is that regardless of my desire to find out who or what God is, I am no closer to solving that puzzle than we were two thousand, five thousand, or ten thousand years ago. Not only can I not say what or who God is, I don't know if anyone can. Having two or three or many schools of thought with as many theories does not change anything: We still don't know! We most likely never will know. And that might be a condition that God— if he exists—created long before we appeared on earth, as sentient, problem-solving creatures.

PART THREE

STEPS OF EVOLUTION

CHAPTER 10

Reconsidering the Theory of Evolution

There is a continuous dispute between literal biblical creationists, who rely on the book of Genesis to explain how the world has been made, and evolutionists, who attempt to prove that we all evolved from one common ancestor due to heritable variations in organisms controlled by natural selection. Do you wish to know who is right? To put it bluntly, neither group has precise answers. I don't claim to possess them either, but my intent here is to explore some explanations presented in this field with a little analysis of several of the most invigorating facts.

I will try to reasonably detail the main tools the contemporary evolutionists are relying on—DNA as a proof that we all came from one common ancestor. I will also attempt to trace the so-called transitional forms that, according to natural selection, appear on the genealogical tree, and by these facts alone, I'll try, once again, to see if this is the one and only proper conclusion that may be drawn.

To make it sound even more dramatic, I decided, once again as I've done it previously, to discuss to some extent the signs of possible manifestation of God in the universe. It is obviously pertinent to this matter that is called evolution. Most scientists believe that the creation of the universe by an intelligent designer and the theory of evolution are incompatible. But there is a growing number today of those

–

who accept both theories. Moreover, there is a growing number of Christian scientists who happily accommodate symbiotic survival of both bodies. I wish to discuss this topic further, as this subject matter is one of the most perplexing in our human experience. I don't mean to take sides. It's been my overall intent to present the arguments aimed at sorting facts from fiction. And though my writing so far might be interpreted as being subtly biased toward creationists, I can assure you that it is not simply so. What I am specifically concerned with is how our friendly Christian creationists handled the possible role of a creator to a particular individual. Not much deviated from such way of thinking is Hinduism, with its insistence of God incarnated in certain humans. As for Judaism and Islam, while those two religions are somewhat more reasonable in the sense that they don't need to designate any human who possesses godlike features, nevertheless, endow their gods with humanlike attributes. To that extent, my understanding of God, if he exists, differs from any religious group recognized today, and I will speak to it at the later part of this book.

With a statement as this, let me begin with a remark regarding the paradox that has reappeared with a new vigor since Darwin's 1859 work on evolution. It has proven one characteristic feature of man: his belief that he can become an invincible and omnipotent creature himself, able to control almost everything. In other words, as man reaches new levels of knowledge, he simultaneously acquires a powerful awareness that he can achieve anything he imagines; to recall a familiar slogan—the sky is the limit. This awareness persuades him that he may control most events in the world without asking who or what provided the material he manipulates or who gave him the capacity to figure out how to manipulate it. True, most of it is lately skewed toward the natural selection, inheritance, mutation, and genetic drift, though not necessarily in this order. But what is characteristic of a man is his growing awareness in infallibility. Scientists claim that there is nothing eternal in their world, and through the experiments they are conducting, they are willing to discard, not withstanding, time conclusions. This is a true statement, but it concerns not exactly all their achievements. Natural selection is that untouchable edifice that is beyond the reach of any careless intruder, with an army of watchdogs inevitably jumping to the rescue each time someone is trying to make a noise.

—

I am not arguing the point that most facts presented in today's literature create an illusion of indisputable proofs. But with a careful eye, one may trace that the reason of accepting those arguments as facts are mostly based on a desire to prove the point and adjust them to accepted rule than to a logic and the obvious certainty in details.

Let's now try to dissect this statement.

Evolution is a process that seems uncomplicated on the surface yet is convoluted and subtle in reality. It requires the existence and operation of a myriad entities, agencies, and forces held in balance.

Today evolutionists have established themselves as a strong, persuasive, and self-affirmed group who should not (they believe) be questioned about their work, especially on the level when such inquiries might produce a negative attitude toward them. This is not surprising, for evolutionists are equipped with more than a few convincing arguments, theories, and facts. They have held their theories up for review by peers in science journals. They continuously brag about clinging to the many repeated and confirmed experiments. Hence, an attempt to take them on might be both dangerous and foolish. And yet after acquainting myself with a number of contemporary proofs presented by notable personalities in the field, I've decided it's worthwhile to speak my mind anyway.

Let me start with a discussion and analysis of a book titled *Evolution: The Triumph of an Idea*, written by Carl Zimmer. Zimmer is a writer, an essayist, and a contributing editor to such respectable journals as *Science*, *Discover*, and *National Geographic*. Paleontologist Stephen Jay Gould, in his introductory article to that work, said this:

> In discussing the truth of evolution, we should make a distinction, as Darwin explicitly did, between the simple fact of evolution—defined as the genealogical connection among all Earthly organisms, based on their descent from a common ancestor, and the history of any lineage as a process of descent with modification—and theories (like Darwinian natural selection) that have been proposed to explain the causes of evolutionary change. (*Evolution*, 2)

The "simple fact" to which Gould is referring might not be at all simple, since in order to conclude that we all came from one common

–

187

ancestor, it must be experimentally proven, as the scientific method suggests. In my opinion, none of the evidence presented so far in the scientific world, such as the anatomical structure of different animals, the molecular similarity or morphology of different organisms, or even the documenting of so-called transitional forms, have unequivocally proven that the modifications that have taken place point to the fact that all organisms descended from one common ancestor.

First of all, let's see if there is a difference between suggesting that all life shares genetic commonality and suggesting this implies that all organisms (whether extinct or extant) must be connected. Sharing common genetic information is not the same as a continuous lineage of multiple transformations connecting all organisms in one chain (or evolutionary tree) to a common ancestor. Certainly all life might have made use of the same available building blocks, but that does not necessarily mean that all organisms must have been transformed sequentially from one species to another before reaching their current state. This is not proven fact, and it is possible that many original (common) ancestors with subtle differences gave rise to the different species.

Before I speak about this in more detail, let me say a few words about the origin of life. The origin of life is an enigma for many reasons. For one, scientists cannot agree whether they should be discussing a single origin event or many origins.

If we use a top-to-bottom approach in an attempt to decipher our origins, we will end up with one maternal ancestor common to all humans—let's call her "Eve." Yet before her there existed many bacteria and archaea and so on, all the way down to the first subatomic particles responsible for the beginning of the world.

At that level, we can only say one thing for sure: Our knowledge is interrupted right there, since we are not able to know from where those particles came. We also do not know why these entities took their particular shapes and forms. What produced the conditions for these entities that they might have replicated, though with modifications, making them relatively stable? In other words, we are in complete darkness as to how DNA and RNA began to function. It is for that reason we puzzle over which came first: the chicken or the egg.

The story of the origin of life, scientifically speaking, begins with the prebiotic synthesis of amino acids arising out of the so-called

—

primordial soup. Amino acids are the building blocks of proteins, the basic ingredients of all biological compounds found today. To say it more comprehensively, proteins are molecules resulting from at least two amino acids connected via a bond called the peptide bond. They are always made out of common atoms: carbon, hydrogen, oxygen, and nitrogen, and, often, sulfur.

What made these atoms so sophisticated? What gave them the powerful ability to produce genes? What made them "alive"?

The famous experiment conducted for the first time in 1953 by Stanley Miller and Harold Urey showed the possible chemical origins of life. By producing amino acids from hydrogen, methane, ammonia, and water, after sending electric sparks into that mixture, Miller and Urey proved that organic synthesis could have occurred on the primitive earth. They did it by simulating conditions in their lab that in their minds existed at the time on earth.

A few centuries ago, when scientists had doubts about how maggots appeared in raw meat, a theory of spontaneous generation was in vogue for some time. Though this theory has long been discarded, as recently as in the beginning of twentieth century, the Russian scientist Aleksandr Ivanovich Oparin proposed that the spontaneous generation of life did indeed occur in a primeval soup when the primordial earth had a negligible amount of oxygen in its atmosphere. His theory was that life possibly originated from nonliving matter through chemical reactions activated by different forms of energy. Today scientists, while denying the ability of organisms to appear spontaneously, are conducting experiments in which they try to demonstrate the spontaneous formation of organic molecules from inorganic molecules.

These kinds of experiments looked simple and fairly straightforward on the surface. But to make such simple experiments, one had to not only known what to do with those molecules but to acquire them from somewhere. It's a good thing they all were around. But rather than trying to qualify such experiments, let's move into a better-researched field of science—the evolution of life.

Let's start with the anatomy of mammals. With some degree of deviation, all mammals have similar bone structure and physiological systems. Morphologically, all mammals have similar cell structures. All mammals rely on carbohydrates, proteins, and fats and we all

—

contain very closely related DNA. Still, one cannot say with certainty whether it developed from only one or a few identical chemical sources that in time were transformed into DNA, if that process has indeed taken place. This particular point cannot yet be proved or disproved.

Coming back to his introduction in Zimmer's book *Evolution: The Triumph of an Idea*, Gould refers to the three categories of evidence of true evolution, or, as he puts it, "the factuality of evolution." First he cites that direct evidence of evolution has accumulated through "the small-scale changes" observed by humans.

"The second category," writes Gould, comes from the "direct evidence from transitional stages of major alterations found in the fossil record." Gould continues:

> *Although the fossil record is indeed spotty (a problem with nearly all historical documents, after all), the assiduous work of paleontologists has revealed numerous elegant examples of sequences of intermediary forms joining ancestors in proper temporal order to very different descendants—as in the evolution of whales from terrestrial mammalian ancestors through several intermediate stages, including Ambulocetus (literally the walking whale). (Evolution, xxxi)*

Then he speaks of a third category of evidence:

> *All organisms carry useless remnants of formerly functional structures that make no sense except as holdovers from different ancestral states—the tiny vestiges of leg bones, invisibly embedded in the skin of certain whales, or the non-functional nubs of pelvic bones in some snakes, surviving as vestiges of ancestors with legs. (ibid., xxxi)*

I see no difference between Gould's explanation of intermediary (transitional) forms and his description of useless vestigial organs. He is vague in distinguishing between these second and third categories of evidence, which underscores how flexible the human mind is to be able to see identical things or events so differently. It might be said that we humans try to prove the only truth seen through our individual minds and that each of us does this in our own peculiar way. And it might be added that this is how an evolution of one's vision of truth transforms into an indisputable fact of many.

When Gould supposes that alleged transitional forms between hoofed animals and whales point to evolution from one common ancestor, his supposition does not automatically make it a fact, does it? One needs to have proof that such alleged connection exists. As I see it, the tiny vestiges of pelvic bones in the baleen whales Gould is referring to could simply be a genealogical mutation or the result of an adaptation of a particular species to the demands of the environment without resorting to a common ancestor. Take for instance people who have six fingers on their extremities instead of the standard five. Being born with six fingers does not necessarily point to an intermediate form of human being but rather to a possible mutation resulting in a physical discrepancy.

We must use not only human knowledge, logic, and abstract reasoning to make sense of such mysteries as vestigial legs in whales. We must possess and present indisputable facts, must we not? Not having those, we are left with no choice but to be persuasive and authoritative. As I said previously, reality may be objective, but human beings are not. The moment that human reason enters the arena of inquiry, objectivity leaves.

We draw certainty though from the positive feedback of people who see things as we do and who support our worldview. That is how we chose the groups of people we want to affiliate with, as the old adage "Birds of a feather flock together" alludes to. We gravitate to people who we think we belong to: scientists, biologists, physicists, believers, nonbelievers, musicians, people who speak the same language, share the same culture, etc.

We settle into such a group, making ourselves comfortable among like-minded people and fighting for the survival of that group and for our own survival within it. This behavior provides us with a complicated network of human relations in which we continue to make even more gradations, assumptions, and separations. A feature of this network is language, terminology that creates meaning—and division.

As the consequence, we end up with a society made up of a conglomeration of such groups in which almost nothing can be seen clearly and objectively.

When people say they are seeking the truth, what they are often saying without realizing it is that they are seeking a body of like-minded people who will affirm their truth. I feel that the truth the way I see it is the real truth, or at least I hope it is. Would that mean I am looking for my constituency? You bet I am. My human nature seeks a body of supporters who will tell me "You are not alone" and "You're definitely right."

Such philosophical justification aside, let's return to a conversation about evolution. There are at least two approaches to making a scientific argument on a topic: one is providing a possible proof (for example, finding an appropriate fossil) and another is providing a rebuttal of that proof (for example, arguing what else that fossil might be).

With this in mind, I wish to discuss a proof posited not long ago (sometime between 2000 and 2004 CE) by paleontologist Dr. Philip D. Gingerich in the petrified remains of an ancient whale. Within the female whale abdomen, Dr. Gingerich claimed, were the fossilized remains of a fetal whale. The fetus had teeth and some bones. Before I proceed to discuss this claim, I'd like to make a short digression into the known evolution of whales.

Whales (along with dolphins and porpoises) belong to a family of mammalian life known as cetaceans. Until the twenty-first century, most paleontologists believed that the whales descended from mesonychids, which were carnivorous hoofed animals, akin to horses, cattle, deer, and so on. The transition from land animals to marine animals took less than eight million years. Mesonychids, now extinct, were a sister group of artiodactyla, a representative of which is the hippopotamus.

Recent data suggests that whales and hippopotamuses are related through a straight genealogical lineage. However, hippopotamuses appear in the fossil record millions of years *later* than pakicetidae—the ancestors of modern whales.

The pakicetidae are ungulates that have been classed with the order artiodactyla, or hoofed mammals, as mentioned before. These artiodactyla lived fifty-three million years ago. Based on the skeletal structure of fossils, they looked like dogs with hoofed feet and a long, thick tail.

As a few evolutionary scientists studying whales tell us, the feature connecting these hoofed dogs to whales was their ears. This

—

specific kind of ear was found in another group of ancient small, deer like creatures that lived forty-eight million years ago in Kashmir, according to Hans Thewissen, paleontologist and professor at Ohio University. He called this raccoon-sized creature Indohyus. These creatures were land-based herbivores, not sea creatures.

Nothing complicated so far, right?

In 1883, Victorian-era scientist William Flower suggested that legless leviathans had evolved from mammals known as ungulates, a group whose one characteristic included hoofed feet. More than a century later, Richard Monastersky wrote in *Science News* an article entitled "The Whale's Tale" that appeared on November 6, 1999. In it he wrote, "It no longer stirs even a whiff of controversy. Dozens of scientific studies over the past three decades have convinced biologists that cetaceans are the progeny of hoofed animals."

So what is this clear-cut proof (or at least evidence) connecting present sea mammals to hoofed land ungulates? Given all of the different forms that any fetus takes on its way to being a viable life, why would that fossil fetus found by the Gingerich team be taken as absolute proof of a transitional form between the early whales that gave birth on land and the land animals represented by a number of different mammalian families?

It is said that a brook can only flow in one direction and not in the opposite one. This has been held to include the evolutionary stream, so no one expressed doubts that this Pakistani fossil belonged to a pregnant female land mammal. However, my question is how was **this** fossil determined to represent a transitional form between hoofed land animals and ancient whales?

Even though the concept of a transitional form is manmade and, indeed, we are all transitional organisms in a constant state of change, it does not automatically follow that we all came from one common ancestor. True, the fossils might have deviated from the original forms of their root species, but that does not mean they are necessarily interconnected with the rest of the species.

What sort of life a fossil actually represents must be factually proven, and, without reference to a deep special knowledge, it seems to me some scientists are merely tossing facts in the air and attempting to adjust them to the requirements of a formula as they fall. So when an evolutionist says something in the order of "How do you convince a creationist that creatures had transitional forms? Hah. It can't be done. There is no convincing someone who has his mind made up already," then this argument goes both ways.

So are there any more convincing arguments, when so few have been presented until now?

The late Dr. Duane Gish, who, until his demise on March 2013, had been a senior vice president emeritus of the Institute for Creation Research was quoted in the "Talk Origins Archive" in January of 2010:

> *There are no transitional forms in the fossil record between the marine mammals and their supposed land mammal ancestors . . . It is quite entertaining, starting with cows, pigs, or buffaloes, to attempt to visualize what the intermediaries may have looked like. Starting with a cow, one could even imagine one line of descent, which prematurely became extinct, due to what might be called an "udder failure." (78-79)*

Mocking one's opponents is in no way evidence against their point of view. Neither is the fact that one cannot imagine the form itself. What is more critical is if, given what we know about how nature works, one can really imagine the *process*.

Michael White, who writes for *Adaptive Complexity* and who is a biochemist working in the Department of Genetics at Washington University School of Medicine, wrote this in a column entitled "The Ambitious Ancestors of Whales" in the February 2009 issue:

> *In what is now central Pakistan, an eight-and-a-half foot long, pregnant aquatic mammal went belly-up, and sank to the bottom of shallow coastal waters. Forty-seven million years later, a huckster by the name of Duane Gish denied that such mammal ever existed . . . . Gish may have found it entertaining to imagine what a half-whale, half-buffalo looked like, but today's scientists don't have to imagine the appearance of land-based ancestors of whales. The fossil series leading up to whales tells a very detailed and remarkable story of how furry, four-legged land mammals eventually gave rise*

—

to behemoth marine descendants. A spectacular fossil find, reported yesterday in PLoS One, reveals some amazing details from the evolutionary history of whales.

Mocking is still not an evidence of truth, but after reading this claim, I was naturally curious about the source to which this gentleman was referring. PLOS One turned out to be an interactive open-access journal of peer-reviewed scientific and medical research. A thoroughly detailed article in it eloquently pointed to the find predating the known ancestors of whales. It looked very academic and quite substantial. So I read it slowly, referring to plenty of other sources when needed to get to the core of it. When I finished reading, this was the conclusion I came to: conjecture had played a substantial part in interpreting the scientists' observations and summations.

Back to Dr. Gish. Gish did not deny the existence of marine mammals—just that this marine mammal was a transitional form for another. Second, there are no contemporary records that offer evidence that the fossils found belonged to transitional forms between the ancient land animals and the whales. It all was an assumption, a possibility, and so forth.

I should note that there are more conflicting opinions about this find. Jonathan Geisler, a paleontologist at Georgia Southern University in Statesboro, warns that it is too early in the game to be assigning absolute attributes or circumstances to the fossil find. To the fact that the fetus in this case seemed to be in a breach position (suggesting marine birth), Geisler noted that many land mammals also give birth in the breach position occasionally, including hippos, which can give birth both on land and in water.

This reminded me of how Charles Darwin looked at his finches from the Galapagos Island. He found many closely related species that looked different at first glance but were similar in most of the features that only an imaginative, sophisticated mind could attempt to connect. That, however, does not necessarily mean that these species relate to each other genealogically in a straight ancestral line. To claim as fact that all species are connected to one common ancestor, one would need to possess a proof that would withstand scrutiny no matter from which angle one approaches it. Do scientists today possess such proof?

—

We could try to trace this process by considering the role of DNA, which is the main engine of almost all organisms present on earth. It is responsible for heredity and evolutionary changes. And yet we are unable to explain how it appeared in organic life. Proteins are needed to package DNA and to control its function, but DNA should have existed before amino acids were given the command to make proteins. What gave that command?

Scientists have supposed that RNA might have been a precursor of DNA. Yet even if RNA is simpler than DNA and presumed to have emerged first, it is still too complicated to have just appeared for the purpose of participating in a previously nonexistent process. Again we have a catch-22: Who or what conveniently provided all those elements, producing a chain of reactions that eventually led to genetically complicated DNA? From where did the impetus for creating something of that magnitude come?

It is true that only a few elements are needed in order to produce proteins. But with a little change in configuration and order these elements are placed, many more proteins come to life. What force has produced such variety? What kind of spark came to life to build so different and yet able products?

With questions like these, let me attempt to clarify a few definitions used by paleontologists, anthropologists, biologists, and geneticists. There exists a generally accepted terminology with corresponding meanings for the following words: *variety*, *sub variety*, *species*, and *subspecies*. The history of how the scientific world arrived at and agreed on these terms is quite long, so I'm not going to go into it. Suffice it to say that it was done over time through the work of many parties. The interested reader can start by going through the works of such thinkers and naturalists of the eighteenth century as Benoît de Maillet, Georges Buffon, and Pierre-Simon Laplace. That will help one conceptualize an evolution not only of life on earth, but also in the cosmos.

Yet all these works, including Georges Cuvier's anatomical reconstruction of extinct animals and his theory of catastrophism, involved transformation: inert matter that somehow came to life. The established terminology of three kingdoms that contain all living organisms (animals, plants, and fungi) places these life-forms in separate groups based on observed behavior, morphology, physiology,

–

anatomy, and genetic distance as well as some experiments. From that placement, the terminology led to the development of an evolutionary tree.

The father of contemporary evolutionary theory and author of *On the Origin of Species*, Charles Darwin, was born on February 12, 1809. He was a naturalist from Shrewsbury, Shropshire, England. His grandfather, Erasmus Darwin, accepted that evolution had taken place in living things, including humans, but he couldn't comprehend the exact cause of it. And yet his grandson did.

Charles Robert Darwin was a pioneer in establishing natural selection as a major vehicle of evolution, producing new species that struggled for life. Still, before he came to such a conclusion, he first had to undergo a transformation from being a devout believer in a literal interpretation of Genesis to a revolutionary thinker acknowledging concepts of gradual uniformitarianism and refuting the fixity of species.

As Ernst Walter Mayr, one of the twentieth century's leading evolutionary biologists, mentioned in his introduction to a facsimile of the first edition of *On the Origin of Species*:

> *Though Darwin was wrong in his discussions of inheritance and the origin of variation, confused about varieties and species; he was successful in discovering the basic mechanism of evolutionary change.* (Introduction, page viii)

NATURAL SELECTION

Natural selection, as Darwin named it, is the key mechanism of evolution. In Darwin's time, people did not have today's scientific knowledge of the genetic ability of an organism to inherit traits from its progenitor. The evolutionary theory of *soft inheritance*, offered by French biologist Jean-Baptiste Lamarck, pointed at the passing on of acquired features of an organism to its offspring during its lifetime. This theory was only partially supported by Darwin as possible reaction of an organism to environmental stimuli. Darwin used the term *pangenesis*, to which he ascribed an ability of somatic cells to collect information of the parent cell that would eventually be passed on to the next generation. Yet these variations among any individual species could not be explained by the observable changes (the phenotype) alone. Another mechanism had to be applied as well. Thus, natural selection came to life and was appropriately determined to be the main instrument that later—along with mutation, sexual reproduction, genetic drift, and genetic flow—allowed complex adaptation to occur in life-forms.

Though I accept this mechanism of the evolutionary process unequivocally, I see the definitions applied to ensued different organisms, such as species and their varieties, slightly different. I am in basic agreement with an explanation of evolution that provides a hierarchy of biological classifications, but I respectfully wish to emphasize that species and varieties can only relate to each other up to a point. What I mean by that is that each species is represented by varieties produced by changing environmental and genetic forces. These varieties, I firmly believe, cannot produce completely new species the way contemporary terminology suggests.

Under the peculiar conditions of nature, organisms change their habits as well as morphological and physiological appearances and functions in order to survive. It is these environmental pressures and the genetic discrepancies that mutations produce from time to time that eventually lead to new varieties. These genetic differences accumulate to the point where it is impossible to recognize that the new organisms might have a common ancestor in that lineage. Thus they are given—and, in my mind, quite erroneously—a new species designation, when in fact they are only a new variation of the same species or subspecies at best.

Such definitional discrepancies could be traced back through the genealogy of any individual human being. If one tries to detect commonalities with ancestors who lived fifteen thousand to twenty thousand years ago, one will most likely find very little if any mutual phylogenetic characteristics with that ancestor due to accumulated mutations and adjustments to the environment. Yet that does not mean that we and our ancestors are of different species.

In fact, the closest species that scientists refer to as our ancestors are separated from us by roughly three and a half million years. Whether a hypothetical interbreeding between a contemporary

—

human being and a distant relative would be able to produce offspring is unclear. Nevertheless, this is the most reliable proof that we are from the same species.

If we trace the latest split in animals, we find that the time span between the closest animal ancestors and present-day species is considerably shorter. Does that difference in producing more varieties in these two classes of species justify the scientific and statistical data applied to animals and humans? Is it possible that our system of distinguishing species is flawed? One can see that such an approach obviously brought us to not only different results, but also different conclusions. We find that animals produce more species in a shorter period of time than humans.

Another trait of species is their potential ability to produce viable offspring. This phenomenon is quite easily observed in nature. Usually the progeny resembles its parents. But when species produce visible varieties in appearance and behavior, the variation can become a discernible point of confusion. At what point do we determine that we are seeing the birth of a new species? Which transitional forms should we use as a definitive sign?

I don't mean to say that different species do not exist. They no doubt do exist, but how they appeared is another story. The conundrum comes from the inability of contemporary science to succinctly show where and how the first species appeared. Did they show up in separate primitive forms one by one, or did they indeed start as one common point, branching into millions of finally recognizable species?

Let's use the evolution of sex as an example. Sex is a late-occurring phenomenon in evolution. Prior to its appearance, there were only asexual organisms such as bacteria. Millions of years later, bacteria are still procreating in the same way, asexually. Would bacteria then consciously or subconsciously seek to develop into more sophisticated organisms in order to satisfy some unfulfilled need? Of course not. Bacteria cannot feel or think. Yet they have somehow developed instincts for survival, and one of them is asexual procreation, which bacteria continue to use about 3.5 billion years later.

At some point, a theory suggested that asexual species had less of a chance for survival than sexually reproducing species. In that case, assuming this theory was correct, we should have seen fewer bacteria and protozoa that developed asexually and more of those that shifted to sexual reproduction. One would think evolutionary steps would have eliminated such primitive organisms as asexual bacteria if sexual reproduction, which is far more efficient than asexual reproduction, was a better adaptation and favored survival in some way. But as we know, not only did such organisms not disappear, they are with us in growing numbers.

The earliest representatives of the three-domain system of prokaryotes are archaea, eubacteria, and bacteria, which are separate groups of single-cell organisms. Because all three groups are no more related to each other than they are related to eukaryotes, their exact place in the evolutionary tree is unclear. Archaea was previously classified as bacteria, but that classification was later overturned. Bacteria and archaea are similar, but archaea are more closely related to eukaryotes in using their enzymes for transcription and translation.

The similarities between archaea and bacteria come from both lacking interior membranes and organelles. The important distinction is that the outer membranes of archaea are composed of glycerol-*ether* lipids, while those of bacteria are composed of glycerol-*ester* lipids. The glycerol-ether membrane provides archaea with better resistance to the environment, as the ether bond is much stronger than the ester bond of bacteria. Archaea are microorganisms that survive in diverse environments, including salty oceans, hot and moist soils, and the guts of humans, where they help digest the various foods we eat. So far they have not proved to be pathogenic, which means they are not known to produce disease in humans. They are what your doctor may refer to as "good bacteria."

Eubacteria is a general term for a true bacteria (true bacteria have rigid cell walls, even though all cells contain lipids in their outer membrane) and cyanobacteria. Most of them are nonpathogenic. They are found on and in animals, including humans. Cyanobacteria, also known as green algae, are believed to be critical to the marine ecosystem. Also, while using light, water, and carbon dioxide, they emit oxygen as a byproduct of their metabolism.

Archaea and bacteria are believed to be the oldest forms of life on earth that emerged at least 3.5 billion years ago, while eukaryotes are believed to have evolved 1.8 billion years ago and animals only six hundred million years ago.

—

Bacteria, which are found almost everywhere, survive in numerous habitats and have played both positive and negative roles in the history of earth and humans. Bacteria are a normal part of our body. Some types of bacteria are helpful in their role of fighting other bacteria that cause disease. Bacteria play an ecologically important role in the decomposition of carbon, nitrogen, phosphorus, and sulfur.

However, even though scientists have learned much about these small organisms, their precursor (or precursors) is not known. These organisms successfully defy extinction, as we find archaea and bacteria alive and well 3.5 billion years after their first appearance. One of the mainstays of evolution is survival of the fittest, which means these organisms have been very successful indeed.

Yet knowing that bacteria are made up of lipids and proteins, I have to ask how they withstood the hot temperatures at the time of their creation without being destroyed. Most proteins become denatured at temperatures above forty degrees Celsius, and it is quite convincingly proven that the temperature at the time those organisms were thought to have appeared much exceeded that higher limit.

Even if the first living organisms were thermophilic (could survive in an extraordinarily hot environment), they should not have appeared earlier than two and a half billion years ago. (Unless, of course, we are wrong in our estimates of what conditions prevailed on earth at what time.) At that point in the Archaic era, the atmospheric temperature must have dropped to seventy to seventy-two degrees Celsius, which is a borderline temperature for bacterial survival.

This fact could direct us to other conjectures. For example, on primitive earth, when the environment had different parameters, archaea and bacteria must have been protected by some additional structures that are not found in them today. The archaea and bacteria possibly survived in places where the temperature could not damage their crucial components. If that archaic bacterium could not use soil as a shelter, then the other way it could safely survive was in water.

We know little about the creation of water. So instead of trying to solve this and all other existing problems at once, suffice it to say that water was present on earth as early as 4.4 billion years ago. There is another way one can account for the presence of ingredients that might lead to the synthesis of lipids and proteins found in bacteria and

—

archaea. This might have happened via meteorites falling to earth, thus providing ingredients from which life began to develop.

I expect to hear a roar from evolutionists in regard to my explanation of why bacteria should be considered as a real guide in deciphering the steps of evolution. Though found in abundance, they do not possess a bony structure, and therefore we cannot know how many bacteria disappeared over the years and how many and which evolutionary changes they underwent. It is impossible to draw any logical conclusions from that point of view. Yet my reasoning is that bacteria, with all these possible changes, still show up as bacteria billions of years after their first appearance.

If these were one of the first organisms from which evolution began, why are they still around when so many species have become extinct? Simply put: They should have disappeared, especially given the assumption that earlier bacteria were tougher in their ability to survive. With the argument that their ability to adapt to the new environment succeeded, the human body, as the most sophisticated newcomer, should have adapted to stave off their harmful effects much better than bacteria does. It is as simple as that. But it is no secret that that is not the case.

Turning next to viruses, I would like to point out that these life-forms are not only involved in symbiotic relationships with almost every other existing organism on earth, they also use such organisms for their own survival. Unlike bacteria, viruses are not capable of reproducing on their own. Their genetic material requires a host to replicate a new virus. And yet they have never (excluding possibly smallpox, which is presently kept only in the lab) disappeared completely, despite numerous attempts by humans to wipe them out.

The origin of viruses is unknown. There is an assumption that they may have evolved from pieces of DNA or bacteria. They are acellular structures and their only role is to infect the living cells they invade. Viruses are composed of nucleic acid (genetic material), proteins, and sometimes lipids. They reproduce using the commands of the host cell to transcribe, translate, and copy. After that task is accomplished, viruses exit the host cell as an infectious agent.

Why the human organism didn't learn how to overpower a virus in the process of evolution is hard to understand. Could it not learn how, if to not kill these pathogens, to at least tolerate them without getting

—

diseased? As justification, one can of course claim that humans, being a recent species, did not learn this simply because not enough time has elapsed. But given the human capacity to advance, it is a fairly weak defense of our deficiency, I'd say. Besides, humans, according to accepted theory of evolution, must be the most advanced class (species) on evolutionary staircase.

Let me now step into the holy of holies: the theory of the origin of species presented by Charles Darwin in the nineteenth century. Today not too many intelligent people would argue that Darwin failed to provide enough evidence for recognizing the process of evolution. But as they also know, each day brings new pieces of information concerning any point of knowledge. For instance, one day it is deemed good for one's health to have a glass of wine or a cup of coffee, and another day it is outright dangerous. Which is it?

That's a trivial question compared to those surrounding the theory of evolution, but it gives the reader an idea of how easily people might be swayed in different directions, depending on the discoveries made every day.

Darwin published his first edition of *On the Origin of Species* in 1859, a little more than 150 years ago. At the time his abstract, as he called it, was written, no one knew about mutations, heredity, and DNA as we do today. He rewrote his work five times, publishing six total editions, with the last one written in 1872.

Yet in spite of the fact that he referred to his original work as an abstract, meaning that it had few references and citations of prior works in it (since those works did not exist), he also had to struggle with the title of the book. As the eighth Duke of Argyll, George Chambers, properly noticed in his remarks, Darwin's book was not about the *origin* of species at all, but mostly about role of natural selection in their evolution.

Besides *Origin*, Darwin wrote a few other important works, one of which he titled *The Descent of Man* and another called *Selection in Relation to Sex*, which, as a second edition, was published in 1879 by John Murray in London. In it, Darwin began a discussion about so-called sexual evolution, a subject about which I wish to say a few words.

While not diminishing his thorough and keen observational abilities, it would be unfair not to mention his weak and sometimes

—

erroneous conclusions. In *Origin,* Darwin did not once acknowledge his confusion about how domesticated animals were produced when he referred to several possible wild species from which these domesticated animals had presumably descended. He supported the evolutionary theory of Jean-Baptiste Lamarck that was widely known to many naturalists of his time. Although Darwin did not deny Lamarck's theories on the use and misuse of organs as progressive steps in evolution, Darwin himself relied on natural selection, which he always considered the main instrument of an organism's inherited features.

Systematically studying the morphology of birds and other organisms, Darwin became a pioneer and foremost observer of the possible "transmutation of species," which he began to describe in his notebooks around 1837. He decisively denied that the Creator produced his creations in mere days. It seemed obvious to Darwin that this process occurred in gradual evolutionary steps. As a naturalist, Darwin always tried to apply the scientific method that would allow him to prove that the variations and speciation of different organisms, animals, and birds were connected and interrelated.

He wrote extensively about why he did not believe in the laws of uniform development, ascribing to each organism the unique ability to survive in its environment.

To that extent, Darwin was an eminent observer who had not have the genetic tools scientists of contemporary knowledge applying today.

Let us now consider another example. Let's assume that someone incidentally had a deep cut. It will most likely scar, even if no stitches are required to close it. This illustrates that the body adapts to damage via stages as best as it can, though not perfectly. This begs the question: When mutation occurs within any particular organ, does that organ improve in function so that it immediately synchronizes with the rest of the body? The answer is—not often. In order for the mutation to be perpetuated, the mutated organ must function efficiently and properly, at least until the organism has had a chance to reproduce and create offspring with the potential for the same mutation.

In his book, *Darwin's Black Box*, biochemist Michael Behe discusses thesis of biological systems as irreducibly complex. I will not describe the many arguments ensued after Behe's book was

—

published in 1996. It is not my task here. I simply wish to bring a point that it is often argued and supposedly successfully introduce a counterargument in such a case, pointing at a fact that if irreducibly complex organ was designed instead of being evolved, it is impossible to prove how it was designed and who the intelligent designer was. Whether or not such argumentation is valid, only time will show.

Another argument was brought by Philip E. Johnson in his book, *Darwin on Trial*. "Living creatures," Johnson wrote, "are extremely intricate assemblies of interrelated parts, and the parts are also complex." (*Darwin on Trial*, 32)

Can one say the same about possible transitional forms? Would natural selection care that it produced improved stock? Why would such a process rely then on random, mostly detrimental mutations that might or might not produce more advanced features? Couldn't an improvement come in some other way?

If this process is really in operation, then in order to survive, new organisms would necessarily always be better than previous incarnations. They would in a sense be more versatile.

Approaching this topic from a different angle, I wish to pose another question: What made DNA so unique that in being deficient it, by continually introducing errors in itself, led to mutations on one side and improvements on the other?

The mutation-natural selection balance is the only mechanism known to advance evolution. But if that were the case, then mutation must somehow happen in ordered and directed fashion rather than be a random process, must it not? Is this the reason why mutations always occur at a rate of around thirty per genome per generation?

It is also known that the preservation of a DNA sequence keeps an organism from destroying itself. Could God be guilty of protecting organisms purposely?

The intermediate forms theory not only makes no sense, I believe, but also is unnecessary as long as present laws of survival have been deciphered correctly. Why would evolution need to produce so many varieties of one species that eventually branch into intermediate and then new species? I understand that variety produces a greater chance for survival. Does it follow that the creation of new species is the logical consequence and that this is why we have so many different species? If this is an infinite process, does it defy the theory that eternality is impossible? Does this mean that we human beings are evolving into something more sophisticated or, at least, into some new and different species? And if that is the case, where are the transitional forms of human species at this juncture?

Humans spread all over the world for millions of years, applying logic for the same reason other populations of animals did. And yet the latest science almost agrees completely on distinguishing *Homo heidelbergensis* and *Homo neanderthalensis* as being, at best, subspecies of *Homo sapiens*. We modern humans consider ourselves to all be of the same species without the possibility of there being subspecies or varieties. Is this taxonomy sound or is it prone to change?

In light of this presentation, the existence of millions of different nonhuman species and yet only one distinct human species in our world cannot be easily explained.

Or can it?

Let's take another example. There is a popular but unproven belief that the first dog was domesticated approximately twelve thousand years ago. Domestication is a process of artificial selection that implies the use of animals by humans. It is also believed that dogs were domesticated from wolves.

The process by which this relationship was achieved must have been quite convoluted. Imagine a pack of unsophisticated humans out hunting for food. Now imagine a pack of wolves running around doing the same. Next, let's assume a wolf pup got lost or injured and picked up by a human, who fed (instead of devoured) that puppy until it became a slightly less wild wolf. Years later, people somehow concluded that it might be a good idea to raise wolves among humans for food. They realized that it was easier to raise pups than to capture adult wolves. After many generations, these domesticated wolves turned into something new and different that people began to call dogs. Simple enough?

Not quite. Contemporary researchers have tried to run the same experiment under faster and improved conditions but so far have not been successful. Wolves remain wild animals with wild habits. If a puppy was older than nineteen days old when acquired, then it was impossible to domesticate. In other words, it had to be born in captivity with people who wished and were able to nurture it and then used to produce a new breed of wolves that later were called dogs.

Let's say this occurred—that somehow humans came into possession of litters of very young wolf pups. Archaeological findings of fossils suggest the probable domestication of wolves was between ten and fifteen thousand years ago. Historically, people struggled and scavenged for food then; thus, it is inconceivable that they would think of feeding wolf cubs to help them survive a hunger. And if the only goal was to use a dog for food, why spend time to change its nature when wolves could simply be hunted and eaten for survival?

I'm also curious about what kind of a dog was the first domesticated animal. From what we know, the German Shepherd and Alaskan Husky are the only domesticated dogs that physically resemble wolves, yet they appeared quite recently in evolutionary terms and did not exist thousands of years ago when wolves were wandering the world. Fossils of ancient dingoes that lived in Thailand and Vietnam are assumed to be five thousand years old and have even been called dogs; these, however, have either reverted to a wild state or were never domesticated. So to conclude, there is no clear explanation as to how the first dogs appeared and from which species.

In line with this scenario of the domestication of animals, what would a similar process be for such predators as lions and tigers? Can anyone point to the transitional form of these animals before they became, if not house cats, at least more peace-loving creatures?

Now I'd like the reader to consider some other curious remarks made by Carl Zimmer in his book *Evolution: The Triumph of an Idea*.

In chapter ten of Zimmer's book (titled "Passion's Logic") he poses these kinds of questions:

> *Why do peacocks drag around such grand tails—but not peahens? Why is it that when Australian redback spiders mate, the male hurls himself onto the female's poisonous fangs, becoming a meal for her at the end of the act? The answers are to be found in evolution. Sex, biologists now suspect, is itself an evolutionary adaptation . . . . It gives sexual organisms a competitive edge over ones that reproduce without males and females. (Evolution, 274-275)*

My only question here is how convincing is this argument of superiority? Would evolution require the death of a mate to show the sexual organism's superiority over the asexual organism? In what way is this advantage? It takes two organisms to produce offspring instead of one. What advantage is it to have the road to birth fraught with peril? Could the answer be somehow connected to the wisdom of an unknown essence? Perhaps spotting a blunder in his logic, Zimmer further writes:

> But while sex may benefit both males and females, it creates a conflict of interest between them . . . . Evolutionary biologists have found that the peacock's tail, sterile ants, and suicidal spiders can all make eminent sense once they recognize the conflict between the sexes. (ibid., 275)

In his commentary in a chapter entitled "Female Choice," Zimmer writes:

> Competition between males was well known to nineteenth-century naturalists, Darwin included. It fit into his theory of evolution without much trouble: if males competed with one another for females, the winners would mate most often. If having a slightly thicker skull gave the edge to the winners, more males of the next generation would have thick skulls. A pair of lumps might make the skull even more effective in fighting, and so those lumps might evolve into horns. (ibid., 282)

Another no-less-strange observation that Mr. Zimmer offers in that chapter is a description of peacocks assembling in groups and drawing females to their cries. Zimmer writes, "As soon as a female comes into view, a male will raise his tail and make it shiver. They [the females] find certain kinds of tails attractive and choose to mate with their owners" (ibid., 283). He even asserts that a peacock having fewer than 130 eyes on his tail is a turnoff for peahens. The explanation is that females choose mates based on the male's strong genomic features (in which the number of eyes correlates to genetic superiority in the eyes of the peahens) that will theoretically produce offspring with a better chance to survive. This sort of reasoned choice would seem to make peahens at least as smart as human females, who possess mathematical skill.

Perhaps that is the reason that we further read, "When animals choose mates they don't make conscious decisions . . . although [adaptive behaviors] are based only on instinct, they can carry out a sophisticated strategy for survival" (ibid., 287). But strategy requires intelligence. Moreover, "sophisticated strategy" requires even higher intelligence. Is this attribute in reality being played out between peacocks? If they find it "sexy," then how might nature have contributed to this? Was the ability to reproduce a factor in the evolution of sex? While not denying the fact that evolution and adaptation continuously happen, I must ask why simple organisms such as one-celled bacteria (or even other more complex multicellular organisms that reproduce asexually) are not all trying to survive by producing offspring? Would the inability to have progeny stop sexual attraction?

Further, what makes birds, bees, and ants care about their genealogies? Is that cognizance somehow built into their natures? How can they experience the need to relate to their own without being directed by someone else who is even more intelligent?

Later in the book, Zimmer reveals just how sophisticated an animal's survival strategy can be. He cites a case from the 1970s in which Stephen Emlen and his colleagues at Cornell University found that what many scientists were hailing as examples of altruism in animals were "actually a complicated family intrigue" calculated to increase the likelihood of birds from a particular family line surviving to adulthood.

The Cornell researchers, according to Zimmer, concluded that only a few species helped out strangers without regard for blood ties (Ibid., 303). Zimmer describes in fascinating detail the behavior of bee-eaters who would, with up to seventeen birds in their genealogical tree, take care of each other. No one argues with this observed behavior among these birds—or among certain animals, for that matter. It is the explanation of what drives this altruism that seems peculiar to me.

After reading that bee-eaters live in a web of family conspiracies— that some visit the nests of strangers to lay their eggs or that some female bee-eaters fly miles away from their nests to consort with males of other bee-eater colonies or that when a male bee-eater tries to pair

—

with a female outside the family grouping, his father interferes in that affair until his son returns back home—one may wonder whether this is a fairy tale or a scientifically discovered game with rules similar to human behavior. To make it even more intriguing, Zimmer talks about some bee-eaters' ability to cheat on their own family members while others act as moral "watchdogs" in that same family.

Does this mean that humans inherited some communal traits from the animal world or that we are compelled to interpret animals' behavior according to our own?

Coming back to the peacock's splendid tail, Charles Darwin considered the reason for its existence. He could not produce any logical theory for several years and finally concluded that the peacock's tail is related to sexual selection dictated by the choices of peahens.

That conclusion, in my mind, would call for a number of questions:

1. Why are only peacocks provided with this particularly colorful tail and not millions of other bird species? The wild turkey, which also possesses a splendid tail (though not even close to the tail of the peacock), might be another example of a flashy species that is of the same order as peacocks (*Galliformes*), but neither are of the same subfamily and genus.

Given that most birds do not possess such finery, where are the transitional creatures?

2. Why would a peahen be attracted to such a tail? Is it possible that it's not for the reasons humans think?

By evolutionary logic, wouldn't such a tail make a peacock a better target for predators?

3. How do flashy tail feathers correspond with an instinct for survival?

This kind of vitalistic evolutionary theory was contemplated by Lamarck, according to whom the long neck of the giraffe evolved due to its stretching to reach the leaves of the tallest trees. My question here would be the same as for peacocks: Why did no other mammals in the same environment evolve a long neck (or legs) to improve their chances for survival? The okapi, which is closely related to the giraffe, does not have nearly as long a neck or legs as the giraffe does and has zebra like stripes instead of spots.

Another point I wish to make is that natural selection must not limit different species to one or two transitional forms in taxonomic rank. Yet we find very few examples of so-called transitional forms. Are those indeed the transitional forms, or are they examples of natural adaptations of species trying to survive the environment?

Besides, who can name a "proper" order in which organisms follow the evolutionary steps? Does a predator turn into a prey or prey turn into a predator? Is the number of chromosomes in each species indicative of an order in which species evolve? Humans, who are at the summit of evolutionary tree according to the number of their chromosomes, cannot point-blank claim to be the last attainment of nature. If our closest "relative," the chimpanzee, has forty-eight chromosomes that by fusion (as it is today an accepted explanation among scientists) gave us forty-six chromosomes, that would mean that the lower count of chromosomes found in the cell must be an example of the more sophisticated species. To no one's surprise, this is definitely not the case. Bats, porpoise chickweed, and coffee, along with some other species, all have forty-four chromosomes in their cells. And in fact, there is no correlation between the number of chromosomes in the cell and the complexity of an organism. But while it is an undisputable fact that the human genome is very similar to the genome of a chimpanzee, it is no less so to dolphins, whose intelligence might, in some cases, be considered on more advanced level than some *Homo sapiens* are and whose chromosomes count is forty-four; their genome is also almost identical to us. Do we say then that we have split some recent time ago from an aquatic ape with one branch turning into humans and the other in to the sea animals? Probably not, as dolphins, besides being evolutionary, separated from the chimpanzees and thus from us for at least ninety-five million years, were evolving in dramatically different environments.

Furthermore, that would make us much older species than it is accepted among scientists so far. Then how do we explain our genomic similarities with dolphins? Does it not support my theory that we were provided by numerous and only somewhat similarly basic ingredients that grew into a structure of DNA? Even if we did evolve from this unknown "aquatic ape," wouldn't our human physiology reflect at least some of aquatic features, say in the vestigial form?

There is sufficiently popular misconception existing today that we, as embryos, are going through the stages of evolutionary steps, inheriting tails, gill sacs, and other similar parts of lower species. In one sentence, it is not so.

ADAPTATION AND MUTATION

When in 1994 paleoanthropologist Tim White and his archaeological team discovered skeletal fossils in the Afar Triangle of Ethiopia, the news that they had found a transitional missing link between an apelike ancestor and the bipedal hominid "Lucy" flew around the globe overnight. Fifteen years later, an international team of scientists (forty-seven authors) finally released their findings with their conclusions. In October 2, 2009, a special issue of *Science* was published by the nonprofit science society Advancing Science, Serving Society (AAAS) to reveal those conclusions. In a series of detailed papers, the team described *Ardipithecus ramidus*, the previously mentioned female hominid. From the abundance of findings—a partial skeleton, skull, pelvis, hands, limbs, and feet— scientists concluded that "Ardi" walked completely upright, had a reduced canine/premolar complex, a predominantly plant-based diet, and was largely woodland-focused. The reduced canines in particular raised questions about this new hominid. The researchers summed it up this way: "Such questions can no longer be addressed by simply comparing humans to extant apes, because no ape exhibits an even remotely similar evolutionary trajectory to that revealed by *Ardipithecus*" (Lovejoy, 74).

The conclusions drawn by White and his team were that:

> The markedly primitive Ar ramidus indicates that no modern ape is a realistic proxy for characterizing early hominid evolution—whether social or locomotor . . . Rather, Ar ramidus reveals that the last common ancestor

that we share with chimpanzees (CLCA) was probably a palmigrade quadrupedal arboreal climber/clamberer that lacked specializations for suspension, vertical climbing, or knuckle-walking. (ibid., 64, 75-86)

Despite the doubts of some skeptics regarding the implications of these findings, one thing became clear: The ancestor humans and chimpanzees last shared differed from extant African apes.

One might also conclude that in a constantly changing environment, creatures would develop so-called transitional features that were either unsustainable in the long run or not optimal even over a short period of time. This might explain some features of the remains of *Ardipithecus ramidus*, including the smaller tearing teeth.

In that connection, I would like to consider one more feature of any species: the ability of an organism to adapt to its environment.

Evolution is a process of change. Adaptation is defined as an attribute allowing an organism to better adjust to its environment over many generations. In that sense, it is almost synonymous with evolution. On a deeper level, though, this meaning suggests that something has not merely changed, but also adjusted to its environment with the qualities necessary for survival.

To put it differently, adaptation is a process in which each individual organism, through the same adaptive mechanism, ends up with different qualities than its progenitors. I believe these qualities can lead to confusion and misinterpretation in distinguishing between species and members of a single species that have adapted to different environments.

Out of the three propositions that Darwin made in his book, natural selection played a huge—if not primary—role in the evolution of species. Evolutionists would argue that nature, with millions of years at its disposal, offered enough time for species to change into many varieties, undergo many mutations, and eventually produce new species by splitting from their previous ancestors.

To see if this theory is correct, let us take as an example the split of chimpanzees and hominids from their possible precursor, an apelike creature. Chimpanzees from the genus *Pan* developed two closely related species: the chimpanzee and the bonobo. These two, it is now thought, diverged approximately one million years ago. Chimpanzees

—

prefer to live in the hot, open spaces of Africa, while bonobos inhabit the humid forests of the Congo. Chimpanzees are more aggressive and territorial; they use violence to get sex. Bonobos, on the other hand, use sex as a tool to overcome violence. Overall, they are not as aggressive as chimpanzees; their males ordinarily submit to females. For instance, males let the females eat first when they find food. They also do not fight over food.

Let's try to visualize this presumed split of two close relatives. One is weaker and less aggressive than the other. Both comfortably live in the forest, where plenty of food can be found. The first individual gradually found comfort in the humid forests of the Congo. Her sister, a more rugged type, did not require such specialized climatic conditions and remained nearby with her parents. Time elapsed. Under different demands of nature, these two members of the family changed until, generations apart, the bonobos and chimpanzees appeared.

There are no doubt other recognizable features that differentiate these two closely related species. Nevertheless, I am not trying to investigate the details of the evolutionary paths taken by these or any other organisms mentioned in this book.

The differences mentioned above between chimpanzees and bonobos may lead to the following questions: What stopped chimpanzees from forcefully pushing the bonobos out of comfortable and reliable jungles where plenty of food could be found?

Would chimpanzees not easily win a battle between the two?

Being aggressive and powerful animals, they would not think twice about waging war against their weaker counterparts and would easily win. The explanation that bonobos developed a milder temperament than chimpanzees because they did not have to fight for food does not hold water. This is but one example of the evidence that—between environment and genealogical changes—genes play the dominant role in shaping the character of species, and the environmental role is somewhat secondary.

Now when we consider the genus *Pan* from the subfamily Hominidae, which includes humans, and take into consideration that according to the latest research chimpanzees and humans share roughly 98 percent of similarly structured DNA, we must conclude that we are very closely related in evolutionary history, must we not?

According to the contemporary theory of evolution, humans and chimpanzees split some seven million years ago from a mutual ancestor. With that knowledge, let's consider a few known assumptions of why hominids moved from walking on all four extremities to upright position using the only two legs. One theory refers to the hominid's need to adjust to its environment. That might seem a valid theory if these animals had acquired human sentience.

A competing theory is that the upright position helped hominids better reach fruits on trees (as giraffes were supposed to have grown longer necks). This supposition would follow if smaller animals had adopted the standing posture first. Yet another theory points to the improved observation of predators the upright stance offers. In such case, most animals would want to move out of the forests to an open space with learned process of how to walk on their hind legs.

This theory also implies the preventive consideration of lower class animals in how to behave in order to avoid being caught by the predators.

Another theory cites Africa's hot climate and the need for hominids to expose less of their bodies to the sun, which would return those animals to the shadows of the trees or cause them to migrate out of the continent to a cooler and less dangerous environment. On the other hand, why would they not have simply grown more hair or fur? In fact, why would they have lost their body-covering protection in the first place?

Let us look at how scientists interpreted the changes that led from apelike creatures to hominids. Scientists found that the major foramina, an opening connecting the spine with the skull, had moved from low on the back of the skull (characteristic of four-legged apelike creatures) to an almost central location on bipedal hominids. This seemed to indicate an adaptation from a four—to a two-legged stance. It might sound right, but it is not easy to visualize this process.

According to Darwin's theory, evolution comes in small, incrementally induced changes. That would mean that the apes' foramina had to gradually move until it enabled a vertical position. But let's say Eldredge and Gould are right and that equilibrium took place in this case.

I don't see how this is possible, no matter how imaginative I try to be. But my lack of imagination isn't germane; the recent discovery of "Ardi" is. *Ardipithecus ramidus* pushes our fully upright, non-ape ancestry back much further and overturns much of what we thought we had understood of our own evolution.

To speculate further on this subject, why can we not see such drastic adaptive mechanisms in relation to other species? Why has no other animal developed the capacities that human beings have in the areas of abstract thought, manipulation of the environment, and communication?

Yet again, why have we not adapted even more useful features than we have? For instance, why was a third eye not produced on the back of the human head, as this protective measure could have greatly benefited our species? Since we have long extended our waking hours into the nighttime, why hasn't the human animal developed better night vision? Why not eliminate the need for elimination (at least in such an unpleasant way as defecation is)? Why evolve bowels at all?

A no-less-puzzling phenomenon is the programmed emergence of so-called adult teeth that start to appear around the age of six in human young. If this process is the result of adaptation responding to the demands of nature, why haven't humans developed a third set of teeth to replace the ones they lose to decay and other stresses?

I'm sure one could come up with more examples like these, but I'll stop here to consider instead how Darwin explained the role of natural selection in the advantageous modification of species. "We have reason to believe," wrote Darwin, that "a change in the conditions of life, by specially acting on the reproductive system, causes or increases variability" (*On the Origin of Species*, 82). He continues:

> *Man can act only on external and visible characters: nature cares nothing for appearances, except in so far as they may be useful to any being. She can act on every internal organ, on every shade of constitutional difference, on the whole machinery of life. Man selects only for his own good; Nature only for that of the being which she tends.* (ibid., 83)

Later, he adds:

> *Now, if nature had to make the beak of a full-grown pigeon very short for the bird's own advantage, the process of*

modification would be very slow, and there would be simultaneously the most rigorous selection of the young birds within the egg, which had the most powerful and hardest beaks, for all with weak beaks would inevitably perish; or more delicate and more easily broken shells might be selected, the thickness of the shell being known to vary like every other structure. (Ibid., 87)

In spite of such extraordinary declarations, Darwin, who was skeptical and intelligent by nature, had also carefully qualified his theory of gradual evolution. It hinged upon a premise that he described in this manner: "If it could be demonstrated that any complex organ existed which could not possibly have been formed by numerous successive, slight modifications, my theory would absolutely break down" (ibid.,198). I must agree that changes in living conditions can cause variability, as nature cares nothing for the appearance of its subjects. Yet nature somehow is not completely detrimental. In fact, we may say that organisms outsmarted nature. So inevitably again the question of an Intelligent Designer (God) arises, not simply out of the necessity to look for one, but as a logical consequence. Otherwise, we would all be victims of blind chance, and the laws of survival, including the world of predators and prey, would make no sense whatsoever, no matter what rational tools one used to assess them.

Now if as Darwin said that nature is blind and does not care how its species might look like, why cannot we see the intermediate forms of unknown monsters that evolutionarily adjusted to the environment with the best chances for survival? I mean, where are the species with two or three or more heads among animals? Why not real dragons, breathing with tongues of flame, fill the streets? Wouldn't all such creatures that humans imagine in fairy tales then indeed exist?

At this point, I wish to bring in a few representatives of different species to see if they fit into currently accepted rules of evolutionary progression. For example, let's dissect the ancient primitive fish, the bichir, which is mentioned in Zimmer's book on evolution. This fish is from the family Polypteridae, and it possesses fins as well as primitive lungs. It lives in Africa's freshwater reservoirs and the Nile river system. It resembles tetrapods in its jaw structure, among other features. Describing this fish, Zimmer writes:

There are still some primitive, air-breathing fish alive today, such as the bichir of Africa. Around 360 million years ago, one lineage of air-breathing fish began spending some time on dry land. As they increased their time out of the water, they adapted their limblike fins to support their weight as they walked. Eventually their gills disappeared altogether. Over the course of millions of years, these early tetrapods became completely dependent on their lungs—a process documented with fossils. (Evolution, 398)

Fossils do not come with explanatory texts that impart meaning and context. As rare as fossils are, fossils that include soft tissue (such as gills or lungs) are even more scarce. Researchers are fallible, and no matter how knowledgeable they are, they must decipher their discoveries through their own subjective filters. Hence, I will try to analyze the above-quoted passage with the full realization that my own analysis might be flawed.

When Zimmer points to the lungs of the early tetrapods—"documented with fossils"—he makes a few assumptions. He explains that primitive lungs found in African bichir were not absolutely essential because they were not the only way to receive oxygen. The explanation that the fish spent some time out of water is even less persuasive, since just making the remark that fish "increased their time out of water" without a corresponding explanation of why they did this leaves the reader without any clue as to the adaptive imperative. This might lead to the question of why the fish left the water. Or even better: Why didn't all fish leave water?

Could it be because the fish, while happy in its environment, nevertheless decided it should explore the land anyway? Exploring the land required a different mode of movement. Could the fish have decided to use its fins as primitive legs, the way someone in a canoe might use his oars to pole his way through the shallows? Possibly, though one new condition still had to be overcome. Land inhabitants require a different breathing apparatus.

Did the fish then devote its time to perfecting its lungs? How might it have done this? And why? Land could never offer better survival conditions than water did, specifically, if one was made for water. Besides, wouldn't such maladjusted-to-the-land-condition fish

—

become an easy target for predators? So what motivated the fish to make such a drastic move? I doubt it contemplated anything at all, and I have my doubts that the fish would have been happy on the land, after all.

Is it possible that the fish decided at some point, during its millions of years on land, that it had made a mistake? Especially since life on earth may have been intolerable from time to time? According to scientists, the younger earth was a place with an unstable environment and extreme temperatures mixed with high winds and beset with erupting volcanoes and earthquakes. That might scare any number of species back into the water.

Although he has not explained why these fish moved from sea to land, Zimmer calls upon the reader to consider another example of fish evolutionary steps. He asks us to consider why Antarctic fish do not freeze to death in their extremely cold environment. According to Zimmer's text, Antarctic fish survive in cold climates because their livers produce natural antifreeze. The antifreeze forms a sugar-studded protein that bonds to ice crystals, stopping the crystals from growing indefinitely and damaging the fish.

This is a perfect example of an organism's ability to adapt to its environment over generations through the combined processes of mutation and natural selection. The question is, what caused the fishes' livers to begin making this antifreeze in the first place? If one succumbs to adaptation process as an appropriate mechanism, the a counter question must exist then—why people do not possess such protective mechanism as those who live for centuries in places like Antarctica or tundra or any other place with a climactically extreme weather?

Would mutation process be selectively in accord with nature and even more selective of which species to be allowed to adapt better and which would not? As one can try to figure out such process, this is not the same as the survival of the fittest.

Zimmer also explains how evolution changed the process of making a blood clot. "If you should cut yourself with a knife," he writes, "some of the proteins in the tissues will react with one type of clotting factor and activate it. Now the clotting factor can start a chain reaction" (*Evolution*, 401).

Zimmer then details the steps of this process. One should note that the chain reaction consists not only of a number of complicated mechanisms, but is also conducted in a strict order, without which blood clotting is impossible. Each action follows its predecessor precisely until a molecule called fibrinogen turns into a sticky mass, thus forming a clot. Zimmer admits that "the complexity of the clotting system is its strength: a single original clotting factor can activate several factors in the next step, and these in turn can switch on many more factors. From a tiny trigger, millions of fibrinogen molecules can be activated." (ibid., 402) He then concludes:

> *It's a remarkable system for stopping wounds, no doubt.*
> *And it depends on all its parts—if people are born without*
> *one type of clotting factor they become hemophiliacs for*
> *whom a scratch may mean death. But that does not mean*
> *that it had to have been Intelligently Designed.* (ibid., 402)

Do you, the reader, feel that Zimmer has persuaded you once and for all of his point of view that no design of any kind went into this complexity? It reminds me of the previously discussed proofs of another Darwinian evolutionist, Dawkins, whose position with regard to evolution—at least in his mind—could not be mistaken. But the most important aspect of his comments is his determination that whatever creationists might have added to this discussion is neither relevant nor worth hearing.

To summarize the facts and ideas I have gathered thus far, let me say that there is no doubt in my mind that signs of evolution, mutation, and adaptation exist all around us. And yet my next question is, why are these processes so complicated? Wouldn't it be much easier to produce an advanced but simple mechanism that makes clots? Why go through such a rigorously detailed process that risks someone's ability to survive a simple cut if any of the steps are performed incorrectly?

Since far more primitive creatures are able to survive bleeding, what was the evolutionary reason for later life-forms, including humans, to make this process so complicated and dependent on chance?

I'd like to close this segment by setting forth my understanding of evolution. Evolution is change. In collective definitions found in the *American Heritage Dictionary*, encyclopedias, and other references, we learn that most sources insist that evolution is actually a movement from a simple form to a more complex form.

I would like to agree with such an explanation but cannot. What of change that moves in the opposite direction—from the complex to the simple? What of change that moves back and forth, from simple to complex, and vice versa? What of land animals that adapt to an aquatic environment or aquatic animals that evolve into land forms? Or even animals that have gone from one environment to another and then back again?

Entropy is a process connected to evolution. Our expanding universe is evolving, but if entropy has its way, it might eventually collapse the universe in what is theoretically described as a Big Crunch—but this would still be defined as evolution. If we assume that this process happened not once but many times, then it might be defined as a revolving or cyclic evolution.

CHAPTER 11

Steps of Evolution with Genetics

Even scientists can only go so far before they hit barriers limiting their knowledge. Such barriers include the lack of knowledge about how atoms like hydrogen, oxygen, and others acquired their properties. They also include the answers to such questions as:

- What dictated the behavior of an electron in relation to a proton?
- What organized the production of amino acids and made them produce proteins?
- How did proteins become able "to consider" building up the material world?
- Why did DNA assume the property of passing on genetic information?
- Which vehicle was designated to supply cells with enzymes that effect the process called DNA repair, in which the enzyme recognizes and corrects damages done to DNA?
- Why do all organisms possess unique features, albeit they are composed of the same elements providing nature's effects on them are similar?

I will not pretend that I am able to give answers to these questions. The reason I ask them is to show that we can't say with any level of certainty that God—that is, intelligence that in some way organized the universe—does not exist. I don't mean to say that he *does* exist. At least, not in the form and shape in which humans have attempted to represent him so far. I will present my understanding of God in another context.

For now I'd like to turn to microbiological changes in organisms, to briefly discuss DNA, RNA, mutations, and genes. My hope is for us collectively to have a deep enough understanding of these things to reach a general conclusion.

Biochemistry might be called a hybrid science. It comes from an amalgamation of biology and chemistry. It is a process naturally occurring in all organisms. A live organism that converts biological molecules—producing, for instance, carbon dioxide and water from sugars that are consumed—cannot do it by blind luck. The biochemical reactions of each individual organism acting randomly and uniquely, rather than according to general rules, would produce millions of unknown molecules performing in bizarre ways.

Separate parts of an organism joined in one single cooperative mechanism could not come from a random submission to an indifferent process of natural selection. Elements like oxygen, carbon, hydrogen, and nitrogen that make proteins, lipids, amino acids, and glucose could care less whether a body will build, combine, or break down any substance exactly as dictated in some blueprint in order to make a functioning creature that can tolerate its environment. As they say, mixing gasoline and oxygen can run your car engine or it can cause an explosion.

How many conditions and preconditions must be met, how many precise reactions, specific catalysts, and enzymes must be forged in order to connect developing organisms via adaptation and evolution from the first second of developing life? It is quite remarkable no matter how one slices it.

At the heart of these processes is DNA. The most simple biochemical description of DNA is that it is a combination of special sugar, deoxyribose (also called *pentose*), two purine bases that are chemically expressed by two nitrogen rings, and pyrimidine bases with one nitrogen ring connected to a phosphoric acid molecule. This combination is called a *nucleotide monomer*. DNA is made up of a chain of these monomers, thus producing *polymers*, many (poly) monomers connected together.

The polymers of DNA are aligned in two polynucleotide strands coiled in a distinct shape called a double helix. RNA, another important structure, is quite similar to DNA but has a few important differences: one in sugar and one in the base of the pyrimidines. A single polynucleotide strand—a structure characteristic of RNA instead of the double helix expressed by DNA—is another difference between these two acids.

To understand the simplicity and fine details of the DNA located in a cell's nucleus—packaged from and consisting of a long chain of nucleotides varying in number but sometimes reaching up to one billion—try to visualize how infinitesimally small all the ingredients are. In that tiny cell, in a much tinier nucleus, there are tens of thousands of DNA molecules that are thoroughly packed with proteins.

The proteins' appearance depends on precisely twenty amino acids that came to the cell from the outside world. The trillions of cells representing humans were collected not just as random cells but as cells with different specialized structures and therefore different functions. Thus, we have muscle cells producing different types of muscles, nerve cells, cells responsible for the sex organs and the complicated functions of the sexual and reproductive systems, blood cells, and so on. All of these cells use the same twenty amino acids that select a frame to produce similar specialized cells.

The specificity by which DNA controls the formation of RNA, while RNA controls the formation of many specific proteins needed for a cell, is beyond explanation. It is also beyond comprehension that these proteins, whose work is so vitally important, are supplied via simple food consumption. Food particles cannot enter a cell without special preparation. These preparations are conducted both on macrobiological and microbiological levels. Food particles are processed and broken into amino acids. When these amino acids enter a cell, the organelles called *ribosomes* use them to construct necessary proteins under the command of genetic code moving from DNA to its subordinate RNA.

The cell provides precisely twenty amino acids, while the number of proteins produced inside the cell greatly exceeds that number. These proteins are not just the particles made from food. They fulfill many different and important tasks, such as making bones, for example. They produce a source of energy and supply catalysts called enzymes, without which the majority of biological reactions would be impossible. This is accomplished not by using many different, independently produced proteins but by folding many *identical* proteins into different shapes. Even under the unfavorable conditions that a cell may encounter, proteins show the ability to self-assemble into their proper shape.

The latest available research reveals that cells assist some proteins to fold on their own by producing an abundance of other proteins scientists have named *chaperonins*. They also sequester proteins in times of environmental stress, releasing them later for continued buildup.

Because RNA is a little simpler than DNA and is under its command, some scientists believe that RNA appeared earlier than DNA. I do not have a strong opinion on that; however, it is no matter which came first in this chicken-and-egg scenario because both DNA and RNA could not come into play without having been assigned a particular task.

What or who assigned that task?

Now imagine the most primitive cell: the bacterium. No matter how primitive it might be, a bacterial cell contains DNA. It has a tremendous ability to survive in many different environments. By some statistics, there are approximately forty million bacterial cells in a gram of soil. There is almost no place on earth where bacteria do not exist. Fortunately, the majority of bacteria are not harmful to other forms of life; man has even learned how to use these primitive cells to his benefit. But harmful bacteria can cause serious, even fatal diseases such as anthrax, bubonic plague, and tuberculosis.

The ability of these cells to harm people is related to their complex associations with other organisms. Bacterial cells inadvertently produce many reactions in the human body as they reproduce, including disabling its immune system and rendering the body unable to remove harmful agents.

Try to picture the subcellular level of bacteria, where proteins are found in a simple bag, *cytoplasm*. These proteins have been named *bacterial hyperstructures* because they show relative complexity. The development of powerful microscopes showed that the genetic material in a single circular chromosome is located in an irregularly shaped body called a *nucleoid*, which is itself found in cytoplasm.

—

The development of nucleoids and circular chromosomes cannot be explained by contemporary science. It is also inexplicable how bacteria have survived under difficult environmental conditions by gathering in highly resistant, immobile structures named *endospores*. This static condition, comparable to hibernation, may last for millions of years.

To sum up: DNA is the main engine that provides future generations with their appearance and behavioral patterns. This information accumulates in genes. Genes are specific nucleotide sequences that collect in different numbers in humans, but averaging twenty-one thousand. Genes form the units of inheritance found in DNA structures called chromosomes. There are forty-six chromosomes in each cell. These cells are known as germ cells or *haploid* cells.

The process of transferring hereditary traits to offspring occurs in germ cells formed from a sperm and an egg, causing fertilization. A mechanism responsible for the reproduction of hereditary traits lies within the structure of DNA that contributes to heredity by copying itself. Both parents cooperate equally in this process, giving twenty-three pairs of chromosomes each to the new progeny.

From time to time, while this copying occurs, the sperm cells introduce a change in matching bases of nucleotides. These changes are called *mutations*. Mutations are believed to always happen randomly and, generally speaking, are of two types. One type of mutation results from changes in sperm cells and the other from changes in other bodily cells. Only sperm cell mutations are responsible for the hereditary changes (those that are passed down to progeny). Changes within cells other than sperm cells are limited to the organism in which they occur.

Many mutations happen because of unstable nucleotide bases in DNA. This instability may result from, for example, the energy produced from water being rushed into a cell. A change called a *tautomeric* shift causes the redistribution of electrons and protons in the bases. The result is that the normal pairing of A-T or G-C (adenine to thymine or guanine to cytosine) does not happen. Remember that a water molecule consists of positively and negatively charged atoms. If a DNA molecule is replicated during that shift, heritable changes may occur.

So next time you come home hot and sweaty from a run and start chugging water, remember that every product you consume can produce changes in your body.

We know that a living organism must adapt to its environment or die. Thus, weak and injured organisms will be eliminated, and only the fittest will survive. However, the strongest survivors still need to adjust. This adjustment will most likely produce the bodily changes that eventually influence the quality of the reproductive system. That would mean that randomly occurring mutations might introduce a new ability to the organism.

On the other hand, these mutations could produce a number of new requirements to which the body would have to adjust. Given such a combination of outer and inner irritants to a body, an organism may change either in small increments (such as in Darwinian evolution) or, according to a theory of Stephen Jay Gould and Niles Eldredge, through "punctuated equilibrium" (observed rapid change after a period of visible stagnation).

In any event, mutations are indeed rebels against the imperatives that drive each organism. The question remains: Who or what made these orderly functioning vehicles? It goes without saying that evolutionists and creationists answer this question differently.

CHAPTER 12

Steps of Evolution without Reference to Genetics

One must accept that everything around us is in a constant state of change. Despite the human desire to live forever, our sun will not shine forever. That means eventually life will not be possible in the way we are accustomed to it, especially for humans. The temperature, the darkness, the atmosphere will change in ways humans will not survive. If we recognize that we are the weakest structures in the universe, we must understand how chimerical our desire to live forever is.

Astrophysicists and astronomers mostly agree that the universe is expanding and that that expansion will eventually produce complete darkness in the observable sky; this means all stars and planets will disappear because of the tremendously stretched universe. But while the theories behind what drives this expansion are not unanimous, scientists agree darkness will occur in a few billion years. (Possible causes for this expansion are discussed in the portion of this book titled "The Strange Laws of Physics.")

Suffice it to say that the universe is not only expanding, it is accelerating. It might sound contrary to the Newtonian laws of physics, but it is now considered fact, especially after astronomer Edwin Hubble proved it in his calculations at the beginning of the last century.

Most scientists today accept the theory that earthquakes, volcanic activity, mountain creation, and sea-floor depressions result from plate tectonics in the lithosphere. This was first expressed scientifically in the theory of continental drift offered by Alfred Wegener in 1912.

The word *lithosphere* is used to describe the rocky crust of the earth. There are approximately seven defined tectonic plates on collision courses within the earth's crust, producing calamitous movements. To ease the earth's movement, nature created the *asthenosphere*, a few-kilometer-thick layer of plastic rock located right underneath the earth's crust and mantle; the asthenosphere allows these plates to move. The boundaries between plates are where earthquakes usually originate. In addition, symmetric magnetic anomalies and the plates' colder temperature (compared to the hot mantle of molten rock below) cause an exchange of heat across the core-mantle boundary. All these movements vary in velocity, thus accounting for drag, topography, and density in the crust.

Other evolutionary geological changes were brought about by water, wind, and glaciers that, over millions of years, produced sedimentary rocks. Sedimentary rocks result from the accumulation of precipitated minerals and organic particles that, after settlement, are eroded by both chemical action and exposure to the elements, such as unstable temperatures, wind, and water.

The majority of people do not know much (and probably don't care) about all the rocks, water levels, and minerals that are the necessary ingredients of our earth. But whether one speaks of the different layers of the atmosphere, the layers of the earth, the variable level and condition of the sea floors, or the changing levels of the oceans that surround us, all these phenomena contribute to making our world much less stable than we might wish it to be.

Is it less stable than God intended it to be? I suppose that might depend on how you view God's interaction with the world. Despite the fact that the book of Genesis depicts God in the role of a laborer working with clay, the creationist view drawn from a literal interpretation of Genesis posits that the earth did not evolve over millennia but rather, the earth in all its complexity, was created quickly, in a matter of six days, seven thousand years ago.

Perhaps this might explain why God decided to recall his creation in Noah's time. In any event, as there was a definite point at which the earth was constructed, and mankind with it, there is also a definite point at which it will be destroyed. At which time, by some beliefs, God will create a new heaven and a new earth. Whether this refers to the literal physical heavens and physical earth or some spiritual reality, it probably goes according to a plan that we were not consecrated into.

Why seven thousand years? It requires complicated math, but basically the creationists have attempted to count the earth's lifespan prior to the advent of Christ by adding up the generations and ages given in biblical genealogies that purport to run from Adam to Jesus. This allows the creationist calendar to work backward from the current year to 1 CE and from there to the dawn of creation.

Some fundamentalist creationists believe that the world will end, in fact, sometime during its seven-thousandth year. I am uncertain whether the rest of the universe will be affected by this.

It should be noted that a literal yet highly interpretive belief in the Genesis story evolved at a time when the human beings involved did not know that earth was one world among many or that our sun was one of a galaxy of stars that might also have their own planets. What biblical creationists make of that, I am uncertain, but it does create a dichotomy. Is the earth billions of years old, as science has been telling us, or is it a mere seven thousand years old as one of many holy books arguably hints at?

It should also be noted that there are many other varieties of creationism, some of which have nothing to do with the book of Genesis. There are, for example, those who believe that God created the universe but that the natural laws are simply the tools by which he chose to do it and that he has—again, like the sculptor with his clay—spent uncounted eons engaged in an ongoing process of creation.

It is only the biblical creationists with their theory of catastrophism (meaning that such seemingly ancient features as the Grand Canyon or the Himalayas are the result of cataclysmic events) who argue that God did his most important work in less than a week a mere seven thousand years ago and that therefore evolution is an illusion.

CONCLUSIONS

In conclusion, I'd like to finish this chapter as following:

Without a doubt it must be accepted that Darwin was a pioneer in his views on evolution. From his first explorations on the similarity of human and animal functions during his medical studies in the late 1820s, to his preparations for the church carrier, to traveling to Galapagos Island as a naturalist, Darwin underwent evolution many times himself. His first work, *On the Origin of Species*, took years to write and was published several times with heavy modifications between editions; a whole new chapter was added in the sixth and last edition published in 1872.

Today, a little over 150 years after Darwin's book first appeared, many works have been written on the subject of evolution. My goal here has been to illustrate some of the numerous attempts to debate this issue by presenting both the creationists' point of view and the evolutionists' point of view. Whether I have been successful is for the reader to decide.

I believe the subject of our origins intrigues us because it is not only relates to our ability to live indefinitely longer, but also relates to our minds' capacity for inquiry. That capacity, unsurprisingly, is comparatively limited. I believe this limitation will always haunt us; no matter how much we learn, our reach will always exceed our grasp.

Darwin recognized, almost from the beginning, that evolution is the result of a two-step process: adaptation and natural selection.

Yet I believe he was wrong in ascribing the main role in evolution to natural selection while relegating speciation to a secondary status. To my mind, speciation is not less important; but regardless of which is dominant, I believe both are being managed by something else.

Perhaps this is where God gets into the act.

Unfortunately, contemporary approaches to the theory of evolution have not changed much, and the description and characterization of natural selection as a process by which species adapt is only correct on a superficial level. With constant changes in nature as well as with everything else in or around us, it is almost impossible to trace those changes in a neat, orderly manner.

That is why, even with the establishment of a plausibly sound mechanism for evolution—and many different additions to it—I

—

come to the following summation: Evolution is a slow, natural process requiring an accumulation of infinitesimally small modifications rigorously screened by natural forces, which eventually improves the organisms that survive the process.

In light of such a description, any experiment in evolution—conducted by breeders of animals, for example—could only work if nature allows the production of a viable hybrid. Sterile offspring would bring the experiment to a quick conclusion. Successful experiments of this nature would necessitate a saltation—meaning a sudden leap when a new species appears in a single generation, which Darwin compared to a special creation.

Problems that arose among the supporters of Darwinian evolution included the impossibility of solving the riddle of irreducible complexity as well as finding fossils that clearly showed the transitional forms of an organism. Such conundrums as the evolution of an eye or a wing, or any organ for that matter, could not be resolved.

This was not because of the quandary over who created the Creator. It was because of an inability to step back from the unproven theory that all animal life began with one common ancestor; this led to continuous attempts at a logical explanation without the ability to provide evidence or to conduct experiments.

While not pointing to the definite presence of a Designer, I think that to reject the possibility that our world might have developed by some other process than a series of fortunate events has produced a gap in our explanation of how the world operates.

Would a theory of slow evolution with the accumulation of intricate modifications work if the preceding life-giving events happened differently than currently accepted by contemporary science? It seemed obvious to me—starting with a theory of catastrophism offered by Georges Cuvier—that Darwin's theories of evolution and Cuvier's theories about the extinction of organisms were not mutually exclusive. Evolution must have been a gradual process, insisted Darwin. No, changes came by way of catastrophes, insisted Cuvier. Is this necessarily a problem of binary thinking? Might both have been correct?

After all, there are such examples of catastrophic events having profound effects on planetary life, such as the extinction of dinosaurs, which could have been due either to a huge asteroid hitting the earth or to volcanic eruptions.

But neither theory explains how the first organisms appeared on earth. They deal with life already established and struggling with an environment that over time becomes more and more amenable to that life. What if we apply the same formula Isaac Newton used to describe the law of gravity? He watched an apple fall to the earth and thus conceived the idea that the laws controlling that movement were the same everywhere. I would say that to grow an apple one has to have proper soil, an atmosphere, and seeds before the apple tree will grow and produce fruit.

With earth in its primordial stage and meteorites bombarding its surface, as well as an abundance of such elements as nitrogen, hydrogen, and carbon, life might have been transferred to earth and nurtured by any of these conditions. That there is much more to understand about the conditions that brought about life, no one doubts.

PART FOUR

BEHIND THE THEORY

CHAPTER 13

How Convincing Is the Big Bang?

Before I begin to describe my understanding of the universe, a few words of introduction to this chapter deemed appropriate.

While contemplating themes of this book, I came to conclusion that topics raised in it must direct me in to a "digging" of a matter of cosmos. That made me terrified and excited both at the same time. To me, everything that requires description of what happens in the universe had to be exciting not only because I realized that cosmos is grandiose, magnificently majestic, and spectacularly beautiful; its orderly conduct could very well be the result of something more meaningful, more rational, and more thoughtful that most people are seeking while hoping to find a reason which many call gracefully and in awe by the name of God.

Scientists are always trying to make a point that only repeated experiment may prove their theory. One example that comes in mind is a hermetically closed glass can that contains equal amount of M&M's candies. One can easily see the borders that separate each distinct color of the candy pebbles that were placed in order—yellow, red, blue, and so on. But by the moment you begin to violently shake a can, all the colors start to mix, and there is no way one can run a course of putting them back in order. That is one of the laws of order and chaos.

With an explanation by the scientists of starting the universe from an event, such as described as a Big Bang, one must assume that exactly the opposite happened. From an explosion that had to occur, the universe began to acquire the orderly conditions. I don't even consider how close an explanation of both theists and scientists of the beginning of the world came together. Both began magically, with theists insisting that God created the universe from nothing and scientists offering no less magical development of the beginning of the universe out of nothing or, as in the case of Big Bang, finding a magical dot that suddenly appeared from nowhere. Without clear explanation how it did happen, to me, it is no better explanation than what the theists provided us. To rephrase today a pretty known title of a book, *A Universe from Nothing*, written by Lawrence M. Krauss, and supported by people like Richard Dawkins and Sam Harris, who are the most known atheists among the other nonbelievers, why not assume that, for God, it would take as much an effort, if not less, to come from nothing as for such an ambivalent entity as the universe itself is. If one does not question who created the universe or, more precisely, who placed the magic dot that miraculously appeared out of nowhere and then exploded, why question who created the creator?

In the meantime, just the same as in the living organisms, cosmos, with all its laws, appeared as managed events. Taking that as a fact, the task that would follow then would be to separate illusion from logic. That seems to me is the only way that has to be placed forward in order to know what is the truth and what is not. And with that, you may then suspect "God's hand" or not at all.

From a philosophical point of view, physicists not much differ than the scientists from the other investigative fields as well as the rest of us are. While pursuing more or less the same goal, physicists firmly established themselves in two visible-but-opposing camps. One acquired the name of particle physicists, another—condensed-matter physicists. It would be much less funny if representatives from both camps realized that either camp helps to solve the same equation, but by different methods. Yet being humans, they don't find it amusing that it is unnecessary to put down anyone while competing and that it does not a matter who is the most important. These scientists do not recognize that they consider both fields of the same structure and that cooperation would only ease and speed up approaching a final goal, in this case, for instance, finding TOE, "the theory of everything."

Obviously, I am not in a position to teach physicists about physics, but I feel quite comfortable to point at improprieties in human behavior.

The other side of that coin is to consider that people finding about cosmos could come from absolutely different backgrounds. Starting with a friend of mine, who was genuinely surprised that our galaxy is not the same as a whole universe, to those who were familiar with the binary stars and space-time as well as with the phenomenon that time warps, the task I encountered was how should I write to be understood by lay people, produce interest in more cosmos educated people, and not to become a subject of mockery by scientists such as, in this case would be, astronomers and astrophysicists.

Tracing the history of experiments conducted by particle physicists for the last eighty-five or so years, I realized that these scientists mainly established themselves by a kind of activity that may reasonably fair be characterized as methodically breaking the smallest things apart. They do it with ever-increasing force that they are certain they need to do in order to understand how the universe came about. And that specific type of activity was not once ridiculed by the other camp, who, for some reason, dismissed consideration that atoms behave differently than when they, *atoms*, join in the molecules as one of the intermediate steps of the complicated processes encountered around us.

With that in mind, I went into self-directed assignment to make a short dictionary of specific words used in cosmic terminology. That way, those who may find the reading of this chapter a little troublesome as well as tedious and boring, an explanation of the words and events according to accepted standards may be meaningful and helpful tool. Thus a glossary of specific terms appeared at the end of this chapter. The rest had become a matter of necessity.

One may skip reading the following pages altogether without jeopardizing enjoyment of the book. But then again, if one finds the topics discussed here as exciting as I had, why not give it a try.

At best, you might better understand why I had been inclined to become an agnostic; at worst, you will waste a few precious moments of your life.

So without further ado let me start to speak about cosmos.

Now as you probably noticed, I thrive on collecting many questions. And here, not to change my long-ago developing habit, I gathered some again:

- What is the universe?
- How does it function?
- How did it come about?
- What is a role of elementary particles found in the universe?
- Where the universe is heading?
- Why did it begin to accelerate again?
- Where do cosmic rays come from?
- What the real goal of the black holes might be?

Any of these questions may easily lead to the big question: How could anyone completely deny the existence of God?

I, for one, do not say anything about it yet.

What I am going to do, nevertheless, I will attempt to tackle these questions on two levels. First, I'll start with a general description of the universe: What kind of matter is found in it, what the governing laws that matter follows are. I'll discuss how (or even if) these laws relate to each other. My second task will be to describe the possible scenario of the end of the world, according to a few accepted scientific theories, as well as inferences and conjectures based on them. Finally, I am going to offer my analysis and vision of where our planet and the universe are heading. With our short presence in this world, it is still a piercing thought—what is the destiny of the stars, the galaxies, of all life in the cosmos?

The universe is vast if one reckons everything known to comprise the universe. In its vastness, only 5 percent of it is ordinary matter. The remaining 95 percent is shared between dark matter and dark energy. Dark matter is invisible; nobody knows what it is or of what it is composed. Dark energy is even less understood. The only thing scientists are aware of is that these phenomena logically must exist.

I will discuss dark matter and dark energy later in this chapter. For now let's talk about that 5 percent of the universe that's made up of ordinary matter.

Everything material in universe consists of atoms. These atoms in turn consist of smaller subatomic particles called *protons*, *neutrons*, and *electrons*. The electron is considered to be an *elementary particle* as it has no known components. Protons and neutrons are made of even smaller particles called *quarks*. Quarks are usually found in groups connected to each other by *gluons*. Different combinations of protons, neutrons, and electrons produce different elements, such as hydrogen (the most abundant in the universe), helium, carbon, and many others. Atoms also make up the stars and galaxies.

Scientists are trying to figure out how the universe came about. Is it static with no end or beginning, or is it evolving and necessarily will come to an end? To give some idea of the nature of the debate, I'll touch on some of the theories as presented by the scientific community.

Scientists are quite often trying to explain the simplest things that make up the physical body. Because of their meticulous work, many queries about physical compositions of these bodies and their diversified functions can be answered in a straightforward fashion. Nevertheless, for better or for worse, we are still burdened with unsolved problems. Some are brand new. Still many are the old ones on which scientists continually shine new light. And some have not yet been precisely defined.

For the last one hundred years, tremendous achievements in recognizing the new laws of physics have been discovered.

The scientific world has learned about quarks, *fermions*, *leptons*, gluons, *pions*, and *muons*. These are now habitually discussed at the dinner table among physicists, astrobiologists, astrophysicists, and other scientists in related fields. (Not to mention science-fiction writers.)

Those words might not mean much to the average person, but everything in our environment, including us, is made of all or some of these particles. Where these particles acquired their features from, and specifically from where they actually appeared remains an enigma even today. The contemporary string and M-theories may shed a light on those questions but they are mostly in a class of hypothesis that not confirmed by experiments. Accordingly, we may say that some theories, such as those describing matter and antimatter (as represented by electrons and positrons, for instance), may not be theories but rather merely logical postulates. And this is why.

In spite of actually a relatively short period of time since 1928, when the only known particles were electrons and protons, over one hundred

—

new particles have been discovered. Some remain hypothetically suggested, others were proven that they do exist. Nevertheless, an electron had begun its own history after J. J. Thompson in 1897 isolated it from atom. A curious thing that was confirmed then was that an electron has not only an electric charge but possessed a quality of magnetism akin to the north pole-south pole duality. Then Paul A. M. Dirac, an English theoretical physicist, published a paper in which he wrote an equation that suggested that an electron might have both a positive and negative energy. The accepted concept was that most of what was seen in the direct observation of matter was likely to possess a mirror image or opposite. The further logic dictated that if an electron has an opposite (it was named a positron) particle, the only difference of which is its charge, then in all probability it is likely that all other particles must have their counterparts as well. In other words, there is *symmetry* in the universe, with one antiparticle for every particle. Incidentally, it was also Paul Dirac who, in 1933, postulated the existence of the antiproton.

There was a problem with this conclusion, though: If each proton, electron, and neutron had an antiproton, positron, and antineutron, then matter and antimatter would annihilate each other when they meet. That also would mean that the world as we know it would end.

Because our universe *does* exist, and even though the theory of matter versus antimatter was almost immediately accepted among many scientists, something else must have taken place that would explain the "survival" of the universe. That "something else" indeed exists, and, as scientists have explained it, the reason we are still enjoying the material world was due to an uneven process by which particles prevailed over antiparticles. That is, matter prevailed over antimatter, and the material universe came into existence. Out of every billion particles annihilated (versus the same number of antiparticles), one additional particle of matter was left intact.

So nature seems conveniently provided the conditions where the matter would have prevailed. Let us now assume that such a scenario is legitimate and balance-imbalance of nature indeed played in to a material (and our) benefit and we all came into an existence. What does not quite fit in to such a scenario neatly is the logical conclusion that providing a huge number of all these presently existing opposite particles, we would continuously witness unsettled particles bombarding each other here and there and, in fact, everywhere. By this analogy, we would also constantly encounter antipeople that time to time annihilate us. As this does not occur, the question arises—is there some kind of misunderstanding related to description of matter and antimatter?

The author of *Antimatter*, Frank Close, writes, "As the positron was discovered in cosmic rays, and as antiprotons also have been seen there, it may be tempting to think that these antiparticles are the remnants of antistars that exploded far away. On the contrary, these positrons and antiprotons are the debris formed from the energy released when a high-energy cosmic ray made of ordinary matter hits gas in the upper atmosphere." (*Antimatter*, Frank Close, Oxford University Press, 2009, page 116.)

In addition, another problem demanded an attention. Scientists argued that while the photons were produced each time a reaction occurred between the particles of matter and antimatter, under certain conditions, if these photons were sufficiently energetic, they could be transformed into electrons.

This begs the question: Wouldn't the photons (in this case called *bosons*), which have integer spin (angular momentum), no charge, no rest mass, and therefore no substance, act as mediators of force only and follow different rules than electrons?

If the photons are merely a force that transmits particles, be they electrons, positrons, or protons, then how do massless, charge-free, nonsubstantive, elementary particles may transform into charged subatomic particles that have different angular momentum (half-integer spin) and absolutely definite mass?

Most important, the Pauli exclusion principle states that each orbital of any atom which holds two electrons allows the two be present together at the same time only if they have different spin projection. This principle maintains that no two electrons can have the same quantum numbers, that is, principal number, angular momentum, projection of angular momentum, and spin projection. Photons, on the other hand, having zero spin, can virtually sit on top of each other without "claiming" an extra space.

Let me go a little further in describing the behavior of the electron-positron pair.

For that, we need to consider the concept of symmetry a little deeper. Specifically, *CP-symmetry*. CP-symmetry is the theory that

—

there are two types of transformation possible in the universe: charge conjugation (every particle becomes its antiparticle) and parity (every particle becomes a mirror image of itself). However, interactions between particles, such as decay, result in variance, so the results are no longer symmetrical. There is a violation of the charge conjugation/parity symmetry, which is in other words a CP *violation*.

When, in 1957, Russian physicist Lev Landau proposed CP-symmetry, it became the basic theory of quantum field particle physics that explained a true and simple symmetry between matter and antimatter. But when James Cronin and Val Fitch announced in 1964 that this symmetry could be broken, it created turmoil in the physics community. It has been experimentally confirmed a few times since—such as in the 2001 experiments conducted at the Stanford Linear Accelerator Center (SLAC)—that, under special circumstances, the symmetry might be broken.

This made a dent in the theory of symmetry and placed a new obstacle in understanding of how the universe works.

So where is the distinctive representative of antimatter, the positron, found? Positrons are a component of cosmic rays. Cosmic rays originate in outer space and are believed to be a product of supernovae. Because they are electrically charged, they are influenced by magnetic fields. These rays may approach the earth from any direction, but because of its powerful magnetic field, the earth is able to deflect and redirect them.

Yet positrons became available to scientists for experimentation through particle accelerators. Before the era of particle accelerators, cosmic rays were the most significant tool for finding positrons. When high-energy cosmic rays collided with atoms in the upper atmosphere, they produced gamma rays as well as neutrinos. Gamma rays are usually blocked from entrance by the upper layers of the atmosphere. The neutrinos, on the other hand, advance freely through it. It is known that these latter particles are passing through our bodies by the thousands every minute.

Don't panic. They're mostly harmless.

Now when you read in a scientific article an explanation such as "Beta particles are just highly energetic electrons or positrons and therefore can take either negative or positive charge," you may wonder: How could that be? If these two particles are opposites and

−

normally annihilate each other when they meet, what makes them act as electrons at one time and as positrons at another? If symmetry is real, how could they be present without destroying each other?

A related problem arises when we consider the motion of particles: If a particle of matter is moving in one direction through space-time, then the antiparticle must move in exactly the opposite direction. Yet while moving in opposite directions, wouldn't these particles eventually collide and annihilate each other? If that happened to all particles and antiparticles, would it not have destroyed the universe long since?

Consider the antihydrogen atom. Theoretically such an atom can exist only in antimatter, and so far has only been created artificially. This has led to the hypothesis that it exists naturally with all the complications that ensue from having to have antiquarks and antigluons to keep it together. But if all these quarks and antiquarks exist at the same time, wouldn't that mean they *must* eliminate each other?

While Paul Dirac suggested that an electron might have both positive and negative energy, the discovery of an actual particle that possesses such a positive energy belongs to Carl Anderson, who used cosmic rays in his experimental apparatus. The physical proof of the existence of antimatter led to a long chain of experiments and discoveries. Based on these, my assumption would be that "antimatter" must be used not only as a descriptive term but to refer to a separate class of entity existing in the physical universe.

As an example, let's take an electron and a positron. In almost all cases, they are identical in all existing measurements except charge. Could they then be a single bipolar particle, the features of which depend on such things as intensity of energy? Could the special conditions that researchers learned how to create in the lab produce "frozen" positrons that could be observed not only as recognizable entities, but as separate particles as well? Could the successful production of positrons ultimately bring hidden dimensions to light?

From just over two thousand years ago, through the time of Isaac Newton's *Principia* in the seventeenth century, to the development of particle physics, to the latest theories on the possible existence of the Higgs boson, to the references to string theory, humanity has lived in expectation of discovering the answers to many mysteries.

—

For over two hundred years, people from related fields were satisfied with an explanation of universal laws that used a classical approach to physics, only to later realize that those fundamental laws could not explain all occurrences in either our lives or the universe. In fact, some newly recognized events contradicted known laws; their discovery required different ways of thinking and sometimes required denying the validity of existing explanations. This led to many upheavals and the discarding of previous explanations of how the universe behaves. For example, the so-called "great debate" between Albert Einstein and Niels Bohr about the determinism of quantum mechanics brought forth many positive, creative thoughts and explanations.

Unfortunately this has not always been the case. There are always conservative loyalists who continue to hold onto the existing laws without acknowledging the validity of newly discovered ones, just as there are people who, instead of finding evidence for what they've imagined might exist, try to simply push their ideas through as valid without that evidence.

IN THE BEGINNING

The contemporary theory of the beginning of the universe was proposed by Georges Lemaître, a Belgian priest and physicist who first described it in a paper published in French by the small and obscure journal *Annales de la Societe Scientifique de Bruxelles*. For the reason unknown today, this paper didn't receive much attention. The year was 1927. Based on Einstein's theory of general relativity, Lemaître came to the conclusion that the universe is expanding. His conclusion was connected to the observation of the Doppler shift of objects outside of our galaxy. This effect, named after the Austrian physicist who discovered it, is observed as a change in the frequency of a wave caused by the movement of the wave's source in relation to the observer. Lemaître's observations indicated that objects in the universe outside the Milky Way are moving away from us, that is, expanding, which also meant that the universe couldn't be in a steady or static state.

In 1946, a Russian-born American physicist, George Gamow, described the beginning of the universe as the primeval fireball, placing emphasis on the superhot conditions with which it began. In 1949, an English astronomer, Sir Fred Hoyle, responded to this theory, sarcastically calling the beginning of the universe the "big bang" and argued that the universe was in a steady state because of the continuous creation of matter. Such a belief in a steady state was also a theory of Einstein who, at the beginning of his career, famously calculated a static universe through a so-called "cosmological constant" that was connected to a countergravity force.

Yet even though Einstein abandoned this theory after the discovery by Edwin Hubble that remote galaxies are speeding away from the center of an expanding universe, it was later proven that Einstein was not at all incorrect in his calculations.

The moments before the universe allegedly began its existence are shrouded; hence, scientists prefer to devote their attention to that moment when the universe began its initial entry into space and time. Today the term *Big Bang* is used to describe the beginning of the universe from the moment when it erupted, according to a theory, from a tiny, dense, hot point to continuous expansion. The observations of the cosmic microwave background radiation, the fleeing galaxies accompanied by the redshift, the uniformity and homogeneity of the enormous universe, all advanced the acceptance of this theory tremendously.

Scientists eventually accepted the idea of a sudden explosion, a singular tiny point developing into a quickly expanding universe. Never mind that such an approach contradicted one of the main laws of physics that "out of nothing comes nothing." There were a number of recognized events that coincided with the Big Bang theory, and that, from time to time, arose to provide yet another piece of evidence.

Still there were quite a few unexplainable details. Scientists would either set them aside, pending further understanding, or point them out as possible errors in observation or logic. Among those details were the following:

After approximately nine billion years of speeding up and then slowing down, why would the universe pick up its pace again?

Why are the farthest galaxies speeding even faster than those closer to us?

What produced a cosmic microwave background spread evenly throughout the vastness of the universe?

How was an equal temperature achieved in different parts of the universe when those parts have not come into contact since the initial event?

There are many more questions like these, and recording them would be justifiable if I were writing a book devoted to cosmology. But I am not; this is a philosophical work, not a physics treatise. I will, however, tackle a few more questions that seem to me to be important in context with the theme of this book.

First, I'd like to briefly consider the pivotal references upon which the Big Bang theory is based. There are actually three models of that theory:

- an open, infinite universe,
- a closed and finite universe,
- a closed and finite universe that expands forever and that is in a quasistatic phase.

While not dismissing the third option completely, let me focus on the first two models.

An open, infinite universe is consistent with the Big Bang and expands forever. By definition, it implies the existence of an unknown, without predictable limits, an adaptable medium that has to be present in some form or another in order to carry such an expansion. This universe must have originated in a singularity. Such implication would require not only the emergence of this ridiculously tiny and dense unit of matter from nowhere, but also the presence of a medium in which it could grow.

Given all of this, along with the heat and force necessary to a sudden explosion, a rapidly expanding universe seems quite speculative to me. This model suggests that the universe was immediately filled homogeneously and isotropically (meaning uniform in all directions) with interstellar dust that turned into stars and galaxies during this rapid expansion. Then the universe began to rapidly cool down, dropping its temperature on a scale of thousands of degrees Kelvin.

Such a picture of expanding space filled with galaxies is quite often compared with some kind of a crumpled fabric or a baking loaf of bread filled with raisins. Not only must the space in such a model provide a firm platform on which massive objects are placed, this platform also must be able to move with everything in it while it sits in turn in yet another unidentifiable medium.

Another process offered by the scientists was that, at the time protons and neutrons were created, the ratio of matter to antimatter somehow shifted toward matter. A process known as *baryogenesis* brought a victory for matter and eventually allowed life to exist. While this imbalance resulted in more matter than antimatter, the protons that were not annihilated could have combined with neutrons to form heavy hydrogen and helium nuclei in a process called a Big Bang *nucleosynthesis*.

Why matter has won this battle of dominance so far remains unanswered, but the search for that answer is continuous and has given rise to the suspicion that some remote structures in space might in fact be composed of antimatter. This scenario offers expectations of a spectacular explosion that might occur in the future when matter collides with antimatter and the universe will finally be annihilated.

Now let me get back to the popularly accepted suggestion that the universe began from a single point, less than a proton in size, which suddenly exploded from a very hot and dense state.

I don't pretend to be a scientist, but let me express some concerns about this model. We have a tiny dense point that appeared from nowhere, reached an unimaginably hot temperature for no obvious reason, and then exploded—again, for no obvious reason.

This begs a number of questions:

- How could such a tiny structure produce an explosion of such unprecedented magnitude?
- What power did this point, no matter how big or small at the time, possess?
- Even if one might imagine such an event, what were the chances that this singularity would turn such immense, chaotic power into a programmed, systematic process in order to produce the galaxies, the stars, and the planets, and connect all of them by observable laws?
- What forces might be in play that gave the universe this overall homogeneity and an even temperature?

—

- And, of course, what possibly could have produced this miraculous invisible dot filled with the myriad treasures that blossomed into stars, galaxies, and life?

One answer offered today by theoretical physicists lies in the idea that the early universe was present in a magical material called a *false vacuum*. False vacuum theoretically possesses a high-energy force that is unstable and can be hidden in an unimaginably tiny, dense particle. After a fraction of a second, it turned into a *true vacuum*, which is the medium in which we live.

True vacuum, according to a contemporary theory of particle physics, is a substance that possesses energy. It may also possess a variety of different states. The forces acting in one such state are the *strong nuclear force*, the *electromagnetic force*, and the *weak force*, those forces needed for life to be present. After a false vacuum decays into a true vacuum, its excess is theorized to produce a fireball of energy that possesses a *strong repulsive gravitational force*.

Einstein constructed his model of a static universe using this repulsive force to balance the gravitational pull of ordinary matter. His theory explained the cycles of an expanding-contracting universe.

In 1980, Alan Guth introduced a theory of the *inflationary universe*. His idea was that a hypothetical, super dense chunk of some unknown material magically manifested itself (but where?) filled with a repulsive force so strong that it began to expand. This repulsive force possessed a strange quality: its total mass would remain proportional to the volume it occupied. Thus, the faster this chunk expanded, the greater its mass and the stronger its repulsive force would become. In fact, it possessed such a strong force that it pushed or pulled the early universe until it blew up.

This unusual expansion Guth called *inflation*, and with this explanation, a new theory walked into the field of physics: *quantum gravity*.

Guth's theory covered such questions as: Why does the universe appear to be flat, what makes it homogeneous, and why it is generally isotropic (identical in all directions)? The inflation theory was supposed to solve the problems inherent in the sudden explosion of a singularity. It referred to an exponential expansion of the universe, driven by the negative pressure of a false vacuum with a density that was three times stronger than the pressure of a true vacuum. Inflation also had to explain the origin of the large structures in the cosmos.

Now this inflationary universe theoretically should have ended fairly soon in the scheme of things. In order to normalize the situation, Guth suggested that repulsive gravity was unstable. While initially producing conditions described as a Big Bang or a hot fireball, the elementary particles flowing within it would now become normal matter. Correspondingly, its gravity also transformed into an *attractive force*.

The only problem was that the theory did not completely work; it had holes in its processes.

The speed at which the false vacuum turns into a true vacuum is so fast that inflation would have ended before the universe became homogeneous and isotropic.

From where did this false vacuum come?

All this reminded me of speculation in a science-fiction novel, and yet, surprisingly, it was broadly accepted by the scientific world.

Einstein contributed much to this body of thought; he first made an assumption that matter is uniformly spread throughout the universe. That is how definitions of homogeneity and isotropy on a large scale came to exist. From this followed the idea that our earth has no special location in the universe.

In his further assumptions, Einstein concluded that the universe is static. What he needed now was some kind of mathematical equation that applied to a theory of general relativity. But here was a stumbling block: the distribution of matter in the universe was not static; it possessed an attractive force. Something else was needed if his theory about the uniformity of matter was the correct one.

Einstein realized that, without violating physical laws, a medium with nonzero energy and tension was needed. He theorized that this constant energy might have existed in a vacuum. But vacuum is empty space. Einstein was the first scientist to introduce the idea that this empty medium has energy. Since then, physicists have determined that we live in the lowest-energy true vacuum. This energy is considered positive energy, and it is stable compared to a false vacuum, which is not. Because a false vacuum is unstable, it eventually decays. Before the universe began to evolve, this high-energy false vacuum produced a hot fireball from the subatomic particles, about which Guth wrote.

—

You may have anticipated my next question: From where did these subatomic particles come? They are predicted by many particle physicists because the roil of primordial vacuum needed subatomic particles in an instant, yet they have never actually been observed.

In any event, to state that the universe began in an almost inconceivably short time, 10-43 seconds, and yet already consisted of photons in thermal equilibrium, governed by fundamental laws dictating their behavior, and providing dominance of matter over antimatter, seems to me to be quite speculative. The formation of elements that would help define an orderly functioning universe in such a brief moment is, to me, more a fairy tale than a rational explanation of the beginning of the universe.

Moreover, one more important question remained to be answered: What kind of cosmic blast had to occur that would send myriad particles flying outward for an unimaginably long time (at least 13.7 billion years), only to slow down after an estimated nine billion years before speeding up again?

No empirical explanation currently exists of a mechanism within or beyond the expanding universe that could first slow its expansion and then speed it up again.

DARK MATTER AND DARK ENERGY

To explain the above-mentioned phenomenon, modern-day scientists introduced the concepts of *dark matter* and *dark energy*, inferring their existence from the discovery of gravitational fields. Gravitation was scientifically proven by Italian scientist Galileo Galilei in his experiments on falling objects. Sir Isaac Newton addressed gravitation in the inverse-square law, and Albert Einstein demonstrated it through his theory of general relativity. And yet gravity is still an unsolved phenomenon. It is one of the main laws governing everything material in the universe; it is also the most widely recognized one because everyone and everything on our planet experiences it.

The simplest way to describe gravity is that it is the attraction of the earth. No matter how much effort is applied, we will always fall back to earth unless some device, such as a rocket, assists us in overcoming that earthly attraction.

This attraction, or gravitational force, might also be expected between any two planets, stars, galaxies, and so on. However, because its force is proportional to the *mass* of the bodies involved and their distance from each other, it might or might not be noticed. Even the tiniest structures can be supposed to have some gravitational pull.

Using different techniques—including the test known as *gravitational lensing*—scientists came to the conclusion that there is much more gravity present in galaxies and star clusters than their measurable masses should produce. This, scientists concluded, implied the presence of an invisible force or mass that does not come from visible ordinary matter but had to come from something else. Scientists named this something else *dark matter*.

The first to propose the concept of dark matter was an American astrophysicist Fritz Zwicky. This event took a place in 1930. Since that time, many new theories have been developed and applied to show that dark matter indeed exists, but so far, no convincing evidence has been offered to explain its properties or origins. Part of such difficulty comes, of course, from the inability to detect dark matter directly.

Another stumbling block arises from the possibility that dark matter has been deduced wrongly; scientists have proposed a "weakly interacting massive particle" (WIMP) as the main constituent of dark matter, but this particle, like the dark matter, could not be detected.

The same problem exists in relation to the cause of gravitational forces; scientists are looking for evidence of another theoretical particle they cannot detect but have already named: the *graviton*.

When Edwin Hubble established in 1929 that the universe was expanding, it was also discovered that this expansion was speeding up instead of slowing down as might be expected. Because such behavior could not be explained by the influence of either ordinary or dark matter, a new explanation was proffered: *dark energy*. This concept, like dark matter before it, was an acknowledgement by scientists that neither of the prior phenomena could be explained.

The nature of dark energy is as hypothetical as its existence. Not only is it theorized to be smooth and constant in the expanding universe, but it does not accumulate. It is further posited to represent

70 percent of the energy density of the universe and to be causing its accelerated expansion.

Meanwhile, dark matter provides the gravitational force that keeps galaxies and clusters together, allowing life to exist. Despite the fact that the reality of these two entities cannot be verified, scientists hypothesize that they represent up to 95 percent of all the existing substance of the universe and are considered the main forces influencing its behavior.

Does this open the door to God's involvement?

It is accepted by most physicists that there is a black hole at the center of each galaxy in the universe, including our own. This is the point around which the galaxy revolves. Physicists now theorize that the pull of dark energy (sometimes called *quintessence*) might actually be caused by massive black holes situated at the edges of the universe and that they are getting more massive with time. Such fields—if indeed they exist—will be responsible for indefinitely expanding and contracting the universe. That would mean that the universe continuously cycles from Big Bang to Big Bang over the eons while we go along for the ride, trying to determine when it started but not knowing when it will end. Interestingly, an ancient religious treatise offers a brief description of this idea:

> *The vast day of Brahma, the Lord of Creation, ever lasts a thousand ages; and . . . his night lasts a thousand ages . . . When that day comes, all the visible creation arises from the Invisible; and all creation disappears into the Invisible when the night of darkness comes.* (Bhagavad Gita 8:17-18)

On February 5, 2008, an article appeared on the science blog The Daily Galaxy—Great Discoveries Channel titled "Is Dark Matter and Dark Energy the Same Thing?" In it, British astrophysicist Dr. Hong Sheng Zhao discussed the idea that "dark matter and dark energy could be two faces of the same coin." Zhao offered the idea that these phenomena may act in different ways though they are a manifestation of the same force.

Another article, published on April 9, 2010, by science writer Ker Than for *National Geographic News*, said,

Our universe may be nested inside a black hole that is itself part of a larger universe . . . According to a mind-bending new theory, a black hole is actually a tunnel between universes—a type of wormhole. The matter the black hole attracts doesn't collapse into a single point, as has been predicted, but rather gushes out a "white hole" at the other end of the black one, the theory goes. (Than, 2010)

Of course, this "new" idea won't bend the minds of anyone who reads much science fiction, in which it's a much-explored subject. Nonetheless, physicist Nikodem Poplawski, who offered this theory in a recent paper published in the journal *Physics Letters*, presented the mathematical equations from which it followed that the matter black holes destroy is, in fact, *not* destroyed but simply absorbed to become the future building material for stars and the rest of matter. According to his theory, black holes play the role of a tunnel connecting the old universe to the new one. This solves the problems inherent in the theory that the universe began as a singularity. It would explain the origin of gamma ray bursts as well as the Big Bang singularity. As Poplawski explains:

Gamma ray bursts may be discharges of matter from alternative universes. The matter might be escaping into our Universe through supermassive black holes, or "wormholes," at the hearts of those galaxies, though it is not clear how that would be possible.

In another article in the same online journal on March 22, 2010, by science writer John Roach, titled "New Proof Unknown 'Structures' Tug at Our Universe," the author writes that there are:

[Unknown, unseen 'structures' lurking on the outskirts of creation . . . . Scientists reported the discovery of hundreds of galaxy clusters streaming in the same direction at more than 2.2 million miles . . . an hour . . . . The researchers made the controversial suggestion that the clusters are being tugged on by the gravity of matter outside the known universe.

A few more theories are being discussed among astronomers and astrophysicists, two of which I wish to mention briefly here. One is the Omega Point theory offered by Tulane University professor of mathematics Frank J. Tipler, who suggested that the universe would come to an end in a Big Crunch. While Tipler possesses a powerful ability to combine invocations of God with a sophisticated imagination and no-less-sophisticated mathematics and computer science skills, to me his hypothesis would seem the most truthful if he had not resorted to so much fantasy to produce it.

Another recent theory offered by cosmologists Paul Steinhardt and Neil Turok was based upon colliding three-dimensional worlds that would produce a new combined universe. This would explain such events as the release of tremendous energy leading to an acceleration of the universe, the so-far unaccounted-for temperature at its dawn, the redshift of galaxies moving away from us, the cosmological microwave background, isotropy, and the spread of cooler cosmic temperatures. But based on simple arithmetic, it becomes unsustainable because a collision of two worlds would mean that another two must be produced for the collision process to be repeated. This would seem to be impossible, as such processes will eventually bring us to zero available universes.

CHAPTER 14

Unidentified Massive
Objects (UMOB)

I'd like to offer here an alternative theory that our present universe might stem from the previously collapsed universe. My assumption is that it should happen due to a massive gravitational pull provided by ordinary matter of previous universe.

Let me elaborate on this.

Imagine a firework set off during a Fourth of July celebration. Its sparks, after the initial shot, would first spread over a visible part of sky and then fall more or less evenly toward the ground in a shape that might remind to an observer either a dome or a vault. The reason these sparks will fall downward is, of course, due to the gravitational pull of our planet.

In the case of the death of the universe, the reason the galaxies and the rest of the star matter will also eventually fall might be due to the gravitational pull of some unknown mass or masses that might accumulate somewhere beneath or around our universe. In other words, the galaxies, its stars and particles, as well as interstellar dust, all eventually will start to give in, providing such a powerful gravitational pull will exist. Now whatever will fall will not assume an indefinite free fall but it will "land" on that original mass, adding to its bulk more and more. Such falling will accumulate at different places, where they were pulled by that mass, creating what I call *unidentified massive objects* (UMOBs). I call them unidentified for the reason that nobody had seen them, and till now they are not even hypothetically present. While spreading around the existing universe in unknown numbers, these massive objects would possess huge gravitational forces. The closer galaxies and other structures approach any UMOB, the faster they will fall toward it. Thus they will gradually produce even more massive balls of matter along with increasing gravitational pull.

In time, these giant balls will become so massive that, in addition to their gravitational force, they begin manifest different qualities. These will depend on the quantity of shattered stars, interstellar dust, protons, neutrons, and so forth that they have collected. This accretion will lead to a powerful dynamic mass, which will become a natural trap in which all the parts of the universe will eventually end up.

When we say that the universe is expanding, that means a little more than just imagining its elasticity. The stars, galaxies, and planets all individually experience gravitational and electromagnetic forces that keep them together without producing any change in their masses. Now try to imagine what would they experience if there were also gravitational forces tugging at them from the UMOB? If these UMOBs are massive enough—exceeding ten billion solar masses, for example—they will powerfully attract stars and galaxies, producing even greater gravitational force than found in normal matter.

This begs the question: Is it possible that UMOBs might be that culprit that scientists mention when speak of an enigmatic dark matter?

What if these UMOBs indeed exist? Could they act the way I just described?

Could they assume even more tasks than just organizing the tremendous pull? Let's give them some additional activity, shall we?

The growing balls of materials may become the participants in a new mechanism—possibly creating yet another universe. Of course, not all the remnants of a Big Crunch will contribute to the cycle of cosmic rebirth. Some will remain in that junkyard I call UMOB. A powerful interaction among those remnants might likely become a source of another mysterious gravitational force now called dark energy. Even though the remnants will act as an attractive force, they will also act as a repulsive force, which actually will depend on their location.

–

It is quite easy to become confused by these separate yet unified forces influencing our perception of events. How is it possible for one force to play two different roles simultaneously, one attractive, the other repulsive? It may be possible under certain conditions.

Let me see if I can explain.

Dark energy is said to be a repulsive force, while dark matter generates an attractive force. While we shouldn't confuse the two forces, we might say that though they represent one and the same force in regard to their source, yet their physical location alone could determine whether they act with the attractive force of dark matter or the repulsive force of dark energy.

In this theory, the falling matter of the universe would be explained by classical gravitation and not by the enigmatic dark matter of dark energy. The only difference between dark energy and dark matter would be that the gravitational force found *inside* the galaxies would be intensified by dark matter, while the force arising from the UMOBs *outside* the galaxies would be considered dark energy.

Hence, the gravitational force that in some cases is called dark energy and which plays the role of a repulsive force comes from UMOBs located somewhere closer to ordinary matter, thus adding more power to an ordinary gravitational force. In other words, two forces (attractive and repulsive) actually represent the same gravitational force.

Theories of cosmic development have generated further mysteries. For example, the flatness of the universe might be easily explained by use of a simple analogy. Imagine you are standing mere inches away from a huge mural, staring directly at one spot on it. From your vantage point, no amount of eye rolling will allow you to see the big picture. It is impossible to fully appreciate its shape while in close proximity.

This phenomenon is persuasively illustrated by the fact that we once thought our planet was flat. The Doppler effect made no sense until we understood what we were looking for. Now that effect tells us about the movement of bodies in the galaxy and even the movement of objects outside of our galaxy. This movement allows us to explain why nearby galaxies, such as the Andromeda Galaxy, have a prevailing blueshift rather than a redshift because we are falling toward a common central point (the *barycenter*).

—

The Big Bang/Big Crunch model was originally considered and dismissed in the nineteenth century because the accumulated entropy would not only cause the debris of broken cosmic parts to amass but also produce shorter and shorter cycles of death and rebirth until such repetition would no longer be possible. Even if such an explanation were valid, nobody insisted that this process must last forever.

However, it might have started a theory of continuously repeated cycles that each time lead to a big collapse and a Big Bang sounds quite plausible to me. The idea that this process might go on forever, from a human point of view (with a nod to existing controversy), seems to me the most reflective of the cyclical events' sequence.

While I agree with the model describing a Big Bang scenario that undergoes a cycle, I do not accept that a Big Crunch must need violently end the universe. To explain further, let us consider a black hole. It is known that the neutron star caused by the collapsed core of a massive star possesses an immensely strong gravitational field. It can hold a *degeneracy pressure* of up to five solar masses before it collapses even further to form a black hole.

So let us consider a scenario: that a black hole found in the cosmic junkyard might play a role as the final destination of falling stars.

Stars would continue to collect around such a black hole until no more stars were left in space, thus ending the universe, correct?

Well, we don't know that for sure. We also cannot say with certainty that a black hole might not produce a passage for escaping mass, as some scientists have begun to hypothesize. The bigger question here is whether a black hole could absorb enough material to become the source of a Big Bang and thus be a starting point for the next cycle. To this, we cannot give a definite yes or no answer. But if we assume that UMOBs have been produced for some period of time and that, after swallowing all possible galaxies, would then become super massive black holes, these black holes will not only produce a super gravitational field, they might eventually start to evaporate into a plasma of electrons, positrons, protons, neutrons, and so forth. These particles might gather on the other side of a black hole through a gateway usually referred to as a wormhole.

Now would these particles be enough material to initiate a new Big Bang and begin a new cycle? One cannot answer that with certainty. But the birth of a new universe might be the result of the death of

–

an existing universe with the consequent production of a gateway (wormhole) leading to a new universal cycle in an adjacent universe.

This theoretical model might very well answer a number of previously unsolved problems as follows:

- UMOBs—multiple sources of giant gravitational fields spread almost evenly throughout space would likely provide evenness of temperature.
- Similarly, the universe would display homogeneity through a mechanism of equally spread quarks and electrons throughout inflated space.
- Interstellar dust particles would gravitate toward each other, therefore developing new stars and galaxies.
- Cosmic microwave background (CMB) radiation will be equally spread throughout space as photons will be produced and evenly scattered around the UMOBs.
- The nature of redshift and blueshift was explained previously as a phenomenon of an accelerating universe, which contributes to the model of a cyclic universe.
- This cyclic model, in my mind, is not only the most logical but also rationally more acceptable without resorting to miracles and impossibilities.

PRIMEVAL EXPLOSION AND OTHER THEORIES

Now let us consider some other explanations offered by various scientists over the years.

In his book *Epic of Evolution*, Eric J. Chaisson states:

> *The entire pattern of distant objects receding more rapidly than nearby ones implies that an "explosion" must have occurred at some time in the past . . . . The galaxies are simply the debris of a primeval "explosion," a cosmic bomb whose die was cast long ago.* (9)

Chaisson explains that he places the word explosion in quotation marks for one reason: "The word *explosion* is in quotes because,

—

technically, most astronomers don't like that description" (9). He further proceeds to explain that the word *bang* does not mean a literal explosion and "that the primordial matter did not actually explode into any already existing space" nor did any galaxies rush into the "empty space" beyond (10).

In *A Briefer History of Time*, physicist Stephen Hawking concisely describes this event as such:

> *In Friedmann's first model of the Universe, the fourth dimension, time—like space—is finite in extent. It is like a line with two ends, or boundaries. So time has an end, and it also has a beginning. In fact, all solutions to Einstein's equations in which the Universe contains the amount of matter we observe share one very important feature: at some time in the past (about 13.7 billion years ago), the distance between neighboring galaxies must have been zero. In other words, the entire Universe was squashed into a single point with zero size, like a sphere of radius zero. At that time, the density of the Universe and the curvature of space-time would have been infinite. It is the time that we call the big bang.* (Hawking, 68)

I find this an eloquent and physically prudent explanation of the events that happened 13.7 billion years ago.

According to conservation law, energy, no matter how weak or powerful it might be, cannot begin from nothing. Yet this is exactly what scientists are trying to justify when theorizing that the universe stemmed from a tiny point that turned into billions of galaxies. If the energy used could not be either created or preserved because nothing existed yet, then the assumption that a hot initial-state singularity somehow began to expand is presumptuous. Not only did it mysteriously acquire the tremendous power necessary to produce something so unimaginably vast, it also presumably began its expansion from a similarly unimaginably hot and dense singularity. How that singularity produced such a temperature is conveniently avoided.

Another weak point of this theory, as I mentioned before, is the medium in which this singularity must be placed. That invisible point must have existed in some framework. So what we are left with is stars and planets falling into a black hole that acts as a tunnel connecting an existing, disintegrating universe with a newly organized one.

CHAPTER 15

The Strange Laws of Physics

Now, leaving further consideration of these ideas to astronomers and astrophysicists, let me turn to a discussion of the possible existence of a theory of everything (TOE), also referred to as a Grand Unified Theory (GUT).

Let me start from the facts presented by science. We can separate our discussion into three distinct levels. At the first, we need to consider the physical macroscopic universe. At the second, we may define our conversation as based on microscopic structures. At the third level, we may refer to quantum mechanics with its reciprocal dependency between classical and quantum physics.

Before we begin a discussion on any of these levels, let me emphasize that in spite of considering these realms separately, no matter which part of the universe is being extrapolated, all the cosmic ingredients are the result of adding together protons, neutrons, and electrons.

On the macroscopic level, there is the cosmos, or universe, or existing space; the three terms have the same meaning with a few tiny differences. The first two terms are almost identical and imply an orderly, harmonious system from which the Newtonian (classical) laws were drawn. The third term, *space*, is generally used to describe the expanse that contains stars, galaxies, and other structures.

All in all, we would not be grossly mistaken to describe the laws of physics as unexpectedly connected and stable.

Today there are two types of physics: classical, founded by Isaac Newton, and quantum or particle physics, the most familiar representative of which is Albert Einstein.

The widely known laws of classical physics are the law of gravity, the laws of motion, the three laws of thermodynamics, and the laws of electromagnetism. In quantum mechanics (another term for quantum physics), special and general relativity were the first important steps in informing the world that not all phenomena are straightforward and obvious. I don't intend to discuss all these laws in detail, but in my mind, each intelligent person interested in how the world functions should familiarize themselves with them.

All of these were not only somehow set in motion by an unidentified force or forces, but all are connected, function in a visibly directed manner, and manage all the occurrences in the universe. Their presence is a strange phenomenon; their origin cannot be traced to its source. In the meantime, the best thing humanity can do is to recognize these laws and try to explain them, to reverse engineer them logically, working backward from their effects toward their origin.

The recognition of existing laws began with the Polish theologian and astronomer Nicolaus Copernicus. Copernicus challenged the hypothesis of Ptolemy of Alexandria, the Egyptian-born Greek astronomer who offered a model that the earth is the center of the universe around which all other planets and stars were moving. From this heliocentric model, it followed that the earth and its companions orbited the sun.

Later, the Danish astronomer Johannes Kepler came to the conclusion that planets orbit in an elliptical motion. Italian scientist Galileo Galilei, who pioneered the use of the telescope, observed many imperfections in the structures of the universe and located four major moons of Jupiter, opened a road to more questions and subsequent discoveries.

Then Sir Isaac Newton came along with his laws of motion. Within two years—1665 to 1666 CE—Newton changed the face of physics through a stroke of inspiration and a series of experiments that resulted in his laws of motion. The main law (of mutual attraction), concerning any two objects of mass, was discovered by Newton via the famous accidental observation of an apple falling from a tree.

Gravitation, as it was named, is a phenomenon that is present in any object as an attractive force. The other three laws of motion were defined by the concept of force that causes mass to accelerate.

One of the important conclusions Newton's laws of forces and motions brought to the scientific world was that the universe was an orderly place. The next waves of laws dealt with energy and defining the mechanics of the universe. The laws of thermodynamics were introduced and expressed through the so-called three (sometimes four or even five) laws of thermodynamics.

The first law states that even though energy may change many times, it is always conserved in a closed system. The second law refers to the ability of heat to spontaneously flow to objects with lower temperatures. The third law considers the properties of a system that approaches absolute zero temperature. It states that the conditions under which an absolute zero temperature may be reached are actually impossible to achieve due to numerous processes that will continue indefinitely before the system dissipates.

A necessary element of the laws of thermodynamics is the process scientists call *entropy*. The word is derived from the Greek word *trope* (transform). In physics, entropy is the degree of disorder or randomness in a system and is found by measuring that part of a system that preserves energy unavailable to drive mechanics.

During experiments, beginning with an attempt to create a perpetual motion machine (that is, a machine continuously powered by its own heat), it became clear that such a concept was not possible for a very simple reason: No matter how carefully such a machine was made, some part of its energy would escape the system. This escaping energy contributes to entropy.

Such a conclusion necessarily violates the first law of thermodynamics, the conservation of energy. In other words, according to the first law, the total amount of created energy must be equal to the amount of energy given off as heat. In reality, it was not so. Thus the second law was born, in which the escaped energy would not be available for work needed by the machine system. With energy leaking out, the machine system would deteriorate, no matter how well constructed it was. The system was experiencing entropy.

Entropy is a versatile concept that best can be appreciated on a large scale. It increases as a system becomes more chaotic, and it decreases as system approaches equilibrium; that is, it does not lose energy. Under those circumstances, entropy becomes not only a measure of order or disorder, it also turns into a bridge connecting the first two laws.

To understand this concept, one has only to consider the big picture, in this case, something *really* big: the universe. The universe, no matter what happens in it, is always organized. Physical laws are always maintained despite problems encountered here and there. And in fact, what is debris or waste energy in one process eventually becomes useful material in another, which seems to be a cosmic illustration of the axiom that one man's trash is another man's treasure.

For example, let us take a collapsing star. The star's death, in compliance with the second law of thermodynamics, produces entropy by breaking into subatomic particles. These particles become the material needed to create a new star. Their energy is a necessary component in the application of the first law of thermodynamics. Thus a cycle of two connected laws is obviously in play and in good order. In this context, a perpetual motion concept might work after all, and the life of the universe might last for the unforeseen future.

I am not going to discuss here such phenomena as magnetism and static electricity, which are quite intriguing in their own rights. This book, as I mentioned earlier, is not about popular physics; therefore we will only touch on those subjects and topics that appear to be relevant to our discussion. So let us move to another realm of physics: the physics of an atom and its particles.

Until fairly recently, atoms were considered the smallest component parts of the universe. They are small enough to be invisible to the human eye without special devices. The size of an atom in mathematical language equals 1.0×10^{-10} meters, which is about the same for all atoms. To understand how small this number is, one can imagine a cube one inch on a side. In that, one inch would be approximately one hundred billion atoms.

Yet atoms possess an even smaller nucleus that is composed of protons and neutrons, each possessing different qualities and structures. The number of protons in a nucleus usually equals the numbers of electrons found orbiting them. Scientists often compare an atom to a solar system. The nucleus is the sun, around which electrons orbit like planets. Electrons that are negatively charged are

—

attracted to protons in the nucleus that are positively charged. When the protons and electrons are equal in number, an atom becomes neutral in charge. Neutrons have no charge and therefore do not influence the charge of atoms, but along with protons, neutrons create a powerful gravitational force. Likewise, in the above-mentioned solar system, the sun attracts the planets through its powerful gravitational force.

In both cases, each of the objects (the sun or the nucleus) are clearly defined. Therefore one may conclude that the nucleus should present an independent structure that possesses its own features.

Now try to visualize this: Despite all atoms being the same size, they possess different qualities owing to a different number of protons gathered in the nucleus. All protons are similar in structure. This means protons could be interchangeably placed in the different nuclei of a particular atom, and it would not affect the atom's features, at least theoretically. The only thing that matters is their collective number.

With that knowledge in mind, let us picture the universe globally. All the large structures of the universe follow the classical laws discovered by Newton. All the small particles, starting with protons, neutrons, and electrons, which follow different types of laws, were discovered in the twentieth century. But when these small particles are gathered together to participate in the large structures of which they are necessarily a part, the laws change.

Again, while I am not trying to push the reader to accept my way of thinking, it seems to me that whatever organized these invisible objects had to be goal oriented and had to have not only a vision of how to make these things, but also a purpose in making them, which eventually connected all the dots of all the phenomena existing in the universe. Therefore, despite the attitude of some scientists who believe that God does not exist and who are instead trying to find a theory of everything (TOE) or a Grand Unified Theory (GUT) that might indeed connect all these phenomena, it seems logical that they should acknowledge the possibility that what we call God might be the unified field that is the source of these physical laws.

I am going to conclude this chapter with the statement that many scientific discoveries not only help us to make decisions in our lives, but also ought to make us thankful for the intellectual journey humanity

–

has been privileged to embark upon. Nor should we be rebuked or mocked as profoundly gullible if we express a belief in miracles. Given our present level of knowledge, we must also acknowledge that we are only moderately certain of a meager 5 percent of the universe's contents.

Glossary

Angular Momentum. It is a product of body's rotational inertia and the angular velocity with respect to a related axis of rotation.

Antimatter. A mirror image of matter that has an opposite sign.

Antiparticle. Part of antimatter hypothetically presented by positrons, antiprotons, antineutrons, and so on.

Atom. The smallest part of an element that chemically corresponds to the element it is found in. Each atom consists of nucleus with specific number of protons and neutrons that are "sitting" inside of it and an equal to the number of protons the number of electrons that move around the nucleus.

Attractive Force. A force of attraction, such as gravity; this is the term applied in physics referring to the principle of attraction between all masses in the universe.

Barycenter. In physics, the center point between two objects, where they balance each other according to their masses.

Baryons. These are triplets of quarks.

Baryogenesis. This term is used for a discussion of hypothetical asymmetry between particles and antiparticles, i.e., matter versus antimatter.

Big Crunch. A scientific theory of the possible end of the universe when all existing matter will collapse.

Binary Stars. A star system in which two stars are orbiting around the common center of mass.

Bosons. The carriers of force. Gluons, photons, W, Z, Higgs are all bosons.

Charged Particle. A particle with an electric charge considered a charged particle.

Conjugated Charge. Denoted with the symbol C. A symmetry provided by particle-antiparticle mirror image or transformation.

Cosmic Rays. The term is given to high-energy charged particles that reach the earth from outer space.

Cosmic Microwave Background Radiation (CMBR). Thermal radiation of unknown origin that uniformly fills the observable universe.

CP Violation. The term used in particle physics describing violation of conjugated charge and parity symmetry.

Critical Density of the Universe. It is a condition of the universe that allows it to stay in balance without jeopardizing its eventual demise.

Dark Matter. A hypothetical matter that is characterized by unexplained gravitational effects on ordinary matter. In cosmology, dark matter that makes roughly 25 percent of the universe is unknown and invisible type of matter that hypothetically accounts for a large part of a total mass of the universe.

Dark Energy. A hypothetical form of energy that plays a role in accelerating the universe through a gravitational repulsive force that permeates all of space.

Degeneracy Pressure. A specific condition found in white dwarf stars, with the pressure set in motion by fermions, such as electrons, keeping cold stars, such as the white dwarf, from collapsing.

Electron. Often considered a subatomic particle that has negative charge.

Electromagnetic Force. Comes as the product of two combined fields—electric and magnetic—that together are responsible for the attractive and repulsive force as well as chemical reactions and different atomic structures and all other electromagnetic phenomena.

Element. Naturally occurring substance that cannot be reduced to any other simpler substance. There are ninety-two naturally encountered elements such as oxygen, hydrogen, etc.

Elementary Particles. The fundamental particles such as electron, proton, and neutron, out of which atoms, elements, and matter are composed.

Fermions. Particles of matter that, according to the Standard Model, have a half-integer spin. Protons, neutrons, leptons, and quarks are all fermions.

Galaxy. Cosmic system that combines billions of stars, cosmic dust, and black holes held together by a mutual gravity.

General Relativity. Refers to the laws of gravity according to which the more massive a body is, the more gravitational attraction it possesses, along with bending the space in which an object travels. The usual example would be our sun that, due to its mass, warps space around itself.

Gluons. The elementary subatomic particles that mediate the strong nuclear force that explains how protons and neutrons are kept together in the atomic nucleus.

Gravitational Lensing. The term applied in the reference to the way of distribution of matter that is far away from earth. A deflection of light that occurs between a very distant bright object found in space and the observer that spots this distorted image.

Hadrons. The collective name for the particles that are baryons and mesons.

Higgs Boson. A hypothetical elementary particle predicted by the Standard Model of particle physics. Named in honor of an English theoretical physicist as in recognition of his many outstanding works, it had been nicknamed originally by Leon Lederman as the result of Lederman's publishing censoring. Peter Higgs, a physicist who came up with hypothesizing of existing elusive particles back in 1960, did not call them as Higgs boson, but reluctantly (not wishing to offend religious people) as "God particle."

Isotropy. This term is applied to describe the universe that is uniform in all directions.

Leptons. The particles that do not have strong interaction and either charged—like electrons—or have no charge—like neutrinos

Matter. Ordinarily defined as the material substance that is found in the universe and that has a mass and volume.

Meson. Particle that consists of two quarks.

Muon. An elementary particle that has mass in the range of two hundred times that of an electron. It belongs to leptons, and therefore has no strong interaction. It has either a negative charge or no charge as in the case of muon neutrino.

Neutron. Subatomic particle that is neutral (has no charge) and that is found as a part of a nucleus of an atom.

Neutrino. Weakly interacting particle that possesses unique quality of passing through matter unimpeded.

Pauli Exclusion Principle. In quantum mechanics, this principle is described as that there are no two identical particles with a half-integer spin that may occupy the same quantum state simultaneously.

Particle. A small substance that is a constituent of matter.

Parity. Denoted as P property of a physical system that, under transformation of a fundamental particle, implies a mirror image.

Photon. An elementary particle that has no mass, electrically neutral, and moves as a particle and a wave.

Pion. A particle that is a meson yet less massive than a meson and heavier than an electron.

Positron. An antiparticle for electrons.

Proton. A subatomic particle that is positively charged.

Quantum. Unit of measurement applied to quantize, for instance, the amount of energy in electromagnetic waves.

Quantum Gravity. The speculative field of theoretical physics which attempts to develop a scientific model that will unify both quantum mechanics and the principles of general relativity.

Quantum Mechanics. The field of physics that considers behavior of matter at the level of subatomic particles.

Quantum Physics. A branch of science based on quantum theory, holding that energy is not continuous but comes in small discrete units called quanta that behave both like particles and like waves.

Quarks. Elementary particles of a nucleus that always bind together by a strong force.

Quintessence. A hypothetical force existing to define dark energy.

Rest Mass. Also **Invariant Mass**. Mass that is characterized by the total energy and momentum of an object that is, at zero speed, relative to an observer.

Special Relativity. The revolutionary insight that the flow of time in the universe differs depending on one's reference frame. In other words, with the same basic laws in the universe, there are different realities that simultaneously coexist.

—

Space-Time. Four-dimensional entity that results from unified combination of space and time.

Spin. An intrinsic motion of particles considered in quantum mechanics.

Standard Model. A theory describing interactions of subatomic particles.

String Theory. A term that is used in particle physics referring to the smallest particles of elements that are theorized to exist in tiny invisible loops that can break into open strings.

Strong Nuclear Force. The strongest of the four basic forces that are present in nature (the other three are gravity, electromagnetic force, and the weak nuclear force). It is also the shortest in its range and acts in atoms by the way of gluons, which hold together quarks, believed to be the smallest particles of the nucleus.

Strong Repulsive Gravitational Force. The hypothesis that antigravity may exist and act contrary to the forces of gravity.

Symmetry. Invariance in physical system that is preserved despite its transformation.

Weak Force. One of the four basic forces and the foundation of some forms of radioactivity, playing a role in the decay of unstable subatomic particles. It has very short range and one quintillion times weaker than strong nuclear force.

WIMPs. Weakly interacting massive particles—hypothetical particles that might constitute dark matter.

Wormhole. A hypothetical "tunnel" connecting two different points in space and time.

AFTERWORD
AND
GENERAL CONCLUSION

If one were to summarize the information collected in the first part of this book, one might conclude that it was mainly devoted to the questions of our origin and purpose: What brought us to earth? Do we owe our presence to chance, to intelligent design, or to some unknown combination of inorganic substances that proceeded with *self-replication* and finally produced us? Those are all legitimate questions, but they are bound by strict limitations. Thus, to this end, scientists seem to answer—almost in one voice—that there is no need (read *impossible*) to explain what happened before the universe came into existence. Our knowledge begins and ends at the horizon, a situation we must accept as we attempt to decipher what happens "on this side" rather than to dwell on some unknown place "over there." There is, though, a new tendency to speculate beyond this realm, specifically if one considers the recent variations of Big Bang theory or the origin of the universe from nothing. There is also an assumption of the presence of *multiverse* that comprises the various universes, including our universe. But these are hypotheses that yet to be proven and, so far, are more on speculative side than anything else.

Theologians, on the other hand, interpret for us the teachings of God by whichever means they find appealing. Thus, we have learned that God is omniscient, omnipotent, and, according to most faiths,

—
277

loving uncreated almighty power. According to those same beliefs, there is no other way, as the case seems to be, in order to win the love of God; people of any society and epoch must realize that there are those who are with the believers and those who are recognized enemies. No matter how much love God is capable of, he does not feel as to love everybody equally. He even reassures people that in order to survive, people must distinguish who their enemies are. So much love coming from God. And absolutely reasonable question must be, why must God love his creation, good or bad? Or perhaps we only imagine he does. Many human beings believe that we are the only sentient creatures in the universe. Can that be true? What if that was true? Does that increase our significance in the universe? Would that somehow explain what God had "in mind" when he decided to create us? Moreover, did he make us with a specific goal he wanted us to pursue? Did he make us imperfect on purpose so we may preoccupy ourselves by trying to improve our deeds and our lot for the most of the length of our lives? Did he really plan to make us eternal? Did he envision what sort of finished product we will become? And if he didn't, would that remove his qualification as being omniscient? Or will that make him more as scientist than anything else? I say that because that will explain many things. Such as that as scientist, God had to conduct experiments with us humans, as well as with animals, birds, flora, and atmosphere. While he envisioned what he wanted to create, he might have needed to see what will become of us. And being a "live body," we had to go through evolution, expecting or not God to intervene from time to time, which he didn't have to. And if that was the case, wouldn't that be justifiable that God didn't get involved in our affairs in order to make some corrections upon humanity that inadvertently skewed toward "the wrong" path while evolving to become eternal?

History teaches us that ancient people while they were preoccupied with inevitable demise differed in comprehension of *death phenomenon* in the sense that we are. Still, the behavior of earth's early *inhabitants* may be easily understood; they were learning how to survive in a rugged environment. They operated by survival instinct supported by observations and experience. Their knowledge about how the world worked was gathered by accident and reflection.

Before religion and doctrine, people had to communicate almost in the same fashion that animals did, struggling for territory, food, and other resources. Language and an appreciation of life and death came much later, and along with them came a desire for immortality.

The spread of people throughout the continents as they sought food and shelter brought about localized ways of thinking and survival tools suited to the immediate environment. The ancients were trying to protect themselves from the unimaginable disasters and events nature would throw at them from time to time. Such developments resulted in many different cultures with different values and comprehensions about life.

If we fast-forward, we may weigh the last five thousand to seven thousand years of recorded history to see what progress—if any—human beings have made. What arose during that time was an established notion that we ought to live much longer than nature had so far allowed. One of the ways that this limitation could have been overcome was through invoking a higher Power—a Power that produced our world and us, gave us the ability to think, and taught us how to be successful and happy.

No wonder early people believed God was a powerful Unknown that could perform all the miracles observed in nature. The Sumerians, the Egyptians, the Hindus, and the Hebrews—all were trying to establish their personal connections with a power that was beyond their capacity to comprehend. But even with these diverse people establishing ties with their god or gods, none could have reached the realm of reality.

For one reason or another, people exaggerate their importance on earth and in the universe, not giving much thought to the fact that our planet is as undistinguishable in the cosmos as a grain of sand is in a dune. Regardless of the fact that contemporary man has learned how to calculate billions of stars or visit our moon and send unmanned vehicles to a few others in our solar system, his ability to influence the universe is about the same as that previously mentioned grain of sand. We are blinded by the fact that our planet seems vast and open to the seemingly infinite skies.

The universe we are surrounded by is not only vast and very little known, but it is also cold and dramatically inanimate despite theologians' referral to spiritualism and pre-determination. In that vastness and uncounted unknowns, the god we have imagined might or might not exist. We are born miraculously. We die miraculously. And between those two phenomena, we live our lives trying to understand the miracles that befallen us. And yet in that picture of wonders, one can easily spot such phenomena as *electro-magnetosphere*, lightning, wild fires, and eruptions of volcanoes to name just a few. Would these protectors of ecosystem and life on earth come incidentally, or are they deeply "thought of" by that same unknown power we cannot figure what it is?

Is that the reason we live in a dream that the Being we call God is appreciative of our existence? What possible role might he have cast us in that would be of use to him? Why in the world would God—among billions of galaxies—need flesh and blood humans to accomplish any serious tasks? Would we be able to collect hydrogen and helium atoms to create another sun? Would our souls? How is it possible for God to be in any form we might imagine? Does he have a brain, so that he might understand us? Can he have human feelings such as love, if he must last forever?

Can anyone answer?

In order to control all these vast cosmic structures functioning interdependently, with all the innumerable details in all the tiniest particles existing in the universe, with cosmic events unmanageable, and often unimaginable, by human beings, how could anyone claim that God is flesh and blood? Could any reasonable person accept a claim that God reduces himself to a bush or a human body and comes to us as Krishna or Jesus and possibly in some other earthly form? How could anyone claim that he or she knows what God is?

We cannot even calculate the limits and vastness of our universe. We aren't even certain there is only one. In a universe reckoned to be at least fourteen billion years old, this planet has only had a human population for the last several million. Did God plan on making humans so much later even as he presided over the birth of the universe?

On the other side of the God-versus-no-God debate, scientists are in no better odds while guessing the question "How did we get here?"

They do not have an answer to what cannot be probed physically or measured by material means. They know that particles do exist but not how or when or where or why they were made. They do not have

–

an answer to what distributed all these ready-to-perform substances and entities across the expanding universe. And they most definitely do not know how to deal with the question: "Who or what has made all this happen?"

So the legitimate question remains: Given that scientists are as much in the dark about the origins of the universe as anyone else, including theologians, does that make evolutionists superior? Are scientists prepared to tell the rest of us how this all came about?

I don't think so. Scientists don't think so either, though there are some people who claim that they do.

At the beginning of this book, I said that no one (including me) has the answer to the question: What is God? I may speculate on the subject (as millions of others have before me), but I cannot escape the idea that we were *made* not to know. Our human capacity, our ways of thinking, whether designed or not, might be incapable of grasping that, even as scriptures old and new suggest.

That God is not what we think or say God is, is obvious. So I suggest we let it go. Let us live our lives without trying to solve this particular puzzle, for our own benefit. Let us consider for what purpose we are here and acknowledge the possibility that we are on a long-term journey with an indefinite destination.

BOOK TWO
HUMAN NATURE

PREFACE

I decided to begin the second part of this book by presenting a new classification system for human beings.

The first attempt of such classification from a medical point of view is credited to the Greek physician Hippocrates (460-370 BCE). Thus a theory of the four major types of *temperament* (the same as *mix* in Latin) was developed. Each temperament—almost never pure, but rather some combination of the four—corresponds to a specific yet different personality type. People were divided into sanguine, melancholic, choleric, and phlegmatic categories, and rarely, if ever, represented one pure type.

Since that time, many physicians, philosophers, psychotherapists, and psychiatrists have contributed to distinguishing people according to their temperaments, psyches, and unconscious minds.

In 1767, Carolus Linnaeus, a Swedish physician and botanist, separated people according to their skin color. Hence descriptions of red Indians, or *Americanus*, yellow Asians, or *Asiaticus*, black Africans, or *Africanus*, and white *Europaeus*, or Europeans, came into existence. Reasoning that there was a connection between skin color and temperament, Linnaeus also attributed to these groups behavioral features expanding to their cultures, religions, and places of origin.

Carl Jung once said:

> *Despite all the psychology we think we possess today, the psyche is still infinitely more obscure to us than the visible surface of the body. The psyche is still a foreign,*

–

almost unexplored country of which we have only indirect knowledge; it is mediated by conscious functions that are subject to almost endless possibilities of deception. (Jung, 74-75)

This particular time at the first half of the last century was marked by many as the dawn of contemporary human knowledge. And yet though much progress has been made in the last seventy to eighty years, we are still in the process of studying humans.

I have devoted well over three decades to some academic but mostly self-study of human psychology. Observing people at different levels of a few societies, I have come to the conclusion that people basically fit a general description, regardless of which society they belong.

While the maturation of an individual might be shaped by education and cultural environment, the origination of the motivations of each individual are the same for everyone. Thus, to understand the thinking process of each person and to follow that person's behavioral expression, some kind of classification system had to be created. The system I have constructed—simple yet not simplistic—has, in my mind, led to a much better understanding of humans' hidden motives and different behavioral shades. With the comprehension that major human attributes are similar in all people, such a classification became feasible.

My classification, like everything else, can be philosophically disputed on many levels. For one, the task I've assumed concerns people, and not the machines. To introduce the gradation of material things—such as, for instance, computers—would be hard enough, but the unavailability of clear physical proof made my task many times more complicated.

In order to convey my point, I would like to bring into this discussion the following example.

When the first people were sent to the moon, this event had a shocking effect on most of us. Our minds, from natural curiosity, excitement, and expectation, went through the stages of pride, to awareness that humans are a capable species, to eagerness at the thought of accomplishing even more breathtaking feats. Still, as shocking as it was, in terms of lifespan, the effect was short lived and eventually it was all but forgotten.

The physical reminder of it came, however, in the formation of groups of people who began to work in that specialized field and who agreed to tenaciously continue their tedious jobs in the space industry, day in and day out, year after year.

If asked to express one's opinion about those people, one would likely say something like those people are mostly a forgotten breed. They are probably doing a routine and regular job, surrounded by boredom. Yet many already are not aware of them.

Indeed, the rest of humanity relatively quickly moved on to other, more exciting fields and busied themselves with tasks no less interesting.

It is also not necessarily true that all those forgotten ones are stuck in boredom, but as long as they are forgotten, our human nature keeps them from being put on a pedestal.

In as small an example as this, one can easily distinguish that there are people whom we call the leaders, and these are in the minority, with the rest of a majority fitting into a category of followers. We could also speak of those who are less concerned about doing something exciting than merely accomplishing their duties and living decent, simple, and fairly satisfying lives. Of course, there is much more to it; behind it all are the human motivations hidden from superficial appreciation. We'll talk about those as we progress in our discussion.

There is yet another, somewhat intermediate way of considering the previous or similar events. When the scientific world discovers something new and unusual, such an announcement usually is taken as true and solid. Despite the fact that we do not possess physical proof of it, we accept it with relative ease.

It is quite the opposite though when one speculates on those things. For one reason or another, we refuse to accept unconditionally what is still unproven by science. In that theoretical period, we find ourselves in curious position: We listen, we doubt, we check the existing sources, we try to bring in our own points and logic, and only after thoroughly weighing the possible facts might we reluctantly come to a general conclusion.

Whether such a conclusion would become reasonable and sound, one can only know after some definite time has passed. But whether it was our lucky guess that we intuitively followed or an unpredictable confluence of circumstances that helped us, most of us would silence the fact that past events, if we could not comprehend them in time, were not at all complicated to understand. Such is our human nature. Such is our brain at work. We do not easily acknowledge that there are things or events we cannot understand at once.

In the attempt to clear it (our nature) further, let us discuss these subjects in a little more detail.

PART ONE

RECOGNIZING THE DIFFERENCE

CHAPTER 1

Mental versus Physical

When Charles Darwin presented his theory of evolution, people immediately fell into two major diametrical camps: those who vehemently began to support it and those who, with no less vigor, disputed its validity.

While there were no clear facts presented, bystanders watched the ensuing struggle between the two camps. The last word, nevertheless, was handed to the general public as a whole package, and humanity accepted it without having a strong opinion on its overall credibility. Not surprisingly, the opposing camps are still battling it out, sometimes enjoying visible success and, from time to time, temporarily obtaining primary recognition.

Since all living things on earth are composed of the same chemicals found everywhere around us, organisms that share a similar taxonomy resemble each other. Scientists have even found a chain that connects us all and theorized from this that we owe our presence to one common ancestor. But do we really expect a dog to ever become a human being through a series of intermediate forms? Dogs are the product of human intervention in nature, and such intervention means that the natural progressive chain of evolution was disrupted.

Here I must remind the reader of the existing *genotype-phenotype* combination distinction, which is drawn on the observable features of an organism (phenotype) and the genetic makeup, which is a particular set of genes (genotype). While the physical properties of an organism

–

are responsible for its survival, it is the inheritance of genes that dictates these physical properties. At the same time, the genotype is not the only factor influencing the phenotype. The climate, environment, and phenotypic plasticity (the ability of an organism to adapt) all contribute to changing the observable features of an organism.

The theory of the gene-centered view of evolution was first suggested in 1966 by the evolutionary biologist George C. Williams, and it has since been adopted as a classical theory. It recognizes that natural selection and evolution together influence all competing genes that play a role in the phenotypic changes.

We also need to understand that we are not frozen species simply accumulating change. While we speak of specific features that were passed down to us, there is often a discernible degree of separation from our biological parents. Our uniqueness is succinctly explained by scientists who show how a process of mutation, followed by adaptation to the environment, gives birth to new species. We undergo many transformations; that process is constantly present in us, but we need to separate our *inherited* features from our *acquired* ones.

To demonstrate this process, I will illuminate a few details in our development. The features that are in our chromosomes, those we call hereditary, bring forth complicated organisms. We are in fact armored with them and trying to learn how to apply them accordingly, especially during the first twenty to thirty years of our lives. We are not simply clones of our parents, getting pushed farther from them by accumulating mutations that necessarily interact with the environment. This is how we become new and complex organisms. We are each a new and complex organism. We become individuals with unique characters, accompanied by the traces of new ways of behavior and thinking.

It is the very reason why siblings from the same parents within an insignificant age gap are so often different from each other.

When a group of teenagers gather at the shore of a fast-moving river and then climb a tree nearby to jump to the other side, not all children are able to perform the task equally well, either physically or mentally. At such a moment, the number-one enemy of these children becomes peer pressure, which is fraught with serious consequences. When not able to say *no*, children take chances that, fortunately in many cases, end without any grave tragedy.

But what in such an episode (besides pure luck) makes any child learn about life, friends, or his own destiny? Does it even become a topic of the day? Is it not true that each individual asks himself a similar set of questions: Can I do it? What if I cannot do it? What will my peers say about me?

I will speak more about "I" and perception of the world through the mind of an individual later on. For now, let me speak on the competitiveness as a trait of living organisms, in particular among humans.

Competitiveness belongs to any live organism, starting with the most primitive entities. In order to survive, all live organisms must compete. Whether it is fighting for a particular place under the sun, getting enough resources for one's own needs, or racing a car on a track, all organisms compete.

The scientific study of the relationship of living organisms to each other and their surroundings is called *ecology*. The competitive exclusion principle formulated by Russian ecologist Georgii Frantsevich Gause states that two species competing for the same resources cannot coexist. Such competition always leads one of the competitors to either go extinct or to find another ecological niche. That way, nature is "allowed" to clear earth from the burden from overpopulation. If nature provided equal conditions for all organisms, and these organisms were equally developed, the competition would undoubtedly lead to the elimination of all species. That in turn would end life as we know it.

Considering the higher kingdoms of species, especially human beings, one may ask: What features must an organism possess in order to compete and win?

While this question plunges into a very sensitive subject, I must carefully present the facts leading to a clear conclusion that will cause no bias yet maintain honesty and truthfulness.

Today, science has proven that genes are the main tool responsible for our ability to compete. Still, they are not acting alone; they are influenced by other genes as well as by the environment. We need to recognize this fact along with the comprehension that the environment is comprised of prenatal, postnatal, biochemical, and social factors. In other words, it is the constant (for the purpose of discussion) combination of these factors that an organism experiences regardless

—

of its positional presence. The features it exhibits are not stagnant but in fact transformable, which is the result that comes from a combination of all three factors: environment, genotype, and phenotype.

Let's now consider the main faculties that human beings must possess in order to compete. One has to include the following: physical strength, the desire to achieve, an ability to strategize, an ability to think in abstract terms, an ability to disengage from pity, endurance, and the desire to be the first or best. This is a schematic detailing of a few principal features required to engage in competition.

We do not usually analyze why we are competing, what makes us want to win, or why do we not want our competitor to win. In some cases, we even allow our imaginable competitor to coexist.

We usually also do not immediately understand why we are riveted by such features as aggressiveness, fear, or envy. But don't they all appear as a result of competitiveness? Isn't this tool of survival, called competition, acting as a basic driver of emotions in a process? Pride, spitefulness, malice—all these and similar features are the result of competition, shaped to maturity by culture and self-control.

I don't know any other way to support these statements but to offer a few small examples from life. Those would be such examples as:

- Not letting someone ahead while standing in line for a rare commodity.
- Not letting someone ahead on a narrow road.
- Competing for things we might not need at all but know they are desirable to someone else.
- Bullying behavior often found among students.
- Laughing when we are the spectators of someone who is hurt while falling or hitting oneself.

These last instances are ample in contemporary television shows such as *America's Funniest Home Videos*, for example.

In that same category is also the paranoid feeling that someone close to us is dead, when we haven't heard from him or her for some period of time, however short.

At this point, I'd like to bring our set of emotions. We can think. We can talk. We possess desires and usually enjoy life. How did it all come to us? How did it happen that we, besides appreciating life, strive for improvements in whichever way it may urge us?

Why we experience all these mentioned emotions come from a complex and subconscious need to survive, to outcompete, to remove any obstacle, and to eliminate any possible hindrance for our success. It often develops into an opposite but still-reflected feature, the fear of being left behind and therefore not being able to compete. Thus humans acquire a sense of haste quite often poorly understood or defined.

It gets even more complicated when we compete with *ourselves*. For example, when you drive a car in traffic, especially in the city, with whom do you compete? Whether it is an imaginable competitor, who is driving slowly in front of you or someone who interferes with your driving on either side, it is always someone who gets on your nerves. The problem with such a scenario is that it is our own *persona* that gets us involved, which, for unexplainable reasons, makes us excited about competing and winning. Never mind that it is our subconscious transformation from human power to a horsepower. Never mind that statistically there are more men (especially young men) who are trying to compete in this unusual way. This phenomenon obviously exists, demonstrating itself differently depending on the driver's intellect or a real success in life.

If one tries to sum up all those above-mentioned qualities that characterize a human, one might conclude that intelligence plays a far greater role than physical fitness. Still, the physical fitness of an individual not only is the basis for many corresponding human qualities, it is also continuously encouraged in contemporary society regardless of the real value of such qualifications. Sports, physical attraction, beauty pageants, all such events are the result of this demand for physical superiority. And, in fact, it starts from appreciation the big things.

On a distinguished and separate platform stands a woman's desire and need to seek physical attraction in man. I will address this issue in the section devoted to the distinguishing features in the thinking processes of male and female counterparts. For now, I simply wish to mention this distinction.

—

While there is no universal agreement on the definition of intelligence, it is a proven fact that there is a gene that influences the behavior of conscious organisms.

In 1999, a scientific article was published by a Princeton molecular biologist, Dr. Joe Z. Tsien, who achieved impressive results by improving memory in genetically engineered mice after manipulating some brain receptors and thus introducing the term an "intelligent" gene. By that time, there had also been conducted intelligence tests, called IQ (intelligence quotient) tests. An IQ test itself, in the climate of today's politically correct society, is a very slippery slope road, yet scientists are still trying to establish its value as a measure.

Such, for instance, was the public statement called *Mainstream Science on Intelligence* issued by a group of academic researchers. Originally appearing on December 13, 1994, this statement came as a response to the misleading and biased reports in the media about the role of intelligence. The statement was an attempt to explain the scientific achievements and breakthroughs in this realm. The group set out twenty-five conclusions of its research. Some of them, though not necessarily in particular order, were as follows:

- Intelligence tests are not culturally biased against American blacks or other native-born English-speaking peoples in the U.S.
- The brain processes underlying intelligence are still little understood.
- Members of all racial-ethnic groups can be found at every IQ level.
- Intelligence is a very general mental capacity.
- IQ is strongly related to many important educational, occupational, economic, and social outcomes.
- Heritability indicates that genetics plays a bigger role than environment in creating IQ differences.
- There is no persuasive evidence that the IQ bell curves for different racial-ethnic groups are converging.
- The bell curve for whites is centered roughly around IQ 100, the bell curve for American blacks roughly around 85, and those for different subgroups of Hispanics roughly midway between those for whites and blacks. The evidence is less

—

definitive for exactly where above IQ 100 the bell curves for Jews and Asians are centered.

The contemporary understanding of heritability is attributed to genetic factors as well as to the environment.

While most scientists today agree that human behavior is the result of a combination of heredity and environment, with the former having an edge, it also must be understood that both human traits producing positive behavior in society and those inducing negative effects are, nevertheless, hereditary.

At this juncture, I'd like to introduce my main reason for human classification. Observing a familiar staircase of evolution, it is not difficult to conclude that people, crowning it generally, combine two distinct but characteristic descriptions: animal and sapient. This combination results in a unique and relatively new creature: the human being. While we have no choice about being animal or sapient, we do have a choice about how we manage both elements.

In light of this, I'd like to break down my classification even further to consider men and women separately.

I will not discuss at any length the original separation of men and women within their visible and defined roles in primitive culture. There is plenty of literature written on the topic with a core description of the physical suppression of women by men and of their separate roles, the former as the provider of food and the maintainer of household obligations and the latter as hunters and masters of the procurement and the means of survival. Suffice it to say that while we as humans are motivated by many characteristic features that in combination produce us, men and women rely from the start on different inherited attributes.

The first half of the last century was characterized by many great achievements, among which psychoanalysis deservedly occupies an honorary place.

Such familiar dignitaries as Sigmund Freud, Carl Jung, J. C. Flugel, Erich Fromm, and others had firmly established themselves as the leading specialists in the field. Among the colleagues of these men, it was surprising to find any female at all. Yet one can learn that talented females had their say, beginning with such pioneers in the field as Karen Horney. Even today, Horney is recognized as an expert of psychoanalysis who had walked confidently into this man's establishment.

While not denying her role among her contemporaries, Horney's theory on neurosis was quite obviously influenced by her own relationship with her father, who had played a huge role in her life while she was growing up. It was not an easy relationship, as Horney recalled; she felt ignored by her father, who treated her harshly and who, in her estimation, favored her older brother, Berndt. Thus we find lines like these in her work *Feminine Psychology*:

> *Since her birth, the girl is subjected to a constant reminder of her inferiority and in response, she develops her masculinity complex. If we add to all this masculine character of our civilization, we can understand why appropriate sublimation channels are hard to find for women. Besides, once unconscious masculinity wishes arise in a woman, a vicious circle develops, which makes things worse: by taking refuge in a masculine role, the woman, developing contempt for femininity and in this fashion, not only is her feminine identity threatened but also any emerging feminine trends will make her feel more inferior.*

No doubt, one must find a balance in analyzing the personal experience of someone so that their subjective experience does not interfere with their professional judgment. But indeed, we are not able to remove ourselves completely when asked to arrive at conclusions, judgments, even diagnoses. Our personal experience is always behind the scenes.

The description of a woman's role brought up by Horney coincides exactly with the place of a woman in today's developed society. One can easily trace many trends in Horney's work in modern community, including contemporary America.

Women in America have come a long way from not being able to vote and mostly playing the submissive role of a quiet and obedient wife to achieving dizzying heights in every possible field of human endeavor. Today many women are found among lawyers, doctors, astronauts, scientists, and politicians. There is presently no place where women do not play an important role in society.

Has ignorance finally been corrected? Has an existing imbalance between men and women been resolved once and for all? Was this imbalance the only or the most important factor influencing societal ills, or there are others? When society changes so radically, the legitimate question that comes to mind is, did such a move help to eliminate previously existing problems, or did it create new and different ones?

These kinds of questions can be asked from a different angle as well. Does societal structure alone assign people their roles in life? Do any personal attributes of the human being—or more precisely, any particular feature of an individual—contribute to his or her personal achievements? Do any physical qualities such as the physiological structure of the human body also place human beings in positions dictated by nature?

If we consider the role men play in society, we will realize that the need to single out each individual man is inevitable. In my classification, however, I speak in generalizations because only in that form does classification make sense. While people certainly continue to judge others *en masse*, and generalization creates a general and not precise comprehension of any specific group, this generalization helped me to see the nature of individual character.

Of course, such general colloquial descriptions of men as "they think with their penises" or "testosterone is the main engine of man's behavior" are widely known. But is it enough to know?

Years ago, a popular psychologist, Dr. Joyce Brothers, wrote these words:

> *Men and women do not think the same way. Their brains are almost as different as their sex organs . . . . Men are right hemisphere oriented and they use this side of the brain more efficiently than women do . . . . Women are left hemisphere oriented, more verbally adroit. Their left hemisphere develops earlier, which gives them an edge in reading and writing . . . . The male brain is specialized. Men use the right hemisphere when dealing with spatial problems and the left with verbal problems . . . . The female*

brain is not specialized. Right and left hemispheres work together on a problem. This is possible because in female brains, left hemisphere abilities are duplicated to some extent in the right hemisphere and the right hemisphere abilities in the left.

Talk show host Phil Donahue said in his book *The Human Animal*, "Biologically, our brains have loose bars with an open door, always." What he meant was that in our nature there is always some tendency toward instability and an ability to change. And indeed we are constantly changing in our perception of the world and our way of thinking. This process is continuously present as long as we live. But what we are changing *from*? What is that original base that we inherited or acquired? When did it become our baseline?

In 1983, an extra bundle of neurons in the female *corpus callosum* (a structure in the human brain) was discovered. The discovery of this extra structure brought us to an era in which scientists and psychologists began to understand how women's brains work. The bulge, which anatomically connects the right and left hemispheres, might play a role in sending more impulses to the neocortex where emotions could be prolonged for quite some time. It would be just as if the neocortex is receiving an unusual number of impulses, as compared to the usual number received by a male. Of course, one should realize that whenever one speaks of a prolonged activity of impulses, in actuality that means a thousandths fraction of a second, which is the time for passing an impulse from one place in a body to another.

Given the elevated number of impulses of this physical structure, it is easier to explain women's display of much stronger excitement when they are stimulated. That might be why we see more emotional expressiveness among women then among men.

Recently scientists from John Hopkins University reported that the left and right sides of the brain called the *inferior parietal lobule* (IPL) are larger in men than in women. Furthermore, this study showed that the left area was defined as responsible for excellence in physics and mathematics. The same studies have also revealed that the right IPL is involved in spatial visualization, particularly the location of natural objects in cosmos.

–

Now scientific studies have never completely stalled, and each day we learn of progress made in understanding humans, however big or small that progress might be.

With that comes new attitude in society.

Today it is very popular to speak in politically correct terms. Therefore, to say that women possess such and such attributes and men other or even superior ones would alarm a substantial crowd of watchdogs spread throughout many layers and fields of society. Yet nature does not care about the sensitivity of some uptight individuals and does not offer different packages of hormones, the ability to conceive and carry a child, or even passing an egg to testicles instead of ovaries. Only a mother can breastfeed her baby because only her body will produce milk.

For a woman relying on herself, who struggles in society, as Horney described, trying to achieve any discernible heights, it becomes an unfortunate reality that such a woman almost necessarily loses her femininity.

Some time ago, the words "feminism stinks" could be found on many street walls, especially on the walls of professional school campuses. Students are the most perceptive part of societal waves. But who could have written such proclamations? Could it be male chauvinists who'd like to see women remain in the kitchen? Or is it possible that some anonymous student did it just to provoke an outburst and indignation in unhappy females?

What did those feminists want? Do all women like what feminists have accomplished so far? How many support them today? At the beginning of that movement, it looked like many of them did. Now very few even bother to speak about it. Is it because it became a norm of daily life? Did women finally get the recognition they deserved among members of society?

We might approach these questions from a different perspective. When women decided enough was enough, advocates of women's rights, such as feminists appeared to be, became fully justified. The roars that accompanied their fights were widely appreciated. Different segments of the excited crowd succinctly pointed to the changing epoch, starting with the sexual revolution, settling on Geraldine Ferraro, Sandra Day O'Connor, and Jeane J. Kirkpatrick. Did all women feel comfortable and elevated? What about those women who felt all right at home and, yes, in the kitchen?

Today, an American woman cannot and will not brag that she is spending the majority of her time keeping her household in order by making a good dinner for her husband and by educating her children. Such an attitude has been unequivocally condemned and cast into the past. Today, most women are those working moms that are going into the many fields previously occupied by men. They are executives, doctors, senators.

Not all women went this way, but enough did to change the equilibrium women were seeking. Did this make women happy? Do all women dream to become Hillary Rodham Clinton?

Statistics do not show how many women want an executive position. There is no answer to this question if we'd ask men either. But most likely only a handful of them would have the goal to become president, even in such a powerful country as the United States.

So why are women still not happy? Why is divorce still a fact of life, even rampant, not only in this country, but also worldwide? Why is an army of women still frustrated and confused in their relationships with the men they married?

There is no one or simple answer to all of this. I will discuss the topic as we progress. Suffice it to say here, statistics show that people are different in their approach to questions of life, and it is not simply a business of educating them as to how they must accept and feel about the tiny details of it. A definite percentage of people are interested in politics or in cosmetics or in sports. Knowledge of this division helps us to see people in groups. The statistical method simply confirms such division.

So what features about men are not considered habitual for most women? Men love to behave as if they are superior. They are stubborn and rarely consider another way of thinking if they perceive it as weak. They enjoy talking politics. They love to watch or participate in sports and war games, and they believe in their superior logic that is usually aided by effective mathematical or spatial ability.

Many of these features are based upon the physical strength of men as well. If physical attributes are not sufficiently developed in them, such men resort to the process of thinking as their main tool of success. In that, men are akin to their counterparts, women, with

—

two major differences. First, the appearance of a physically inferior man does not occur within the expected norm. Second, the hunting reflex is at the level of a long-passed inheritance. So by pursuing the same goal, of higher achievements in different fields that now require mental superiority, men continue to strive for better results, and that indicates a desire to compete.

This competitive reflex also leads to the need to be noticed. It covers a number of features that start with the desire to be a leader— or if a follower, then better at executing a specified task—along with a stubborn insistence on considered and applied logic.

With this almost-constant desire to win, men have a sacred belief that their deeds are always appreciated. This plays into their often inadequately expressed desire to be recognized. Depending on background and circumstance, one may see that manifestation of pride in different behaviors. This feature is not necessarily on display, but more often than not it is present in the majority of men.

So how does the general thinking process develop in a man's head? Excitement is a core feature of all live organisms. In humans, it arises from sudden changes in circumstance, whether expected or unexpected. Again, depending on the circumstance, we may see a manifestation of that thinking process, or we may not. Because a man perceives his presence among fellow humans as an event of an extraordinary personification of him as individual, depending on such self-gratification and connected to his background, he will apply the willpower to either control himself or not, and that will show through the signs of excitement elevated to a certain degree. If for some reason a man's perception of an event pushes him to think that to express his emotions is inadequate, that alone will keep him from showing those emotions externally. This feature of a man, unfortunately, often leads to the need to consume alcohol in excess and, on rare occasions, to even use drugs, although there are many other reasons for drugs and alcohol abuse.

The existing differences between men and women, thus mentioned, have been applied to a mature audience. But do these differences appear in adulthood, or do they roll back to infancy?

Based on the works of Anna Freud, Melanie Klein, Ernest Jones, and other earlier psychologists, the analysis of children has carried many useful, theoretic, fundamental principles into the contemporary

—

psychoanalytic approach. Such understandings as ego, fantasy, and the love-hate relationship were scientifically substantiated and developed.

Today, after learning the role of genes and after many careful studies of controlled groups, scientists have decisively proved that environment and social learning, while tightly entangled with genetics, play a significant role in constructing a neurological profile of a child.

A child in its early age requires not only the careful evaluation of its still-developing physical and mental systems, as both are not complete, it is also of the utmost importance to protect and navigate a child's behavior under the careful supervision of adults. Without proper navigation, a child will resort to any kind of behavior to feel comfortable, relaxed, and protected.

I also wish to point out here that a different approach to a developing male child versus a female child must be carefully exercised. It concerns not only the physical and physiological differences between both genders, but because of a different approach of society to raise and nurture male children versus female children, the steps both sexes are following are distinctly contrasted.

Let's trace a baby boy's advancement. Born with the expectation that he will develop physical superiority, a baby boy is shaped by society into a creature with strong and superior qualities. The nature of those demands depends on the culture of the society, of course. Yet overall, most contemporary societies encourage either physical or mental superiority, and sometimes both, with an expectation from a baby boy to compete and to win at the end as a result of such competition. With thus conditioned predetermination and with an undeveloped ability of mind, a boy, nevertheless, is placed on a road to be molded into a Herculean type. In contrast to such expectations, no matter how much effort is granted, if a male infant doesn't inherit the necessary strong male features, it won't become what was anticipated. The wrong approach and the lack of understanding by young parents and society with its establishments is a very important reason to consider why a growing child may develop inadequate behavior and possibly become an impediment for society.

In the case of a female, society rarely, if ever, cares how much femininity a female child might display. Starting from the time of her

—

birth and up to when she becomes a teenager, a girl is often left alone. The female child is mostly expected to play with her dolls, to be compliant, and not to behave in a rebellious or disagreeable fashion.

The young female in that sense is much less abused by society than her male counterpart. But by the same token, she is mostly shaped by peer pressure and very little by the individual rearing of her family unit.

So right from their birth, female/male creatures are necessarily placed in a "specific box" in which their development is actively-passively shaped. This preconditioning leads to specific problems that obviously influence the further development of a persona.

I will return to a discussion of other problems existing in the education of boys and girls later on in other parts of this book.

CHAPTER 2

Classification

Long before I decided to separate people into categories, I learned the two major properties that human beings possess and that connect all people on earth:

- Willpower
- Human Emotions

While both attributes are the result of the thinking process, they are often in opposition to each other.

Willpower or self-control is that necessary tool that humans need to learn how to employ in order to survive. Our emotions, on the other hand, almost constantly fight each other, thus producing an imbalance, the inability to be organized, and even chaos in our lives that willpower is destined to control. With this in mind, I constructed a classification system that should help us understand people's reaction to specific circumstance, their motivations, and the possible rationale behind it.

All three categories in the classification describe a distinct group of people that are usually bound within the particular borders. Yet while each category reveals a definite group of people who necessarily belong to it, each category allows some mixture of any of them. What that means is that some people do not exactly fit into a specific group but might float into an adjacent modality despite the strong emphasis of designated borders. In other words, people from one category may be close to the fringes of any other group or even interlaced with it, such that they display some features from another group.

It is of utmost importance to realize that features humans possess come in specific sets, and while they are not necessarily all expressed at once, they are embedded in us, waiting for a special event to be revealed. Therefore it is necessary to understand that while some individuals, for instance, do not visibly display certain features (or a trait or a faculty for that matter) in any given time, it might very well be present but not necessarily revealed. It all depends on the education a person received, his ability and desire to control himself in specific situations, as well as his falling into one of the categories described below.

The lack of knowledge of this detail may cause some degree of confusion, especially in those inexperienced in categorizing people. Therefore it is essential to understand that in order to properly approach each and every individual, some special training might be required. Having said that, I need to warn the reader that there are no schools or training programs that currently exist, as my classification is, not only a new one, but also not yet known to formal academic circles.

As a measure of precaution and for the purpose of clarification, I feel that it is necessary to inform everyone who is going to carefully explore the system presented below that it is merely a sketch or an outline of the subjects upon which I continuously enlarge in the pages of this book. Therefore readers shouldn't feel confused or embarrassed if they disagree with or misunderstand my classification at first. I also suggest not forcing oneself to an immediate adoption or rejection of it right after the first reading.

One more thing I wish to say here: the purpose of creating this classification is not simply to separate people into categories, but rather to illuminate the differences between us so we can learn to accept our fellow humans the way we are. It is my hope that those who acknowledge my system will not rush to conclusions and flaunt to others their suddenly superior knowledge.

Now with this improvised introduction, let me start from the physical birth of a child, in other words, the physical appearance of a child into this world. Besides inheriting specific traits, a child immediately is exposed to environmental conditions, including the quality of nurture by those in charge, which is often connected to the baby's parents or a mother. The ability and desire of the guardians to satisfy the needs of an infant elicit a corresponding reaction. Beginning with the baby's health, a capacity to tolerate external irritants, all incoming impulses are interpreted by a newborn on an individual basis. The demands of a baby to be satisfied and not to be overly disturbed depend mostly on the two factors mentioned earlier: inbred features and nurturing guardians.

The first attributes of humans, *self* and *ego*, are the original primal features that begin to show themselves at a very early period of our existence. They are not only the first platform on which comprehension of the world begins; they are also the main features that require satisfactory interpretations of all the irritants coming from the outside, surrounding as they contribute in the shaping of the character of a future person. While both are connected, the first faculty to announce itself is *self*. At the time an infant is born into this world, it learns his own self while getting food, expressing different feelings through laughter and crying, taking his first steps, and so on. Self is that voice in our head that pretty soon finds itself arguing with another voice (the *ego*), letting us know what it wishes to do. Ego, on the other hand, arises with the development of the conscience. The more maturity the conscience reaches, the more pronounced the ego becomes.

According to Freud, "the ego is that part of the id which has been modified by the direct influence of the external world" (Freud, 363-4). While this definition of ego probably sounds right, it might be added that ego starts with establishing oneself in this world. In infancy, it begins with eliminating, for example, the feeling of hunger. A child uses any means available to be fed and not to feel hungry. His demands vary, but with time, they turn into craftiness, aggression, charm, the ability to please, and so on.

At this early age, a child cannot understand many things and mainly behaves according to the actions and reactions of surrounding adults. There is no doubt that by coming in this world, he almost immediately begins to experience frustration along with curiosity and expectation of someone close to him being able to calm unknown feelings and hurts. A child's perplexity is tightly connected to an instinct of survival and a sense of fear. Being inexperienced and therefore quite brittle, a child naturally accepts a softer, gentler approach from an adult, whoever provides it. Therefore it is not necessarily a sequential chain that puts a mother in front of a father in the satisfaction and acceptance of nurture by children either male or female. There is no ambiguity that a natural bond occurs between an offspring and a feeding mother. But it is not a mystical attachment. If a father figure is able to demonstrate to a child mild and tender behavior, such a child would not distinguish between the two parents right away.

With a child getting older and therefore acquiring comprehensive skills, such a child would either admire a father figure as powerful, strong, and protective or pull away from such a person, scared by the magnitude of strength displayed.

It also comes into play with such other human qualities as the need for a search of new expectations. Thus while a child's appreciation of the events of the world begins to take some definite shape, such a child begins to distinguish between what is an immediate feeling and what is long term. Quite often, a feeling of saturation and thus dullness in perception of the event takes place, and a child may drastically change his priorities to prefer either a parent or a guardian.

When Freudians (Sigmund Freud and his students) were describing a child's feelings, the interpretation of reality that a child would perceive through sexual arousal, they meant that the child's sexual apparatus is much more mature than his thinking apparatus or that he is sophisticated enough to use any irritant or outside stimuli via his sexual perception to understand the world. That could not be correct, as such an explanation had to place the interpretation of all people in one category without distinguishing between them. As we will imminently learn, people are not the same, and they could fall into one category only if they possess similar features.

In this regard, I'd like to say a few words concerning the *Oedipus complex* and the early stages of psychoanalysis.

The Oedipus complex, so thoroughly described by the Freudian schooling in an attempt to generally explain the development of an infant child was, in my mind, far-fetched with an approach based on the wrong interpretation of a child's entrance into the physical realm.

Let me elaborate on this.

When a child is born, it is equipped with so-called unconditional reflexes, such as the gag reflex, breathing, hunger, bowel movements, unlearned reactions to such stimulus as abrupt, loud sounds, and powerful sexual impulses. The other reflexes were learned and arise as a result of the interpretation of inherited features. Fear, a sense of guilt, self-awareness and ego, aggression, jealousy, and the desire to possess, all of these are acquired features that come to us as the result of interpreted inbred traits. They are also learned through behavioral modifications of a child by surrounding adults, as in that early age, children begin to appreciate the power of ego, the ability to influence people, along with manipulation, adjusting, and, most importantly, child's comprehension of the events.

While the psychological apparatus of a child, among other things, depends on an inherited nervous system, the result of this inheritance leads to a different degree of action, toleration, and development.

It is also important to understand that many features normally not revealed during a period of one's life may suddenly appear under certain circumstance. That does not mean that such an individual acquired previously not-existing features, but that they were in a dormant, latent condition until certain circumstances revealed them.

Following is my understanding of how people are appropriated.

—CATEGORY I—

This category is represented by a small group of unrelated people. It consists of those individuals whose thinking process is much stronger than their sexual needs.

People in this category are obsessed by one large idea. They are almost blinded by it. They are vigorously energized by it and therefore very persistent in many attempts to achieve their goal. They can rarely be distracted from this goal to accomplish something else. Their logic can yield visible superiority, but if that logic is proven to be in error, instead of acknowledging their mistake, these individuals will look for other ways to prove that they are correct.

People in this category are not easily affected by depression, embarrassment, vulnerability, boredom, loneliness, or laziness. To reach their goals, they may often use means that could be considered unacceptable to the majority of society, but to them this no acceptance might be irrelevant. These people are prone to become leaders, which often turns them into tyrants, autocrats, and dictators.

Depending on the goal these people are pursuing, the rest of humanity may see them as noble or fanatical and sometimes even insane. They may use malice to achieve their goals, and this particular feature—while planted in our genes—does not have to be immediately revealed. Yet malice is quite often present as a useful tool in achieving the desired results.

The remaining gamut of human features such as lies, intrigue, intolerance, and so forth all may appear if they become particularly helpful to these persons' aspirations. These individuals need no more logical justification for their behavior than that it will aid them in fulfilling their goals.

Sex often plays a very small, almost rudimentary role in their lives. Human sexual variety is not in their repertoire. They may choose one or two ways to express their cravings, but whatever they choose, sex, as a rule of thumb, will not be a major issue for them. Obviously, history knows such characters as, for example was the Roman Emperor Caligula. But his character does not fall into the first category, as his pursuing the inherited role of a leader was secondary compared to those people who belong to the description.

—CATEGORY II—

In trying to explain people from this category, in which sexuality approaches the level of a thinking process, I came to the conclusion that these people have to be divided further into two separate subgroups: A and B, with a sandwiched middle layer of the subgroup B. While people of each subgroup can be separated without difficulty, they also are often interlaced in their behavior. If one takes into consideration that there is no such thing as pure type but there are many sprouted features connecting different groups, it will help to understand that such division is mostly conditional. Thus, when I mention both subgroups A and B enumerating people involved in the same profession, it does not mean that same person may fall in either category. It simply means closeness of these subgroups with possession of joined modality.

SUBGROUP A

The people in this subgroup of Category II tend to be very goal oriented, although not as much as in the group of Category I.

Here we find scientists, teachers, engineers, doctors, accountants, composers, and performers of classical music. Sexually, these people are somewhat subdued, but not so much that they do not consider sex a necessary pleasure. They enjoy it very much. Yet their thinking process prevails over their sexual desires. This becomes especially clear when these people experience any obstacle to achieving their goals in life. They may easily abstain from sexual escapades or even casual sex to concentrate on their goals.

SUBGROUP B

Subgroup B, on the other hand, is represented by a quite interesting group of people. First of all, these people have almost equally divided their rational thinking processes and sexual needs. One cannot say that these people are animals with human traits or humans with strong animal instincts. It is simply not so. Their mentality is basically equal to their sexuality. And in this combination, these people are the most variegated group, with many different representatives in it.

To characterize these people, one must approach them as objectively as possible. In doing so, I divided this subgroup into two levels. In the upper level, one can find doctors, writers, artists, and some actors. Depending on the level of their achievement, these people are almost equally divided into optimists and pessimists.

Sandwiched between the upper and lower levels of this subgroup is the crowd represented by the butchers, barbers, shoemakers, tailors, and similar craftsmen. They are not necessarily educated or goal-oriented people. They devote themselves as much to their work as to their sexual escapades. They are the foundation of any society, and they are not burdened by the need for a special position in it, as long as they manage to provide themselves the means for a comfortable lifestyle.

At the lower level of this subgroup, we find a mixture of actors, musicians, dancers, and other representatives of the entertainment industry not mentioned earlier.

–

This level is intermixed with people we consider unstable. They are often in search of a role in exciting new fields. They seem overly optimistic yet rarely satisfied with their achievements. Their behavior is reminiscent of teenagers, but thanks to them, we enjoy many exciting moments in our lives.

—CATEGORY III—

This group occupies a special place in any society. I call these people to some extent unfortunate, as representatives of this category have their animalistic tendencies so well developed that it is stronger than their apparatus for rational thought. The lower the level, the more the animal is expressed.

When this category is subdivided, the upper level would be represented by thieves, shoplifters, drug addicts, and prostitutes not driven by concurrent circumstance but by an uncontrollable animalistic desire.

The middle ground of this category is marked by those who are drug dealers, burglars, robbers, and accidental killers. The mutual feature connecting these people is their opposition to the rest of the world.

Finally we encounter those we still must consider as people, but who are known to society as murderers, cold-blooded killers, sadomasochists, rapists, and child molesters. This group lives more by instincts for survival than anything else. Their mental processes are quite confusing even to them. It gives them a mixture of pleasure, guilt, excitement, and satisfaction. They kill or rape for moments of simple enjoyment brought by rage and the fear they elicit in the people they victimize.

They also possess the desire to be independent and powerful people, and this desire is driven by their enjoyment of seeing fear in the people they closely encounter. Overall, they are envious of people who are successful, and this envy often produces in them a split personality.

Most of these people—probably all—cannot be rehabilitated, not because of the lack of educational tools humanity possesses today, but because they are seriously sick. They need, along with medical attention, psychologists, and behavioral specialists, to manage their disease. Unfortunately, doctors today don't possess the means to cure their condition. So the only treatment for them at the present time would be separating them from society until scientists in genetic engineering find an effective treatment for them.

I would not advocate sentencing these people to death in spite of the gravity of their crimes, as it does not serve as a deterrent to crime. Besides, it is not simply the fault of these people. They are born with genetic deficiencies, and the role of society for now must fall mostly on the preventive side.

While not advocating capital punishment for these people, I believe they nevertheless must be punished. If they've committed a crime, they must suffer the consequence. Still, the crime they performed was as much their fault as the society that overlooked it. Crime that society didn't know how to prevent became a reality.

Using today's available means, society must be educated in how to recognize these individuals in advance of their crimes, rather than expressing indignation at the tragedies they cause after the fact. People must learn how to protect their family units. They must be educated to recognize the subtle signs of the developing creature and always reinforce strong moral values. The signs one must look for are very subtle, almost invisible, and only highly specialized training may reveal indirect signals that might be revealed in these people. These would be the ability to manipulate, the desire to sneakily hurt someone, pretentious politeness, and a readiness to please. These would come along with indifference to other humans' needs, a lack of remorse for doing wrong, and an overly exaggerated ego. I will speak more on this matter later on.

To summarize, I wish again to emphasize that this classification is a naked structure that still needs to be dressed in proper clothes. One may use it only after obtaining a thorough understanding of it and familiarizing oneself with the many variations described on the pages of this book, as well as in many other existing sources—but not otherwise.

As our human tendency to exaggerate reality, to overreact to uncontrollable events makes us much less objective that we desire to be, it is important not to jump to conclusions or, even worse, to sincerely believe that we are finally equipped with the universal solutions to all possible occurrences in both the present and the future.

To finish this important division of people, I'd like to repeat that same thought that was provided at the beginning of this chapter. We are not simply made-up machines intended to accomplish a specific task. We may, in spite of definite inheritance of genetic traits, confirmed influence of society, our own upbringing and concurrent situation in our personal life, still exhibit fluency in displaying different traits. Whether these traits are prevailing at specific circumstance or they are subdued due to conditional reasons, we must possess them in order to be displayed.

CHAPTER 3

Race and Humans

In his book *What Evolution Is*, Ernst Mayr placed a very short article (exactly one page in length) under the title "Are There Human Races?" In it the famous biologist and evolutionist—possibly trying to sound politically correct, and in fact not answering his own question—confuses the reader repeatedly by swinging back and forth without saying anything to clarify this issue.

On the one hand, Mayr says that people "cannot escape recognizing the so-called racial differences." On the other, he suggests that it "is important to realize that these differences also exist within all of the human races" (262).

In the introduction to *Mapping Human History*, which is titled "The Human Pageant," Steve Olson wrote these words:

> *Anyone walking along the sidewalk of a large city can't help but be struck by the incredible variety of human beings—tall and short, fat and lean, hairy and hairless. Some have skin the color of heavy cream; others are as dark as bittersweet chocolate. The shapes of people's faces, the colors of hair and eyes, the contours of eyes, noses, and lips are marvelously unique. Partly we're attuned to these differences because we use them to identify people we know. But our diversity is not an illusion. Human beings really are one of the most physically varied mammalian species on Earth.* (1)

–

Then we read from the same source that:

> *Given this extensive history of mixing, the strength of*
> *racial prejudice in the United States can seem perplexing.*
> *Throughout the country's history, Americans have drawn*
> *rigid distinctions between black and white, Indian and*
> *European, Asian and non-Asian, Latino and Anglo.*
> *Furthermore, these distinctions have been rooted in the*
> *belief that sharp genetic differences separate groups,*
> *differences that shape behavior as well as appearance.*
> (55)

The conclusion to which Olson comes is that "scientific research has shown that these claims have no merit. Given the history of our species, the behaviors characteristic of a group must be the product of culture—of what people learn—not of genetics" (Ibid, 55).

Almost indoctrinated by such statements, one might realize how difficult it is today to elucidate on a subject without weighing how much and what precisely one should or shouldn't say. It also becomes quite obvious how prejudicial our dependence on the physical description of an organism is. And possibly because of that prejudice, we are warned that the genetic apparatus, while playing a somewhat important role in people's lives, still is not the dominant one, especially if one reflects on the behavior.

But let's refresh the definitions of race and culture. According to *Encyclopedia Britannica:*

> *Race is neither an artificial construct, a collection of*
> *individuals arbitrarily selected from a population, nor a*
> *religious grouping, linguistic division, or nationality. A*
> *race is a population or a group of populations distinct by*
> *virtue of genetic isolation and natural selection.* (vol. 18,
> p. 984)

Webster's International Dictionary defines race as "A division of mankind possessing traits that are transmittable by descent to characterize it as a distinct human type (Caucasian, Mongoloid)."

Collier's Encyclopedia defines races of man as *the divisions of mankind which have sufficient constant, inheritable traits to identify them as separate groups.*

In a more recent article on race and culture published on the Progressive Scholar blog on May 13, 2010, M. Kean writes, "Race is a social construct that is used to categorize and divide people based on physical characteristics, which often lead to conflict and oppression." In this last statement, it is distinctly shown how extreme human beings may become in their desire to not be singled out, diminished, and disparaged.

It is a proven fact that people carry the whole gamut of genes that play a role in diseases, human essence, and the behavioral changes that make us human. Whether it is an extra copy of chromosome 21, which produces babies with Down syndrome, or Klinefelter syndrome—in which males get an extra X chromosome—or a hermaphrodite (a person having both female and male sexual organs), genes are a small but nevertheless quite important part of the world that exists, that has always existed, and that most likely will exist for a long time to come.

The role of genetics is fairly easy to identify, as one can appreciate the material proof offered by nature. Genes play a distinct role in providing color to our eyes, hair, and skin. They are responsible for the physical appearance of our body, and its function and adaptation to environmental demands. These genetic differences are clearly recognized by society. But are they responsible for behavior?

At the beginning of this book, I discussed the influence of physical fitness via adaptation to the environment. Adaptation is also often caused by the surrounding human network or society. In that society, built on past understandings of good and evil and common wisdom, people create the virtues by which the majority likes to live.

Thrown in this whirlpool is our understanding of hereditary features. They necessarily play a role in each individual's behavior, do they not? Even with some level of hesitation in accepting this proposition, it is a different story when it comes to a discussion about race, gender, intelligence, variant abilities, and the success of an individual and overall behavioral display. People grow alert, mindful not to be offended or to offend, and quite often are inapt in their conclusions.

–

So intending no offense, I'll consider the behavior of animals. For instance, the tidiness of cats is known not only to the owners of felines, but also to the general population. Birds build their nests not by the instructions of a teacher but by the natural instincts most likely inherited through their genes. Dogs dig in soil, hiding a bone or covering their excretions, without copying their older peers. Such examples are plenty and may point to one thing.

Heredity undoubtedly plays a role in the behavioral inclinations of the animal kingdom including its highest form, humans. Then the legitimate question must be—is behavior shaped by the complicated interweaving of acquired factors and inherited features?

Without lingering on Linnaeus's description of ill-tempered red Indians or the supposed nobility of white Europeans, I wish to ponder a proper conclusion, and not necessarily one that society recognizes and agrees with today.

With segregation, whether forced upon or self-imposed, people gradually become alienated, prejudiced, and inexplicably hostile toward unknown or lesser-known subjects. There is no secret that people prefer to stay in ethnically akin communities. It is psychologically easier to understand, to follow, and to imitate. For one reason or another, it is believed that people of similar ethnicities carry a kindred alliance.

Yet it is no secret that people of one ethnic community still develop habitually familiar traits of envy, animosity, and even hatred toward each other. Intercommunication is not necessarily sincere within even small family units, in the daily gatherings at workplaces or in social groupings.

While these specific features can be found in any society—which again definitely points to heredity—it is also a fact that the gravity of these features depends on the cultural habits of the society. The culture of any society does not develop separately from the abilities of a single individual. That individual is transformed by the society and in turn contributes his own understanding to what ultimately is a society of individuals. Thus, the tool for survival—and therefore the longevity of any society—becomes tightly entangled with the heredity of each individual and the environment the combined individuals happen to create.

—

This raises a question: Is human division into race or ethnicity valid enough to make the distinction among people? Has race been erroneously defined while playing an important role in human lives?

This underscores another question and a feature of human behavior: How valid is the ability to generalize while making one's own observations?

Who are the Germans, French, or English? How reasonable is it to separate Indians from Pakistanis? Do we have any doubts about who the Mexicans or who the American Indians are? Do the Chinese people have a merit not to be called Japanese?

Here, we must go back in time to when civilization left us a few examples for contemporary science to draw seemingly logical conclusions.

Early archaeological findings show that people were quite often separated geographically. Yet our propensity to establish cultural differences has inadvertently interlaced with our search for other more substantial human attributes.

We read that the Celts were a diverse group of people, out of which possibly originated Irish, Britons, Scots, and Gauls (French). Does that mean that Celtic people were one and the same? The astounding answer is, "not necessarily." They might have used a similar language or had closely related cultures, but that's about it.

We further learn that the country by the name England originated from a tribe of Germanic people, the Angles, who invaded Great Britain in the fifth century CE and occupied it until the eleventh century. The Saxons are the other Germanic tribe responsible, along with the Angles, for Anglo-Saxon England. Another group of Germanic tribes, known as Norsemen, is responsible for Scandinavian countries and Normandy (France).

By which standard might we classify Chinese people and Anglo-Saxons, for instance? Did they have a common ancestor, but through the conditional changes of the environment become different peoples?

Could Jewish people, Mongols, and Germanic people come from the same stock?

Such examples are bountiful and may lead to one conclusion—that there are no "pure" races.

—

Today, sensitivity of a contemporary society becomes so problematic that it leads us nowhere in our attempt to define race without fearing to offend. Many cultural anthropologists refer to race as a social and mental construct rather than an objective biological fact. Enough works, written articles, and scientific conclusions bring additional confusion to our understanding of race. Traditional references to skin color, hair type, bodily proportion, et cetera, effectively only describe the superficial distinctions of races among humans.

In light of this approach, it is paradoxical that ethnic data is collected by the United States Census Bureau. While the Federal Office of Management and Budget (FOMB) defines the concept, saying that "public testimony and research indicate that race and ethnicity are subjective concepts and inherently ambiguous," it suggests that

> *For purposes of collecting data in the United States, race and ethnicity are cultural concepts and social constructs. As stated in the current version of Directive 15, the racial and ethnic categories are not intended to reflect scientific or anthropological definitions of who should be included in a particular category.*

Yet it still allows the collection of such data.

Not dismissing a discussion on race, let's turn to another social portraying of different groups of people. Why do so many types of people exist? What makes them gather in different groups? Are they influenced by kindred physical aspects? Do they have similar ideas that bond them together? Why do they appreciate many incongruent events in similitude? What produces in them that feeling of belonging?

It is a known fact that people from the same race or ethnic group under some circumstances feel affinity, while under other circumstances they may be hostile to each other. Does that mean that our reading of human race is misapprehended?

What constitutes the notion of race? A definition provided by the *American Heritage Dictionary, Second College Edition* reads thusly: "A local geographic or global human population distinguished as a more or less distinct group by genetically transmitted physical characteristics."

—

Stephen Jay Gould, Niles Eldredge, and Australian anthropologist Colin Groves speak of the evolution of large mammals in a distinct pattern. Today this is known as *punctuated equilibrium.*

Punctuated equilibrium is described as a long period of stasis interrupted by rapid catastrophic change. It is an alternative to the theory of *gradualism* (proposed by Darwin) that describes evolution as uniform, steady process with gradual transformation of a whole lineage.

According to this theory, the process of evolution happens in distinct patterns. Species do not change for a long period of time. Then a small group of animals diverge into a new species.

This happens under certain circumstances such as a geographic separation of a population by any natural or manmade barrier. Separation for a long period of time leads to a divergence in traits in such a population with the gradual development of new traits and finally, an inability to breed, thus producing a new species. This logic is not that easy to swallow, though, especially if one tries to visualize this process of transformation from one species to another.

Let's try to trace the split of humans and chimps from apes. The genetic material inherited from our common ancestor appears to be almost identical. Still we are not the same species, and our separation must have been quite complex. Research points to changes in the environment that is mainly responsible for the evolution of humans and chimps.

The change is described roughly like this: Over twenty million years ago, there were vast regions of tropical environment accommodating the survival of apes. Gradual climate change and broken regions of forests and savannas created conditions to which primates had to adjust. These new conditions dictated the gradual adaptation of primates in their habitat along with changing feeding habits.

One of these changing habits, scientists believe, brought the necessity for apes to walk in the upright position. Logically such an explanation might very well be accepted, but after I learned of certain differences in the skeletal framework of apes and how those affected their first attempts to walk on two hind legs, it seemed to me that it couldn't have been such a smooth transformation.

First, the big toe of an ape is not parallel to its other toes, but opposes them, which impedes its balance while walking upright.

–

Second, the largest thigh bone (femur) that in humans is the center of gravity is, in apes, turned so as to produce an amble, rather than a bipedal stride. Apes' arms are much longer than their hind legs, and that most likely comes from their use for climbing trees walking on all fours. Apes' spines are relatively the same in size throughout their bodies, while ours are longer, especially in the cervical, thoracic, and lumbar areas. The major aperture (*foramen magnum*) connecting the spine with the skull in humans is located centrally beneath the skull, allowing our vertical stance. In apes, it is more toward the rear of the skull.

Taking into an account all of these differences, it is hard to comprehend how the proposition, that apes adapted to an upright position to see predators better in the new forest-free environment and thus to more readily escape, in any way coincides with reality. Not only can I not see how any awkwardly and slow-moving primate species on two legs could outrun a predator such as a cheetah or a tiger, it is hard to imagine a contemporary human being that would think of changing his posture in order to live a better life in the future. The reason animals are forced to change their habits must be beneficial not in the long run, but immediately.

Trying to adjust to a new environment, mammals like us do not rely on cultural offerings either but mainly on our own genetic ability to survive. If natural selection demands that the fittest survive, how could any creature contemplate what future benefits should be expected if the present use of them seems detrimental?

While doing his research on evolutionary patterns in large mammals, Groves came across a mechanism that differed from what we had thought about adaptation following geographical separation of groups. He found that most changes happened in the middle of large groups of species. It ran counter to the accepted theory, but it seemed to be a definite fact that most changes happen at the highest density of population.

Why?

With punctuated equilibrium described as part of gradualism, the features that appear in a new distinct group or species must have been connected not only to the demands of a changing environment but also to a combination of genetic drift and random mutations. While the adaptation of an organism is dependent on the demands of nature, any

—

organism has its limitations. When it cannot adjust to ever-changing demands, it faces extinction.

Organisms respond to the demands of nature by producing a wide variety of new traits. A trait is a distinct feature of an organism, such as the specific color of an eye. The trait is usually environmentally dependent or genetically inherited. If the trait is of a hereditary nature, it is a product of genes. If it is connected to environmental conditions, it can produce changes in the phenotype without dependency on genetic shift.

According to the central dogma of molecular biology, offered by Francis Crick, a trait is the final product of many biomolecular processes. It describes the transfer of sequential information that starts from DNA, proceeds to RNA, and finally to protein. DNA, speaking in relatively simple terms, is the main engine of inheritance. It contains the substances adenine, guanine, cytosine, and thymine (A, G, C, and T). These substances interconnect in a strict order. Their number is sufficient to provide the genetic information of an organism from generation to generation.

We are not going to inquire into how these four substances acquired the ability to accumulate and provide the necessary information. This is not due to a lack of curiosity but because it has so far been impossible to decode.

What scientists *have* learned is that all live organisms have similar DNA, with slight differences found in each individual. These differences produce many physical variations. The contemporary approach to this is that differences among groups began with mutations in DNA structure.

This raises a series of questions:

- What caused cells to acquire DNA to begin with?
- Did the very first cell possess DNA?
- What gave it its hereditary ability?
- Why are all people born with unique fingerprints yet very closely structured DNA?

Tracing the genealogy of contemporary humans led to Africa, thus leading scientists came to the conclusion that all the peoples of the world originated from that continent. If this is so, why are the most diverse groups found there?

If people came from one female (mitochondrial Eve), say two hundred thousand years ago, what made the following generations so diverse?

Let's consider this hypothetical example. Mitochondrial Eve (mating with male Adam X) gave birth to two daughters. One got married and moved to the south of Africa where, under different climatic conditions, this lineage developed mutation "a" The other daughter didn't move and married a local guy. Therefore her progeny didn't acquire a similar mutation to her sister's.

Would these two lineages finally diverge so much so that new subgroups with racial overtones develop? Is it possible that one group would eventually turn into, let's say, white Anglo-Saxons while the other might stay black? Is the theory of African descent challenged by the discovery of forty-seven million-year-old primate Ida in Germany, so that a new suggestion that the earliest anthropoids colonized Africa is more valid?

There are basically two approaches to trace our descent from mitochondrial Eve: physiological and arithmetical. The sample above is a physiological one, and it refers to a phenotype based on genotype and environment. One can see how unreliable it must be, as new discoveries overturn previous suggestions at the speed of light. I am going to use the arithmetical method, which is fairly simple and straightforward and which was used successfully by Steve Olson in his book *Mapping Human History*.

This is the calculation Olson offered: With the generations apart an average of twenty years, any given person was supposed to have in his genealogical tree approximately 1,024 great-grandparents who formed part of his bloodline over approximately two hundred years. Why it is not an exact figure? Because not all of the parents might have had children, and we are considering an ideal situation in which everything went smoothly regarding the procreation and survival of offspring.

Now if we go back forty or even fifty generations, we will come to a much larger figure than the existing number of people on earth at that time. So if each of us had two parents, four grandparents and so on, fifty generations ago our distant relatives had to exist in a number counted in

—

the billions. At the dawn of agriculture, about ten thousand years ago, the population of the world was roughly five million. So right there, one can spot a discrepancy. Instead of having a larger and larger number of ancestors, in reality it must have started to taper at some point with the number of the participants gradually decreasing to just one.

With this exponential regression backward, it is impossible to see how the population would come to a halt with the production of one mitochondrial Eve. But let's assume (it is not that difficult in our case) that our calculation is flawed and that instead of getting a bigger number, eventually we come to that one person, our mother, Eve. Which method of calculation must be applied then so that we might definitely say that mitochondrial Eve appeared from another (unidentified) world as a winner and that she was the only mother humanity had? Was an Adam (or many Adams) conveniently present as well at the time? Were they competing among themselves in order to mate with mitochondrial Eve?

Other important questions might be how did the split from the apelike creature to humans and chimpanzees occur, technically speaking? Here I am questioning the possibility of interbreeding among different species. What exactly triggered such a split? What kind of drastic environmental conditions must have been present that such a split took a place? Should one apply a theory of gradual (a million years of) changes and adaptations or swift, sudden transformation as the theory of punctuated equilibrium suggests?

The theory of common descent, presently accepted by the scientific world of evolutionists, has supposedly explained the diversity of life and the sharing of common traits. It implies that despite numerous other differences, the most taxonomically close organisms share similar traits because they also share a common ancestor. As evidence, the scientific community puts forward a few fossils and the anatomical similarity of a number of related organisms.

Ernst Mayr said it this way:

> *Life as it now exists on Earth, including the simplest bacteria, was obviously derived from a single origin. This is indicated by the genetic code, which is the same for all organisms, including the simplest ones, as well as by many aspects of cell, including the microbial cells.* (40)

—

The question is, did that single representative of many similar organisms come into the world ready-made or did it arise from the phenomenal combination of inorganic substances? That is not known, and it looks like it never will be.

So let's turn to the facts and from that try to draw a conclusion once more.

- The existing genetic code is the same for all organisms.
- There are millions of different species in the world, some more closely related, some less.
- There are predators and prey, domesticated animals and wild stock with different habits and abilities to survive.
- According to evolutionists, we came through the steps of being insectivores, prosimii, anthropoids, and so on.
- When we speak of race, we mean certain physical characteristics that are found in the majority of a particular ethnic group.
- Varying environment and cultural traditions influence the anatomical traits of the body, promoting hundreds of new traits.
- People from different ethnic groups often interbreed with each other.
- Besides obvious differences in physical appearance (phenotype), there are genetically transmitted traits that are found in specific groups.
- The main tool that produces constant genetic change in an organism is the mutations in DNA.
- Natural selection is the main power in conducting evolution.

With this in mind, let's again ask a question: Are there genetically produced races, or is race a product of the genetically changing organism combined with changes impelled by the environment?

Were that question to produce a simple and clear answer, there would not be so much difference of opinion about the subject.

Why are there unique friction ridges on the skin of every human being? What produced DNA structures so distinct that science can unmistakably identify any single human being?

These questions require one mutually recognized answer, but they don't yet have one.

—

PART TWO

THE NETWORK OF SOCIETY

CHAPTER 4

Culture and Society

The definition of culture is actually straightforward: "The totality of socially transmitted behavior patterns, arts, institutions, and all other products of human work and thought characteristic of a community or population." *The American Heritage Dictionary* provides at least six definitions of such culture, with an emphasis on patterns of art and style, religious beliefs, intellectual activity and particular institutions, as well as accepted norms of behaviors of its population. Culture is the result of a definitive style of life accepted and followed by the majority of the members of any society managed by and entrusted to a particular form of government. There are presently a number of different societies based upon such accepted scheme.

For example, a society might be a constitutional monarchy, where the monarch is a ceremonial head of state and whose power is limited by the constitution. Another type is an autocracy, a society in which one individual accumulates unlimited legislative and executive power. Yet still another structural organization is when the authority is placed in a constitutional republic so that there is a head of the state as well as representatives of the people, who have limited power over the people that elected them to govern according to constitutional laws. There is also the parliamentary system, in which members of the cabinet or ministers are accountable to the legislative body. Then there are democracies and republics.

Democracy happens when government rules by and for the people. A republic is a form of government in which the people can exercise indirect control over their representative government. The definitions that apply to these forms of governance are theoretical, of course, which is why people struggle to clarify the existing ambiguity, a task that is often accompanied by intense internal struggles.

In the twenty-first century, many states that are not monarchies call themselves republics. Such entities as parliamentary republics (India and Poland), federal republics (Argentina, Germany, the United States), socialist republics (China, Vietnam, and, at one time, the Union of Soviet Socialist Republics, or USSR), and Islamic republics (Afghanistan and Pakistan) are, again in theory, governed by the people. There is another political system that is popular today in many countries. Such countries as the United States, Germany, Italy, France, and India are all structured as liberal democracies. Liberal democracy, also known as representative democracy, and besides the protection of the rights of minorities, implies universal suffrage, granting all its adult citizens the right to vote and the right to pursue freedom without the infringement of their human rights as defined by their society. As history has shown, however, whoever gets the power, regardless of societal structure, tries to use it with all his or her conviction and might.

Why is that? To this simple question, an even simpler answer would be such is human nature. How does it manifest itself is the subject of the second part of this book.

With this remark, let me begin with a question: What precipitates the pattern that produces the characteristic face of any society? For centuries, different societies pursued the same goal of happiness but by different means.

Would it then be possible to construct a generic society that is indifferent to ethnicity, race, or nation? Why does any root-stable society—while always dynamic—eventually becomes obsolete? What contributes to such instability? What role, if any, does environment play?

As I discuss elsewhere in this book, people have a tendency to cling to each other in order to understand natural events and to overcome a multitude of impediments mutually handling such phenomena as loneliness and fear. If we add to this trend the physical proximity of

–

relatives, friends, and like-minded people, we find the nucleus of an organized group that is growing into a society.

On the other hand, individuality plays an important role in achieving those goals.

Homogeneity, displayed on the surface by any joined group of people, does not exclude but actually requires the distinct heterogeneous qualities brought by the separate individuals. These differences—combined, entangled, and molded in one melting pot—usually become a productive tool for a specific group of people and culture.

In fact, one can consider such joined group of people as a specific body that includes a number of disparate parts. They visibly function independently yet supplement each other, playing a role in creating a complicated mechanism. Eventually, it becomes obvious to them that as an organism, they may produce more accessories with much less effort, and this knowledge becomes their voyage road.

On the other hand, no matter which society one might refer to, it always based on characteristic similarity of people. Let's consider an autocracy as an example. Let's assume an autocrat or an absolute monarch acts out of his own despotic rules, completely neglecting the wishes and yearning of his own people. Yet no matter how devilish, unabashed, or ruthless such tyrant might be, he would still be surrounded by bootlickers, go-getters, butt-kissers, and pretentious flatterers with very little stock of like-minded people that eventually will produce the likeness of a monolith society.

When we speak of the homogeneity of a specific ethnic group, the accepted wisdom is that ethnically akin people can be visualized as one characteristic mass, if not homogeneous, then at least possessing special generally recognizable qualities. It is an accepted notion that ethnically related people, while clinging to each other, display analogous desires, possess the same appreciation of things, and are joined with similar understandings of splendor and opulence. They express like vision of happiness, sense of humor, feelings of pride, values, and morality. Thus, ethnicity plays a huge role for closeness of people. Adding to this pure genetic closeness, the environment in which such group of people resigns plays not a small role in creating characteristic features of any particular group.

The society, thus molded, gradually outgrew roots that are in fact another characteristic feature of humans (as well as all life organisms) to establish firm presence in generally unstable world, defying necessary coming eventual demise whether sooner or later.

Now let's consider what else might be influencing the structure of society.

In countries where religion still plays a significant role and becomes the monolith with the political governing of the country, people are indoctrinated at the level in which an individual does not have an ability to choose his or her style of life not related to religious preferences. Such examples in the contemporary world are the countries of the Middle East. The extremes that become prevalent are usually supported at the government level, resulting in necessarily dictated uniformed society. It is not surprising then that any deviations from the main course of such thrusting vision is punishable by law. In other words, this pressed-upon cultural attitude becomes, on the surface, accepted style of life for people of such society without recognition of obvious brainwash and coercion of its members.

This type of manipulated society, though from diametrically opposing approach in considering a role of religion has encountered in such countries as China, North Vietnam, and North Korea. Here we have a political party indoctrinating its people into an atheistic consideration of events, prohibiting interpretation of those based on religious beliefs. Owing to an inability to appreciate the reality of such closed society, the outsider, as a rule of thumb, makes an improper judgment of all the people that belong to this society, forcing to see its people as monolith body. In any event, gathering of humans leads to the production of a nucleus that finally turns into a society. Such a society struggles to survive by producing a multitude of means for living. Depending on the contribution by the core of its people and its natural resources, the society evolves into a definitive community. By pursuing concrete goals and establishing a form of government, a particular society adopts definite policy, or a constitution, depending on its organization. As time goes by, it achieves a distinct place among other communal organizations of similar or different structure.

In reality though, to achieve stability and recognition, society never develops as a monolithic body. With many undercurrents present, it is influenced by unceasing internal strife. After nurturing dreams

–

and hopes, different groups of people (read: the individuals) become progressively disturbed as that promise is not realized. Depending on its organization and the course it pursues, a society may find its goals either pushed further into the future or postponed indefinitely. As a consequence, societies come and go. No society may last forever, no matter how desirable such a project might be.

Originating in eighteenth-century Europe with the Age of Enlightenment, the argument arose that all people are created equal. Enlightenment thinkers tried to prove that, despite the unpredictable evil and violent nature of humans, people should be guided by reason and objectivity. Such approach, along with the human desire to be free, led to the formation of governments that would support constitutional laws created to protect the people within a society.

Yet while people are born with the same set of emotions, the display of these emotions differs, also differs is the individual ability of each member of society to adjust to existing circumstances.

This is one of the reasons why, in any society, there are those who are at the top and those who are on the bottom, with many levels in between. No matter which society one might consider, it is always schematically the same. People are born with different mental capacities. They are born with different levels of desire and ability to reach for their envisaged goals. These unique qualities bring unique destiny and success to each individual, despite seemingly similar overall mutual appreciation of life.

The simplest and easiest way to see it is by giving an example. Let's take for instance a structure in the army. There are soldiers, and there are generals. The soldiers are those who take the orders, and the generals are those who give these orders. There are many soldiers, while there are only a few generals. It is a fact of life. People, long time ago, figured it out, realizing that not everyone can be a general. It is with that same way of thinking one can surmise that not everyone can be CEO of a big corporation. It usually involves more than one or two corresponding qualifications. Of course, there are some cases when a soldier may turn into a talented general. But these are rare occurrences, and normally, such individual would have possessed hidden abilities that under certain circumstance were revealed. It is also resoundingly clear that to become a successful CEO involves even more than just ability and talents. One must possess endurance, the desire to achieve along with the ability, and a little luck that could be more appropriately referred to as favorable circumstances.

Yet more often than not, these basic requirements don't come together at once in one package.

With incompatibility between the desire and personal ability to achieve planned or established goal, it becomes noticeable that many discrepancies can be revealed that actually characterize each human being. Thus, we encounter people who are successful and those who are not. We come across people who are "chronically" lucky and those who are "chronically" not. We come across people who are happy and warm and those who display such negative feelings as envy, meanness, and pleasure derived from the misfortune of others. Yes, we are burdened with feelings, and those feelings are also a part of our lives. If they are positively expressed, we accept them with joy and belief that it is somehow an expected norm. But if a person possesses the prevailing negativity, we are having different reaction toward such an individual.

If we consider these feelings as negative, we begin to wonder why people are permeated with them. Those feelings often concern us; from time to time, we wish to know why we possess them and why some people express them more often than the others. We also wish to know how to correct those so-called abnormalities, quite persuaded that this is all possible.

For that reason, we create schools, academies, organizations, and institutions that provide us with special knowledge that are not necessarily always and especially equally comprehended. Thus, we get an army of psychologists, sociologists, and so on. Adding to it, we have those who feel that they are the masters in comprehension of fundamental reasons of problems in society and that are not necessarily connected to either talents or endurance or luck and the least of all some bad feelings.

In that sense, I'd like to mention some of the most virulent views of Noam Chomsky. In his book *Making the Future*, Chomsky not once (as well as in his many other books and numerous speaking events) peremptorily declares on the surface caring words, that for unsophisticated listener or reader sound like expressing concern, yet

—

at the same time they devoid of deep meaning and without making much sense. Thus we read, "The resulting concentration of wealth [since the 1970s] yielded greater political power, accelerating a vicious cycle that has led to extraordinary wealth for a fraction of 1 percent of the population, mainly, while for the large majority real incomes have virtually stagnated" (Noam Chomsky, *Making the Future*, 2012, p. 13).

These and similar remarks of people like Chomsky might influence some to believe that our world is full of injustices. It directs us to think that this impudent and ruthless 1 percent of people sneakily grab the opportunity, having in mind one specific purpose—to take the power in their own hands and to subdue and demolish the rest of the citizens. Such approach almost necessarily causes the turmoil that usually starts with an expression of rebellion, followed by quick progression to demonstrations, a.k.a. occupying public and personal properties, and eventually might lead to an attempt to overthrow the existing regime and government. Finally, if these compassionate self-proclaimed righteous people become successful, they might further the reconstruction of the particular society and eventually lead to a collapse of the existing model with the necessity of creating a new one.

A dawn of new society comes to existence with all the unavoidable changes. Now no matter which societal structure will be created, it will follow the same set of rules. Most of previous regulations and laws will be discarded. Those that a new society will reconsider may or may not be reestablished. People that played a role in throwing the previous model will be reshuffled and either become useful or with the firm feelings coming out of necessity and without real remorse will become obsolete.

An era of new enthusiasm and mistakes will crawl in. A child is born destined to live or die, whether achieving its maturity or regressing in premature and quite painful demise. But if it lives, it will go in steps of all previously existing societies.

So now our generic society, after achieving the heights of a harmoniously organized culture, begins to conduct a full-fledged style of life. But nothing in this world is forever, and our society gets very close to the point of exhausting its resources. If this is the case, it must necessarily seek the means for survival to avoid the collapse of its culture.

—

The task of finding new resources suddenly comes with a new goal. In times of peace, diplomatic attempts are made to solve the problem. When that does not produce positive results, those in charge of the society might consider military actions upon a neighboring population in order to achieve their goal.

Often a different scenario takes place. The society of a lower culture with fewer natural resources begins to lose its members to migration. This brings a depletion of human resources, the destabilization of culture, and, if no measures are taken to stop the free fall, such a culture eventually disappears.

It might also transpire that the whole society undertakes the new task and moves into another, more favorable geographical location. Such migration is a fact of history and is dependent on the availability of the needed land.

To finish, the scenario we considered not only would be theoretically possible, it indeed existed in many historical epochs with different degrees of success.

But thus far, we have discussed societies of ethnically similar and related people. Yet ethnic similarity is not always a given. A new and unprecedented example came with the United States of America.

Let's see what's the scenario of this new society might be.

CHAPTER 5

American Society

American society is unique on many levels. While it began with exploration by Spaniards looking for new sources of gold and more convenient routes to China and India, it quickly degenerated into bootlegging and the near elimination of the native population. The colonization of the American continent, initiated by Spain and Portugal, followed by the French, Dutch, Swedish, and finally the English, changed this unknown part of the world into a vibrant-yet-promising milk-and-honey region almost overnight.

For the first 150 years, this vast, mainly alien territory turned into separate, mostly belligerent colonies, occupied by settlers from a number of European cultures. These settlers had different religious affiliations, individual motives, and distinct claims on the land. With no desire to act as one community but energized by disparate ambitions, the colonists inevitably engaged in internal wars, forcefully removing many aboriginal cultures in the interim. No aristocrats came from European countries at that time, but instead many tradesmen, speculators, and vagabonds arrived in a new land. These settlers laid the foundation for a new and distinct culture, eventually acquiring the name of the United States of America.

The Wild West, inescapably wild by origin, had begun its remarkably hyperbolized and grotesque history and life. People gunned each other down without hesitation as soon as their sense of self-importance was infringed upon. They cared little for the lives of any stranger. Looting, robbery, and theft became the constant norm. Thankfully this period was relatively short-lived. By the end of the eighteenth century, settlers began to realize that laws were necessary in order to pursue the freedom they all craved. Relying on experience in the countries they'd left behind, they began to imitate their old cultures in a new environment.

That was also time that acquired the historical term of spiritual awakening. After the Spanish built their missions in Florida, Georgia, Texas, New Mexico, and California, the French established their footholds in Louisiana, Illinois, and Michigan, and Great Britain settled the East Coast, the people began to realize that their gathering must be brought into some order, however incongruent it might be, if they wanted their new society to last. Whether because of the proximity and geographical exposure to the civilized world of European countries like Spain, France, and Portugal or the particular and somewhat unfounded attitude of the English colonists as being superior, the main engine for the establishing of a new rule sprouted on and from the East Coast.

Starting with the creation of committees of correspondence in 1772, the British colonists increasingly raised their voices against the illegitimacy of a series of taxes that Britain imposed on them. During the next few years, these committees organized the Continental Congress, declaring that their own laws took precedence over the laws of the British Empire. New colonial militias began to gather in cities such as Boston, readying to withstand the British forces. To suppress the protest and to restore British rule, the English sent combat troops; fighting between the colonists and the British Empire began. The year was 1775. The war, today known as the American Revolutionary War, or the American War of Independence, which began with the Battles of Lexington and Concord, led the victorious settlers of the East coast to declare their independence from the British Empire in 1776. In issuing the Declaration of Independence, they proclaimed the right of a cooperative union for self-determination. In that year, thirteen former British colonies founded the United States of America. This union included only colonies on the East Coast without reference to the South, West, and Northwest.

—

The newly created country laid its foundation on the idea that "all men are created equal." Never abandoned, but somewhat modified over the years, the concept was meant to protect its all enfranchised citizens through a Bill of Rights, which was adopted in 1791.

Since that particular time, for the relatively short period of a little over one hundred years, the United States had drastically changed their territory, acquiring and annexing Louisiana, Florida, California, Texas, Alaska, and Hawaii, along with a few more independent countries and territories.

Fast-forward, by the nineteenth century, major acquisitions, expansions, and annexations, were completed, establishing, for the most part, one monolithic united country with one government in charge. Occupying the most substantial part of North America, today the United States is the third-largest country in the world in both area and population.

After introducing its governance framework, the United States, in September 1787, adopted a constitution as the written law of the newly organized nation. The federal government was assigned three branches: the executive, the legislative, and the judicial. Each branch was endowed with specific powers and duties. This division was designed to distribute the power and authority of the government to prevent it from falling into an authoritarian system. And with that, the United States of America became the oldest democratic society in the world.

Today, the executive branch of the United States consists of the president, the cabinet, and the federal departments. The executive branch has the responsibility to enforce existing laws, to determine foreign policy, and to manage the armed forces. The president and his cabinet cannot make new laws or interpret them. The last two roles are respectively assigned to the legislative and judicial branches.

With the federal system as the main instrument to keep the country's political platform sound, the power of government is conditionally divided between the central agencies and the states. The federal government wields the authority according to the principles of federalism, which imply a shared power between the federal government and the state government. The federal government is the national government of the constitutional republic of fifty states.

—

The term republic implies that the heads of each state and the other government officials are elected representatives of the people. As such, government officials cannot represent any special group without considering the interests of all the people equally.

The states were given the freedom to adopt local governing agencies to make decisions about local taxes, fire and police protection, education, and other commonwealth issues of the local community.

The first political party, founded by Thomas Jefferson and James Madison in 1790, was the Democratic-Republican Party. The Democratic-Republican Party contrasted with the Federalist Party formed by Alexander Hamilton. One of the major points of disagreement between these two parties was related to the Federalists' supposed inclination to prefer the monarchial principles of Great Britain.

The Democratic-Republican Party lasted until 1825, after which it was dissolved. Besides the many innovations in elective processes and the detailed organization of the new governing system, one of the major effects the party had on society was the creation of a network of newspapers.

While the party members, including presidents, called themselves "republicans," the term was used to describe the overall political values of the new nation. Today the Democratic and Republican parties exist as opposite and often countering forces. The modern Republican Party, not related to the former Democratic-Republican Party, was founded in 1854. It used the term republican in memory of Jefferson's party. The Democratic Party had officially been recognized since 1832. In our days, the Democratic Party is often called "the party of Jefferson" and the Republican Party is called "the party of Lincoln," which only serves to emphasize the instability and confusion originally existing in the terminology of both parties.

Despite ideological disagreements between the Federalists and the Democratic-Republicans, both parties contributed to the future strong national government of the United States of America.

History, nevertheless, has shown that people remain people in spite of beautiful and noble slogans. At every level of the American society, starting with the federal government, down to the African slaves, fighting had broken out among the opposing sides. Whether it

–

was a diplomatic effort or a duel or merely squelching the discontented by force, fighting quickly became an accepted practice of ideologues. People began to realize that their inalienable rights must be fought for, though they didn't have to fight the deep-rooted, inveterate conservatism characteristic of the European countries from which they came.

But what was taking place had led to the separation of people based on different understanding of religion, freedom, lifestyle choices, and, yes, the inalienable rights not equally accorded to all or accepted by all.

As it is usually the case of any establishing society, an American society began from an agrarian development of the newly acquired lands. Along with it, the characteristic feature of human beings and, in this particular case, of the American farmers, came that in that early period; people began to exhibit the signs of defiance to everything that was considered as an infringement upon their newly acquired freedom. The so-called excise tax that government decided to apply to farmers in a form of a new taxation for the leftover grain and corn led to the fighting of the farmers against the government official that came to be known as the Whiskey Rebellion. While the rebellious farmers didn't like the law that asked them to pay more taxes than they considered their fair share and while they somewhat logically rejected the idea that they had to pay for the financiers and speculators, an old genetic imperfection interlaced with an imperfect mind brought to the surface the sickening features of human nature: envy and blame. Without going to the core and without trying to analyze the necessity of paying taxes to help to reduce the national debt, farmers immediately began to blame the political ploy of the federal government and, as a result, the Democratic-Republican party came to power in 1801.

Yet by consolidating and expanding to the west, north, and south and by using indentured workers and slaves, America gradually found itself reintegrated as a country. With the substantial influx of new immigrants, the United States stepped onto the fast track of urbanization and industrialization.

By the early twentieth century, America was a sovereign country effectively declaring its status as a political, economic, and military power. It was accepted as a major player not only regionally by neighbors to the north and south, but everywhere else in the world.

—

Was the United States a monolith country inhabited by tightly connected people recognized as ethnic Americans, or was it somewhat of a myth? Did the outside perception differ from that of its insiders?

Strangely enough, more and more people realized that in America, as well as anywhere else, the rich got richer and poor got poorer. Whether it was a trade union, a band of brothers, or a religious and similar affiliation—like the Freemasons, the Knights of Columbus, a political party, or a criminal gang—it was always considered wise to come together under a gregarious slogan: "United we stand; divided we fall."

The logical question that followed was, "Is it possible to achieve this ideal on a large scale?" Theoretically, as many would agree, it sounds plausible but is most likely impossible in real life.

Of course, there is nothing wrong or unwise in trying to overcome obstacles or fight jointly. There are many examples of people doing exactly that in the face of catastrophe or hardship—but it is hopeless when people's interests do not coincide in the long run. That often was the case and cause for major upheavals, as history has proven time and again.

While America justifiably accepted the notion that it was the best country in the world, with its mostly proud citizens, it also realized that no paradise existed anywhere, including their own land and regardless of how exceptional her people may be.

Thus the removal of Native Americans to reservations, the slavery of blacks, the suppression of the rights of women, immoral experiments such as, for instance, the Tuskegee syphilis research from 1932-74 and the detainment of Japanese citizens in internment camps during World War II, were among the most awful mistakes young America made. Yet I believe she made these mistakes not because she wished to act barbarically but from a sheer lack of experience coupled with a desire for self-affirmation and defense of her interests.

With this assertion I would like to conduct my own analysis of contemporary America as a country, her cultural achievements, and her strong and weak points. I hope to do this without undue criticism and hopefully in a constructive manner.

The United States of America resulted from the enterprise of disparate people joined by a similar wealth of energy, willingness to assume unforeseen risks, and little doubt in their ability to succeed.

This country is viable and vibrant and invigorating for one simple reason: It did not abandon one of its truths, that America is a country of immigrants. This idea surely deserves some attention.

Today people mainly come to the United States from less-developed countries compared to the times of the original settlers. Since these new immigrants' roots and background are so different from that of the previous waves of the majority of immigrants, some of those Americans who were born here do not find many things in common with these later, continuously arriving people.

These Americans try to justify their pride, resistance, and unfriendly attitude by citing their government's attempts to try from time to time to open the country's borders wider. While heated arguments about immigration bring to a discussion such volatile issues as illegal ingress through the borders of the southern states, human trafficking, gang violence, and overburdened social services, naturally these Americans want to protect their nests from being disturbed. They therefore seek conciliatory excuses when they are asked to be friendlier, warmer, and more welcoming creatures than human nature disposes them to be.

Probably the most tangible reason for their resistance is established American culture, which is the best in the world in their eyes.

To those who resist immigration as a whole, the hodgepodge of immigrants from South America, India, the Mediterranean region, Africa, and Asia are often too much to take. Their different and often-foreign languages along with distinctly peculiar habits from poorly understood cultures force over the threshold of comfort of some Americans, denying larger society's desire to produce a melting pot.

The government called for further immigration control, often uses the influx of the newcomers as a political ploy. And as consequence, the results are less than satisfying. Some statistics even show that America is moving backward. Particularly in education, infrastructure, and the prosperity of its people, America is becoming less and less competitive on the international level. It is no longer considered avant-garde in important fields.

To top it all, the people who are flooding the country less and less remind those established through generations Americans who proudly call themselves an *exceptional* people.

—

That bothers some and disturbs many. So people begin to search for an answer. Why is this happening? Who is that person or distinguished group of compatriots who are guilty of polluting the society? Who can protect as well as restore the famous American pride? More and more people question America's ability to maintain its established place in the world. More and more people begin to question the role of government in achieving this goal.

Might the solution be easier to find if the real cause or causes of existing problems were defined? But who can say what the real causes are? What would a balanced, if not close to objective, recommendation look like?

As a starting point, why don't we begin by realizing that no matter how justified the pride of those Americans who were born here might be the longevity of this prosperous country is partly based upon a constant inflow of newcomers? Why then do the majority (as realized mainly through the perception of the media) not acknowledge that the zest for success displayed by these newcomers conforms to the country's norm? Immigrants, in their majority, are eager to study, to work, to create decent homes, and, overall, to live their lives according to the rules of the society they have chosen.

They do not fight working lesser-paying jobs or longer hours if those things offer success or survival. For the most part, they exhibit willingness to enjoy and not to complain. Therefore, rather than blame the new uncertainty on the newcomers, Americans should recognize that other obstacles must be keeping the country from climbing back to its previously earned and deserved place.

So let's try to dissect the arisen questions by providing corresponding answers. Who are the *American* Americans? How did they manage to create a superior society? How did they manage to create a society at all?

These are the kinds of questions asked by many new arrivals to America. They don't necessarily ask them in a straightforward fashion, but they do ask them.

Between the slogans about freedom, American pride, and constitutional protection of the rights of its citizens and people, a collection of amendments were introduced that had to be considered and reconsidered in the short life of this fairly young country.

—

Did America become the promised melting pot? Have people from so many different backgrounds, ethnicities, and nationalities at any time since the establishment of this country acted as one unit or as one family? Or does it remind more of a "salad bowl," as current sociologists have recently began to use this new term?

Let's consider some important facts and events to better understand this country and analyze a few cultural incongruities as they indeed exist.

Only recently, such minorities as blacks have been elevated from the level of second-class citizens with the rights to vote, build communities, and get an education. This is not necessarily so regarding their acceptance as equal applicants for jobs, especially where private enterprise is concerned. No wonder the number of unemployed blacks exceeds that of other ethnic groups and minorities. According to the Bureau of Labor Statistics in October 2011, the employment situation among blacks, is still around 15.1 percent (at the time of writing this book) compared to whites at a little over 8 percent.

Their obstacles amount to a number of different reasons, some of which I speak about in the article devoted to blacks in the United States.

Yet blacks are in a sense provoked by long-existent government programs. While not losing their desire to enjoy the better things in life, they got used to the obligation this country felt to fulfill the minimum resources needed to provide decent living to all its citizens.

The lot of the minority group we know as Hispanics, or more recently as Latinos, is not much different. Latinos suffer from an identity crisis. What I mean is that they do not object to being identified as Latino, but they do not wish to be profiled based on that label. Some states apply a practice of extrapolating information according to characteristic traits of Latinos. Those who look Latino, especially in southern states, might be the suspects of being in this country illegally based on their appearance. While there is nothing wrong with maintaining the accepted laws of this country and not giving in to pressure from different concerned individuals or groups that often are based on a false sense of the pride of the oppressed, by the same token, it is nothing but prejudice that would be based on an ethnic consideration that places a limit on an individual, denying his or her achievements or talent and thus depriving someone of their individuality.

We see people as groups: whites, Jews, Asians, and so on. We see people as religiously affiliated: Catholics, Mormons, and Protestants. We see people as minorities: homosexuals, the homeless, and the disabled.

We see people with hereditary diseases or those who were born into recognized labels without any choice in the matter. We categorize people according to their affiliation with a party, a club, and so on. Then we create further gradations for those belonging to such a group.

In that regard, let me speak of a few such groups, starting with homeless people.

With our tendency to generalize, we may speak of them as a minority group, as a separate few, or as individuals. But how we speak of them is dictated by our task. What do we need to accomplish? If we need to understand who homeless people are and why they are on the streets that would be one part of our task. If we try to solve their homelessness as a societal problem, than that will clearly be a different mission.

First and foremost, we need to understand that homeless people have one thing in common: They can no longer struggle in the community in which you and I still function with different degrees of success. The reasons why this has happened might matter only if we decide we want to help them. And by help, I don't mean hand them a dollar or two just to make ourselves feel better. By help, I mean long-lasting and objective programs that will direct these people to recovery. Schizophrenics need to be treated in institutions (and we need to make sure these are available). Drug addicts must be placed in rehab centers. Those who have simply lost their means to survive must be offered shelters along with training and retraining programs. No person must be left behind, no one.

It is ridiculously irresponsible to speak of aiding these people in terms of transgressing the Constitution—as if to protect their right and freedom to be homeless. They are not on the streets out of a desire to be free. It is not their choice to be happy on the streets. Pride, ambition, and the pretense that everything is under control are all *the excuses for inaction*, whether we acknowledge it or not. It is also absolutely wrong to imagine yourself in the place of these people. It

–

accomplishes nothing if you weigh your understanding of freedom to choose. Nobody in his or her proper mind would choose to stay on the streets, scrambling to survive.

There are of course those who might fall into a category of runaway teenagers, who, while having different agendas in each particular case, are still out there mostly because of mishandled family matters. These will be addressed later in this book, in a chapter called "Rearing the Children."

For now, let me go back to the homeless people who are not related to the issues of runaways. How do we help these unfortunate people? How do we prove that the melting pot actually exists and that Americans are warm, thoughtful, and caring people?

What if we were to establish a federally run bureaucratic unit that would be specifically responsible for the welfare of homeless people? I am not going to provide here the details of who would be doing what in such an organization. What I am concerned with is justice without overblown mistrust or possible corruption and, therefore, the need for double—and triple-verifying agencies with the involvement of profiteering lawyers. I do not imply the service of social workers, although there are among them encountered those who nurture a thought to establish their names and prospering career more than they should care about people they were elected to help. But most of all, I don't wish to produce a fight about the validity of withholding an extra dollar from your (as a law-abiding citizen) paycheck that would probably be the result of such step.

With necessarily emerging opposition who would fight anyone who brings a new idea how to improve health of the established society, it would be no wonder to hear many objections, including that the government not being able to do anything good or that the bureaucrats will impede any good or novel ideas.

While the reader will consider how to object to this sort of unlikely coming intrusion into your business, let me discuss yet another dilemma somewhat unrelated to the one described above. Let me speak of homosexuals.

Are homosexuals perverts? Are they abnormal or sick people?

A man starts to speak. He speaks eloquently for a while. Suddenly he becomes irrelevant and irrational. He speaks nonsense. He is disconnected from reality. That is how psychiatrists usually define

—

schizophrenia. Schizophrenia is a pathological illness. It is a disease that is treated with varied levels of success in special clinics or institutions. Schizophrenics are not normal people.

But how does one define abnormality? Is it what isn't normal? Then what is normal? Could abnormality be a phenomenon that is characteristic of the majority? We all know that the majority could be involved in, for example, smoking marijuana, gluttony, or acts of war.

Abnormal usually means not typical or deviating from some typical standard. It could be something physical with an exact value. Or it could be some abstract concept that serves as the reference of a medium value.

Abnormal often means pathological, whether one refers to a physical proof or the human mind's way of thinking that is habitually compared to a standard.

With that comes another question: What is standard?

It has not been proven that homosexual people are born with some genetic difference although it is a possibility. Yet it is a proven fact that homosexual inclination appears from early childhood, when a child's sexual orientation, as well as many other psychological inclinations, are still in development. At that age, children may experiment with new forms of excitement. But while the prevailing majority discards the idea of planned or attempted coitus with someone of the same sex sooner rather than later, homosexual individuals continue to experience substantial same-sex attraction.

Could we then conclude that homosexuals are abnormal? Not according to the provided definitions. So while recognizing gay people as normal, we should also realize where they stand, what their rights are, and what means they apply while struggling and demanding their rights and recognition.

For one, we need to appreciate that homosexuals have a full set of feelings, the need for excitement, and a sex drive just as all other humans do. They enjoy things everyone else enjoys with some variety from person to person. They try to achieve success in the same ways as most of the rest of humanity pursues.

Yet they have sexual needs the majority of people either don't display or have subdued. They are no doubt acutely aware of being different, and for that reason alone, their own sense of belonging to general society can become twisted, and society has been slow to accept them.

—

When someone feels different from everyone else and tries to succeed in a society that does not seem much concerned about unusual individuals, it often produces a psychological hindrance for such an individual. On the other side of the spectrum, such a person might display an obvious and exaggerated type of behavior that the majority of others would perceive as extravagant, which can slow the society's ability to be accepting.

Today, American society mainly tolerates gay people. There are some outbursts against homosexuals, and especially against gay men, but the more people become aware of homosexuality, the less they express negative feelings toward gays and lesbians.

The question that must be answered first of all, I believe, is who, or rather what, is homosexual?

Sadly there are still a number of people in our contemporary world who do not have a clue about gays and lesbians. These people believe that homosexuality is simply a wrong way to express beautiful sexual needs that are ingrained in humans. These people believe that homosexuals are perverts who were not reared properly. These people insist that in any moral society, with proper religious and social education, it is possible, if not of the utmost importance, to convert homosexuals into heterosexuals regardless of the effort involved. In other words, they believe in the possibility of "rehabilitating" gay men and women, because, to them homosexuality is a moral condition that under special circumstances might turn into an acquired disease.

If this were the case, there would be many occurrences of converting gay people into straight people, would there not? If perversion or a dissolute lifestyle were actually the cause of homosexuality, it would be "normalized" with time under the proper circumstances. Suffice it to say, history has not presented us with such statistics.

Whether it starts from the mental interpretation of enjoyment or the physical location of erogenous zones different from those of heterosexual people, or even a combination of both, one must agree that moral perversion has nothing to do with homosexuality. For those who might see examples of homosexuals married to opposite-sex partners and producing offspring, my suggestion would be to better familiarize themselves with my classification: There is no precise type of people, according to Hippocrates classification exists, and which I mentioned at the beginning of this book.

—

Those who are attracted to those of both sexes are most likely bisexuals, who sometimes have an exaggerated inclination toward one sex. But usually bisexuals equally enjoy relationships with either sex.

Homosexuals in the United States are a distinct group. They have been able to rid themselves of many obstacles that gays and lesbians experience in other cultures and countries.

In this country, many homosexuals went through the steps of being in the "closet" for a distinct part of their lives to becoming outspoken individuals who were not necessarily always discreet in their confessions. And this might be one of the ineffective moves homosexuals make. There is such a thing as the norm of social decency and tolerance, which is the accepted standard to which people are accustomed, and people in any culture try to adjust themselves to these norms either willingly or through an enforcement of the law. But those who make themselves outcasts by differing from these norms usually experience different degrees of estrangement.

To start, it is hard to understand why people need to be aware of a person's sexual orientation to accept them. I am not particularly suggesting that gays would be better off back in their closets, but a policy akin to the military's "don't ask, don't tell" (whether repealed or not) sounds fairly reasonable to me. Such an attitude toward gays would accomplish a dual task. First, I am probably not the only person who does not want to know about the sex lives of other people. Not because it is somehow offensive to me but because it is usually more information than I normally would wish to know. Second, it is easier (and again I speak for myself) to accept a person without bias without knowledge of their sexual orientation.

In other words, a person who insists on defining another person on the basis of his or her sexual orientation promotes a label of prejudice along with all the other invented labels mentioned elsewhere. Why? We do not talk about straight people emphasizing their sexual preferences unless it presents a particular concern. The majority of heterosexuals do not discuss their sexual encounters with strangers.

Surely there are other signs that might reveal who is gay. But so be it. Why must it concern me? People are different. We constantly learn how to tolerate each other or how to accept unusual events and behavior. Must it bother anyone, then, that many homosexuals love to dress in more extravagant ways than most straight people do? Must it bother anyone that gay people often find themselves in such fields as fashion design, interior decorating, and some forms of art? This might be explained, though not always, by a psychological pressure exerted by heterosexuals on homosexuals, who make gay people feel the need to prove their "normality" despite their obvious differences. They seek more like-minded people through the Internet, the organization of spectacular parades, and special nightclubs. One might say that there is nothing wrong with it. And there might not be. But why do we need to emphasize sexuality? Why force someone else's sexual preferences on someone who is not interested? Why create the illusion of being in the majority when you are not? You cannot prove much by your openness in such a manner, but you may evoke estrangement by, if not the complete disgust of someone who is not into the same whirlpool of your sexual appetite.

There is one more thing that needs to be mentioned here. Even if people finally recognize that you were born this way, don't insist on having all the privileges heterosexuals have. Don't insist that your right to have children is equal to those legally provided to heterosexual couples who might find themselves medically unable to have children. Don't try to convince the authorities and the concerned public that you can nurture and educate your child as well as the next straight person might, or possibly even better.

This really does not matter, especially given the case of what motivates you.

Without a doubt a heterosexual couple deserves to adopt a child more than you do. Why? Because that would be a socially accepted way that children are usually raised. Even if you anticipate your relationship working well for a long time, or even if you might take care of a child much better than a heterosexual couples or a single parent, as long as you don't deny or hide your sexual preferences, others will assume your children will be exposed to all types of sexuality.

Despite all of your flexibility, skill, or experience, in the long run, you will experience most of the problems heterosexual couples do. You will possibly separate from your partner and form a relationship with a new partner. Have you sincerely thought of such a scenario, which would require your answer to a future child? What if your heterosexual child would not completely accept your, and therefore his, circumstance? What if your child started to feel different, perhaps ashamed, or maybe depressed? Shouldn't you consider this part of your story as well, not only, selfishly, yours?

But then again, would it put more restraints on you than on your heterosexual fellow human? Does it imply a suppression of your rights? If that is the case, ask yourself more questions. Do you need a heterosexual partner to produce children? Can you blame anyone that you were born different than the majority of people? Is this the main motif that forces you to insist that you are entitled to get married?

Well, no one in their right and unprejudiced mind would deny you having a relationship with your partner. No civilized person devoid of prejudice would deny your unification either. But why do you insist on calling this unification a family? I do not consider the legal nuances of defining marriage. My question is why aren't you satisfied with having a legitimate union between you and your partner instead of insisting on getting married the way heterosexuals invented for themselves? What is wrong with legitimizing just the union and to call it what it is?

Think about it. Don't play the role of the oppressed in this democratic society. You cannot complain, if you are sincere enough to appreciate your status. No one on a large scale, except for a few antigay bigots, is trying to offend or diminish you. Be thankful for what you've gotten without constant pressure on the rest to give you more and more in this life.

There is no paradise on earth. Each one of us gets his or her own portion of share either as the rewards or a point at issue that one has to tackle with. You and I must be perfectly aware of it. Each one of us must accept it. And each of us must truly be thankful for it.

CHAPTER 6

Pro-Choice versus Pro-Life

On the subject of whether to have or not have an abortion, I am not going to provide you with Solomon's decision and say who is right and who is wrong. Both sides are correct in their interpretation of a dilemma, and my only role is to substantiate both positions.

The latest discussion on the topic in the United States commenced in 1973 with the controversial *Roe v. Wade* decision. When the Supreme Court decided on a woman's right to have an abortion, the decision gave way to many legal issues that flared up from time to time but were never finalized.

Discussed at the federal and state levels involving different supporting and opposing groups, the debate soon reached national, religious, and political arenas. The reason so many groups got involved in the issue was in fact quite simple. Each group pursued their own interests under the umbrella of fighting for a good cause. But on a surface, it had never exceeded the two opposing forces fighting each other to the tooth and nail.

Thus, today the controversy is not less intense and relentless than it was some few decades ago, with different layers of society supporting the right of a woman to choose and different conservative groups against it.

How does a child get into this world? Does it become the product of an effort of a man and a woman? Does it become a fruit of an undisputed love between two people? Or does the birth of a child

–

come from an undisputable match of the mysterious energy finalized in the continuation of life?

To no one's surprise, the answer to the question like this will be "Any desirable or undesirable coincidence may eventually produce life."

Could that be another cruel joke placed upon us by an unknown source?

How did people learn about birth? Who was the first teacher to explain the nature of pregnancy and labor?

These are not idle or silly questions if we wish to try to answer them.

People don't get representatives from another world to help them learn, acquire knowledge, be warned, or receive explanations. In a general sense, people are always the pioneers in their beginnings.

First, they start by experimenting. Then they learn that some of their experiments turn out to be mistakes. Soon they begin to apply rules to satisfactory outcomes. They begin to learn how to avoid bad judgment.

When society discusses issues with moral linings, such a society is considered civilized. From here on, people consider their motives to be logical explanations and acceptable norms.

Do we have to blame a woman for having an abortion? Do we have the right to decide on her behalf to abort a fetus (or child) or not? Is it godless for her to kill an unborn child when she, due to her nature, acts as a vehicle for future human beings?

When we plan to have children, it is noble. But most of the times we are simply obtaining pleasure from our sex games. We'd love to think that we wouldn't mind having children as a result. But what if procreation were not connected to sex? Very few of us would really want to have children then. Why? Because with children come responsibilities. And with that also comes a different level of sacrifice. Why then would we still consider having a child? Probably the next few answers will encompass the majority of the offered theories: ego, loneliness, some amount of nobility, and curiosity.

If God created the poor and rich, the famous and obscure, and contributed to creating the sick and healthy, then he was most likely the one who gave us the opportunity to continue life. With that, he must have allowed a woman to be relieved from pregnancy by different means and yes, till today, by an abortion. Perhaps by this gesture he gave us some kind of task that we have yet to solve, while weighing if we have the "right" to kill an innocent child. To those of you who believe that they know the answer, I have a question: How many possible future lives are destroyed by masturbating youth, and what harm if any is produced by the ejaculation of sperm without a sex partner?

On the other side of the coin, do you feel that you have an answer to what kind of a person, good or bad, might have been born if an abortion hadn't prevented it?

To take a more responsible approach to this dilemma, a few more questions need to be asked, not so as to point at hypocrisy but to further signify people's awareness.

What motivates either camp, pro-choice or pro-life?

Let's first consider pregnancy from the mechanical point of view. A woman who becomes pregnant is condemned, in a sense to months of exhausting her body and overcoming such common complications as severe bodily swelling, severe, long-lasting headaches, gestational diabetes, high blood pressure, and uncontrollable vomiting. She may even suffer a miscarriage or an ectopic pregnancy (when the fertilized egg implants outside the uterus). There are many more severe complications not mentioned here because this is not a medical study forum, but rather a written discussion to make a point. Psychologically, a woman may also undergo such ordeals as depression, suicide attempts that will actually be propelled to the end, or be frightened of harming her future child while caring it.

Does the conservative camp of prolife advocates really care? To them, the life of a defenseless fetus has a stronger right to be protected than a pregnant woman has to relieve her psychological or physical turmoil. Yet should we label them as insolent and callous people?

Must the behavior characterizing any opposing camp be taken into account while we consider a motivation of a particular individual?

From the ethical, humane, and moral points of view, the behavior of each individual counts. From the position of the advocates of any particular group, it always reflects a general platform on which such a group stands.

Certainly the life of a fetus has to be weighed against the sufferings of a mother. But, as in the case of a transgression of law, there are motives and circumstances that must be considered; such must be taken into account with the case of a pregnant woman.

I do not wish to introduce in this discussion the position of the churches and different religions. Each without any doubt brings a positive point or two in such a debate. But this book is not a proper forum for such discussion, suffice to say that whoever speaks on this particular topic is mostly correct if a speaker is not an extremist in any direction.

In other words, each representative has a legitimate point. One might be on the surface more obvious than the other. But while I personally would not recommend an abortion, to me, proper (and strict, I might add) education beforehand, contributing to the possible prevention of an undesirable pregnancy, must take place rather than an unnecessary blame of a platform of an opposing camp. I will speak about that in more detail in the chapter titled "Society and Its Morals."

CHAPTER 7

Animal Abuse and Sacrifice

There are at least two ways to approach this dilemma: popular and religious.

To consider the abuse of animals under a popular umbrella, one must include such little-justified means of cruelty as the disfiguring of dogs and cats when we thoughtlessly neuter or spay them. This act alone is done for the sole comfort of humans, who in the majority use these domesticated pets for selfish pleasure. There is also little consideration for malnourished, feral cats and dogs that for this reason alone are having short, unhappy lives in the wild.

The Humane Society of the United States has been doing a tremendous job starting in 1954 in providing shelters for stray, abused, and rescued animals. Their mission to create a sensible human-animal bond cannot be over exaggerated. But while this organization has achieved substantial improvements for the protection of animal habitats, it is clearly not enough, as abuse of animals sporadically continues, not only in this country, but all around the world. The practices of dog fighting, the clubbing of different exotic animals for the commercial fur trade, and euthanasia are the more obvious signs of the mishandling animals by humans.

And yet there are other, more severe and obvious displays of human cruelty, such as hunting, fishing, or placing animals in restricted human habitats known as zoos, which are used merely for pleasure and are inconsistent with the survival of human habitat.

–

The world in which we are residing has at its core a cruel reality: We cannot survive without eliminating other lives. We need to devour animals for food. Even those who have proudly announced themselves as followers of plant-based diets eradicate fruits and vegetables along with different grains, all of which belong to a world that is the least comprehended and appreciated. Whether or not plants express their "feelings" in way humans or even animals can understand becomes irrelevant, as we do not know for a fact whether plants are suffering while being eliminated.

At that point, we realize that our world has been made this way, and it is not always up to us to change it. Yet while we are powerless in that sense, we might learn how to make this place of our survival more equally serviceable for all life provided.

But to kill for reasons such as to prove someone's point, to save someone's honor, or out of revenge would be immature if the matter were not so grave. There is a difference between killing for survival's sake (one bad example would be an act of war) and killing for spectacle and entertainment, although both could be prevented if people had more control of their violent tendencies. There is such a thing as an accidental killing, and in those occurrences, we are powerless, trying to find justification for how this could happen.

On a different platform stands (though mainly in the past times) killing for religious sacrifice. First of all, it would be absolutely godless to request humans to kill an innocent animal on God's behalf. Secondly, God, if he were around, wouldn't need a man to kill someone to prove man's loyalty. Third, God—or gods, for that matter—do not need food of any kind in order to survive. Hence, killing a defenseless animal is not only a cruel and unjustified act, but it is definitely irrelevant to God's existence also.

That animals are also killed by those sadistic creatures sick in their minds, such people may be substantially ill and definitely need medical attention. But among these people, as usually the case is, there is a different degree of their illness. Thus, their disease might be transient, and while not in any measure benign, it still comes in early childhood and disappears with the maturing and learning the proper morals. It becomes profoundly sickening when such an individual carries this enjoyment to adulthood. I somewhat mention why that is the case in the last part of my book titled "My Thoughts on a Few Other Dispositions of Humans."

—

CHAPTER 8

The Crowd and a Hero

People by nature possess tribal instincts that make them cling together. Together they appreciate the power of events, develop general attitudes toward newly learned phenomena, and decide on acceptance or rejection of the lifestyle they want to conduct.

The fabric of society is such that it might be easily compared to a fiber rope. It seems monolith from a distance, but the closer one approaches, it the better one can see the structure of which it is made. It is a recognized fact that belongs to our material world, yet it is much less understood compared to the explanation of our individual appreciation of events along with corresponding behavior.

This phenomenon, pointing to the mentality of a crowd versus the mentality of an individual normally is expressed in the powerful urge of finding a hero. A hero who would be able to connect us all and who would prove that our desires, our quest for life, are not whimsically strange and a lonely road must not become our unfortunate destiny.

And when a rising star comes along, declaring through different means of his arrival, the majority of a crowd rushes to the claimant with open arms.

In other words, people always need someone who will be able to lead them. This desire expressed by expectation of someone, allows people to acknowledge a sudden star almost instantly.

An expectation of such a leader lies dormant but always present however subconsciously.

This need for a hero is actually self-explanatory. People are often confused and unsure of their general direction. They are often not happy with the produced results. A hero or a leader who appears quite suddenly and who could be the navigator for a few or hundreds or thousands and sometimes even for tens of millions of people is always welcome and is always expected. Following the acceptance of such an individual, people generally feel temporary relief yet almost immediately scramble to test the new hero by his or her performance. Therefore, designating someone as leader does not necessarily mean that that person will last.

The simplest illustration of such a hero, along with proof of people's submissive nature, can be easily spotted on a road. Many times when a reckless driver hits the road, he immediately produces at least one, but most likely a few others, not as much as the imitators of the false headman, but rather those insecure and unstable individuals who are expressing the need to find a leader. The less conspicuous desire to reduce stress by lifting constantly self-applied practice of being under control of one's own will power is another, more subtle but nevertheless present feature about which I am speaking in more details somewhere else in the book.

To say that this hero follows or makes rules often not characteristic of the majority is mostly exaggerated. He or she might grossly distort the wishes of one's own people or even follow the interests of a few, but as a rule of thumb, this hero is always a reflection of the people's longing.

Depending on the specific agenda involved, he might or might not reflect on the wishes of the majority. The larger the crowd he gets, the more complicated it becomes to focus its attention on individual and mutual goals.

In a large society, a newly produced leader might be perceived as a hero, as inspirer, and sometimes even as a traitor, which depends on the structure and the vision of any particular society.

Do people need a hero? Can they do without one? The answer I wish to offer is that people are mostly idle in their behavior. They need someone who is energetic, passionate, and reflective of their aspirations. If the chosen hero shows the qualities necessary to lead, he becomes a real leader; but he is also placed on a shaky pedestal by the yearning crowd.

That doubt that people express is something embedded in all of us. We doubt our friends, our neighbors, and our relatives, and we doubt ourselves. We need constant proof that we are on the right track, and we aspire to get it from a chosen hero.

CHAPTER 9

On Patriotism and Loyalty

There is nothing wrong with being loyal to friends or to a country or to the government that represents it. People usually feel faithful to an ethnic community of the country in which they were born. They feel patriotic and obligated to protect their land in times of danger. They develop a true love for their place in this world. These feelings are especially prominent in people who—besides feeling kinship among themselves—are aware of being the core of the land's inhabitants.

There are times, however, when a government uses the loyalty of its subjects to its own advantage. When that is the case, it is not only using its truehearted devotees but the populace as a whole, regardless of what is best for their welfare. Such a government is methodical in its pursuit of producing as many robotic humans as possible. The more robotic a member of society becomes, the better the results are in terms of what is expected of such individual with regard to his loyalty to his comrades and the country he defends.

The message is, don't think much. Don't question the validity of an order. Don't question the need to accomplish a given assignment, task, or mission.

Aren't these the main rules in the army or any other force we designate to be our guardian angels?

I will repeat that same sentence with which I began: There is nothing wrong with being loyal. What is wrong is for a government—or, for that matter, any agency with such power—to cynically and insincerely use loyalty to its own advantage without love for its people.

Does this happen? Does it happen everywhere or in some places and not others? I will let you decide.

CHAPTER 10

On the English Language

While this country is perceived as an English-speaking country, it is far from certain which tongue will become the most popular. Spanish conquistadors were not only the first people who began to settle in America after encountering Native Americans; for some time, they were the tangible majority among the later-appearing French, Dutch, and English colonists. Today the Spanish-speaking population again becomes a majority as an ethnic group that lives as a major minority group in such large states as Texas, Florida, California, and New York, easily conversing in both Spanish and English.

There are, of course, more subtleties than this, such as Spanglish in Arizona or Nuyorican in New York. Asian communities, while sufficiently spread all around the country, use different dialects as well as languages. This segregation of language into dialects is not characteristic for other communities such as the Russian, Muslim, Greek, and Italian communities are. But their population does not come close to the number of Spanish-speaking people in this country.

The topic of what language should be acknowledged as the United States' official language has become the subject of discussion, especially in the last few years. With the increasing numbers of Hispanics as well as Latinos from South America, Spanish looks to become our second language. With such an obvious use of Spanish, some authorities should not declare English as the only official language.

On the other hand, this declaration has a legitimate point as English (though not American English as we know it) was the official language that the colonists used when they created the United States of America. The English colonists were successful not only in achieving independence but also in expanding and empowering this country, turning it into a subject of admiration and respect—though not always and not for all its deeds.

Nevertheless, it is due primarily to the efforts of British, Scottish, and Irish immigrants that this country became what it is today.

With today's need to speak two languages, as is usually the case for any civilized bilingual country, the Spanish language seems to be the most appropriate choice.

CHAPTER 11

Society and Its Morals

Before I will discuss this topic, I wish to clarify a definition of moral values. I'd like to introduce my understanding of what are objective moral values and what is the base for sound moral values.

Objective moral values are those that exist in human appreciation of life, thus are man-made definition. They mean that true objective moral values could only be those that imply not intentional and not without justification harm induced on other live organisms. Sound moral values, on the other hand, are based on positive reflection of the majority of any given society.

As usual is the case, there are two main approaches to this topic, one is offered by an atheist and the other by a religious advocate. The theists always connect their explanation to an existence of a god, while from an atheist point of view, moral values develop along with evolution of humanity that cares about its well-being. In my mind, both explanations are only partially truthful, mainly for the reason that they are not objective. They each pursue a hidden desire to prove their base. They much reflect on contemporary achievements in particular society. And they do not project all-embracing ideas of what is moral and what is not.

Let me explain why I say that. From a religious perspective, the moral values of a man are always projected through God's assumed attributes: compassion, love, kindness, and so on. We discussed those attributes before, that humans somehow handed them to God, and here I wish to underlie that religious advocates seek to prove them, along with other imaginary descriptions of God. Simply put, this kind of god could not and would not exist or rather last forever. And while theists do insist that a moral person can exhibit his best qualities only when he is connected to God, there are plenty of examples that this is not always the case. The premise that atheists have no reason to be moral is based on a wrong assumption whence the need for morality is coming from.

Morality is coming from an individual appreciation of an accumulated general wisdom brought about by the multitude of societies. This wisdom suggests that not being moral will lead to self-destruction of an individual in a much faster pace than of those who are trying their best to accommodate that magic desire to be moral and become adjusted to the rules of a society. Not knowing what is good and what is bad for one's well-being may lead to a destruction of that individual, however fast or slow it might be. Such an individual without a clear conscience that leads him to analyze his behavior will come to a conclusion of possible detriment of his behavior sooner or later. Accepting true and objective morality as a way of life will only help an individual survive in a particular society without jeopardizing one's own ability to last.

With regard to not intentional or not without justification harming another life, the way we exist is eventually placed in front of a dilemma—what is the lesser evil? As long as this rule is followed, it will be considered as sound moral value in any particular society.

Now with this general description of moral values, let us proceed to a concrete narration of moral values in a particular country, the United States of America.

You and your destiny
You and your mood
You and the accident
You and disease
You and the galaxy

You never know what is going to happen tomorrow or a month or a year from now. Take from life everything you can today. Enjoy it as much as you can because tomorrow may be too late. You could get into an accident and become paralyzed. You could die from disease. Isn't it a bit strange that while you did not choose this galaxy, you are still stuck in it with all its preconditions?

Besides, who can tell you that if you follow the regulations with which you have been provided, you will definitely live a longer, happier, and healthier life?

Let's consider these questions from another angle.

How much should the government have the power to dictate, to make rules, and therefore to intrude upon your understanding of freedom? Do you trust that the people in charge somehow know what could make you feel happy?

Do you trust them to decide what you should do and what you should not do?

Should they dictate whether you must have an education, even only on an elementary level? Should they tell you what or how much you can eat and drink?

Do you have the answers to any of these questions?

Why do people still feel unhappy even though they claim that they have almost everything?

Why do people often become bored and discontent with what they have?

Do we need any laws and rules? If yes, then *why*?

A single woman who is a teacher becomes pregnant. Should or should she not continue to teach your child or other schoolchildren? Is she morally adequate for such a role?

Would you like to know what people think and say these days?

First of all, they say many different things but instead of listing them all, I'll just mention a few.

Those on a board of education might consider whether a single, pregnant teacher should be fired. Among the young, single, and the majority of women, the opinion might be that the teacher should be given the choice to abort or not abort the baby. Among the majority of men, one might hear that she has undermined her credibility and therefore must be fired. And the schoolchildren involved? They generally could not care less.

Who is right? Why is it only the woman who is scrutinized in this circumstance? What about the man who made her pregnant? Why does he get away with his inadequate behavior? And why, most of

—

the time, is it a man who is criticizing, judging, and speaking about ruined morals?

When Americans fought for their freedom, what did they have in mind? Is it too vague and ill-defined to give a clear and precise meaning today?

Should a man be sued for sexual harassment for trying to flirt with a woman?

United States Equal Opportunity Commission (EEOC) guidelines state:

> *Unwelcome sexual advances, requests for sexual favors, and other verbal or physical conduct of a sexual nature constitute sexual harassment when . . . such conduct has the purpose or effect of unreasonably interfering with an individual's work performance or creating an intimidating, hostile, or offensive working environment* (29 CFR & 1604.11 [1980])

Have Americans finally gone overboard in their zeal to reach moral superiority? Wouldn't the interpretation of such wording imply broad modifications, which what lawmakers probably had in mind? Didn't they (especially women from the feminist camp) achieve careful and often inadequate conduct of a man, who at the least has to hide his feelings so as not to be misinterpreted as a predator?

No one denies that there are men who try to seduce a woman just to have sex with her. But that is a nature of men, of any man, whether feminists and lawmakers like it or not. Yet most men know the boundaries and would not pursue a woman beyond an accepted norm and standard. The sad and at the same time funny thing is that the contemporary attitude of American society has changed the norms of human nature to abnormality.

An adult single male might go to jail for soliciting sex from a prostitute in states other than Nevada. Are people in Nevada immoral? Do people in Nevada know something the rest of Americans don't? Do such diametrically different laws in this country mean that people are different in their desires? Society promotes sexual appetites throughout the country via explicit or implicit commercials, *Playboy* magazines and TV channels, porn shops and strip clubs and by many other hidden or obvious means. They provide intense suggestions that another world exists, and it is far from being of poor taste or choice or what have you. In the meantime, the society tries to claim superior moral cleanness when it comes to a punishment for crime that had taken place.

In a hypothetical situation, a young woman fell in love and had a romantic relationship with her boyfriend, or so she thought. This fancy lasted until she got pregnant. Suddenly their relationship went sour. Being somewhat religious and scared by her first pregnancy, the young woman makes the decision to carry her pregnancy to term. Is she right in her decision? Did she consider all possible arguments and courses of reasoning?

Where did she go wrong, if she indeed did? Was any of this her fault?

She fell in love. Their relationship was so beautiful. Why did she have to even consider stopping it, when everything seemed so radiant and shining? She could not foresee that her boyfriend would suddenly leave her.

Did she turn out to be immoral? Did she turn out to be a weak creature for not standing her ground and instead allowing a sexual relationship?

Who has the answer?

When, some years ago, the host of a television talk show discussed strip clubs, the lives of the strippers, and how they are perceived by the general public, the studio audience had all kinds of opinions. The questions that were raised stretched from how these women got involved in such a business to whether any of these women were married and had kids.

During precisely one hour (including commercials), people tried to understand why stripping still attracts the attention of many, with some hue of perversion in mind. The host of the show, Phil Donahue, seemed completely lost, from time to time suggesting a caller "loosen up" and "not to judge too strongly," only to come to the hasty decision that he, Phil Donahue, would wish "to run away" from that particular program.

What is wrong with us? Why can't we decide what is good and what is bad?

Today stand-up comedians must use foul language, speak and make the explicit gestures of soft porn encounters, and generally portray some kind of rebellious behavior to arouse what looks like a bloodthirsty crowd.

There are more than a few advocates, of whom we most likely have heard, who insistently recommend: Life is short. Get whatever you can now.

An unmarried woman teacher became pregnant. Nobody blames her for the desire to get excited, to find joy in her life, and to be happy. Yet most people would probably agree that it was her responsibility to think of possible consequences when she involved herself in sexual activity with a boyfriend while not being married. Her morals at some point became subdued to the point that she allowed herself to step onto the wrong path. Was it a lack of guidance by her family? Was it a missed chance by her school to educate her? Who is responsible for the seemingly insufficient care she received?

Never mind the frame of mind of her male partner. Never mind that in the United States establishing female fertility was always considered highly important prior to marriage. When young people accept marriage as a traditional way of building a family, it should occur to them that sexual activity before being married usually implies consequences.

For the last few decades, an impression has been created that the word virgin is somehow a dirty word unless divinity is attached to its meaning. No one knows why this is the case. Why are we born in virginity? Why was a physical sign of untouched purity provided along with a female's attributes and beauty?

One still might ask questions like: Is it a sin to lose one's virginity before marriage? Is sexual activity before marriage immoral? Is becoming pregnant out of wedlock immoral?

We might also consider such questions as: Must all people get married? What if marriage while on rare occasions still cannot and will not happen, such as gay couples as we spoke about earlier or cases of accidents, crippling diseases, and other similar events? Could these unfortunate circumstances be somehow foreseen in advance?

With questions like these, one can easily see how unsubstantiated or rather complicated such matters can be.

—

Let me ask you this: Is cheating on a husband morally wrong?

A young virgin woman marries a self-satisfied, possessive man. A few years later, after ever-increasing marital tension, she one day asks herself a question: How did she sink into such misery of daily boredom? What happened to her expectation of being happy, vivacious, and fulfilled? What happened to the beautiful dreams she longed for when she imagined marriage?

She finally rebels and finds relief at a part-time job. She comes home reinvigorated, but her husband does not like it one bit. They fight more often, and she realizes her illusion of being happily married is gone. She is fed up with her husband's perception of her as his slave. Still she tries to be responsible, not being argumentative, and always there for him; however, he is never happy or satisfied with her. She is frightened of him and cannot even mention separation or divorce. Finally, another man appears in her life. He is warm and kind, and besides sympathizing with her, provides means of a little comfort to her as well.

Can anyone blame her for trying to live a happy life, even if it sounds morally unacceptable? And why is it morally wrong?

A young couple stays together as roommates and lovers after turning eighteen years old. A few months later, they break up due to irreconcilable differences. They can no longer tolerate each other and decide to go different ways. Are they immoral people? Should we condemn their behavior because they did not wait until they reached a legal age to get married before their decision to share a bed together? That way they might have avoided making a few more mistakes. Besides, sex before marriage does not necessarily reveal how much in love a young couple is.

Or, as what often occurs, another scenario happens: only one of the two wants to end the relationship. If the other partner is still in love and does not yearn for separation, she or he is condemned to suffer. But the other party does not care much. The other party wants out, and the sooner the better. Who is morally right? Is it possible that it was not a correct decision in the place to live together before marriage? Still, don't we all make mistake? Don't we all agree that it is better to learn from others' mistakes but rather rarely, follow this popular wisdom?

Now we need to consider another issue. Why do people get married? I see three main reasons:

1. People get married when they fall in love.
2. People get married to overcome loneliness.
3. People get married to oppose an acute sense of transitory existence.

These three are the most powerful forces that always act in combination, whether humans are aware of them or not.

Many times, especially when getting married for the first time, partners confuse sexual infatuation with platonic love. These two types of feelings produce powerful attraction along with a romantic attachment, and it is not that simple to separate one feeling from another.

Platonic love produces an inspirational appreciation of beauty, nobleness; even the divinity of the person upon who love is projected. In ancient Greece, such love was usually found between two males. Love between a man and a woman was always looked upon as sexual.

All kinds of love are expressed through emotions, being more often a virtue than not. In the case of romantic love, its anatomy may be portrayed as follows:

We find our object of attraction to be the most appealing. Quite often, people become attracted to something extraordinarily beautiful in their eyes, as in the quote, "Beauty is in the eye of the beholder." This vision of an object translates as perceived beauty or as an object of attraction without much distinction between them.

Such is the most frequent reaction that people might experience, and it usually leads to the sudden impetus of "falling in love."

We might also notice that observing a beautiful object often leads us to expect it to be as flawless inside as out without any reference or specific knowledge. What do we do then? We confuse what is anticipated with our exaggerated feelings.

We, and, I might add, especially men, see a sexually appealing woman as an object of our admiration. Then we ask ourselves: Can we fall in love?

What really is love? Is it a mirage we invented and want to believe in? Or is it the highest level of selfishness that humans may reach along with their willingness to sacrifice? Love is an ephemeral faculty of mind, as is everything else in this world, yet it also can last.

A famous philosopher of the last century, Nikolai Berdyaev, once said, "Love is an individual and personal phenomenon, which is directed toward a single irreplaceable individual" (translation mine).

—

Despite the observation that love has to be directed toward a particular individual, it is not always the case that love is irreplaceable, despite what Berdyaev asserts.

Let's speak of an imaginary young man who suddenly develops an incredible, almost irresistible desire to buy an expensive and beautiful wristwatch. What is going on in his mind? At first, he feels unusually excited. He does not want any other watch but that specific one. He needs to save a little more money, and the purchase will be within his reach fairly soon. The cherished dream makes him a bit agitated, but it is not much to be concerned about. Finally the day to buy has arrived. This is one of the happiest days in the young man's entire life. The dream watch is on his wrist, and it is almost impossible to describe his feelings in words. Suddenly everything around him seems wonderful. The whole world is celebrating with him.

The next day, the young man wakes up quite early. He slept more lightly than usual. He looks at his watch with warmth and admiration. He listens to the ticking of this wonderful and unique device. He is not getting tired of repeatedly eyeing his wrist. He knows that he will never stop admiring the new purchase.

But time is passing. A month is gone, and the young man realizes that he does not pay much attention to the unique ticking any longer. He checks the time only when he needs to know it. He doesn't wipe off the glass as regularly as he did in the first few days after its purchase. Scared by this, he notices that he does not feel the same tenderness for his watch as before. He also recognizes that his feelings of happiness and warmth somehow began to disappear.

He now realizes that he has other things on his mind about which to worry.

What happened to him and why? Is he negligent or too busy with other things? He tries to tell himself that he hasn't lost any of those beautiful feelings. But it is all in vain. He has probably disillusioned himself. Something has already died in him.

Is this squandering a law of ephemeral existence governing all life on earth and anywhere else in cosmos?

A dark thought enters his mind. We are all condemned to die. We yearn to obtain the subject of our dream; when we reach it, we inadvertently lose our need to dream and that means we rob ourselves. Could that mean that it is better to dream than to achieve a dream?

—

Let's check on our imaginary young man with his watch. Surprisingly, we may learn that far from being disenchanted, our hero dreams with no less enthusiasm about acquiring a new Porsche. The same unyielding fire sets off the same set of emotional waves in his soul. As we say, it is *déjà vu* all over again. Some would call it an abjuration of death. Some will see it as readiness for progress. If we had limited ourselves to dreams, the invention of a simple tablespoon would still be in process; we would continue to eat with bare hands.

But why do our feelings toward a specific subject run short? Why, once satisfied, can we never rekindle the same excitement that overwhelmed us for the very first time?

Would the truth be a novelty in itself?

We need changes. We need fluidity. We need an expectation of a new and better life.

Is this an explanation of instability in marriage? Does the mystery of a happy marriage lie in such a simple explanation? Is this the only reason why people file for divorce? Is this a possible explanation of why people lower themselves to being unfaithful?

When the inevitable exploration of two people united as a family comes to an end, each partner in the marriage begins to look for variety to oppose the boredom of life.

Two young people love each other deeply and sincerely. But an unexpected circumstance suddenly separates them for a substantial period of time. At the beginning, they regularly write to each other. They suffer, and they both wish they could speed the time up. But there is nothing they can actually do about their separation.

A year or two later, disheartened by the rarity of their latest correspondence, the young man comes home for a short while to learn that his girlfriend is engaged to someone else, not even a friend of his. And the worst part of it is that they are going to marry soon.

Is this a familiar story?

Why didn't she wait? They were so much in love. They promised each other to wait, no matter what.

A suspicion crawls in his mind: Did she really love him?

She tells him that she loves her present fiancé. But how and why did she betray their relationship?

What is love?

"Great hope for a man to overcome loneliness is tightly connected with friendship and love," writes Berdyaev, and "the meaning of humanistic love is a justification and salvation of an individual through his sacrifice of selfishness," writes another philosopher, Vladimir Soloviev (translations mine).

In his novel *Cancer Ward*, Aleksandr Solzhenitsyn portrays a heroine, Dr. Vega, as a profound and unusually complicated soul. Relatively young and healthy, she devotes all her private and professional life to terminally ill patients on a cancer ward after she learns that her sweetheart, a subject of admiration in her youth, has died in a car accident. The accident happened sixteen long years ago, but she continues to deny herself any intimate relationship, devoting all her life to gravely ill patients.

Despite such self-imposed isolation, this woman feels accomplished and happy. Permanently touched with the cold breath of reality, she bravely overcomes the barrage of restrictions that she levies on herself and that eventually separate her from the whirlpool of a whimsically extravagant and never-quiet world. Still, somehow, she does not believe that she is sacrificing her life in any way.

Finally she meets a man for whom she develops strong feelings. The man is one of her patients. She does not feel pity for him but instead realizes that this man brings her warm memories from her past. She is confused since these new emotions remind her of the feelings she used to have for another man such a long time ago.

Is she falling in love again? Can she fall in love? Can she have feelings toward someone who is condemned to die?

Amazed at first by the strong character author portrays, we see a morally sound woman who simply feels that she is able to love again.

Despite her extraordinary morals and unusual mentality, this woman has ripened again, in this unusual environment, in this unusual circumstance, with such an unusual man.

It just happens, and she loves a man who is diagnosed with a mortal illness.

The writer-psychologist masterfully shows that human beings possess many qualities that are simultaneously personal yet hereditarily transmittable. We learn that we are able to develop the same feelings in many different places under many different circumstances toward absolutely different and unrelated people and things.

Could sex and intimacy be interlaced with love? Could this combination, if repeated an unpredictable number of times, be consistent with sexual promiscuity? These questions come inevitably to our minds after reading this book, which the author skillfully titled *Cancer Ward*.

Sigmund Freud devoted all of his life to that same topic. One can find many works written about those most intriguing phenomena: sex and love.

When it comes to a combination of these two, only humans may experience such two marvels simultaneously. But can we define love and sex and give them a strong analytical explanation?

We are not rational beings from the beginning. We all start from the subconscious and use our rational thinking afterward to justify our acts with a good reason.

Freud, this giant of psychoanalysis, didn't believe that we use our minds independently of a sexual influence. He suggested that any of our thoughts, feelings, and impulses is necessarily transformed by sexual arousal. He spent most of his life preoccupied with those two phenomena.

Was he ultimately right? Are we irrational beings mostly directed by sexual inclinations?

A child is born with underdeveloped yet powerful tools: sexuality and comprehension. While these two properties are somehow implanted inside of each of us, they are continually fed by the outside environment via our senses. Our body is covered with receptors that interpret all those sensations coming from the outside world. A myriad of different irritants such as temperature, light, and pressure constantly bombard our body. These irritants are interpreted in our minds, and we perceive them accordingly.

Should they all be perceived as negative, we would necessarily suffer from pain, would we not? Fortunately, humans learned to adapt and therefore do not suffer from either too hot or too cold water in the shower. Our receptors became used to extreme changes of temperature, and we can easily tolerate them, from time to time pushing the envelope and longing for even more extreme fluctuations.

Do these fluctuations necessarily have sexual colorations, hidden or overt? That is hard to say.

When someone caresses a newborn child along the arm, neck, or shoulders, does a child necessarily interpret its feelings as sexual? Freud was inclined to think that it is almost always so.

When a baby cries in hunger, he needs to be satisfied not only by sucking his mother's breast, but by any means of feeding. Of course, the mechanism of interpreting the feeling of hunger, even in a baby's mind, is quite complex. But for the purpose of our discussion, we might say that it is not complex enough to be interpreted as sexual enjoyment, obvious or hidden.

As we grow older, we become more confused than when we were children because we cannot say for sure that these are just regular reflexes originating in the receptors on the skin, and not the sexual ones. Why? Because by that time we learn how to transform many positive feelings, we experience into sexually colored ones. But while we are residing in our childhood and our emotions are underdeveloped, our animalistic part is underdeveloped as well. That is why I do not necessarily agree with Freud's premise that every touch and every need we have is colored by sexual impulses.

Up until now, we have discussed fairly stable features. We also bring into this world other types of features, such as human curiosity. Our curiosity manifests itself by our need to explore the unknown. We often yearn for new, exciting things. We hope that along with these discoveries, we'll find absolutely new and extreme pleasures. These expectations might explain why we are in a constant search for novelty, even though we often feel satisfied with our achievements.

Did all these descriptions mentioned so far really add up to defining love? Did we reach a clear understanding of what love is?

Let's try one more time.

Love is a product of extreme thinking. It is a peak of human mentality. Love develops through intimately interlaced desires that often include sex. Love is based on the personal ability of an individual to express him or herself depending on someone's background, temperament, culture, and education.

Love has many contradictions in its fabric and to understand them it is simply not enough to study it. One must experience it.

Overall, love is affection that a person might experience and express with different intensity, as well as has a different ability to communicate to another individual. Love can be expressed and directed either in positive or negative ways. In the case of the latter, it is often finalized as a selfish desire to possess without consideration of the opposite party; in that sense, love may be expressed through such negative feelings as hatred, a desire to harm the object of admiration, and even mutilation and extermination. Such extremes are widely known throughout history, with or without proper explanations.

But for many people, love is a beautiful thing that is compared with the highest achievements humans are able to feel and express.

HUMAN SEXUALITY

Sexuality, sexual attraction, sexual behavior—all of these terms imply a different degree of sexual arousal, with or without culminating in a sexual act. Sex or sexual acts (excluding masturbation) usually but not necessarily mean an involvement of more than one person in sexual activities. Normally it is accompanied by the penetration of a male's penis into the private parts of a male or female partner.

Sex among humans is distinguished from sex among animals in that humans cannot avoid thinking of sexual activity for long before, during, or after the sexual act. The degree of individual sexual behavior varies from person to person and depends on inherited sexuality, ability to fantasize, education, and cultural environment, all of which often manifest cumulatively.

Purely mechanistic sex in humans, although possible, is encountered among men more often, and it takes place among those who is under the heavy influence of drugs, alcohol, or is known for promiscuous behavior.

Sex, for disparate reasons, is often confused with love, yet it always belongs to our animal instincts. As such, sex would be easier to comprehend if it were not embraced and interpreted by humans. To understand it, we need to approach an explanation of sex not simply as an animal part embedded in us, but as one of the two sides of human nature.

Sex, on the surface, looks like a true partnership. In reality, it is quite distinct from friendship. It is nothing more than a selfish desire to experience enjoyment achieved through the manipulative usage of one's partner.

—

Sex is perceived by men differently than by women, and this fact alone becomes one of the major obstacles between the two sexes. To say that the main role belongs to a man would be inaccurate; to say that a woman enjoys it much less would be irresponsible. The role of both is definitely different. Yet the craving for pleasure by both women and men originates from similar sources.

Whether through the power of nature or God's will, men are the inspirational forerunners in sexual activity in the majority of cases. For them, sex is an exciting game. It is a variation of their hunting reflex, and to play it they must follow some general rules, from time to time inventing a few conspicuous modifications. Depending on individual sophistication, the male hunter starts to chase a woman, often directing her into a trap that he methodically and sometimes skillfully creates.

Does that mean that a woman is always a passive and innocent victim? No, she certainly is not. Her role is different, often hidden from immediate comprehension and observation. That brings an element of mystery into the sexual game. With the two sexes playing by different rules, often the game becomes not only mysterious but exciting as well.

Another characteristic feature of men is their possessiveness. This places many obstacles in the way of the male and female relationship. If a woman allows a man to act as if he owns her, then to some degree she becomes his possession. In that case, if she tries to act independently, their relationship, as a rule of thumb, turns sour. Contemporary and sophisticated women who do not want men's possessiveness to run wild must take careful steps. If a woman masters her skills, a man is kept at an appreciative distance for a long time. If she does not know how to handle the situation, they end up with woman becoming submissive or such relationship is ending with a couple breaking up.

Most men usually are curious about a woman until she is beyond their reach. They fairly easy lose interest in a woman the moment their goal to get her is achieved.

Stating that, I will also say that the majority of men do not fall in love with a woman who is not sexually provocative. Every behavior of a man, from that of the gallant hero to the passionate lover, is directed by his sexual attraction. Certainly a man can be a gentleman with all the prerequisites that would fit in such a word, but if he is not sexually attracted, there most likely can be no love.

Does a sexually objectified woman lower herself in the eyes of a man? The answer is both yes and no. In any event, men do not look upon women through the eyes of feminists. The majority of them do not pursue a goal to diminish a woman or to make her a sex machine, as some feminists claim. With the recognition of the existence of the hunter-man, as well as his constant eagerness to have sex with women, a woman's skillfulness and dexterity is an important armament if she wants to keep a man around.

So those who do not mind playing need to realize that most men are attracted to a woman by certain qualities. Such are a woman's ability to be mysterious. Whether this feature is connected to her walk, smile, dress, or even fragrance, any of this should work as long as a woman knows how to use her wits.

And with that understanding, a woman must realize how truthful the saying "if you plan to win something, you must expect to lose something as well" is. A sexily dressed or provocative woman is actually tempting man's sexual appetite. Hunting reflex or not, men perceive sexy women as desirable objects. That is, until he is in play. The minute the game has begun—this often-shy creature called man turns into a lying machine. His blocked mind doesn't realize that his animal part is distracting his morals. He is tortured by his desires, and whenever he can, he directs his eloquence toward reaching his goals.

I am not going to judge who is playing more dishonestly: the man who enjoys every moment of it, or the woman who provokes his desires (however innocently) hoping that this will lead to a long-lasting relationship with a possible marriage.

What I am going to discuss here is why a man who stays with a woman for some time suddenly becomes an adulterer, not once but quite a few times, during what seemed to be a happy marriage.

It is actually quite simple to understand. A gambling man who never stops playing has no way of changing himself; as soon as his woman forgets the rules of her game, he will start looking for another player.

Does it go only one way, and do women do not get involved in extramarital affairs? The astonishing answer is that a woman usually

—

looks for romance with a passionate man who is able to love her madly. And that brings us to a somewhat unusual conclusion: both men and women are hunters by nature. Yet both are using different methods and passages.

The man needs novelty in sex appeal, and the woman needs novelty in passionate love and romance. Can the two be happily married still? They probably can if they learn how to play by the rules. Otherwise one can definitely acknowledge that marriage, while the invention of which was a highly noble idea, was not thought through enough.

Human beings are not designed to last forever, and people therefore were not equipped with the everlasting ability of continuous admiration of someone or something in particular. I wouldn't go so far as to say that the family therefore should be recognized as an inadequate union and become obsolete. But to regard infidelity as bad and immoral behavior or, even worse, to condemn such behavior, does not necessarily reflect on what is the right thing to do.

Two people fall in love for the first time in their early twenties. They both come to this period of their life being morally pure. They both have waited for the right person to come along to marry and didn't experiment sexually before. Finally, that day has arrived. The two have exchanged their vows and their first lawful kiss. They are now a husband and a wife, legally, as it meant to be. They could have had sex before they were officially married, but they didn't. Should we praise them for such highly dignified moral behavior, or should we not? How many couples like these still exist?

Our pure couple begins a new, exciting, unknown cycle. They cannot compare their feelings to their past experiences, as they have none. They could have heard about those feelings from different people, but they haven't experienced any of their own. So they try their best, and while they learn a lot, they also learn from their own mistakes. A year or five years later, they are the same happy couple with a child or two.

But are they? There is a fifty-fifty chance it is so, and there are data and statistics that might be showing different results. Still, this is not the point. The point is that while our couple could not tell themselves what could be the best solution in each small event of their lives, they might have perceived those events differently, including the satisfaction they expected and received, whether romantically or sexually.

Some twenty or thirty years ago, young people's attitude toward marriage was, first, that the average age to marry must be connected to graduating from college or establishing oneself in a profession, and second that one should obtain experience with more than one partner before marrying a sweetheart of some sort.

There was no dilemma, especially for men, of whether or not to get married. With sexual desire fulfilled, it became easier for men to separate romantic involvement from sexual attraction. Marriage meant maturity, a conscious step into a different style of life; it meant loyalty, along with many obligations and the possible procreation of a new generation. Marriage also meant overcoming one's weak areas, such as loneliness, the need to share one's true feelings and appreciation of life. It also meant the prevention of depression or depressive thoughts, overcoming the anxieties connected to the constant struggle for a better place under the sun, and, finally, camouflaging one's fears of one's unavoidable demise.

Rather subconsciously, people are seeking stability, moral support, appreciation and confirmation of good deeds, as well as hundreds of more related essentials. Happily, such support often comes when we get married.

What people rarely recognize, though, is that the later in life marriage occurs, whatever reason could be substantiated, the more mature we become and the less likely we are to change and thus to adapt. Sometimes it even turns into a reason for fighting and miscommunication between married couples, with the worst end of it leading to divorce.

But whatever the consequences might be as a result of our decision, we prefer to trade our independence as a single soul for the married state.

Of course, there is another scenario that can take place. Two sweethearts madly fall in love and get married, promising to keep all those vows that come with it. Thirty, but more likely forty or even fifty years later, they are still madly in love with each other. There might be sexual intimacy between them, or there might not. It does not really matter. Their love is the true love of two people.

—

Why and how did they manage to save what the majority of us do not? They may have had, besides true feelings for each other, many other mutual qualities such as respect, understanding, and, very important, communication to bridge their connections. Or they learned to see each other as never boring or as a dying novelty. Whatever it is, what counts is that it worked.

And with that remark, I am going to stop any further investigations of such deep and never-dull topics with the hope that the questions raised here were sufficiently answered, or at least that they forced us to think not only more often of our deeds but also in a more proper way.

CHAPTER 12

Rearing Children

The first question that comes to mind is: do we really believe that educating children makes much difference? The truth is that in a family with a small number of siblings from the same biological parents, different results ensue even when parents apply the same teaching methods. Children display disparate levels of comprehension, ability, and desire to learn. You may find all kinds of different talents among youth.

Why is that? Why are some children more energetic than others? Why some of them are shy, and why do others enjoy being praised and recognized? Why does each child react to the same event differently than the child next to him?

We previously covered inheritance, as we all are linked to that faculty of traits. Our connection is inevitable even if children are adopted or brought up in foster homes. Heredity is a complex process; while an offspring inherits the majority of traits from his biological parents, some traits might come from other members of his genealogical tree. But it is mutation that rounds off our character. And we are finally completed by such concomitant circumstances as education and environment.

Within this combination of inherited and acquired provisions, an individual is crystallized in a somewhat peculiar, singular creature marked by unrepeated destiny.

Should we then consider each human being separately or join them as one people?

"No boy is born with aggressiveness and violence in his genes," writes Phil Donahue in his book *The Human Animal*.

Isn't it true that no one would be able to evoke violence if it had not been present in us from birth? It comes with our genes, and it manifests itself in early childhood more obviously in some children than in others. How much it is displayed depends on two factors:

- The degree to which it was inherited.
- The quality of education a child has received.

While inheritance is a powerful tool that science has only begun to learn how to manage, education is the only useful resource people possess at present.

But if we unconditionally accept heredity, what role could education play? Could it eradicate our gene of violence? Can something acquired, such as education, remove such an inherited feature as fear? How wise an approach to the matter would be if we acknowledged our inability to eliminate what has come to us in a permanent package?

First, let's agree that traits like violence, anger, fear, rage, and hundreds of others do not go anywhere. Second, if we want to oppose these traits that we were provided with, we must use a property called willpower. While willpower develops in us accordingly with time, it is a consequential property designed for our genes. It usually acts powerfully as it is dictated by the correlation between society and an individual. When it is properly applied, it becomes an invaluable tool for our well-being. There are also circumstances when willpower becomes so subdued, that an individual must first recognize that it indeed exists.

With education, an artificial instrument that becomes an invaluable tool for educating people, we also learn how to suppress our bad inclinations until they become negligible, using that same willpower. Through an effort of a family unit, school, and societal rules, we can tolerate and become tolerable to those among whom we live. In other words, the main role of education is to postpone our bad inclinations

—

or diminish them so that we will become an addition to the societal network and not an impediment.

Where do we start?

Being brought up in a different society, I had a rare opportunity to observe, to compare, and to see the results. Today I can admit that education in both countries (Russia and the United States) showed both positive and negative outcomes. Yet neither country is willing to acknowledge the mistakes, with a slight edge displayed by the Americans, who were somewhat able to criticize themselves.

A child is born. Innocent and defenseless, beautiful and fragile, it conforms much less to a harmony of nature than the majority of animal cubs. Left alone, it probably would fairly easily return to the lifestyle of primitive man if indeed it was able to survive at all.

Why is that? What makes us stand on a lower evolutionary staircase when born than most animals?

I don't have an answer to that.

The answer I have instead is that all people have an ability to learn and to memorize events and things and to comprehend and analyze many disparate deeds and acts. But the most important intricacy is that we all have inherited genetic traits that declare themselves within different times of our lives and with varying force. The trick of it is that the longer we live, the more stubborn and resistant we become in our learning and relearning. In this process, the time comes when a person becomes saturated up to the point of feeling completed and well rounded.

Exposed to the reality of circumstance from birth, a child immediately starts the cognition process. Biological parents, social establishments, and any other concerned adults who exercise careful control over a child's rearing all influence what kind of a person this child will become.

The paradox of such education lies not in the variance of educational sources, but in the similarity of methodology applied to each child.

With uninterrupted proclamation and bragging about freedom in the land of the free, it is quite surprising how Americans agree about most of their habits. Shaved armpits and legs for women, licking fingers while eating in fast-food restaurants among those who do eat there, the code of dress for the hip-hop generation, piercing or tattooing the body—from where does this all similarity come?

The media, the Internet, and commercials all contribute to a framework of society. But how does it come about that they all carry strikingly similar messages?

What does freedom really signify? Does it come with commercials that bombard the minds of innocent bystanders? Does it come with amendments to a constitution and a bill of rights? Do you think that those commercials selling a product deemed essential by a manufacturer and injected with portrayals of sexually attractive females do not grab the attention of an unsophisticated child?

How about the pornographic magazines on the shelves of the newsstands, partially covered yet unequivocally pointing to their contents? Don't they provoke the same wondering and curious immature minds of young boys and girls? If this is not enough, why not stimulate the inquiring minds with sex education in schools and provide children with condoms? Does this age of puberty sound well rounded and mature to anyone? Could such practice be healthy, or does it deserve to rescind the experiment?

The most bold and absurd explanation for the distribution of condoms comes along the lines of, "The kids are doing it anyway. So why not at least protect them with safe sex? In this day of sexually transmitted diseases, it would only be thoughtful to prevent those dreadful diseases, would it not?"

Would providing children with alcohol and tobacco along with smoking marijuana be a step in the right direction, had those substances had no harmful samples among them?

Why, in such a morally sound society, as the United States claims to be, violence, sex, gangsters, and drugs directly or indirectly are promoted through the media with graphic reports on the news, television, and talk radio shows? Why do an army of unscrupulous Hollywood producers feel entitled to claim their success according to how much money their movies make rather than according to the immediate harm done to the minds of youngsters?

Do children have enough sophistication to properly perceive graphic depictions of rape and murder as a picture that is not ordinarily encountered in the real world?

Do all parents receive divine instructions on how to protect and timely educate their children? Will overstepping parents' responsibilities and rights be perceived in stride and not as an abuse of power by the designated authorities?

There is nothing wrong with the definition of a young person as a legal adult between the ages of eighteen and twenty-one when the law prescribes the responsible use of alcohol, the right to vote, and other mature steps of behavior. Yet this age separation is rather artificially inserted, which is not always based on any particular case.

To rear a child means many different things, the main of which would be as following:

- Each child requires an independent evaluation of his or her physical, developmental, and emotional needs.
- Parents must firmly know the role they assume with a birth of a child.
- Communication is one of the most important tools to reduce and possibly eliminate a generation gap.
- Responsible parents investigate all possible inclinations that are inherited and mutated in their offspring, which might or might not appear right away.
- Raising a child with only rare occasions of inability to provide adult guardianship implies allowing the child's hands to take the reins of governing.
- Responsible parents do not transfer their role in educating children to a schoolteacher or teachers.
- Responsible parents clearly take a different approach in childrearing for an infant, a toddler, a preadolescent, and an adolescent.
- Finally, responsible adults do not make a child out of an incidental (sexual encounter) circumstance.

Although adolescence from the point of education is often the most rebellious and difficult period of a life span, the preceding age periods should not be neglected. The adults who recognize this steady links in formation of an individual, most definitely will be successful, despite the fact that a significant role could be played by the peers

—

of the teenager. The most successful parents are those who tirelessly continue to be actively involved in their child's education.

Of course, it is not that easy to apply one's knowledge even if one believes it is correct in the contemporary society of a free world. Between the hundreds of bureaucratic organizations instilled in the United States and the ability of a parent to rear a child lies an abyss of obstacles, inadvertently leading to such extremes as inciting a child to sue his parents, the fabrication of child abuse by an adult, even the occurrence of murder, which is often looked upon with the sympathetic comprehension of society and the lenient punishment of a child.

There is no doubt that such abuses exist, but to what degree, statistics reflect the real stories behind it.

In any event, with an accepted premise that this is what it is, the parents, and especially the first-time parents must go through all possible directional instructions that they can afford, as we discussed earlier. Each age limit requires special, general, but also individual corrections, which, if a parent has no firm knowledge of, it will be permanently lost.

Parents also need to realize that we all are born with features that, if not timely corrected or curbed, might quite easily turn into our detriment.

We are all prone to express anger and some even use violence under specific circumstances, because these traits are planted in our genes. At the age of puberty, when the organism of a youth is growing faster than in previous years, when peer pressure, studying, and the demands of nature all are intermixed to the point of possible breakage, it is no wonder that we experience the rebellious type, who often seems impossible to manage. Bullying, destroying someone's property, unprovoked taunting of a weaker fellow human—these all are the conspicuous signs familiar to most of us. Could they be prevented if a child had a firm parental-societal grip since much earlier childhood years?

Should one unequivocally agree that such behavior had to be characterized as a result of insufficient nurture?

The answers might be found elsewhere in this book, but to reiterate, one cannot perceive another human being as in an extreme polarities of both black and white and nothing in between, simply by reading

–

the signs that come to the surface. We are complicated in many ways that are beyond any presumed design. Our expressive ability is often exaggerated or subdued up to the point that we are destined to fail to recognize our real selves. We are often read in the wrong way, we are often appreciated in the wrong way, and we are thus often recognized in a way we cannot recognize ourselves.

Without proper navigation, a child will resort to any kind of behavior. An all-embracing willpower at an early age is not conspicuous enough to be relied upon.

Therefore, the teacher accompanying a developing child must play not only a significant role in educating this child. He also must remember that he is a navigator of a particular child, never forgetting that he is one of the captains chosen to lead.

CHAPTER 13

Drug Users, Willpower, and the Power of Addiction

Regardless of whether we are discussing a drug that the majority of people consider harmless (such as marijuana) or addictive drugs such as heroin, opiates, and crack cocaine, we need to understand why people often get hooked on them. Or to put it in other words, we need to understand what produces a different degree of dependency in humans.

We need to understand why some drugs act as harmless stimulants and others produce a strong dependency called addiction. We need to understand why some people need to consume caffeine, nicotine, or alcohol and others don't feel the same urge even if they also have tried these products.

Such substances as caffeine and nicotine normally act as natural killers (pesticides) of some insects. Caffeine also acts as an inhibitor of seed germination in seedlings other than coffee, thus improving the chance for coffee beans to survive. Alcohol is normally found in trace amounts in the human bloodstream, even without its consumption. In other words, the body may manufacture alcohol by itself, specifically in people who thrive on the consumption of grapes, sugar, and other sweets, or who have an overgrowth of yeast inside their bowels.

To understand why people abuse drugs, we need to quickly move through the basic functions of the brain.

The human brain is not only the most complex organ in the body. It is also the main engine for interpreting negative and positive emotions, complex or simple thoughts and controlling basic functions such as breathing, heart rate, the enjoyment of food as well as many other everyday activities.

The human brain is equipped with billions of nerve cells that transmit, coordinate, and regulate all incoming and outgoing impulses. These functions are carried out by chemicals naturally found in brain cells.

To function properly, the human body must:

- Have close to flawlessly, if not flawlessly, developed nerve receptors.
- Have sufficient, balanced, and precisely functioning chemicals.
- Have ability to timely and precisely release and shut those chemicals by neurotransmitters.

When drugs are used (either medically prescribed or introduced without medical advice), a neural cell will respond correspondingly.

With the realization that we all are born into different environmental conditions, accumulate different mutations that help us to adapt, and have different structural qualities of our bodies that contribute to our ability to survive, we may appreciate that we react to all encountered irritants with different response gradations.

When some people are trying to overcome stress or are bored with the opulent, copious life that abounds around them, they look for relaxants or stimulants of any kind. Drugs become the quickest way to reach such a relief, with alcohol being a close second.

All drugs interfere with our nervous system, making it react in compensatory way. Many prescribed drugs produce directed and controlled reactions. Drugs that are not prescribed by a doctor may elicit unpredictable responses, often uncontrollable and fraught with serious consequences. For many reasons, including the one that an individual body can tolerate any irritant up to a point and that human body has tendency to restore its function again and again, some people do not think much about the possible long-term consequences and dangers of drugs that were not prescribed.

But the main reason drugs are used repeatedly, in spite of the user's awareness of the many dangers that might happen upon their use, is their powerful effects and suppression of willpower.

Addiction—which is produced by a number of drugs, as well as alcohol, nicotine, gambling, eating disorders, and other types of compulsive behavior—must be understood as an uncontrollable habit that makes an individual become dependent and unable to cease their addictive behavior without assistance.

Under this formula, marijuana, tobacco, and alcohol (if used for socializing) should not be considered addictive substances. They might, however, be considered as means that are used for extra excitement or relaxation. The problem people fail to see does not lie in whether drug use is considered to be recreational or medicinal. The problem lies in the addictive personality of an individual.

If someone who uses marijuana can prove to himself that his brain does not require any stronger drug to feel joy, can be productive, can be in control, and does not harm anyone including himself, that should be enough not to create a fuss about the issue. Alas, no such criteria exist that can definitely warn us about possibly losing our will to prevent addiction. None of us are equipped with such a majestic mechanism to spot it on time and to be able to stop an addiction. None of us are perfect and flawless enough to be called gods. So we need to be vigilant but not paranoid at the same time.

Another problem with using drugs lies in that some drugs are so addictive and so powerful, that no matter how strong an individual's willpower might be, the threshold to resist a drug wavers. The precise mechanism of drug activity on receptors or the amount of neurotransmitters involved is not as important to know, so long as the unlucky individual recognizes that his problem has become unbearable and that his addiction no longer can be controlled by willpower alone.

At this point, an addict must realize that his addiction has crossed the psychological barrier that was protecting him as a casual drug user and has overpowered him, denying him any control whatsoever, despite the promise that this individual is still under control.

Now, let us try to understand why some people, despite the obvious danger of using drugs, nevertheless engage in such risky behavior. There are a few reasons.

Most of the time, drug usage starts innocently enough, when youngsters experiment out of curiosity with the expectation of unusual excitement. Thus this behavior is mostly a result of peer pressure, popularly expressed as, "Everybody is doing it."

The second most common reason is that an individual cannot reasonably deal with stress.

The third reason is attributable to depression.

And the last reason is connected to the incidental exposure and usage of drugs.

Does any effective addiction treatment exist as of today? Truthfully, there is none, only a somewhat effective organization named Alcoholics Anonymous. The Twelve-Step Program consists of twelve principal steps designed to relate to each person separately, and mostly relies on the cold shoulders of relatives and friends calling on a diseased, presumably worn-out soul to recall his own strength and to overcome his own problem. These programs advise that an individual may be helped only when he or she hits the bottom. In that free fall, relatives should not provide any allowances or stretch out a helping hand; as such moves are usually counterproductive and actually help to enable an addict along his convoluted path, instead of opening the path to recovery.

At best, it advises a person to rely on a higher power—whatever that might mean—along with experiencing a spiritual awakening and making amends for the errors he or she has made. For a religious soul, this program is as much help as for a parishioner visitor who expects to find a miracle (leading hand of God) in a particular church, synagogue, mosque, or any other such institution.

The reason I am saying this is that while some individuals are inclined to be programmed (deeply and wholeheartedly accepting a higher power), the others, with more suspicious and analytical minds, would find it difficult to blindly follow the existing instructions.

Besides, should those who were destroyed by an unknown spiritual force now call for it to bring them up from the bottom they have hit? If it sounds ridiculous, it is.

Another form of help comes from a sponsor, who is, in fact, usually a recovering drug addict and who, at best, can share his own experience, on which an advice is based that most likely will not work. What is then offered is for people to come together, united by similar problems. The only positive side of such gatherings might be that people realize that their disease does not belong only to them.

If this program claims success, at least temporarily, and points to those who do not use drugs after heeding to the suggestion that a higher power indeed exists, it might be the result of their religious belief in a higher power. There is nothing wrong with such a belief, and people should not be sarcastic to those who find it helpful to climb the road to recovery. But for those who are agnostics and nonbelievers, a different approach must be exercised.

Addiction destroys whatever small accumulation of willpower one has left. With that in mind, one must understand that an attempt to help an addict should be done on a case-by-case basis.

An addict, first of all, must acknowledge that he is sick and needs help. He needs to accept the notion that while recovery will necessarily be unpleasant, he will also be tempted many times in the future.

Realizing that there is no effective treatment other than to learn how to harness willpower, after all chemical and holistic medicine has been used, an addict must immediately begin an incremental organizing of his life. There is no place for the chaos that most likely accompanied an addict's daily routine in the past. The addict must understand that his daily routine should be devoted to moderately rewarding duties without undue stress and excitement.

It would be a perfect solution if the addict will find an occupation that will not only take most of his time but will coincide with a specific and desirable aim. While an addict will not be able to rid himself of the cravings with which he was born and developed, he must understand that finding something equally exciting but harmless would be an ideal solution.

The last thing I wish to emphasize here is that this process of recovery is not one straight road. Life demands devotion while it offers stress. People don't live in a vacuum, and to expect not to fight is not only naïve, it is also dangerous.

With these words, I wish to all those who unfortunately find themselves in such a situation real and lasting success.

—

PART THREE

ETHNIC GROUPS AND SOCIETIES

CHAPTER 14

The Jewish Paradox

I will start my discourse by stating that, despite their minority, Jews are disproportionately notable all over the world. For one reason or another, Jewish people get the most recognition among the denizens of different countries and nations. Fifteen or so million people that are labeled as Jews—so diverse in cultural aspects—are recognized as a separate, conspicuous, and often foreign body within any society. While enormously scattered geographically, Jews are joined by thousands of years of a similar destiny, traditions, and mutual understanding.

Notwithstanding the relatively small numbers of Jews settled in any one country, they arouse an enormous reaction and, as a rule of thumb, a negative one.

Often-exaggerated and often-no-less-distorted myths and fictions overlay the real faces of these people to whom justice is long overdue.

With their history not quite four thousand years yet the Hebrews (the Jews) became known as a people around 1900 BCE, owing to the recording of them in the Torah (the Hebrew Bible). The name "Hebrew" arose incidentally and is indebted to a description of a few people who crossed the river Euphrates. It was originally pronounced as "br," which in Hebrew means people who "crossed over the boundary." With the further developing of language, it became the word *Ibri* or *Ivri*, suggesting "Hebrew." The word "Jew" originated

—
401

from an Old English language, pronounced in Hebrew as "*Judah*" (*Yehudah*).

The Latin version (*Evrei*) is in use even today in major parts of Eastern Europe predominantly inhabited by Slavic people.

If it were not for the Bible, the Hebrews most likely wouldn't exist at all, as the Bible is the only original source where Abram and a few members of his family were born. In no way do I deny that the Jewish people have existed as an ethnic group for thousands of years, but who were the original people that became known to the whole world as Jews? Besides the dubious story in the Bible, there is no definitive source that points to their genesis. It is impossible to trace the representatives of that family, if they were indeed real.

Which ethnic group did they belong to while in Babylonia? Did they have any other relatives in that land?

Despite that, the Hebrew Bible contains few unoriginal stories taken from somewhere else, the story of Abram's family—from which the history of the Jews begins—belongs specifically to that and only that book. For this reason, we have no choice but to attempt to uncover, however indirectly, how it all began.

First, let me try to speculate on what made Terah, Abram, Lot, and Sarai, all blood-related members of that family, one day get up and leave the opulent city Ur of the Chaldees. What made these people, who were surrounded by the sophisticated Babylonian civilization and culture, move to an unknown land? The Bible is silent on this point, and we therefore cannot responsibly adduce a motive for such a decision.

It was a time when the neighboring country to the north, Assyria, began to flex its muscle, but that most likely was not a threat to these particular people more than to the others that lived in that region. We may learn that the citizens of Babylonia, while not barbarians, were hardly virtuous. The Bible does not tell us if Terah and his family were strangers in that land or natives. The annals of history also do not document any mass exodus from Babylonia at that time. The family's desire to move, therefore, is an enigma.

Tracing the reasons why the Jews historically have moved from country to country, it is easy to deduce that these were the main three:

- They were thrown out.
- They were threatened and had to leave to save themselves.
- They were seeking a better life, which they were usually denied where they resided.

As one can surmise, none of the above-mentioned reasons could be applied here. Terah could not foresee that the unknown land of Canaan, with its rugged and difficult climate, might provide an acceptable lifestyle for him and his family. There were no relatives or friends mentioned in the Bible who invited this family to relocate there either.

Therefore, one should not be terribly surprised to learn that this family first moved north and arrived in Haran, a city located in contemporary Turkey.

A few years later, after Terah died, the remaining members didn't go back to their original habitation. Neither did they stay in Haran. The Bible tells us that Abram simply met God, who told him that he must move to the land of Canaan, and that he would become the father of a great nation, which God would bless.

Whether the Biblical account of God's personally approaching Abram is a fairytale or a weak narration by the scribes does not much matter here, as we discussed it in detail in the first part of this book.

To me, God's strangest behavior involves *whom* he picked to accomplish his tasks and *why* he specifically chose this one odd family. What made God choose a childless man and tell him that he would become a father of a great nation? Abram does not seem to be recognized for any outstanding qualifications. His female companion and nephew didn't possess any special qualities either (at least none are described in the Bible). Why then did God chose these particular people remains quite obscure.

With God's unsupportable decision to designate Sarai, the wife of Abram, as a mother for the Jewish people, it is even less logical. It had to take a miracle to make Sarai pregnant at an age well past menopause. Isaac, the father of Jacob and the grandfather of Jacob's twelve sons, was miraculously born out of that marriage, the marriage of two very old people indeed.

—

Even if we agree to accept this Biblical story as true and to relate it to the appearance of the first Jews, we still would not be able to describe who those Jews were.

In addition, the five books of Moses, which tell the story of the ancient Hebrews, were found a few hundred years after Moses' time among the ruins of the Second Temple by a scribe named Ezra. These books shed no light on the origin of the Hebrew people at all. Were these found books factual or simply a compilation of popular folklore? Today, none of it can be proved. That this was an exceptional story, though, is inarguable.

In any event, God chose this specific group of people, giving them one strange precondition—ordering that their men had to be circumcised. God even points to a specific date: circumcision must be performed after the eighth day of the birth of a baby boy. Without much logical explanation, except that such would produce the covenant between the Jews and God, the Hebrew Bible does not find it necessary to ponder such a serious offence.

Would God authorize this unjustified method and subject an innocent infant child to such a sudden assault? Would God be concerned that Jews discard the foreskin of their boys' penises before he would promise recognition to all Jews? Yet this widely accepted tradition among the Jews became generally enforced into perpetuity.

Another no-less-puzzling parable is told about the tree of the knowledge of good and evil. Having created man, God warned him not to eat from that tree, thus prohibiting men knowledge that was accessible to God. Since God chose a band of people who are among the most educated people on earth, God apparently did not have a problem with sophisticated human beings.

The question is, why the anomaly? Did God foresee that the Jews would become a people who would incessantly accumulate knowledge? Did he mean to praise or to punish the Jews for expressing such a desire?

In any case, to make at least an attempt to describe who the Jews are, let me make a short summary here.

After the progeny of the twelve sons of Jacob (the Israeli people) came from the desert near Mount Sinai and occupied Canaan, the people that descended from his sons became known as the ten tribes of Israel. These people were located more to the north part of that land. The remaining two tribes eventually formed the country named Judah that was located in the south.

Were they all Jews?

To begin with, half of Jacob's sons were not pure Hebrews, as they were born from non-Jewish mothers.

Second, those Hebrew blood relatives that didn't move to Egypt, but stayed in Canaan for 430 years, had become strangers to the returning Hebrew stock.

History tells us about a protracted (one-hundred-year) war between the kingdom of Israel and the kingdom of Judah. Were the representatives of both kingdoms blood-related people who were killing each other?

It is interesting to remember that after Assyria captured the people of Israel during their war with that country, the destiny of the Israelites became unknown. Most likely, they were assimilated into a new culture. Hundreds of years following their captivity, these people were completely lost to history.

The only Jewish people to whom we can presently trace and connect were the Jews (Hebrews) of the two remaining Judean tribes forcefully taken to Babylonia as the result of yet another war, but who were freed just fifty years later. These Jews are the only connection to the contemporary Jews historically proven. They eventually were dispersed from their land by the Roman Empire, which brought the end of the people known to the world as the Hebrews who lived as a nation in the Canaan land till the beginning of our era (135 CE).

From that particular time, the Jews became known as the scattered Jews of the Diaspora (exile). The new history of the Jews began for the next two millennia, during which the Jews were moving through many places all over the world. They fell into two major and different types of Jews: Sephardic and Ashkenazi. Sephardic Jews are those people who lived in medieval Spain (the Hebrew word for Spain is *Sephardim*), with many of them being converted to Marranos, Jews who ostensibly converted to Christianity during the Spanish inquisition but continued to practice rabbinical Judaism in secret. The Ashkenazi Jews, on the other hand, came to live mostly in Eastern Europe some 1,200 years ago. The word *Ashkenazim* is the Hebrew name for the Jews who lived in the region of Germany in the middle ages, which literally means the "German Jews." These Jews spread all over Eastern Europe, keeping the same German name, Ashkenazi. Whether they remained separate as Jewish people (I am excluding that small percentage of Jews who had intermarried with other races) and can trace their roots to the original Judeans is hard to say.

There were such nations in the past as the Khazars, who lived in parts of Russia, but who were not Jews by birth and who converted to Judaism. There are also the Mizrahi Jews, the Ethiopian Jews, the Jews of Morocco, and even the Lemba people who have Jewish genes going back to the tribe of Levi. All of these people claim their Jewish identity connected to the Jews who returned from the Babylonian captivity in 538 BCE. But how did they manage to remain Jews after they were scattered in small numbers all around the world? Why are the ancient Israeli Jews all but gone while the Jews of Judea managed to survive?

This begs the question: Who are the Jews, collectively speaking? Are they a nation, a race, a bunch of religious zealots, or the separate groups of people wrongly joined by one common denominator?

The Jews are unique; they are simultaneously an ethnic group and, in majority, a religious one. They are widely spread in different parts of world, independently picking their places to stay and are tightly connected to the tolerable indifference of local governments. They are the only nation that for over three thousand years had to struggle to gain acceptance and approval by anyone else in their own country. If you ask a Jew to define who the Jews are, he won't be able to give you a satisfactory answer. If you ask a Gentile who the Jews are, he won't be able to give you a proper answer either.

The establishment of rabbis is in attempt to connect the Jew to his birthright through a Jewish mother, emphasizing that a Jew, no matter whether he is religious or irreligious (or even converted to a new religion), is still a Jew. But no rabbi will get into a deeper discussion about what makes him say that, especially when it comes to explaining the non-Jewish mothers of six of Jacob's sons. What started as a friendly conversation may end with you being labeled an anti-Semite.

Is there any genetic proofs to clarify who then the Jews are?

"A genome-wide genetic signature of Jewish ancestry perfectly separates individuals with and without Jewish ancestry in a large random sample of European Americans." This heading appeared in a

—

research study published by the scientists from the Center for Human Genome variation of Duke University in the journal *Genome Biology* on January 22, 2009.

The abstract read, in part, "Using the principal component analysis, we found that individuals with full Jewish ancestry formed a clearly distinct cluster from those individuals with no Jewish ancestry."

Would such a conclusion possibly point to the fact that no matter how demographically diverse, mixed, or religiously disconnected the Jews are, we can still consider them to be one people? Would that research undermine the main tenets of those advocates of political correctness of the nonexistence of a genetic separation of race? Would these genetically savvy experiments prove that the Jews belong to one *haplotype*? (A *haplotype* is a set of genetic changes characteristic of producing similar diseases, for example, or physical appearance.)

Thus, recognizing that the Jewish people are specifically known for two or three traits, one faces the necessity of considering such an important trait as intelligence. The research conducted by the University of Utah concerning the Ashkenazi intelligence genes revealed that Ashkenazim scored twelve to fifteen points above the test's mean value. (The 2005 study "Natural History of Ashkenazi Intelligence" by Gregory Cochran et al.)

Of course, Jews do not talk about this. They even invented a quite clumsy explanation that seems more an excuse than anything else, such as owing their intellect to their number of hereditary diseases.

American Enterprise Institute (AEI) adjunct fellow Jon Entine spoke these words at a forum at the AEI, on October 28, 2007: "All this (intellect) might be traced to diseases that afflict Ashkenazi Jews from Eastern Europe; these genetic mistakes may promote the growth and interconnection of brain cells."

To counter such a conclusion, one example that comes to mind is the disease sickle-cell anemia found among blacks. It is a hereditary disease that inflicts blacks but, as it turns out, also protects them from getting malaria. Still, no one tries to connect these changing blood cells to, let's say, the physical superiority of African athletes.

Another less-obvious excuse comes with the equation of the roles of nurture versus nature. Although it would be foolish to argue the obvious role of the last two, it also would be irresponsible to equate them.

An interesting study in that regard was conducted by J. Philippe Rushton, a psychology professor at the University of Western Ontario and Arthur Jensen, an educational psychologist at the University of California, Berkeley. "Race differences show up by three years of age, even after matching on maternal education and other variables," concluded Rushton. "Therefore they cannot be due to poor education since this not yet begun to exert an effect."

It would be interesting to note that there are a number of different explanations about why Jews steadily exhibit a thirst to pursue all types of education. Jews' prevalence in accounting fields, for instance, has this poorly related explanation: "Because Jews were discriminated against in medieval Europe, they were often driven into professions such as money lending and banking which were looked down upon or forbidden to Christians" (unspecified source). To credit such explanation, one would have to suggest that because blacks were discriminated against in contemporary North America, they were driven into such fields as music and hip-hop culture.

Reading from same or similar sources on what discrimination usually produces, we learn that Jews with lucrative jobs often have four, six, or sometimes eight or nine children. Follow this logic and observation, wealthy blacks (successful in sports, for example) must have more than one child in one family unit. As this is not necessarily the case, it might be a contradiction to know that Hassidic Jews, whether poor or rich, have on average three or four children in their families.

On the subject of harsh winters, which must explain the high average IQ of Ashkenazi Jews, then the Gentiles from Scandinavian countries with their even harsher winters must be smarter than Jews. It would suffice to know that this is not always the case.

Now let us read from the blogs of anti-Semites.

> *Ashkenazi Jews are smart because they have a lot of German blood and also Mongoloid (Khazars) both of those have high IQ.* (A neo-Nazi blog)

That is nicely said. Does it make German people particularly proud or squeamish?

Concerning the IQs of Khazars, I must wonder how and where the test was conducted, as Khazars were gone long before IQ tests were invented.

Another myth generally ascribed to the Jews is that Jews always help each other. I might dispute this opinion with just one abstract answer from a Russian joke: When two Jews gather for a meeting, their conversation becomes a three-way argument.

Does anyone dare ask why?

Is it because Jews do not respect each other? Is it because they do not feel that their counterpart makes any sense? Is it because each is trying to show his superior knowledge? Or is it because the Jewish independent mind is looking for an answer?

The answer is, all of the above.

Do Jews help each other? Well, first, one needs to define the kind of help. If we refer to moral support, then the answer is yes. If we refer to the solidarity of Jews in the face of oppression, then the answer is yes. If we refer to discovering improper behavior and rebuking it, then the answer will be yes in one case and no in another. But if we refer to lending money without interest or opening doors for a poor neighbor, even of the same faith, or of showering the needy Jew with gifts, then the answer might be "Not so much."

Jews often do not hesitate to express their opinions or to criticize a fellow Jew if they find his approach to a subject unacceptable by their standard. They do not feel the need to stick to any particular agenda unless it conforms to their own. Yet in times of persecution, the Jews had always kept together, helping each other, joined by mutual adversity and danger.

With this brief excursion into the long and short history of the Jews, who are definitely leaving their mark on human endeavor, I must regrettably say that the question of who the contemporary Jews are still has not been sufficiently elucidated. Are the Jews a nation? Are they all connected ethnically or even religiously?

What makes these people—widely separated in different societies and communities—claim that they are all Jews?

In each country, the Jew had to comply with existing rules and order. Whether following these rules or all but ignoring them, the

—

Jews remained the distinguished nucleus, that surrounding outsiders were always able to recognize.

It is not easy to comprehend what joined these people, who have lived in many different countries, under different regimes, in one monolithic nucleus. It is even less obvious what made these separate nuclei of different societies join together as one nation.

Is there an answer to this? Can we define a formula that won't be based on prejudice? Who can say who is a Jew, without either straying into hyperbole or being labeled an anti-Semite?

What makes the Jew a Jew? How has Jewishness become a phenomenon that most people of the civilized world not only know about but—even after having intimate contact with Jews—are unable to define? What secret lies in the core of these people that causes them to be negatively profiled? Why has country after country thrown them out?

Why has this small band of people—only one twenty-fifth of 1 percent of all humankind—created, if not paranoia, then real fear and hatred that have historically resulted in carnage and oppression?

Questions like these seem to have no end. With that in mind, let me digress to consider some of the attributes of man in general and, in particular, the Jew. Maybe this approach will shed light on these complicated questions.

THE ROOTS OF FEAR

Fear, according to the *American Heritage Dictionary* is "an emotion of alarm and agitation caused by the expectation or realization of danger." We find this worrisome emotion among most primates as well as lower organisms (although there it may not necessarily rise to an emotion).

Fear is an inherited feature brought about by the instinct for survival. While fear is an innate trait, the higher in the ranks of taxonomy an organism is, the more obviously this feeling can be connected to its emotional roots. Fear is expressed in different ways, including prolonged worry, phobia, horror, and panic. When it comes to the mass fear that grows suddenly, as in the case of natural disaster, people always combine fear with panic.

–

Ideation of the possible consequences of danger is tightly connected to the ability for rational thought. Therefore it is no secret that in many armies, alcohol was often used to suppress clarity of thought in the face of danger on the battlefield.

Despite the general source from which fear emanates, it is expressed differently depending on the vision of an individual and therefore the promising ability to eliminate it.

In the case of the Jews, when these people were told or shown that the land they inhabited was not really theirs or that they were an undesirable part of society, or, even worse, were to be eliminated, a generic sense of fear arising from such an invisible source enveloped many minds and led to the development of specific traits characterizing that group. The Jews had no choice but to stay together to overcome a mutual sense of fear. They had no choice but to share their angst among themselves. The majority of people, who were constantly reminded that they did not belong to a particular society, inadvertently developed estrangement in that society.

Connected to a particular regime and the politics conducted by a government of that regime, Jews behaved correspondingly. A handful of them who would not be scared found themselves among the revolutionaries, the rebels who were fighting for better living conditions or the advocates of social justice. A handful of them were social organizers in the midst of the habitat of their people.

But the majority, as happens with any other ethnic group of people, was building their own nests, cherishing their dreams and hopes.

In that regard, the Jews of the United States represent a somewhat different breed. Despite the fact that most Jews came to America after being prosecuted in their country of birth, generation after generation, they have shed that feeling of not belonging and that crippling sense of fear. Jews in America felt equal to the rest of their fellow citizens, and this must be solely accredited to the democratic policy of the United States.

No other country on earth came into existence the way the United States did. Different nationalities, ethnic groups, and cultures have all gathered and joined as one people, with one constitution—that of the United States of America. Melting pot or not, the Jews in this land have always felt and feel equal to their countrymen, rarely, if ever, sensing that their rights could be undermined on the basis

—

of alienation brought by their government. That brought about the American Jews—people who don't know fear and who finally can claim this country as their own.

THE ROOTS OF ENVY

Envy, according to the *American Heritage Dictionary*, is "a feeling of discontent and resentment aroused by another's desirable possessions or qualities, accompanied by a strong desire to have them for oneself."

To elaborate on this definition, we need to ask and try to answer the following:

1. Is envy an acquired feature, or it is implanted in our genes?
2. Is this a positive, a benign, or a malignant feature?
3. When it comes to a specific group of people—the Jews, for instance—why are the feelings toward them mixed?

To answer the first question, let's create a hypothetical situation. When someone with the desire to acquire something sees that object in the possession of a neighbor, someone he just met, or a stranger, feelings of envy might range from a desire to acquire the object by any means to an inferiority complex born out of the inability to have it. People might envy different things, such as someone's imagined beauty or an expensive automobile.

When envy is mildly expressed, it usually spurs one to compete, to try to reach somewhat similar results, and even attempt to imitate the subject of admiration. If this is the case, our efforts might result in progression and benevolence. But oftentimes envy can spawn a vicious circle of negative feelings. The resentment that arises in such cases, along with an inability to get a desired object, can produce a whole variety of expressive behavior including an unfriendly attitude and even an expression of aggression. I assume that many readers have experienced such things at least once in their lifetimes.

But no matter what the end results of envy might be, it would not be produced if the drive to compete were not implanted in our genes. So while envy is definitely connected to our competitive side, competitiveness is that defining mechanism from which this whole process starts.

On the other side of equation lies envy of a whole ethnic group, such as envy of the Jews. The strange thing is that when it comes to Jews, people experience quite complicated feelings. Those who envy Jews express their feelings not to the individuals but to a whole group. To figure out why that is the case, we might consider a few possible answers. People might envy the Jewish ability to create and maintain good and solid family units. They might envy the perseverance of Jews in obtaining an education. They might envy Jews as a group of people who don't get drunk, who help each other in good and bad times, and who overall are perceived as the exemplars of an accepted standard on many issues.

Yet people rarely envy the rich Jews. It might seem somewhat paradoxical, but in the majority people do not envy Jews who become lawyers, doctors, musicians, or writers. They do not envy Jews who live in closed communities dealing exclusively with each other. Why should they? Who needs to study that much? Who wants to spend years of youth, beauty, and adventure in studying books? Who wants to follow restrictions of eating kosher foods, wearing the same clothes, or incessantly read the Jewish Bible?

In sum, Jews, for one reason or another, often produce negative feelings among non-Jews.

THE ROOTS OF ANTI-SEMITISM

A few years ago, I encountered an article in a Russian paper addressing the infamous The Protocols of the Elders of Zion. The article was devoted to the one-hundred-year anniversary of its publication, since it first appeared in Russian magazine *Znamya* in 1903. In short, the Protocols were presented as a document with a written plan of the Jews to achieve world domination based on the mass manipulation of people.

It turned out that the Protocols was a hoax. It had been deliberately concocted by the Russian Secret Police to incriminate the Jews. Never mind that originally the text was written by French satirist Maurice Joly and was directed toward the regime of Napoleon III, which had nothing to do with the Jews.

—

The Protocols became available in many countries and was translated into many languages, with printed copies exceeding the combined publications of such famous Russian writers as Leo Tolstoy and Dmitry Dostoyevsky. Despite the fact that the Protocols was proven to be a libelous and falsified document, the intention to use it as an incriminating document against the Jews remained firm.

This document is still available on many Internet sites and continues to be a topic of vigorous discussion.

But let's first define anti-Semitism from a Jewish point of view. Austrian Jewish scholar Moritz Steinschneider first used this term to characterize Ernest Renan's description of the inferiority of Semitic races when compared to the Aryan race.

It was the second half of the nineteenth century in Europe. A Prussian nationalistic historian, Heinrich von Treitschke, declared that the word *Semite* is synonymous with the word *Jewish*. Thus the use of the term "anti-Semite" came to be associated with the Jews only and no other Semitic nation.

The general meaning of anti-Semitism consists of hatred and hostility toward Jews, their ideology, their way of life, and their traditions.

Starting with the venal kiss of Judas that presaged the crucifixion of Jesus Christ, Jews time and again were plunged into a long history of blood libel, exclusion, hatred, and isolation. Alternating between being blamed for killing Christian children, plotting subversive acts, and causing epidemic diseases and plagues, Jews have been imputed with such sins as greed, usury, and scandalous manipulations and machinations used to deceive non-Jews. They have been portrayed in caricatures that denigrate their looks, behavior, and nature. No other nation or people in the history of mankind have experienced such a long-lasting persecution and victimization as the Jews.

Anti-Semites believe that all Jews are bad by nature, without exception, and that these bad features are hereditary. They see the segregation of the Jews in society as a result of the desire for exclusivity expressed by the Jews themselves. This despite the fact that Jews were often forced to live in ghettos, segregated communities in which no other ethnic group would or could live.

The Jewish preference to live in distinguished communities at present is reflective of those past times.

–

Yet most of the intelligent world knows that Jewish problems are many sided. These are:

- The continuous struggle for the unconditional right of Jewish people to exist within the state of Israel
- Holding the Jews collectively responsible for the crucifixion of Jesus Christ
- Ascribing the connection of the Jews to plotting international conspiracies in order to undermine and govern the world
- Placing the Jews in the category of an inferior race
- Implying unacceptable behavior and negative features to Jews

At this point, I am going to change my approach and pose a set of questions that no Jew would like to hear. They are the questions that a few non-Jews might and do ask.

- Why are the majority of Jews often found in the business of commerce?
- Why have more than a few Jews become bankers, economists, accountants, doctors, and lawyers?
- Why are there very few Jews among lay people, miners, laborers, construction workers, and so on?
- Why, after over one hundred years since the first publication of the Protocols of the Elders, do Jews still mainly fit into the description of "The International Jew" written by the anti-Semitic Henry Ford?

Before I offer my opinion, I wish to refer to people like Ford and others in his camp of hatred. You might say that Ford was a paranoid racist and xenophobe although he didn't call for the extermination of Jews (at least publicly). Ford and people like him was representative of a mere handful of sick elements of society possessed by the devilish idea of ridding the world of a small group of people that the majority of humanity hated anyway.

Yet Henry Ford was no dummy. He was a successful industrialist and the founder of the Ford Motor Company. Why did he write so negatively about Jews? What was his score with them?

—

He actually explained it in his infamous set of articles titled "The International Jew: The World's Foremost Problem."

Why am I bothered by this? Because today not only does this attitude still exist, but those who hold it can more and more openly express their negative feelings about Jews as individuals or a collective entity.

For those individuals who, while not denying the Holocaust, still insist that anti-Semitism is almost gone among the majority of people, I would say that sadly, time and again, it's been shown that this is not so. One might hope that people would become tolerant of the Jews, but is that really the case? Is anti-Semitism not a flickering flame that appears here and there from time to time, increasing with each new uproar over Jewish behavior?

Why do the Jews continue to produce such potent feelings of negativity? Why today in countries like the United States, Great Britain, France, and Spain are there more and more people wavering in their position toward the acceptance of the Jew as an equal partner, as a role model, or as a sincere friend? Why are such small countries as Uruguay or Latvia, with such few numbers of Jews, still able to erupt with feelings of animosity toward them?

Posing questions like these, one must again return to the original one: Who is a Jew? Did the American Jews of the first and second waves of immigration become mutually compatible? Does Soviet Jewry in any feature remind us of American Jews? What makes the Gentile say that these or those people are Jews? Can Jews be described without bias as family-oriented people or as people who know how to make money and who always help each other no matter what?

So much conjecture, so many questions.

The Jews who came to the United States, the land of opportunity, should not complain. Whether these are lawyers, doctors, or small and large businessmen, they almost all made it. In fact, the average Gentile would be pretty sure that the Jewish people have found success and have made it in America. They have money, good families, and good work, and often are free to pursue good education. Why would any of them even think to complain?

And they don't. At least no one has heard such complaints.

But what about the other people and ethnic groups, do they complain? How do these people see Jews, generally speaking?

—

"Jews are progressively spread in highest and influential circles." "They are mostly stuffed with money." "They had occupied Hollywood, media, Wall Street, and Forty-Seventh Street." "They are in private sectors of huge corporations and, as a rule of thumb, being the employers." "They are financiers, bankers, the economists, and such." "They are the most visible doctors and lawyers when you need one." "And they are in all other intellectual endeavors such as famous musicians, writers, biologists, geneticists, physicists, chemists, or, otherwise, scientists." These expressions could be heard or read today in America in different places. I would not be as bold as to say that one does not hear those words a lot, but I can assure you that people talk this way. Not often and not in many circles, but they do talk.

The question that must be asked then is "why." Let's start with the big "why" first.

Why are Jews so fond of money? The answer to this is fairly simple and might be explained by another question. Why do most women like money? To an anti-Semite, this is the Jewish method: to answer a simple question with a counter question to confuse and avoid, or, in other words, to not answer.

No matter which answer one might appreciate the most, here is my understanding of why Jews love money. Money is that reliable shelter that gives human beings calm, confidence, the elimination of the fear of hunger, and the fulfillment of many basic human needs. Why does the Jew have such an enormous appetite for money? Bet you thought I wouldn't ask that question.

Clearly I don't have to justify such questions with answers. Any apple tree produces rotten fruit, and although such fiscal inclinations might exist within the Jewish community, I'd have argued that this prejudice is tightly connected to the Jews' two thousand years of deprivation of human rights and habitation.

The Jew's tenacity was developed as an anchor that would allow him to survive. Whether one will agree with me or not, there are the Jews who do not stuff themselves with money, although those Jews are ordinarily invisible. While such a Jew might also exhibit a sampling of a well-to-do family, be focused on the education of his children, cultivate in his children good manners, and so on, such an individual would likely be perceived as a rich man who purposefully hides his richness. Thus a random visitor to that family might not accept the idea that this Jew might be poor.

Now let me try to speculate on why Jews are mostly found in commerce. The answer, although unacceptable to the anti-Semite, is that the society in which the Jew lived often prohibited him from entering certain professions. Depending on the severity of the law, Jews had to do what they were allowed to do.

Were they also looking for ways to get into the prohibited fields? The answer is obviously yes. This is the way most human minds work. People try to succeed any way they can.

Another explanation of why a Jew in business or commerce might be connected to a Jew's ability to excel in accounting. Inherited or not, Jews had to use their heads in order to achieve similar results to those that physically gifted people achieved. Using their brains instead of their muscles, the Jews realized that intellect is superior to physical prowess and therefore is more useful. Jews continuously show a superior ability in math and physics, whether connected to handling money or not.

Finally we need to consider the most complicated question. Why were the Jews thrown out of many countries such that today they remain categorized as the most unstable and unpleasantly visible breed of people?

Most contemporary Americans (although some sources bring the figure down to 22 percent, which is considerably lower than most) would agree that Jews came to dominate Hollywood. The same statistics can be applied when one considers the number of Jews who become doctors, lawyers, or successful businessmen. Jewish doctors and lawyers are everywhere, many times more present than Gentiles of the same profession. How could that be the case? Are they helping each other to get into those lucrative fields? Could it be a simple coincidence?

Let's compare Jews in similar professions within two different countries: the former USSR and the United States.

It is a matter of fact that the USSR State Committee for Cinematography, as well as their theater and art, had always been represented by talented Jews. They had their own Stephen Spielberg, Robert Iger, Michael Lynton, and Michael Eisner. They had their own composers, film producers, and actors.

—

Joel Stein, in an article dated December 19, 2008, in the *Los Angeles Times* wrote these words: "As a proud Jew, I want America to know about our accomplishment. Yes, we control Hollywood. Without us, you'd be flipping between *The 700 Club* and *Davey and Goliath* on TV all day long."

I cannot say that the Jews controlled the Soviet film industry the same way the American big shots did for one simple reason: they were not allowed. But as the American Jews of Hollywood made themselves noticeable, the Jews of the film industry and other forms of entertainment in the former USSR were and are known to the majority of intellectual people all over the world for their indisputable talent.

But there are two conspicuous differences between the film industries of these two countries: first, the Jewish wizards of Russian industry had to be represented and managed by non-Jews, preferably Russians, and second, the Jewish geniuses in that country were paid by the Russian government an amount not anywhere near what the Jews in Hollywood were paid.

Exactly that same formula might be applied in regard to Soviet Jewish doctors, scientists, and musicians. They were devoted to their fields, not because of the money, which was meager—especially if compared to that made by the professional laborer and often not sufficient to live on—but because they loved the work they did.

Onto a more grievous matter of how the ordinary Gentile views the fairytale about Jewish doctors killing Christian babies so the community of Jews can use their blood for making matzos, the unleavened bread traditionally used in Jewish feasts. Although it is not a topic of the day in this country, it is still believed by more than a few contemporary Russians. It speaks ill of the level of intelligence of these Russian folks that one can still find among them people who believe that a Jew must have small horns like the Moses of Michelangelo seems to or that he must have a small tail because the Jew is a literal devil. The unfortunate fact is that anti-Semitism is rampant and widespread.

And with these words, I'd like to engage in some sort of screed directed to those extremists, mostly of Christian and other similar faiths, who had inherited from Jews their beliefs, grace, and the glory of God by the name Jesus Christ, but who are engaged in a vitriolic campaign against the Jews.

—

Your faith, you believe, is the only proper one. You live your life hoping that one day you will end up in paradise. You might admit that you've sinned a little here and a little there, but not to the point that you could be denied entrance into eternity.

The reason you think this way comes from a comparison. In your case, you compare your religion to other religions about which you know little, your group of believers to other groups of people you hardly know, your achievements to their achievements, and your deeds to their deeds. Whether they are neighbors, friends, companions, mates, or children, you compare their beliefs to your own.

You might have achieved a lot or a little, spiritually speaking, but your assessment of your achievements might not correspond either to reality or to what other people think of you when they do their own comparison. To some, this does not matter, and to others, it matters a lot. In any event, you trust your own intuition and reason when it comes to making decisions about life, and yet there are inevitably times when you feel confused. We all are confused occasionally, whether we acknowledge it or not.

The only person, in your mind, who supposedly was not confused was Jesus Christ, whom you accept as the answer to life's questions. Therefore, for you, there is no question about who he is or was. There is no doubt in your heart when your faith is concerned. Anyone, who raises doubt about the divinity of Jesus Christ must be blasphemous, or a fool, or at least a dangerous person. There is no reason to argue with or listen to such an individual character.

Then again, by answering the following questions and analyzing the facts, you might see the truth, not through the cover of your subjective opinion, but as things really are. Anti-Semitism aside, do you consider yourself a truthful person? Or do you consider yourself weak and confused to the point that you do not want to hear something that might confuse you further? Are you afraid of someone else's opinion? If not, read on. You don't have to agree with me on any level. Or at least not right away. You decide. It's your choice.

But here are my questions and some facts:

- Who was Jesus Christ?
- Were the Jews instrumental in creating the story of Jesus Christ, the Redeemer?

–

- Could Christianity have been born independently from the Hebrew Bible?
- When Jesus Christ returns, would he accept the notion of hostility toward Jews by non-Jews?

FACT 1: Hebrews—that is, Jews—wrote the Holy Bible. All of it. Both the Old Testament and the New Testament.

FACT 2: Throughout the Old Testament, the Hebrews refer to one god who does not have a son, who is either human or not.

FACT 3: Gentiles and pagans did not know or care about Jesus when he appeared in Judea and began to preach his way of life to the Jewish people.

FACT 4: Jesus of Nazareth was born into a Jewish family.

FACT 5: He came (as the Bible explains) to save his people, the Jews, from their sins.

FACT 6: The Bible says that Jesus was born to a Jewish woman named Mary (*Maryam*).

FACT 7: God, as described by the Hebrews, was the Almighty God, the only god, who made a covenant with the Hebrews and not with other groups present at the time.

FACT 8: The authors of the canonical gospels, Saint Paul and the twelve apostles, were all Hebrews (Jews) who were in disagreement with their brethren (other Hebrews) who did not consider Jesus Christ as the Son of God.

FACT 9: From the very beginning of Christianity, Christians have held a number of different interpretations of the essence and role of Jesus in their lives.

FACT 10: Saul of Tarsus (Paul) was the first missionary to preach the new faith to Gentiles. Paul never met Jesus in person and seemed an unlikely candidate for the role as his representative. Yet this new role elevated Paul to sainthood and conferred on him the authority to make doctrine.

FACT 11: Because the first Christians were all Jews, they didn't know better than to tell the Gentiles that they had to convert to Jewish faith and undergo circumcision in order to become Christians.

FACT 12: Some Christians came to vilify the Jews and their god, transforming their Judeo-Christian roots into purely Christianity as time passed. In other words, while the very first Christians were Jews

—

or had to become Jews in order to convert to Christianity, after the teachings of Paul (as well as Peter's vision), the Gentiles did not have to proselytize into the Jewish faith any longer to be accepted into Christianity. Eventually some sects became so divorced from Judaism that they no longer saw Christianity as being related to Judaism and began to find fault with the Jewish religion.

FACT 13: Historically some Christians completely separated themselves from Judaism and began to deny the goodness of the god of the Hebrews along with the divine nature of Moses' mission.

FACT 14: Throughout the long history of Christianity, various Christian groups have claimed that others are doctrinally incorrect or even heretical. This often gave rise to new denominations and sects within the faith. Each newly organized religious body would insist that they were the righteous, with many of them not reverently recognizing the Hebrews as the forefathers of their faiths.

FACT 15: To say that Christianity is the only religion of just and righteous people is demeaning to all non-Christians, but especially to the Jews whose faith gave birth to Christianity.

FACT 16: Jesus was, before anything else, the Messiah of the Jews. To pry him from that context is to lose a great portion of the meaning of his ministry.

More importantly, while Jesus criticized the Jewish religious leaders for their materialism, hypocrisy, and emphasis on ritual, he showed great love for the Jewish people. "O Jerusalem, Jerusalem," he said, "the one who kills the prophets and stones those who are sent to her! How often I wanted to gather your children together, as a hen gathers her chicks under her wings, but you were not willing!" (Matthew 23:37 NKJV).

Moreover, he clearly revered Moses and taught that his followers should have love for all people, even those who hated and persecuted them. He did not exclude the Jews or make it a mission to punish them for perceived wrongs. Perhaps Jesus, like Buddha before him, understood that hatred does not cease by hatred; hatred ceases by love.

We know that the Jewish people arose in the history of mankind with a covenanted relationship with their God. Yet history shows that God abandoned them more than once (or perhaps they abandoned him), sending them into the worst possible trials that nature and other humans could offer. In spite of this, the Jews continued to believe in their god.

Christians, who have had a history of elimination and persecution no less disastrous than the Jews, continued to believe in the divinity of Jesus Christ.

What makes these two groups of people such staunch loyalists to their religions? What makes them so stubbornly proclaim that their shared god is the only true god and yet see him so differently?

Questions such as these beg for an answer. To say that people do not see the weaknesses in their own religion would be superficial. Could the desire to believe in a Supreme Power—by whatever name and description—possibly be connected to the human fear of being mortal and powerless, with no guiding hand toward salvation?

These questions are valid enough to be asked again and again. And although their repetition may not produce an answer, we ask them anyway in order to understand.

Whether we are Jews, Christians, Muslims, or Hindus, we cannot deny that we appeared on this earth somehow, and somehow we continue our evolution, hoping that one day all will become clear and we will be granted, if not eternity, then a long life with the possibility of transformation into a better form. Until such transformation happens, we will go on relying on miracles and hope.

To summarize, I wish to say this: It is very possible that God had in mind to keep the number of Jews in the world at no more than around fifteen to eighteen million. You can imagine what might have happened if the Jews were counted in numbers, say, ten times that. But then again, it is not for me to decide.

What I would say though is that the greed of some Jews became dangerous for the rest of Jewry in the same manner as the kiss of Judas was fraught with serious and grave consequences for all Jews. And while not too many Jews rebuke a fellow Jew who is unscrupulous in the practice of making money, the majority of Jews today would certainly not want the rest of humanity to remember words of Henry Ford expressed some eighty years ago in "The International Jew": "Greed of Jews led to the economic 'pogrom' of helpless humanity."

As long as the Jew is willing to learn, he will be present in the world of wisdom and scientific achievement. Both Gentiles and Jews must live with this reality. Gentiles must reconsider how to be

—

respectful of Jews, instead of constantly rebuking them or seeking to humiliate or harm them. This does no one any good.

Jews, on the other hand, must learn to respect Gentiles and their work. And, most importantly, the Jews must learn to be modest in their deeds and to stop bragging about their achievements or riches. Modesty may bring both parties to a mutually beneficial coexistence.

As to the ability of Jews to permeate any society and "spoil" it, non-Jews must realize one thing: While the general consensus about a specific ethnic group is a generalized opinion, it still concerns each individual member of that group separately. How many Jews do you personally know that you must hate because of their nature?

A few words need to be said about Jews in politics and economics. There are two ways to see their role and influence in any particular society: via references based on statistical facts and via the conclusions drawn from opinions accepted by society.

The United States would be the democracy best reflective of Jewish influence in politics, economy, and culture. The success achieved by Jews in this country is tremendous. Senators, representatives in congress, and justices—Jewish elected and appointed officials are disproportionately high when compared to the number of Jews in the electorate.

No doubt such statistics can be credited to the climate of the country with regards to the Jews living in it. Whether it is a new phenomenon related to the fact that this is a country of immigrants, or the relative youth of the culture, remains to be seen.

What does not change is the attitude of the Jews. Out of one hundred senators and 435 congressmen, the Jews are the most vocal. The same can be said of lobbyists, litigators, doctors, and so on. Jews in the majority are often flashy, whether one perceives that quality as negative or positive.

Does this perception make a Jew think twice about his attitude? I really doubt it. That is the nature of a Jew, and if people around him see him as different or even as an alien creature, that for some reason does not bother him a bit.

Everybody is different. Everybody has flaws. So why should a Jew worry about something he most likely holds in common with everyone else?

To finish the story about the Jews, I wish to say this to the Jews of the world: Your people were the first to invent a covenant with one god, and your people were the pioneers in providing Christians and Muslims with a similar idea. That fact alone, no doubt, should make you a proud Jew.

But as powerful and truthful this statement is, no less important should be the fact of how you relate to earth's citizens. Don't look for excuses. Don't support the general expression approved among Jews that people will always dislike Jews. Ask yourself why this is so. Ask yourself a few times, if one time is not enough. Ask yourself if any of this negativity is your fault? Ask yourself what you can do to fit among the rest, if you want to be tolerated, respected, and accepted as equal.

These are not just a few empty words. These are offers for survival. Think about it.

CHAPTER 15

Arab Muslims

The history of the Arab people began much earlier than the religion of Islam came into existence in the seventh century CE. Still, not much information about the origin of Arabs has been collected from that pre-Islamic period. In fact, the origins of these people that available to us are often confusing. As in the case of the Hebrews, the word Arab has its meaning in Semitic languages. It might be translated as merchant, nomad, or person of the desert.

Under this etymological explanation, the Arabs could be the people that were recognized as Nabateans, Qedarites, Ishmaelites, and a few other tribes of the Arabian Peninsula. In other words, the term Arab is the collective term that has been transformed into a definition of a specific ethnic group. Today the belief is held that whoever is connected through their genealogy to the tribes of Arabia can be considered an Arab.

This is the reason why it is hard to do justice when one tries to elucidate the features of the Arab people. That they originated as the inhabitants of the Arabian Peninsula, there are enough documents pointing to it. Besides the Arabian Peninsula, which simply by its name directs us to an awareness of the existence of Arabs, there were places in the whole region of the Middle and Far East where Arabs might have moved and settled. Still none of the available sources clearly state which people were Arabs among those who lived there.

There were plenty of cultures in the Mesopotamian basin that might or might not point to the ancestral roots of the Arabs. Many cultures there rose and fell during the period of a few millennia, starting approximately in 4000 BCE and ending roughly at the beginning of the new era. We will consider some of those cultures, however brief this excursion might be.

The first known civilizations in Mesopotamia were the Sumerian, the Akkadian, the Babylonian, and the Assyrian.

The Sumerians were, in a sense, a "sudden" civilization, as by the time they appeared, they were advanced on many levels. In the year 4000 BCE, they had all the signs of contemporary civilization. In fact, they were the first people who not only knew many details of cosmology and had the political structure of a bicameral congress, they also gave us literary works, libraries, medicine, and many other achievements of civilization. Despite all this, in about 2270 BCE, they were conquered by the neighboring Semitic nation, the Akkadian Empire.

While Sumer was geographically located in the land of contemporary Iraq, they were not Semitic people, and this fact alone excludes the possibility to trace Arabs or, for that matter, any other Semitic nation to these ancient people.

Akkadian culture had prospered in the second and third millenniums BCE. Although its main city, Akkad, has never been found, it is known that this culture achieved its greatest prosperity under the chieftain, and later king, Sargon. The goal of this king was to obtain all the lands with its people of southern Mesopotamia. His policy led to a gradual replacement of the previous Sumerian culture.

The Sumerians tried to return, but they were completely gone by the twentieth century BCE. The major role in their demise, though, was played by the Amorites, whose invasion brought the Sumerian culture to a complete halt. Amorites were the nomads who lived near the mountain areas of today's Turkey, Syria, and Palestine. They'd moved to the Mesopotamian basin after being forced away by a continued drought in the area they had lived.

While it appears these people did not have their own literature or anything specific characterizing their culture, their king, Hammurabi, created the state of Babylonia out of the territories of the Akkadian and Sumerian empires. Hammurabi was a powerful king who created many laws of order known to us as Hammurabi's Code. Nevertheless, his empire was subjugated after the Hittites conquered Babylonia in 1595 BCE.

Hittites originated in Anatolia (Turkey). Out of the traditionally divided three periods, they reached the most power in the second period, lasting from 1500-1430 BCE. The biblical Hittites and people who, by the year 2000 BCE, lived in Anatolia might or might not be the same people; this is a matter of continued debate.

The Kassites' dynasty in Babylonia began after a Near Eastern tribe (from an area of modern Iran), whose origin and rise to power is also unclear, gained control of that land in 1570 BCE, overpowering the Hittites. They were not a Semitic people nor did they belong to the Indo-European family. The Kassites ruled Babylonia for a little more than four hundred years. The kings of this dynasty established trade and diplomatic relations with their neighbors, in particular with Assyria.

Assyria was an ancient kingdom in northern Mesopotamia that competed for its dominance with Babylonia in the second millennium BCE. It was a Semitic kingdom that experienced periods of prosperity and fall during different fortunes of its history. In the third millennium BCE, Assyria was under the domination of Akkadian and Sumerian cultures, later to become an independent kingdom. With its politics of wars and expansion in a period lasting almost a millennium, Assyria began its steady downfall in the first millennium, and by 626 BCE, it fell under the rule of Babylon.

The ruler of Babylon at that time was a king by the name Nabonidus, who himself was an Assyrian. As history continued to dictate inevitable changes, Assyria in the years from 539 BCE to 330 BCE came under the rule of the Persian Achaemenid Empire. In the year 330 BCE, Assyria spiraled into her final breath, when Alexander the Great, the Macedonian emperor from Greece, conquered it. Greeks, not knowing better, confused this kingdom with Syria, and under the Seleucid Empire, Assyria was renamed as Syria.

Today, Assyrians mostly live as a Christian minority in Iraq, although Muslim extremists want to get rid of them. Some of them have relocated to Western countries where they experience very little recognition.

—

Ancient Syria was one of the oldest Semitic cultures in the region. It comprised the whole region of Levant (generally known as the eastern region), an area that included the eastern coastline of the Mediterranean along with the lands of peninsula. The inhabitants of Syria belonged to such great kingdoms as Ebla and Mari, Canaan, Babylonia, and Persia, spreading from the Red Sea to the north as far as Turkey. It was one of the most ancient civilizations of the region and, for that matter, on earth.

Yet during the second millennium BCE, Syria was occupied by the Babylonians, the Assyrians, the Canaanites, the Arameans, and the other sea peoples. In 64 BCE, Syria was turned into a Roman province. It played an important role in strengthening the Roman Empire and later on in establishing Christianity. Saint Paul had his faithful vision of Jesus Christ on the road to Damascus of Syria. It fell to the Islamic conquest and rule in 637 CE, turning into an Arabic Muslim country.

Arabs as a distinguished group of people are first mentioned in the eighth century BCE of the Neo-Assyrian Empire. At that time, Assyria achieved its greatest power in the Middle East. One of the peoples they describe as a tribe paying them tribute were the tribes of Qedarites. Qedarites are believed to be an ancient Arab tribal confederation that lived in the Arabian Desert. They became an influential force, especially between the eighth and fourth centuries BCE.

According to the Bible account, Qedarites were the descendants of the second son of Ishmael, Qedar. Excluding the account connected to the Bible, Qedarites were, in fact, real people who most likely were the first Arabs. Whether they were the only nomadic people that might be considered Arabs or simply the most prominent ones among other nomadic peoples is a matter of believing in different sources. According to sources other than the Bible, Qedarites were polytheists who worshipped different gods, female goddesses, and even water.

There were also the Thamud people mentioned in an Assyrian inscription dated 715 BCE, during the time of Sargon II and, before them, the tribe of A'ad people, who, according to the Qur'an, were the people who disobeyed Allah and were destroyed. Whether all these and the many others vaguely mentioned in different accounts were the Arabs is impossible to say.

—

The other practical approach to decipher the origins of the Arab people could be an attempt to trace their language or languages. There are four distinct Old South Arabian languages that date to the tenth century BCE and the languages of the Ancient North Arabian of the sixth century BCE that are known to have been spoken in the Arabian Peninsula. Yet the Classical Arabic that is spoken today by Muslim Arabs distinctly differs from the Old Arabian, and no clear evidence can be established of their linguistic connection. The many languages that existed in the region in that period have even fewer supporting documents and therefore cannot produce any clear understanding on the subject.

Despite the fact that many names of kings, cities, and states came to us by the reference of a few archaeological findings, tablets, steles, scarce papers, and later the writings of the Hebrew Bible, it is impossible to establish the origin of the numerous tribes that lived in the Mesopotamian region at that time. Neither can much information be drawn from such credible sources of antiquity as Egyptian, Greek, and Roman writings.

With the appearance of the Qahtanites in the Levant and the rise of the Himyarite Kingdom (geographically related to Yemen), more tangible information on the Arabian people came to light. Early Islamic historians connect those people to the biblical Yoqtan, which, though a semi legendary figure, is believed to be the ancestor of all Yemeni tribes.

With all of this presentation, it is logical to conclude that, as in the case of the Jews, the Arab people are impossible to trace to their ancestors. Their identity, again as in the case of the Jews, is independent from their religion. In our times, the term "Arab" is applied to a group of different people who speak in a common Arabic language. But this language is not the original tongue for the ancient peoples of the Mesopotamian region, such as were the Akkadians, Sumerians, Assyrians, Syrians, and Babylonians, to name but a few.

Today the countries in the Middle East are no doubt Arabic countries in the eyes of an outsider. However, historically, it is only recently that such a large country as Egypt, for instance, has been recognized by its dwellers as being ethnically mainly Arabic.

Not all Arabs are Muslims either. Still, because the sheer majority of Arabs are devoted to Islam, it is feasible to speak about that

—

particular group, not diminishing the significance of Arab Christians, Arab Jews, or any other Muslims in different parts of the world.

With that in mind, let us proceed forward to the period of the seventh century CE, when Islam began to flex its muscle, with Muhammad as its divine messenger.

At that time, the old world of many struggles between the Roman Empire and Persia had stalled into a brief period of peace. Ruled by the Byzantine half of the Roman Empire and its capital, Constantinople, on one hand and the Sassanid Dynasty of Persia on the other, these two dynasties were the last citadels of civilization before they fell under the influence of Islam.

Overcoming the influential family of Quraysh, to which Muhammad was related and was a member, the support for Muhammad's new faith had grown as he began more explicitly to behave like a prophet. He had to leave Mecca, as it was still a stronghold of Quraysh, and he moved to north, settling in Yathrib, a place known now as Medina, contemplating one day to return and not to leave without victory. This move of relocation is considered the beginning of the Muslim era.

Soon after, the fight with Quraysh began. Whether it was presented as the need to win control of the trade routes or Muhammad finally concluded enough is enough, he naturally explained this fight as a requirement to restore the goodness and righteousness of God's servants. Allah was the only god the people should serve and that faith in the one powerful god had succinct preeminence over the idolatry and idealization of many.

With such an attitude, the exclusivity of Islam's adherents began to crawl in the consciousness of people. The phrase *Ummah Wahida* (One United Community of Muslims) began to circle at that time, serving as the reference to the unified Islamic world. As a consequence, the phrase "You are the best of peoples, evolved for mankind. Enjoining what is right, forbidding what is wrong and believing in God" became known as the expression found in the Qur'an (3:110).

Gradually intensifying the teaching of Islam among pagans and encouraged by the accompanied success, Muhammad tried to involve the people of other faiths such as Jews and Christians. Although the Jews of Medina had originally supported Muhammad, their position began to change with the expansion of Islam.

Around that time, the Charter of Medina (also known as the Constitution of Medina) was devised by the Prophet Muhammad to provide a formal agreement between Muslims and the tribes of Yathrib. That agreement spelled out the rights as well as the responsibilities of Jewish, Christian, and pagan communities. While this decision of Muhammad was directed to unifying the different tribes of Medina, in reality, the elite merchants of the Jews' largest tribe, Banu Qaynuqa, refused to accept the main tenets of the new rule and for that reason were ordered to leave the region.

Another reason explicated by different investigative sources was that most of the Jews who lived in Medina felt, with the increased power and influence of Muhammad, that their own religious interests were losing respect and importance. They finally refused to accept Muhammad as a genuine messenger from God. In turn, after a few attempts to persuade the Jews to support his teachings unconditionally, Muhammad began to accuse them of transgression and perversion. "If only the People of the Book had faith: it were best for them: among them are some who have faith, but most of them are perverted transgressors" (Qur'an 3:110).

After the unsuccessful attempt of Muhammad to add to his base the Jews living in Medina and other neighboring regions of Arabian Peninsula, he initiated a campaign of open terror of Jews. By different sources (as none clearly explains the main reason for the split between Muslims and Jews), the starting point of separation came with the Battle of Badr that allowed Muhammad to claim victory over the Quraysh.

The Jews, who began to increasingly feel unhappy with the demands the Muslim community directed toward them, finally switched their allegiance from Muhammad and allied with the Quraysh. While Muhammad later on showed great generosity and unusual kindness to the denizens of Mecca, he still cruelly punished the Jews of Medina, killing all men, selling them into slavery, women and children.

The complete separation of the Muslims from the Jews and Christians took place in that time. Nevertheless, the idea of the spiritual continuity of monotheistic faith that Muhammad had preached as coming from a founder of it, Abraham, continued at full speed. Muhammad insisted that Abraham was the father of all three monotheistic faiths, Judaism, Christianity, and Islam.

The methods he applied, though, were muddled up in his unplanned stand toward disbelievers versus the faithful. A point of interest in that sense can be seen in the Hadith, where it is written in chapter 9, "Command for fighting against the people so long as they do not profess that there is no God but Allah and Muhammad is his Messenger" (Sahih Muslim1:33).

This attitude was also mentioned in the Qur'an, which it meant that the words came straight from concerned God:

> *And fight them on until there is no more Fitnah [disbelief and polytheism: i.e. worshiping others besides Allah] and the religion [worship] will all be for Allah alone [in the whole of the world]. But if they cease [worshiping others besides Allah], then certainly, Allah is All-Seer of what they do."* (Qur'an, Sura 8, Section 5:39)

This connection of all the major religions at the time was a powerful tool, most likely instinctively chosen by the prophet, who not only had to overpower the resisting base of those who already had faith, but to convert unbelievers to its ranks. It also helped the teachings of Muhammad, as many native denizens were illiterate.

As a result, a growing number of the merchants in Mecca began to adhere to Islam. That movement was mutually benefitting for the merchants, who felt safe with Muhammad in their trades, and for the people of Medina, who needed such a union to subside the hostility of their neighboring brethren. By 630 CE, the leaders of Mecca surrendered to Muhammad, and the city became the place of pilgrimage for all Muslims in the region.

Soon Islam became the dominant religion, gaining influence in country after country.

When considering why Muhammad and Islam were so successful, the same formula might be applied here as with any other faith.

People's awesome veneration of a Supreme Being who promises eternity after a short time of struggling and suffering on earth naturally creates a tendency to affiliate with any morally sound, superficially true doctrine. Whether those who proclaim themselves as messengers believe in their divine mission completely and unequivocally or not is irrelevant as long as they find a propitious environment in which they are finally and unconditionally recognized and accepted.

The legacy of the Qur'an as a gift from the transcendent god played exactly the same role for Muslims as the Old and New Testaments did for the Jews and Christians.

While that belief on its surface reflected divinity, this religion, as well as any other faith, was a reflection of the aspirations specifically related to Muslims and therefore played a distinctly divisible role of that community from the rest. No matter how beautiful and convincing were her advocates, acceptance and conversion in to this faith could not and did not suggest the involvement of Almighty God. God's evocation, this time by Islam, could not convince people other than Muslims that a role God wished to play would be in the separation of people.

Today Islam is a religion that has spread among almost two billion people and that has been accepted by the rest of the world as a monolithic, monotheistic faith. On the other hand, Islam not only has been adopted by different people from different cultures and countries, it's been revised within Arab Muslim communities quite a number of times.

After the Qur'an and Hadith were accepted as God's and Muhammad's words respectively, while the Qur'an was announced as a record of the exact words of God, the Hadith came as an accumulation of the words and the way of life led by the Prophet Muhammad. Soon after, there appeared Islamic scholars and philosophers who began to interpret the laws drawn from that religion.

It is not so much surprising to see the sudden effect of Islam, which proceeded to spread quickly in the neighboring regions, as it is to see the willingness of people to accept it as their new religion. Human nature always remains the same, and people of different backgrounds and cultures accumulate numerous questions that must answered. The appearance of theological scholars became a necessity to ease the human quest, to interpret, and to explain why this perception of God was the most truthful and transcendental.

Islam, that is, a set of beliefs, is a strict and unyielding religion that refers to God in his authority as an unquestionable ruler with his requirements.

–

Taking the Qur'an as divine revelation, despite the fact that it appeared late in the history of civilizations, no person according to Muslim beliefs has the authority to question the validity of the text in it. Still, from the time the Qur'an was accepted as canon, about 1,200 years elapsed, with hundreds of new denominations founded in different religions. In that regard, it is quite a statement coming from the Muslim clergy that the Qur'an is the last revelation of God. Claiming that Allah is one and the only god as well as the unquestionable Supreme Power, Islam takes on itself the authority to state that it is the last religion of humanity.

Is this a human or divine feature to declare one's superiority among others? Must it not be only the power of God that will decide the future of humankind? Wouldn't it be the case that if this were coming from God, then all people would accept such a doctrine?

Having said that, it is not my intention to suggest that Islam is any less a religion than Judaism or Christianity is. But as in the case of Hebrew scripture or the New Testament, Islam is hard to follow without additional explanations, and that is what the Muslim scholars had to do. Thus the *Sira* (the description of the life of the prophet), the *Hadith* (the narratives of the sayings and deeds of the prophet), the *Ta'rikh* (the chronology of the prophet's life), and the *Tafsir* (the exegesis on the Qur'an) came into existence.

To legitimize all of the sacred revelations of the Qur'an and the sayings and deeds of Muhammad, Muslim clerics needed a law. This came under the umbrella of *sharia* (Islamic) law. All Muslims believe in sharia, but, depending on their school, they interpret it differently. Sharia is actually a collection of codes that encompasses many topics such as politics and economics, traditions and ways of life for Muslims. There is no Muslim that exists that does not recognize sharia.

At the same time, Muslims had split into two major factions or sects, depending on who is speaking of them. Sunni Muslims, who are one of the two major factions, recognize that reasoning and analogy might be needed for the interpretation of sharia, while Shi'a Muslims do not.

In modern times, Muslims are faced with the realistic need to interpret and adjust the sayings of Qur'an accordingly. Therefore, today, sharia in secular Western countries, where it is forcibly applied personally or in families rather than to the whole country, differs from sharia in Muslim countries and states, where either the symptoms of democracy took their course or religious clerics are still in power. In those countries, sharia ranges from obligatory type of behavior to recommended ones.

Muslim communities, depending on their geographical locations, find themselves among secular, traditional, or reformer types of governing systems.

Without considering the possible motifs of relocation of Muslim families from their motherland to the Western world, Muslims tend to stick together on alien soil, gathering in small but homogenous communities. It becomes almost natural that with the strict rules of their religion, Muslim quasi-communities (*Ummah*) continue to follow their accepted laws of how to conduct their lives. It is when such a community becomes large enough to be noticed by society that government begins to issue rules in an attempt to adjust this foreign body to the accustomed rules of the majority of the country.

The majority of Muslims, for whom the unquestionable authority is the Qur'an and the sharia law, do not perceive democracy as a possible substitute for their lifestyle. No matter how liberal, righteous, or legitimate democratic rules are, they are established by humans and can in no way be reconciled with the authority of God. Recently coming from the colonial period, Muslims believe that despite declaring democracy as the great way of governing, it is often undermined by errors in justice, temptations of power, and the fallibility of human morals and principles.

With the Muslim belief in the supremacy of sharia law, they do not easily accept any criticism or arguments against it, including punishments for adultery, consumption of alcohol, and other such human sins, versus fundamental moral commitments.

To ensure protection of *sharia* law, Muslims designate jurists (*ulama*), to perform administrative functions and act as guardians of Muslim traditions. The head of the Islamic state is the *caliph*, who is considered the "successor" of the messenger of God, Muhammad.

The designation of such a ruler split Muslims into two factions, Sunni and Shi'a. Sunni Muslims believe that a caliph must be chosen from the Muslim community merely by election, while Shi'a Muslims insisted that the ruler has to come from the immediate family line of the prophet. This schism has brought great turmoil to Muslims with

–

the subsequent elimination of a number of caliphs as well as upheaval between the two factions.

Today Sunni Islam is the largest body of that faith in the world. They encompass about 90 percent of believers all over the world. Shi'a Muslims believe that the successor of Muhammad must not only be his blood relative, but this rightful successor must have special spiritual qualities and be able to display an authority over the Muslim community. Such a leader is called an imam.

An imam is a leader who does not receive divine revelation from God yet is guided by God and, in his turn, guides the people. According to the Hadith of the successors of Muhammad, it is believed that altogether there are supposed to be twelve imams, and today the world is waiting for the appearance of that twelfth and final imam. It is believed the twelfth imam or *Mahdi* (Guided One) will emerge along with Jesus Christ and will rule for several years, right before the Judgment Day.

In the last few centuries, Muslim Arabs had lived under the occupation of the Ottoman Turks, and that fact actually played a somewhat positive role in their relationship.

The Shi'a and Sunni relationship right after the collapse of the Ottoman Empire was relatively friendly. The Shi'a scholars even attended the Caliphate Conference in Jerusalem in 1931. But the last two wars in the Persian Gulf revealed a major uprising of these factions with unnecessary and unfortunate bloodshed from both sides. This mostly religious civil unrest nevertheless laid the blame on outside provocation and forces, including Zionism as the main provocateur. This tendency to blame Israel, the Jews, and Zionism for the misfortune of different groups of Arabs, especially the Palestinian Arabs, became the usual method among some disconnected Arabic countries and people.

CHAPTER 16

The Israeli-Arab Conflict

In the very short version of historical events, let me bring to you my analysis of what had led to this continuous and almost never-disquieting conflict. I decided not to detail a number of attacks that happened almost immediately after the first *Aliyah* (immigration of the Jews) began to arrive in Palestine by the 1880s. The generalized anti-Semitism and pogroms in Europe sent thousands of Jews to seek refuge in the Holy Land, the land quite forgotten yet always remembered by many Jewish minds and hearts. Not quite discouraged by the difficult climatic conditions, multiple swamps, malaria, and rugged terrain, Jews were astonished and perplexed by the hostility of the Arabs, who had themselves subjugated by the Ottoman Turks for centuries and felt more entitled to that land than the Jews were.

The United Kingdom, Germany, France, the Netherlands, and a few other less powerful European countries in the early nineteenth century commenced an aggressive expansion of their territories. Exploring the new markets, areas in which to settle, and captivated by their domineering influence, they initiated a fairly vigorous wave of colonization.

The industrial revolution and the growing population desiring to migrate allowed Britain to spread the fastest among the rest, especially into the countries of the Far East. The new phase of that expansion soon brought Britain into the northern part of the African continent. Unchallenged as a major player of the seas, it colonized country

–

after country, to further rule them as dominions, protectorates, and mandates.

In the meantime, the former great power of the Ottoman Turks in the Middle East slowly continued to crumble, not keeping pace with the occurring transformations of the world. By the end of the nineteenth century, the influence of the Ottoman Empire was mostly in name only.

After the unsuccessful campaign of Napoleon Bonaparte and the impressive British sinking of the French fleet, Britain, along with many attempts to establish business trades in the Nile Valley region, was considering its role in Egypt.

With the occupation of Egypt starting in 1882, Britain established itself as a new ruler of this indebted country, overpowering the Urabi nationalist movement and suppressing the influence of Ottoman Turks. Claiming that they responded to the request of Tewfik Pasha, the governor of Egypt and vassal of the Ottoman Empire, Britain invaded that country, supposedly for a short while, although they remained until 1956.

Not wasting any time, the British government bought a significant portion of shares from the Egyptian company, who, along with the French, rebuilt the Suez Canal but who had ended in financial crisis. Thus the Egyptians were out of the game while the British got in. Then the major European powers at the Convention of Constantinople in the year 1888 signed an agreement with the acknowledgement of the need to declare the canal's neutrality and that all vessels would be allowed to use the canal in times of peace and war. The guarantor for the neutrality of the canal became Britain. When Britain declared war on Germany and its allies (the Ottoman Empire in particular) in 1914, the Suez Canal was no longer owned by the French and Egyptians. The canal, connecting the Red Sea to the Mediterranean Sea on one side and to the Indian Ocean on the other, became a vital route for the British, as it was used for military purposes.

In December of 1914, Britain declared Egypt as its protectorate. The Ottoman Turks saw the created situation as a signal to call for *jihad*, hoping to involve as many Muslims as possible in fighting the British. The protracted war had ensued with the resulting successive few campaigns of the British forces. The military operations lasted until October of 1918, when the Armistice was signed between the

—

Ottoman Empire and the Entente Powers, with the Turks accepting capitulation. Overall, the campaign of that period was quite a success for the British Empire, allowing them to occupy most of the strategically important Arab countries, including Palestine.

In that campaign, the Great Arab Revolt played not a small role, initiated and led by Sharif Hussein bin Ali. After meeting in Damascus with the Arab secret societies al-Fatat and al-Ahd in 1915, Hussein received the so-called Damascus Protocol, a document that specified the need to establish an independent Arab state with borders that would include the Persian frontier down to the Persian Gulf, the Red Sea, and the Mediterranean Sea in the west, and the Indian Ocean in the south.

It was a magnificent demand after almost four hundred years of darkness and marginalization of the Arab people by the Ottoman Turks. To fight the formidable forces of the Ottoman Empire, the Grand Sharif Hussein was asked to enter into an alliance with the United Kingdom and France. Such an alliance, as it was understood by both parties, but mostly by the Arabs, would require Britain and France to recognize the independence of all Arab people with the creation of an Arab empire, excluding Kuwait, Aden, and Syria.

The price of such a union in reality was the two separate and somewhat unrelated documents signed between Britain and France on one side and the Arab coalition forces on the other. The first one was the 1916 Sykes-Picot Agreement that effectively divided the Arab provinces of the Ottoman Empire into the areas controlled by the British and French Empires. This agreement was actually a secret document signed between France and Britain that also promised to Russia a sphere of interest in the region of Constantinople.

When the Bolsheviks came to power in 1917, they exposed that agreement, sending Arabs into the appalling disillusionment of fairness coming from any occupying force. In the meantime, England and France were awarded the mandates for administering the control of different regions in the Middle East. Britain received the territories spread from southern Iraq to the ports of Haifa and Acre with an access to the Mediterranean Sea. France received control of the northern Iraq, Syria, and Lebanon.

Not to evoke the discontent of local authorities, the Sykes-Picot plan also stated that it would recognize and protect an independent Arab state, for which that Arab people had longed.

–

Another and more grievous (for the Arabs) document was the Balfour Declaration of 1917. This document was a formal British recognition of the rights of the Jewish people to have their homeland in Palestine. While this document became a reason for celebration for Jewish people all over the world, the Arab countries immediately took it as an insult and announced it as a day of mourning. Such a reaction of the Arab people could not be easily explained, especially if one would consider the fact that the leading figure of the early Zionist movement, Chaim Azriel Weizmann, and the leader of the Arab forces, the Emir Faisal, reached an amicable agreement by issuing a 1919 document in which both parties recognized "the racial kinship and ancient bonds existing between the Arabs and the Jewish people." Still this sustained and reasoned-out document was rejected by the majority of Arabs at the Syrian congress in Damascus in March of 1920.

If one takes into consideration that the Jewish people were forcefully kicked out of Palestine in 135 CE by the Romans living in that region and who had had not had their homeland for over 1,500 years, it is hard to understand the hurt feelings of Arabs. The latter had occupied Palestine with the rise of Islam in the seventh century CE, and although they were not dissipated as the Jews were, they came under different occupations, including the over four-hundred-year domination of the Ottoman Empire. This fact alone must speak for the legitimate reasons of both peoples to share the land with each other. Yet that was not the case.

The role of Britain at that time, on the surface at least, pursued two main goals. On one side, they promised to the Arabs its constant support; on the other they behaved as the supporters of the yearning of the Jewish people to reacquire their homeland. That could satisfy all involved parties, but not the Palestinian Arabs. In April of 1920, the Arabs of Palestine rioted, protesting any erection of Jewish settlements on Arab lands.

By the time of the brewing disagreement of the Arabs with the imperial world, a few conflicting events took place. First, the publication of the Sykes-Picot Agreement was found to be in contradiction with the earlier correspondence between Sir Arthur Henry McMahon, the high commissioner of Egypt, and Hussein ibn Ali, the sharif of Mecca, with many promises to the Arab people not mentioned in the Sykes-Picot report.

It also didn't play well when in 1921 Sir William Joynson-Hicks, the solicitor and politician and, later, home secretary of the British cabinet, questioned the British mandate allowing the Jews to settle in Palestine. He objected to the appointment of Jews to senior positions in the civil administration and, along with others, considered it a mistake to give national loans to the Jews. He insisted that the Jews were the richest people in the world and that they should have to pay for themselves (while purchasing plots in the Palestinian land) instead of taking money from British taxpayers.

Another British conservative, Alfred Charles William Harmsworth, who rose to the rank of viscount as Lord Northcliffe, pointed to the change of the policies of his two newspapers when a leading writer of one of his papers, the *Daily Mail*, attacked the Palestine Mandate. In May of 1921, this newspaper suggested that the British taxpayer was forced to fund Zionism.

When in March of 1922, the Palestinian Arab delegation had arrived in Britain for the recurrent and sequential meeting with the British, members of Parliament, and other conservative notables, they referred to the Balfour Declaration as one of the mysteries of modern politics, which had been engineered by the Zionist organization. It must be a point **of** interest that right from the first British Mandate, the Southern Levant (the original territory of ancient Israelis) was not in the consideration of divided Palestine. In fact, the borders of Palestine offered by the mandate were a much different version than either biblical or historical sources suggested.

Those territories that the Jewish people regarded according to biblical and historical sources as Jewish lands were viewed by the Pan-Arab nationalist movement as appurtenant to the Palestinian Arabs, including the West Bank, the Gaza Strip, Jordan, and part of Lebanon.

When one tries to learn the details of the Arab-Israeli conflict, one will quickly understand the difference between the description of that conflict by the Arab scholar, such as, for example, Rashid Ismail Khalidi is, or a subjective approach of the historical Jewish writer with socialist ideas as Tom Segev, and the toned and objective description of someone indifferent seeking to represent the true story of those historical events.

—

Palestine was the land so-named after the Philistines, a seafaring people who had lived in that area since 1250 BCE. The conquering Romans, who expelled the Hebrews from the promised land of Canaan, named so according to the Hebrew Bible and at that time known as Judea, renamed it as Palestine.

To simply compare Palestinians to Arabs is misleading, as Palestine had known Arabs, Jews, Jebusites, Phoenicians, and many other different tribes and cultures for the last five thousand years who inhabited that land. The claim that Jebusites, Phoenicians, or some other tribes were the ancestors of the Arab people is sheer nonsense and simply directs an intelligent thinker into no less confusion as to giving an explanation of who were the Jews.

When the British had drafted a legal document named the Mandate for Palestine, which was confirmed by the Council of the League of Nations (presently known as the United Nations), it was formalized at the San Remo Conference that took place in Italy in April of 1920. The southern part of Ottoman Syria was divided into two newly created administrative regions: Palestine and Transjordan. The region that acquired the name Transjordan was immediately excised from any consideration of possible inhabitation there by Jews. This territory, three times larger than Palestine, was given to the rulers of the Hashemite family by the explicit statement of the Lord Curzon, the British foreign secretary at the time, stating that it must be exempt from the mandate decision and should not concern the Jewish people as their homeland, leaving for them the much-smaller part bordered from the east by the Jordan River.

That might have made sense if the possession of the territory the British Mandate allotted to the Jews would be based on the same strict rules that were applied concerning Transjordan. But that was not the case, and the British government sternly emphasized that the Jewish state should not infringe upon the rights of any and all inhabitants of the territory designated as new Palestine.

Yet the Zionists didn't object to such a decision, although they might have if, according to the instigators of the hatred of Zionism, the Zionists would have to pursue a goal of claiming the eastern part of that land as well. Transjordan, although not named so during the time of the King Solomon, was under the control of the Israelites.

—

Now the remaining ten-thousand-square-mile area that was declared as Palestine would have to be partitioned between the Palestinian Arabs and the Palestinian Jews. However, the Arabs, right from the start, argued that Palestine must be purely Arabic.

The first incident connected to such a claim began with the blunt refusal of Arab milkmen to sell milk and its products in the Jewish neighborhood. The next step was the Nabi Musa riots that consequentially grew out of the religious and national holiday usually observed by the Muslim Arabs in April.

At that day, Muslims had flooded the Old City of Jerusalem. The pilgrims were greeted by the initiators of the event, which quickly turned into provoking speeches about massacring the Jews. "Palestine is our land, and the Jews are our dogs" was one of the slogans chanted by the Arabs. The mob moved to the Jewish Quarter, on their way looting shops, assaulting pedestrians, and destroying properties. The violence soon jumped into the Jewish settlements outside the city, spreading north into Galilee, with the Arab villagers increasingly attacking Jewish settlements all over the place. The assaults were mainly related to the inability of the Arabs to recognize any major changes in Palestine with the possible allotting of land to the increasing number of Jews and their settlements.

The first reaction the British government displayed concerning the disturbed Arab population was to limit the immigration of Jews to Palestine. Out of not even twelve million Jews in the whole world at the time, a few hundred thousand were willing to relocate, but the number of Jews were already too many for those who were in a position to decide where the Jews must be allowed to live.

Realizing the support of the British, Arabs continued to press for their right not to share the land now claimed as merely theirs. They began to attack the *kibbutzim* (farming communities) and burn Jewish settlements, killing scores of innocents.

The most prominent attack yet in that period had happened on May 1, 1921, when the Jewish communists from the Soviet Union organized the Labor Day march starting in Jaffa and marching to Tel Aviv. After a scuffle between the two Jewish group marchers took place and the Arab policemen got involved to disperse it, forty-seven Jews altogether were killed by the Arab extremists. Such attacks began to increase with more Jews being massacred, each directly

–

connected to Arab nationalists frustrated by ever-increasing Jewish immigration.

Were the Jews not responding to these attacks and behaving meekly? Not at all. Despite the laws introduced by the British government prohibiting people of the Palestinian land to possess firearms, Jews not only acquired them, but they felt that it was completely justified to use them. The counterattacks were kicking up swiftly, with each such episode increasing violence many times over from both sides. Notwithstanding this elimination of people on both sides, the Jewish and Arab populations in Palestine continued to grow.

At that time, a major role in relocating Jews to Palestine was played by Zionism. As Jews never completely abandoned Palestine from the time of the Bar Kokhba revolt in 135 CE, the Zionist movement was not based solely on the religious fanaticism of a few idealists but had been mostly directed to the organized return of the Jews to the land they had once called their own and that they so sorely missed.

The first leaders of such a movement were Theodor Herzl, Leon Pinsker, Ber Borochov, Asher Ginzberg, Chaim Weizmann, and Ze'ev (or Vladimir) Jabotinsky. They approached their role to solve the Jewish problem not as zealous Zionists per se, but with the goal to help the Jews get rid of anti-Semitism once and for all and to help the Jews become a nation again.

Between the years from 1924 to 1947, Zionists, who, contrary to general belief, were not forcing every Jew from all over the world to end up in Israel, had been focusing on the legitimization of the Jewish people to have a sovereign homeland. Meanwhile, the Arab nationalists, who were glorifying Arab civilization, had called for the union of Arabs in their effort to eliminate any foreign body from the Arab lands, first off meaning the Jews.

With the increasing waves of anti-Semitism in Europe, Jewish people began to move to Palestine in droves. For Arabs, that meant only one thing: the more Jews would come, the less chance they would get to claim Palestine as their own. By the time the Nazis began disseminating anti-Semitism beyond the German borders in 1939, the British authorities, strangely enough, came under the pressure of the Arab nationalist movement, issuing the so-called MacDonald White Paper, in which was a recommendation that Palestine be governed by Palestinian Arabs and Jews according to their numbers

—

in the population inhabiting the land. The policy dictated to limit the number of Jews that would be allowed to immigrate during the five-year period from 1940 to 1944 to seventy-five thousand. After that, immigration would depend on the approval of the number by the Arab majority. Along with this quota, the rights of Jewish settlers to buy land were also severely restricted.

As it became obvious that neither Arab nationalists nor British representatives in the region had equal interests for all the inhabitants of the land, Jewish nationalists began to gather in militant Zionist groups, avowing to fight not only Arabs but also the British. Some paramilitary Zionist groups such as Irgun, Lehi, and others were founded at that time, and British authorities immediately began to call them terrorists, as these groups were attacking the British officials residing in Palestine.

In the years from 1920 until 1936, many violent attacks between Arabs and Jews happened, often ending in murders, burning of the settlements, lootings, and arrests, which the British officials confusedly tried to quiet if not to solve the ever-increasing problem.

Finally, in 1936 to 1939, Arab nationalists organized a second Great Arab Revolt directed toward the termination of both British colonial rule and the mass immigration of Jews. While this uprising was unsuccessful, with thousands of Arabs being killed, the revolt had direct consequence in brewing the 1947 civil war that was followed by the 1948 Arab-Israeli War.

Sickened by this endless skirmish between the Jews and the Arabs, Major General Montgomery famously forecasted, "the Jew murders the Arab and the Arab murders the Jew. This will go on for the next 50 years in all probability" (Segev, 442). In 1946, the British notified the United Nations that it was ending the British Mandate rule in Transjordan. That same year, the United Nations approved the termination and, almost immediately following that decision, the Transjordanian parliament named King Abdullah as the first leader of that kingdom. The country was officially renamed as the Hashemite Kingdom of Jordan.

But the minute the United Nations, in November of 1947, approved the Partition Plan of Palestine, the Arab-Palestinian community began to express their discontent. The violence became even more prevalent, accompanied by open murders, sniper firings, and the planting of

–

bombs and mines along the roads. The Jews responded with equal, if not more virulent, violence.

By 1948, the Arab-Israeli War had erupted. The war was not the first attempt of Arabs to destroy the Israeli settlements, but it was the first such war free of the British Mandate of Palestine. The Arab forces, who continued to clash the whole previous year with Israelis while the Brits were readying to leave, had the same agenda in mind they had from the very beginning: not to allow the partitioning of Palestine. By March 1948, thousands of Jews and Arabs had been killed. There was no city or place in that land where fighting wouldn't occur.

On May 14 of the same year, the British Mandate had officially ended, and the Israelites proclaimed their land as the state of independence. It was not a clear-cut sovereign country in the way countries are procuring their integrity. The land the Israelis might have pronounced their own had interruptions, enclaves, and partial owning.

Although the borders of a new state would not change once since then, owing it mostly to the subsequent Arab-Israeli wars, the Jews right from the beginning welcomed the notion of their own country without any hesitation and objection.

In the meantime, the Arab world had exploded. First, the secretary general of the Arab League sent a cablegram to the United Nations, stating that the United State of Palestine was about to be created instead of partitioned as offered by the United Nations. Second, they announced their duty to restore a democratic Palestine as a part of an Arab state. Third, they claimed that by reason of the absence of any authoritative organ in Palestine, they must assume their duties to maintain an order in this Arab land. Of course, the main and only motif of such behavior was to force the Jews out of Palestine. The Palestinian Arabs claimed that the Partition Plan was illegitimate, and, with such a claim, they appealed to all Arab nations to help them in their "natural request." All neighboring countries, such as Syria, Lebanon, Jordan, and Egypt, including the volunteers from Saudi Arabia, Libya, Yemen, and the Iraqi forces, cooperated by invading the new country of Israel from every part of the land. With alternate success and inevitable changes in possessions of the land, the end of war spelled the new borders.

—

By the end of the summer of 1949, Israel controlled about three-quarters of the territory allotted in the original British Mandate. At the same time, the Gaza Strip and the West Bank (the lands of former Samaria and Judea), including the eastern part of Jerusalem, came under the occupation of Egypt and Jordan respectively. Still, many Palestinian Arabs (by some conservative figure up to 750,000) lost their possessions where now Israelis came to be in charge. Despite that, in the following three consecutive years, the Palestinian Arabs staged demonstrations with the demand to allow the return of displaced Palestinians. In the meantime, the Jewish state managed to add up to 750,000 of new Jewish immigrants.

The war of 1967, or the Six-Day War, that followed was the third Arab-Israeli military conflict. It lasted only six days, but major damage was done, and Palestinian Arabs and Israelis became two confrontational camps for a long time to come.

At the end of the Six-Day War, Israeli general Moshe Dayan gave the order to his soldiers to remove the Israeli flag that had been hoisted over the Dome of the Rock, after the Israeli victory over the Arabs in the war. His action relinquished the authority to manage the Temple Mount to a Muslim caliph, Haram al-Sharif.

But while this gesture of the Israeli general became a topic of polemic in many years to come, since exactly that time, the dispute over who should control the area around the Dome of the Rock (Muslims or Israelites) has never been dropped.

Nevertheless, the war of 1967 gave Israel the reputation of a formidable enemy in the Arab world. It also placed the small country of Israel into a new category: the *aggressor*. No matter how scholars present the affair, there are plenty of facts that intelligent minds without undue prejudice will be able to connect in order to appreciate how this event really happened. The sad part of it is that the majority of people perceive the Palestinian Arabs as a much-suffering, innocent people who got caught between the Arab nationalists and the Zionists, as aggressive Israelis sought to clean Palestine of anyone but the Jews.

Still, these are the facts:

On June 4 1967, the Israeli government made the decision to go to war with neighboring Arab countries Egypt, Syria, and Jordan, and on June 5, it launched the attack. According to the majority of opinions in the world, Israel acted without provocation and super aggressively

–

against its neighbors, trying to persuade the West of the necessity of the preemptive strike.

The finale of this six-day war deepened the Palestinian refugee problem, adding new territories to Israel, raising the issues of international law, and producing almost unanimous criticism among the majority of countries, including members of the United Nations.

Yet these were the chronologically preceding events:

On May 29, 1967, Egyptian President Gamal Abdel Nasser, in a speech to the United Nations General Assembly, reasoned closing the Straits of Tiran to Israeli shipping on the basis of their mistreatment of the Palestinian people. This act alone was a direct, unprovoked confrontation aimed against the state of Israel by the Egyptian government.

By May 30, Egypt gathered one hundred thousand troops in Sinai along with all of its armored brigades, infantry brigades, and the reservists, and 420 Soviet-built combat aircrafts in its Arab air force close to the Israeli border.

On May 30, Jordan and Egypt signed a defense pact. Jordan immediately placed fifty-five thousand troops and three hundred tanks along its border with Israel.

On May 31, one hundred Iraqi tanks along with infantry forces and two squadrons of fighter aircrafts began deploying troops in Jordan. At the same time, Syria brought its army of seventy-five thousand troops to the northern border with Israel.

On June 2, Jordan called up all reserve officers, instructing them "to be ready to be in Tel Aviv".

Volunteer pilots with aircrafts from Pakistan, Libya, Algeria, Morocco, Kuwait, and Saudi Arabia were added to the Arab air forces. Paratrooper battalions trained in United States schools, twelve battalions of artillery, six batteries of 81 mm and 120 mm mortars were all placed along with Jordanian forces.

On June 5, Israelis went for a surprise attack.

As a result of the war, Israel got new territory: Golan Heights was cut from Syria, Sinai and Gaza Strip from Egypt, and the West Bank from Jordan. Jerusalem was now completely an indivisible part of the Israeli state and ruled by Israeli law.

Encouraged by the unprecedented support and unilateral provocation of the Soviet Union, the Arab countries, after meeting in Khartoum in August 1967, accepted a new policy of a three-part decision: no peace with Israel, no recognition of Israel, and no negotiations with Israel. An immediate plan for the Palestinian Arabs expelled from Israel was to get back the West Bank and the Gaza Strip. In the meantime, Palestinian Arabs relocated mainly in Jordan, but after the refusal of that and other Arab countries to provide Palestinian refugees with a permanent place, the majority of them found different territories in Syria, Lebanon, and Jordan, where they built for themselves the refugee camps. They stay there, to no one's surprise, until today, in miserable conditions.

Terrorist attacks and almost constant artillery bombardments of the newly developed country became a norm of life in Israel, and Israelis, once in a while, were forced to respond to these provocations with short military excursions beyond their borders.

Today, ordinary Arabs do not perceive the Israelites in any other way but as an armed aggressor, who, because of a disproportionate possession of sophisticated military, might allow themselves to oppress, to attack, and, from time to time, to get into a small (or not-so-small) scale of military offense upon defenseless Palestinians (Arabs).

The world is habitually forgetful of the initiator and the reason for the aggression, but it is faced with the reality of the offended sufferer, and this is usually enough not to justify or support the aggressor.

In 1974, the representative for the Palestinian Arabs, the Palestinian Liberation Organization (PLO) was granted an observer status in the United Nations (UN). In 1975, the UN General Assembly adopted a resolution declaring Zionism to be a form of racism.

In 1979, Israel returned the Sinai desert to Egypt after these two countries agreed to sign a peace treaty. The return of the Gaza Strip and the West Bank didn't happen because the Palestinians refused to accept the limited autonomies of these two areas offered by Israeli government. Yet when PLO renounced violence and recognized the legitimacy of Israel in 1990, Israel agreed to reconsider the Palestinian Arabs' wish and gradually to transfer these lands to the Palestinian Authority.

From the year 2000 CE and forward, with many acts of terrorism from the Arab states and no-less-severe responses by Israel, any attempt to find a peaceful solution has been cut short and failed.

–

Today, an Israeli-Arab conflict is considered to be a much more complicated issue than before, crippled by the new and old preconditions coming from both sides. While polls on both sides show that majority of Israelis and Palestinian Arabs accept a two-state solution, Palestinians almost unanimously insist on allowing all the refugees to return to Israel; Israelis do not accept it as a possible solution, for that will suppress their rights as well as the majority of Israelis. They believe in one and an undivided Israeli capital, Jerusalem, which must solely belong to the Israeli state.

Thus, the conflict continues, along with growing population on either side of these two peoples.

To this end, it is impossible to predict a possible normalization of the dispute that exists between these two peoples. The only hope that the final decision will bring to this land a reasonable peace every civilized mind wishes to prognosticate without much base in it.

CHAPTER 17

The Real Russians

In the title above, I refer to the contemporary Russians who presently think and feel about themselves as purebred Slavic people. In fact, I am not going to conduct a full investigation here of the historical establishment of Russia and the origin of the Russian people. I am simply going to elicit a few facts, which contemporary Russians have based their claim on. My goal is to show who the *contemporary* Russians are, how they came into existence, what cultural roots they are enjoying, and how much they differ from the Russians of their fellow countrymen in the time before the October Revolution of 1917.

Russia became a country when a Varangian (Scandinavian Viking) chieftain of the Rus founded the Rurik dynasty in the Eastern part of Europe in the ninth century CE. About that time, an old literary Slavonic language, along with Christianity, came to the scene. Both events had been attributed to Cyril and Methodius, two Byzantine Greek brothers born in Thessaloniki, Greece, and who were on a mission to spread Christianity in Slavic lands.

With the establishment of the two main cities, Novgorod and, a little later, Kievan Rus', the history of Russia begins. During only a few centuries, the princes of Rurikid dynasty separated the vast Slavic land and its tribes into the principalities. Historical documents do not point to any invasion by the Varangians and instead mention that Scandinavian Vikings were invited to rule the Slavic tribes. Whether it is true or not, the many Slavic tribes acted territorially and didn't care much about their conflation as one country. Rurik princes (originally three brothers), on the other hand, saw their opportunity to rule through a policy to divide and conquer.

By the twelfth century CE, the Slavic people of Eastern Europe were divided into three distinct nations: Russians, Ukrainians, and Belarusians. This split facilitated the invasion by the Mongols coming from the Far East and occupying most of Eastern Europe.

A separate principality, the Grand Duchy of Moscow, while originally remaining a tributary to the Tatar yoke by the middle of the fourteenth century, became a predecessor of the Tsardom of Russia.

With Ivan the Terrible (Tsar Ivan IV) coming to power in the sixteenth century, the Russian multicultural tribes began to emerge as one unified force. This monarch conducted the policy of expansion and annexation of the vast Slavic lands, and through the military operations, he managed forcefully transfer power from the Rurik to the Romanov Dynasty. Under his domain, the Tsardom of Russia was formed. It is considered by some historians that Ivan IV arguably contributed to contemporary Russia an important political structure of an independent sovereign country.

Under Peter the Great (Tsar Peter Romanov) and his even more aggressive politics of expansion, the Tsardom of Russia grew into a huge Russian Empire. Peter the Great is known for modernizing Russia while traveling abroad and inviting many architects, engineers, and advisors to his country. He also acknowledged that some European customs were superior to Russian traditions and was not afraid to apply sweeping reforms he believed would make Russia a superpower. In this, he superseded the quest of his predecessor, Tsar Boris Godunov. Peter the Great also continued to suppress boyars as did Ivan the Terrible, once forcing them to cut their beards, as that distinguished them from the nobility of the foreign countries.

As authoritative power continued to accumulate in the hands of the Russian tsars, the governing role of nobility such as *knyazya* (dukes), *dvoryane* (gentry), *boyars* (landed lords), and many others began to steadily decline. Not to completely alienate these powerful and rich people, tsars increasingly would grant them lands and commoners.

Serfdom, practiced since the eleventh century, took on the form of law during the reign of Ivan the Terrible. By the end of the eighteenth century, it became rampant, involving the vast majority of the Russian

—

peasantry. Russian landowners had unlimited ownership over them, restricted only in the right to kill a slave. Runaways had no chance to be pardoned or obtain mercy, and, in fact, the legislations starting in 1653 spelled the severity of punishment for those who tried to escape.

By the years 1800 to 1805, more than half of factory workers were serfs. Emancipated serfs could not receive land and therefore were denied real freedom. As a result, stagnation along with waves of suicides and alcoholism enveloped most parts of Russia. Such grievous conditions led not only to a depressed mood among the educated and nobles, it also necessarily revealed people whose foremost task became the freedom of all oppressed and enthralled members of society.

With this very-short-indeed excursion into the history of Russia, let me jump into the year 1816, when the first secret society of the Russian compatriots was founded. They began to call themselves the Society of True and Loyal Sons of the Fatherland, changing from the original name the Union of Salvation. The times were turbulent.

The first serious uprising, known as the Decembrist revolt took place on December 26, 1825. Originally led by the Russian officers, the movement later acquired such figures as the idealists Pavel Pestel, Nikita Muraviev, Eugene Obolensky, and Sergey Trubetskoy. Acting on two different platforms as two different groups, the radical movement of Southern Society insisted on abolishing the monarchy, equality before the law for all people, and redistributing the land among the peasants, while the Northern Society, based in St. Petersburg, inclined toward a British style of governing.

Eventually, the uprising was defeated with all 124 Decembrists convicted and sentenced with different degree of punishment.

The Russian monarchial absolutism that had begun with the Grand Duchy of Moscow would continue until the October Revolution of 1917.

The beginning of the twentieth century was marked by the formation of the Union of Zemstvo Constitutionalists (1903) and the Union of Liberation (1904) that led to a resolution passed by the Moscow City Duma, calling for an elected national legislature and the establishment of a limited constitutional monarchy.

As the vast majority of the population lived under severe economic and social conditions, many ordinary people were in support of changing trends. By October of 1905, the Constitutional Democratic Party was formed.

The year 1905 was characteristic of increased workers' strikes, peasants' unrest, and the October Manifesto that Tsar Nicholas II signed against his will. This victory of the people led to the granting by the monarchial regime civil rights to all citizens, universal suffrage, and establishing the Duma as the central legislative body. The Duma was the first Russian House of Representatives, granted by Nicholas II.

The word literally meant *thought*, and the assembly had been presented by electors from the land proprietors, capitalists, middle class, peasants, and workers. The liberal party or the Constitutional Democratic Party, members of which were called Kadets, had been the left wing of the Duma with 30 percent of their members, but after it joined the peasant faction, it became the largest party in the House. It was the party supported by the intelligentsia, prominent, highly educated people.

But in 1906, Kadets abandoned their aspirations and declared their support for a constitutional monarchy.

The botched involvement of Russia in World War I (from 1914 to 1918) also played a role in the upcoming revolution. Casualties of Russian soldiers were conducive to poor supplies of food, clothes, munitions, and a disorganized transportation system. Fifteen million men serving in the Tsarist army were mostly hungry, poorly dressed, and overall in discontent, prone to defeat.

Such was the political mood in the first quarter of the twentieth century. People grew increasingly intolerant of multiple injustices. Different groups of people expressed discontent, staggering from changing the regime to complete elimination of monarchy and imperialism.

The revolution of 1917 orchestrated by the Bolsheviks and supported by the intelligentsia on one side and left liberal factions on the other, came as an unavoidable event. While theoretically it began in Germany, prepared by the works of Karl Marx and Friedrich Engels, Russia turned out to be that exactly fertile soil these communist ideologues were longing for. Thus it eventually led to a country that began to build socialism with a communist regime in mind.

As peasants and workers were mostly poor and little, if at all, educated, the leaders of newly established party found it

—

beneficial to get along with liberals, intelligentsia, and sympathetic bourgeoisie. In time, when such a relationship became unnecessary and counterproductive to the Bolsheviks' cause, they began to rid themselves one by one of those now not-needed factions by any means possible.

They began by overthrowing the provisional government led by the moderate Alexander Kerensky, secretly and cowardly killed the last tsar and his family in 1918, and proclaimed the Soviets as the new government of Russia.

The period from 1917 to 1923 was a turbulent time for the Bolsheviks as the Civil War erupted, with the Red Army fighting the White Army and the loosely allied anti-Bolshevik forces fighting everyone else. Many foreign armies also fought the Red Army with some fewer fighters on her side. That was the time when many nationalistic groups were formed, each having separate agenda and platform.

In the light of aspirations for a world revolution and the possible destruction of capitalism on the European continent, Lenin and his loyalists in government had decided to sign a peace treaty with the Germans. The communist uprising at the end of World War I in 1919 led to the replacement of the German imperial government with the establishment of the parliamentary republic or Weimar Republic, which acquired this name from the city where the constitutional assembly took place.

Fortunately (or unfortunately, depending on who discusses it) this uprising had not been as successful as it was in Russia. The reason the revolutionaries in Germany had failed to take control a la Russian style was due to the refusal of the Social Democratic Party of Germany to work with those who supported the Bolsheviks.

With their hopes flying high, Lenin and his loyalists founded the Comintern (Communist International) in Moscow in 1919. Its aim was to overthrow the international bourgeoisie in as many countries as possible and to create an international Soviet republic.

The mentality was once the fire starts, it might as well consume the neighboring structures—in their case, desired. Their dream to destroy capitalism along with active involvement in the regimes of the other countries lasted until WWII.

That particular task eventually died out, and in 1943 the Comintern was finally dissolved; that's how long the government of the Bolsheviks had hoped to sweep world capitalism under the rug. But as soon as, one by one, European countries failed to conduct the revolutionary overthrow of capitalism in their countries, the Bolsheviks adopted a new strategy—of building socialism in one country only. This was put in a thesis by Joseph Stalin in 1924 and was elaborated by Nikolai Bukharin in 1925.

The slogan "Proletarians of all countries unite!"—the appeal of which was directed toward all the workers of the world, the unions, and the socialist parties—nevertheless lasted much longer, almost till the dismantling of the Soviet Union.

Josef Stalin rose to power first gradually but steady, along with slow comprehension and support of each member of the party. After Lenin's stroke in 1922, which forced him into semiretirement until followed by death in 1924, Josef Stalin wittingly and insidiously consolidated the government's power into his hands. In that he showed outstanding leadership qualities, despite V. I. Lenin's warning in 1923 of Stalin's inadequacy to be a leader, recommending his dismissal in his written testament. After his second and third strokes, Lenin became paralyzed and unable to speak.

Stalin did not lose a moment.

With the suggestion to remove him from the position of the general secretary of the Party, Stalin stood to lose a lot. He suppressed the document. Having experience in spreading propaganda and raising money through criminal activities for twelve years before the 1917 revolution, Stalin engineered a hard-line approach to his political opponents, isolating his major competition one by one. With Josef Stalin usurping power and a leading role in government, he initiated a series of large purges that only ended in 1953 upon his sudden death.

The years 1918 to 1921 were characterized by a quite exhausted and failing economical system. The military communism, as it was called and that was adopted by the Bolsheviks during the Civil War, did not and could not work. Its policies included the following:

- Nationalization of industry with centralized management
- Rationing of food and commodities distributed in a centralized way

—

- Declaring private enterprise as illegal
- Obligatory labor duty onto nonworking classes

These requirements were mostly lacking an ability to be accomplished, as they were introduced during a civil war and therefore could not be controlled. With war ending, Bolsheviks began unequivocally suggesting that these implementations must be considered normal in order for proletariat to win.

To make orders more official, the Russian government in 1922 declared that the ownership of land and properties would be considered illegal, and it would be transferred to the possession of government-controlled communities. These repressive measures brought mostly chaos among the frustrated peasants, who, on one hand, were not allowed to have their own land and, on the other, were in jeopardy if they tried to sell their agricultural produce.

As a result, most peasants refused to cooperate. On their side, workers began to migrate from the cities to the countryside, looking for means to feed their families. Eventually the two major cities of Moscow and Petrograd had begun to substantially lose their population. That contributed to a black market that emerged with people dismissing the threat of martial law against the profiteering established by the Russian government. Realizing that such brutal policy was counterproductive and might not work, the Soviet government changed their tactics.

The New Economic Policy (NEP) was introduced. It was done in order to save the young Soviet country from collapse. It was called the state capitalism under which some private ventures were allowed. It was not much, as the state continued to control banks, large industries, and farmers, along with the agricultural products. What the government instead required was collecting specified amounts of agricultural products from the farmers as a tax in a kind. That was a bold move in order to modernize the failing economy. Peasants, after paying the government with food products, could then sell surplus on the private market, making some profit. This had accomplished a twofold benefit for farmers and the country. Inspired by such policy, peasants worked harder, producing even more goods.

But in 1928, the politics of NEP had ended. It turned out not only to be unpopular among the left opposition of the Bolsheviks, it was also considered as an interim measure in an economically difficult time. Pretty soon, the NEP was labeled as a compromising capitalistic element that led to the betrayal of the communist principals. Communist advocates from the left began to quote the NEP as an enemy of the working class, who were forced to buy agricultural goods for high prices from the rich farmers. The peasant traders now were considered enemies of the working class.

The next new economic policy, invented and introduced by the Bolsheviks, had been called collectivization. Farmers were forced to give their agricultural hoardings, livestock, land, and other assets to collective farms. Those well-to-do farmers, who refused to give their possessions to the state were labeled as *kulaks* (tight-fisted). Their possessions were forcefully taken from them, and many of them were exterminated or sent to Gulags. These measures inevitably discouraged the peasants, and starting from 1928, much less grain was produced than in previous years. A new class of unhappy and therefore unreliable peasantry that was often considered as a potential enemy of the Soviet regime had suddenly developed.

It is established that, all in all, six million peasants lost their lives while working in the camps into which they were forcefully transported. Many peasants began to arm themselves, fighting communists by any means they could. Again, the result was the major reduction of livestock.

To correct the situation, the party sent twenty-five thousand industry workers to the countryside. They created *shock brigades* that forced undecided more or less well-to-do peasants into the collective farms. After giving much of the time and effort to these collective farms, the peasants were paid in the established rationing food products along with symbolic salaries.

It created the environment in which the peasants began to sabotage collective farms, burning the grain, slaughtering the animals, sometimes physically eliminating a number of outstanding officials. The immediate effect of such resistance led to substantial losses in the agricultural industry and overall the economic decline of the country. By the year 1950, the number of animal stocks was at the 1928 level.

In the meantime, Stalin had concentrated all the power in his hands, not trusting anyone, and from time to time getting rid of one of his most important and talented compatriots, who in his mind

—

might develop a plan to depose him. It was the time when the politics of mistrust and often the replacement of high-ranking members of the party by unknown and often dull officials began to proliferate at all the levels of the Soviet machine. This policy of the removal of fallen-out-of-favor comrades actually never ended in Russia. Yet it never was on the same scale as during Stalin's time.

The horror of purges, incarcerations, and the killings decimated the entire country on each level and in every walk of life. Politics of suspicion and persecution, with the relative ease of labeling innocent people as traitors and spies, permeated the country, spawning a chilling effect and an atmosphere of depression and fear.

The draconian figure of thirty to forty million people dead, killed, sent to Gulags, or allowed to die in this period of the history of the Soviet regime has most likely not been exaggerated.

Such a regime of repressions suddenly disclosed the many ugly sides of human nature, the ordinary lethargic one that during a period of relative calm and indifference would be hard to spot.

What has been most surprising than anything else though was the fact that many common people, otherwise peaceful and generally friendly, had been suddenly displaying such awful features like intolerance, indifference, mistrust, and even sadistic masochism.

People were easily swayed into believing that one's neighbor had been subversive if state officials said so. They did not express indignation or suspicion that someone might be unjustly indicted or imprisoned. But worst of all, the new politics of the Soviet government revealed plenty of willing executioners who had no regrets or a second thought of the possibly occurring calamity.

The word propaganda, according to the *American Heritage Dictionary*, is defined as such: "Propaganda is the systematic propagation of a given doctrine or of allegations reflecting its views and interests." In Russia, it had been used not only openly, but with a conspicuously positive connotation.

Vladimir Ilyich Lenin, while emphasizing this tremendously helpful tool in advancing his revolutionary ideas, had substantially broadened its methods. Such organizations as *agitprop* (an abbreviation of *agitation* and *propaganda*), sabotage, and the use of media were not only the tools, but as in the case of agitprop, for instance, the Communist party created a specialized unit designated

−

to arouse, influence, and direct the masses. Given the history of the systematic elimination of intelligent and highly educated members of society, the remaining masses in Russia were much easier to be kept in the dark. With little or no education, those who were labeled as working class or a class of peasants were comfortably manipulated by the Russian state officials. Even the word agitation was presented as educated persuasion, that millions of Russians had learned its meaning for years to come.

The rest of the methods, like distortion and concealment of the facts, deliberate lying, and censorship, even messing with statistics along with influencing the people's minds, all of those were brought to the level of unnoticeable, believable likenesses of truth. Its subtlety increased with the increased sophistication of the propaganda machine.

As the Russian economy, education system, and cultural and moral principles were mostly if not all started from scratch, they were manipulated by the Russian leaders in visibly necessary channels.

When accumulated statistics had shown that people were and are able to learn, the repressive measures escalated, and between Stalin's paranoia and the people's resilience to become the puppets of a tyrant, the Iron Curtain was eventually invented and applied with much success from the years1945 until the dismantling of the Berlin Wall in 1989.

People had to be isolated from the rest of the world in order to hide the truth from them. It was a doubly bold move as the rest of the world could not learn about the Russian people either.

The behavior and mood typical for Soviet people after World War II was characterized by the replacement of ideologues and former enthusiasts into the army of career seekers and subsequent bureaucrats.

As I can speak from a position of the insider who has experienced the real climate of the country firsthand, let me give you here a short analysis of what had taken place in that country specifically after the WWII had ended. First of all, most ordinary people were not aware of the problems captivating the country as one might have expected. The system applied by the *apparatchiks* (governing party leader), especially before World War II and immediately after it, had deliberately and constantly perfected their propaganda tool. Reality was skillfully disguised from the masses, and those who knew the real

—

deal being made frightened to speak. Even if they had knowledge of what was going on, they had to be silent under the threat of possible elimination.

The first postwar years had been characterized by even more consolidation of power of a few. The rigid hierarchies of the party members were efficiently reinforced. The propaganda machine along with the resurgence of the military arsenal ever increased the role of the secret police; the centralization and governing of different institutions by state officials had created unparalleled network of bureaucracy and paid the efforts plentifully.

While the country experienced numerous problems in financial, economic, agricultural, and industrial systems, including the inability to provide a satisfactory place for living for her people, the main efforts were directed to an improvement of military might. The command system, using every chance of centralization and repression, had one goal in mind: to bring the country to the status of a military superpower.

People could not use electricity during their leisure time, not because they couldn't pay for it, but because country announced the rational use of it. People did not have enough food or clothes at the stores, as the factories were not restored or sufficiently equipped, not to mention the lack of raw materials. And yet for the West, the Soviets possessed the magic wand, possibly called "building communism," which if decoded meant sophisticated propaganda. Surprised enough by their victory in World War II, outsiders perceived the Russian success as real. The misery of their lives was obvious for the ordinary Soviet citizens, but for those beyond the borders, Russia was an unsolved puzzle.

With the first new type of Russian leaders after Stalin's time, trying to shake an epoch during which the country accustomed to repressions and scare tactics, it began to intensely watch the moves of Nikita Khrushchev to decide if this new leader would bring anything good to his people or if in fact he would repeat Stalin's times.

Yet when they learned that Nikita, as he was often called among the Soviet people, began to clean the shelves of *bulochnaya*—the specialized places where only bread and bread products were sold, which, along with vodka, were considered the main produce—in an attempt to substitute the whole wheat and rye bread with corn (maize) products, they began to question his sincerity and understanding of his own people.

To top this, they began to feel uncomfortable learning of an imminent threat he gave us by showing our military might in the Cuba crisis and the unexplainable and rude behavior at the podium of the United Nations. From his speeches that we must not only equal America (the United States) in economy and infrastructure, but bury it while building communism, people realized that a new autocrat, despotic by nature, had come to power. Thus, a slogan that "a new broom is only as good as by whom it is used" began to circle among people.

While people felt proud of having the first man sent into space, they did not much enjoy the rest of reality, finding very little improvement in the remainder of their lives.

And when, a few years later, they understood that the country did not achieve any substantial progress while occupied with a communist agenda, or rather propaganda of it, they began to slide into the nostalgic mood of repressive behavior reminiscent of Stalin's times. Not losing any time, Nikita Khrushchev began to look for someone he could blame for his failures.

As with previous politics of Communists, state officials began to produce new decrees pointing to the rich, who, according to accepted socialist standards, were people who could afford a little better, if not opulent, lives than the majority could, stating that these elements were of a capitalistic nature with subversive states of mind and therefore were the enemies.

A new wave of fear mongering spread across the country. State officials began a campaign through media, encouraging simple people, especially those with low income, to report any person they believed did not live on honestly earned (meager) money. Anonymous letters were recommended and encouraged that turned out to be enough for the legal searches and possible arrests of unsuspecting and often-innocent people.

As the government portioned salaries according to people's occupations and professions, it was easy to see who allowed himself to live better that his salary might. The people who suddenly became the most feared were the street sweepers, as they were usually among those who began the day at dawn and were the last at dusk on the streets,

—

ending it. They saw all and everything, many times exaggerating the presumed misbehavior by the Russian norm. If one did not want to be scared, one had to pay these street sweepers a bribe, thus asking them not to write anything bad about them to the state officials. As before, people became suspicious of each other, not trusting anyone and not saying anything extra that could provoke persecution and repercussions.

These were the circumstances in which people grew up, making their minds. They knew that if they wanted to have some decent way of living, they must work in industrial fields, not to talk against the regime, or, better yet, to become a party member, to know people with connections, and to try to be happy no matter what. The easiest and the simplest way to achieve that state was found in a tremendous consumption of alcoholic beverages.

It was a different story for people who had to choose to become a doctor, a teacher, or a musician; in other words, those who did not produce anything. These were almost an unwanted class, and the reasons were at least twofold. An experienced machinist working at the factory would make two or even three times more money than any doctor or teacher; in addition, he would be covered by health insurance, usually a member of both the union and the Communist party with visible protection of his rights, provided some type of dwelling, and, above all, offered more quality vacation spots than any medical professional. This dispersion was done on purpose, to keep a worker happy and to make him obedient and not to think twice. Because he produced the necessary goods, the comrade communists occupying the highest government, positions as a rule of thumb, indefinitely, would be able to build whatever they were trying to build.

On the other hand, for those who had strived for education, while not officially rebuked, officially were not praised by the government, excluding single geniuses who could provide the society any advantage.

Believe it or not, this class-free country had definite separations of people according to income, professions, intelligence, and even nationality. If one had been of Russian ethnicity, a worker, having good hands and knowledge of his labor, he was in a higher bracket of paid members of society. He had been a reliable dupe who would not be dangerous as long as his simple needs were satisfied.

With the intelligentsia, on the other hand, they could be dangerous and therefore must be closely watched; and watched they were. Each small clinic, hospital, university, or college had in their staff a *partorg* (party representative) whose single duty was to maintain an ideological spirit among all the employees. Therefore, to become a doctor, one had to be either an idealist and really feel an urge to get into a specific profession or not willing to work physically and therefore not considered a very desirable element for the society.

Besides keeping an eye on these professionals, government always had a quota according to the ethnicity of each individual, providing these limitations to the deans and party managers of each and every professional school in the country. They had a clear directive for how many would get into one of those professions, where they could go for studying and work, and, depending on that, where would they be forced to live. It goes without saying that under such circumstances, people were trying to do everything possible to accommodate their needs. This was usually accompanied by the size of an illegal pay that mostly depended on the caliber of people they knew. No wonder corruption and bribery prospered, along with the domino effect expressed through the massive theft in any possible field one can imagine.

The result of such mentality immediately showed in production of ill-intentioned, career-oriented people.

By the years of the late 1970s and early 1980s, the majority of graduates from medical and other like professional schools didn't know much, with one small exception of the Jews and a few minorities and idealists.

While repressions of Stalin's type have finally stopped, there were separate outbreaks of show trials in which profiteers, breakers of the law, and grand-scale thieves were sentenced, some to life in prison and some to death, with confiscation of their properties and belongings.

In that atmosphere of communist propaganda and the portrayal of its ideas, it was unusual to see how, and not if, religion played a role for its people. Those who were from the Soviet republics located in Asia were considered to be people who had never abandoned their Muslim religious beliefs. The problem was far more overt for people of such republics as Ukraine, Belorussia, and Russia. People of these republics were continuously denied the ability to worship any god.

—

They were closely watched by the communist puppets along with, in fact, absent or active any churches, mosques, or temples.

Under such scrutiny, it was nevertheless the spirit of many Russians who strongly supported the idea of being Christian Orthodox. They had their Bibles, secretly kept their crosses, and when finally government allowed a limited number of churches to restore their function, they began to visit Sunday prayers in droves. The paradox that revealed Russian Orthodox dogma came with the inability to properly learn the history of Christianity on one side and constant propaganda of the Soviet propaganda machine on the other.

As a result, Russian Christians believed in Trinity as one god who came to earth in the appearance of Jesus Christ. The Virgin Mary had him as a child, and Jesus was miraculously conceived through his father, God, who impregnated Mary via the Holy Spirit.

Had the Jews anything to do with it? Only one thing: They betrayed Jesus and participated in his suffering and crucifixion in the face of Judas. For that, all the Jews had to be hated and never forgiven. Such were the circumstances, and no one either was able to change anything or (Jews for instance) wanted to.

When Western countries led by the United States began to insistently demand that the Russian government must not infringe upon human rights of its citizens, the Jews, who felt it the most, began to leave the country for good.

Russian propaganda at that time reached its apogee, blaming every possible failure on Jews. The Soviet machine began methodically suggesting that the Russian people would be better off the sooner the Jews would leave the country.

Russian chauvinism began to grow again. They felt that the rest of their problems were connected to the Jews. The more Jews that left, the better it had to be for the remaining people from the poisonous influence of the Jews. It didn't matter if the Jews helped to build their country or if they were born there for a few generations. They suddenly became the worst foreign part on the Russian morally clean body.

And as much as it was ridiculous and not comprehensible to an intelligent mind, that much it was believable for the ordinary Russians, who didn't read much, didn't think much, and in fact were

—

the classic example of becoming a product of sophisticated, long-term propaganda.

After the so-called second revolution of 1991, Russia began to experience the all old-new problems, along with a visibility of changing polity and installation of a new regime. Nevertheless such discernible instability had quickly led to a recovery in a matter of one decade and people began to feel real changes from the past swerving upheavals. Alas, this old-new Russian country began constructing quite chaotic type of society with old roots of corruption, theft, violence, the lack of vision, along with drastically increasing ignorance. A new wave of Russian gangsters, anarchists, go-getters, bootlickers, and bureaucrats arose in multitudes.

Candidates for Russian leadership were not able to grab the power firmly and for long, and fight for the throne increasingly intensified from one leader to another.

Yet, somehow, after a number of quick changes and different directions, Russian leadership playing on tired, irritated, literary hungry and ready to explode crowd almost mystically surfaced in a new type of powerful government behind which were same party apparatchiks led by the former KGB agent and his fawners.

Vladimir Putin, quietly yet with an iron hand and cool head began to navigate the country in the direction of possible restoration its previous prowess preserving the pride and satisfaction of its people.

CHAPTER 18

The Blacks

This part of the book turned out to be the most difficult in many aspects. Whatever one chooses to say about blacks might be construed as racist if the person who speaks about them is not himself black. Blacks have often suffered from injustices, oppression, degrading humiliation, and the demeaning of their character. And the worst crime they've experienced is slavery, despite the fact that this subjective behavior had been practiced since the dawn of civilization, for centuries, including in the African continent. The unfortunate experience these enslaved blacks endured was much harsher than those African blacks who did not end up as slaves, but who continued to struggle while trying to survive not less harsh natural conditions in their own countries while being relatively free.

Also, blacks are usually considered as one people by non-blacks based on the color of their skin, and that alone might be perceived as offensive thing to do.

As if this was not enough, today many African Americans suffer from an inferiority complex, methodically changing their outer appearance as well as their attitude toward whites, and every decade or two, African Americans present a new, barely recognizable face. They are acutely aware of the perception most whites tend to have about the black people. To complete this picture, they know that whites judge them on the whole and not individually. And because it is a generalization, for instance, to speak of Christians as one people, there is also no justice in such a description of blacks.

Never mind that blacks may often be doing the same thing by judging all whites as one people. Never mind that this is the way we judge other people or other groups. It is habitual and customary for most of us. This itself is a different subject, and I discuss it at more length in some other parts of this book.

The many problems blacks experience are based on the fact that blacks, for one reason or another, cannot tell the story of their history and roots in one voice. You might hear that the story in the Old Testament about the four hundred years of slavery in Egypt is actually not about Jews but rather about blacks. You can learn from some groups of blacks that Jesus Christ was black, that the ancient Egyptians were black, that all non-white people are black, and that whites are a mutational error of the black people. Some even insist that Allah is their god and the Honorable Elijah Muhammad is the last messenger of that god, or rather, the incarnation of God.

While many messengers before Elijah Muhammad had turned to their own people, bringing them a word from God, this messenger spoke specifically about righteous black people and the evil (devil) white man. He believed that the Bible is devoted to the righteous black men who were for one reason or another overpowered by the white devils (white race). He believed that the involvement of God (Allah) would imminently restore the true justice that black men had been deprived of until now. Yet not knowing any better, this prophet continuously called for separation between the whites and the blacks. He actually became a precursor of the most extreme black militants, such as the Nation of Islam is, today visibly represented by Minister Louis Farrakhan.

The rift between blacks and Jews occupies a special place in history, as the two so-called minority groups continue to clash despite each having felt general animosity from core groups in a number of societies. I will discuss this intolerance further.

Black people, if we specifically refer to the color of their skin, nevertheless belong to separate lines of descent which all began in Africa. Today many tribes in Africa exist (Bantu, Bushmen, the Khoikhoi, the Nilo-Hamitic peoples, and the true Negroes from West Africa) independent of each other with their own history.

—

There are also the blacks who live on islands in the Caribbean region, the blacks of European countries, and the blacks of North America. These blacks are mostly separated demographically. But as everyone knows or should know, this is not a strict division of the black people, and they naturally or conditionally change geographic locations from time to time.

I will speak first about the blacks who live presently in the United States. Then I will move to other continents and locations.

The history of blacks in the United States begins with the settlement of America by white English colonists. Soon after was established an organized system of bonded labor. Workers under this system were also called indentured servants. Bonded labor meant lending passage fare at high interest rates to workers who wished to come to America, then having the workers labor without pay until their loans were considered to be paid off. With the introduction of slavery, bonded labor became less desirable and therefore less practiced.

Slavery as a form of forced labor on this continent came into practice more than a century before the United States of America was founded in 1776.

As a part of a new contract, the slave owner had the choice of whether to free a slave or to keep the slave indefinitely after the term of a contract had expired. The decision was directly made based on the owner's sentimental or benevolent nature. This process was called *manumission* and was practiced before the law of slavery was enacted.

Slavery in Colonial America was legalized in 1654 and lasted until 1865, the year when the passage of the Thirteenth Amendment abolished the practice as unlawful.

Forced labor in the form of slavery was nothing new and had been practiced among many countries since ancient times. According to some sources, slavery began after the invention of agriculture about eleven thousand years ago. It was widespread in most ancient civilizations including Egypt, Sumer, Assyria, China, and India, to name but a few.

In colonial America, the first documented record of African slavery dated to 1619. Officially begun in 1654 in Virginia, by the year 1705, every colony in North America had slaves. Slaves in the South worked mainly on farms and plantations, while in the North they were primarily house servants. Although the number of African slaves brought to the Americas amounted to twelve million people altogether, out of that figure only 650,000 actually arrived in the United States by 1705. The census of 1860 showed that the number had grown to four million people in that time period.

The largest number of slaves who arrived in the Americas were shipped to Brazil. Another large number went to Portuguese colonies in the Caribbean Basin and Mexico. With the diminishing number of European indentured workers, slaves were a handy and cheap workforce.

While the consensus is that the majority of African slaves came from the regions around Ghana, Sierra Leone, and Congo, they came from many different tribes and places.

Because they had a very dark skin, not characteristic of that of Europeans, starting with Portuguese, the term *negro*, meaning "dark" was applied to the African people, without any pejorative meaning. Classically, there were three groups in the world recognized by skin color: the Negroid, the Caucasoid, and Mongoloid. Etymologically rooted in the Latin word *niger* which in that language means black, this spelling is still used to point to *substantia nigra*, the dark substance of the human brain that plays an important role in producing melanin as a by-product during the synthesis of dopamine.

While in the beginning, *negro* was used more as a distinguishing marker, by the 1900s the word acquired a belittling tone. Since then, a few alternate words have been in use with their frequency, depending on individual political and social climates. In different languages, the meaning of the word still directly relates to the way it is pronounced and used.

Besides the African slaves who were brought to the Americas forcefully, at that time there were many indentured white workers from Ireland, Scotland, Holland, and Germany. At the end of their indentures, the freed workers were given a chance to buy a lot or to use a piece of another landowner's land for themselves. The problem was that in addition to the formerly indentured servants not having enough money to buy land, there was not much land left, as by that time the best lands were in the possession of the wealthiest families. This created a situation where the freed workers began to realize that freedom was not coincidental with prosperity.

With slavery came a stereotypical vision of a new black person that was not characteristic of those who remained free. This meant,

—

among other things that the accepted practice of the antebellum slaves was an artificial submissiveness toward their slave masters. This way, the slaves had a better chance to survive without being beaten. Yet physical abuse was quite often administered without real provocation. Part of the harsh treatment of slaves was based on the demands of the state to punish a black person, to establish a "better bondage" with a master, and to "persuade" a black person to work, as expressed in the Jim Crow laws.

Another traumatic experience came from the forceful relocation of slaves. An estimated one hundred thousand slaves were moved in each decade between 1810 and 1860, the main reason being the sale and resale, for the purpose of speculation. The transportation of slaves was carried out by marching them in groups; to prevent sudden revolts, their armed overlords often tightly chained the men. The separation of families was habitual, and often men, especially those who were young and strong, were sold separately. Because slaves were considered to be the property of their owners, female slaves were routinely raped by their masters. The children born as a result of these rapes continued to carry the status of slaves.

By 1860, the presidential election revealed a deep split between the Southern Democrats, who supported slavery, and the Northern Republicans, who denounced it. In 1861, when the South decided to secede from the Union, the Civil War erupted. The blacks, who sometimes tried to escape from their Southern owners, now were leaving their households en masse, hoping to find better conditions in the North. When Congress passed the Confiscation Act in 1861, escapees from the South were considered confiscated property. Many slaves for that reason began to join the Union forces in Union territory.

On January 1, 1863, President Abraham Lincoln issued the Emancipation Proclamation, promising freedom for all slaves, including those who were within the territory of the Confederate states. By that time, hundreds of thousands of slaves had escaped over the Union lines, tremendously weakening the ability of the Confederates to resist the regular Union forces.

With its vote on the Thirteenth Amendment, Congress announced universal and permanent emancipation. Slavery in America officially came to an end.

The abolition of slavery in the United States produced millions of people who were a new class of freed people without any sense of direction. Not exactly Americans, they had lost their African identity over generations. They became a new category of people who had been previously told what to think, what to do, how to do it, and how not to do it. For almost a quarter of a millennium, African Americans had been denied human dignity. They became inured to the violent outbreaks of white people, sudden torture, and the institutionalized denial of their affiliation with their country of origin, be it Africa or the United States. Black people developed a sense of inequality due to a perception of their race as an inferior people—even subhuman—who, for the most part, were looked upon with pity and scornful indifference.

With slavery abolished, blacks began to establish congregations and church facilities, creating a new form of Christianity that related more to the African traditions than anything else. They could not feel or accept the Christian faith of white people as their own, as they knew that white people believed the Creator did not have them in mind when he created humankind.

As they had been denied self-determination and self-expression for many decades and were denied education and cultural teachings, the only way to maintain human decency, as they could see, was their spiritualism and work that connected them to survival. Not only did blacks have to provide their own living, they had to secure decent-paying jobs, acceptable housing, medical care, and education, if not for themselves, then for their families and children.

They might not have cared much about all of these at once and not right from the start, but they had to find their place in the society in which they were trying to live. Yet the road to prosperity was littered with obstacles, both natural and manmade.

Still, given the sheer size of the black population, they became the second largest ethnic group after the English colonists. Whether due to the fact that they grew in large numbers or other factors that brought them together, black people found enough endurance to organize their first segregated communities and schools, eager to lead normal lives. Motivated to succeed, blacks initially began to make huge progress in the postwar reconstruction era, marking the transformation of the

—

Confederacy into the Southern states. Despite the fact that they had been knocked down, these black people were ready to live again.

At the same time, whites, in general, had no idea how to behave toward a significant group of people who were not exactly equal to them based on the simple fact that they had come to America not of their own will but as their property. The two groups were on a collision course, one weakened and partially illiterate, the other aggressive and shrewd.

The end of the Civil War was marked by legislation in the Southern states limiting migration, labor, and other activities of newly freed slaves. The so-called Black Codes of 1865 became the accepted practice of treatment of the freed black population. The codes enforced racial segregation, criminalized interracial marriages, and restricted certain rights of freed people with the strong message that blacks, while emancipated, were not full citizens. These laws clearly stated that blacks were a second-class people who could not testify against whites, who had no right to vote or to express legal concerns, and who were limited in occupations otherwise available to white men.

With the era of Reconstruction ending in 1877, and the era of "Redemption" (as it was labeled by white Southerners) taking its place, major steps were taken to limit the rights of freedmen. One such step was the legislation called Jim Crow laws.

Under these laws, racial segregation was required in all public places. The right to vote became more complicated. Blacks were denied permission to serve in local, state, and federal offices. In such an atmosphere, all three amendments banning slavery (Thirteenth Amendment), guaranteeing civil rights (Fourteenth Amendment), and prohibiting the denial of voting rights (Fifteenth Amendment) for all citizens had died for African Americans.

While blacks' official equality was accepted by the Constitution of the United States, its de facto meaning was "separate but equal." The trick was not in the word equal but in the word *separate*. The first real proof of such interpretation came in 1887 when Florida passed a law stating railways would provide "equal but separate accommodations for the white and colored races." Other states soon followed suit with their own Jim Crow laws.

The first declaration of the unconstitutionality of these forms of segregation, starting with a public school system, was announced by the Supreme Court of the United States on May 17, 1954. The remaining Jim Crow laws were overturned by the Civil Rights Act of 1964. Equal rights to vote were enacted by the Voting Rights Act in 1965.

Why it took such a long time for Americans to change their core thinking is not that simple to explain. But when viewed by future historians from the height of at least one or two centuries from now, it will probably not be considered as dramatic as today in terms of elapsed time.

Yet while these discriminatory measures lasted for another one hundred years after the abolition of slavery, blacks could not and did not have many chances to get on their feet, due to their lack of education, poor living conditions, and overall low expectations from those around them.

The period of social activism and justice known as the Progressive Era that began in 1890 turned into a movement characterized by exposing corruption in local government, the political power of bosses, and the engineered suppression of the rights of blacks, women, and poor whites.

This was the first time when a Southern-born Democrat, Woodrow Wilson, became president of the United States. As a leader of the progressive movement, Wilson began his presidency by bringing many white Southerners into his cabinet. His views, having been shaped by his own Southern heritage, would explain his acceptance of demands by these members to expand the politics of segregation. While he would introduce reforms concerning the legalization of unions and the protection of workers' health and safety, he believed that these measures did not concern blacks. The reforms Wilson introduced had to protect white workers but were not expanded to African Americans.

Running the gamut of dehumanization that lasted not less than three hundred years, blacks from Africa finally developed into a people who were different from those who remained in their original lands. So-called African Americans, or blacks who live in the United States, because of people's inherited and individual ability to change, each became their own person yet nevertheless displayed two or three characteristic norms of behavior that join them together as one group. These are as follows:

- Blacks in America are always interconnected by the color of their skin.
- Blacks who were born in the United States are acutely sensitive to long-lasting discrimination against them.
- These African Americans are not ready to dismiss their past experience and to trust white people without questioning their sincerity.
- What distinguishes blacks?
- They are not a uniform or homogeneous group.
- Each black person has distinct abilities and the endurance to achieve his or her individual goals, using different approaches to reach those goals.
- Each black person has distinct values and understanding of happiness.

While realizing that such a network of tremendously diverse people exists, one should not be surprised that blacks have always been represented by diametrically different leaders. From the militants and rebellious types to the submissive and nonviolent, from W. E. B. Du Bois to Martin Luther King, Jr., from Malcolm X to Jesse Jackson, from Elijah Muhammad to Louis Farrakhan, they all looked for ways to achieve true freedom as an oppressed people. Whether they enjoyed successes or encountered setbacks when striving to achieve their goals, nevertheless, they went forward. This success must be analyzed further, and I will do so later in this chapter.

For now, let me evaluate blacks from the position of whites.

To say that all whites think of blacks in the same manner would be a huge misrepresentation. Today, we may absolutely confirm that opinions on blacks differ among younger and older generations as well as educated or not. Yet the majority of whites still judge blacks according to some standard mentality, and that generalization, while today is categorized as politically incorrect, nevertheless exists and is expressed with different degrees of openness and sincerity.

So what is that general opinion? Acknowledging that it might be not pleasant or even fair, one still needs to speak about it in order to come to closure. I must warn the reader that the next few paragraphs might sound politically incorrect, but, as I said, I see no other choice

–

but to speak about it in a straightforward fashion and, by doing, so attempt to understand it and make it go away once and for all.

The following is a characteristic description of blacks that is can be associated with African Americans, although these behaviors are widespread across humanity.

Blacks are loud, lazy, do not want to work, have no morals, do not keep their family units intact; they are looters, angry, easily provoked, insolent, demand to be treated as equals but are often hateful of or at least are trying to make fun of whites. Those who benefit from government programs do so not because they desperately need the funding, but because they are using these programs without any responsibility toward the society they live in, most likely feeling that whites owe them. The most they can do successfully is play music and sports, yet only those at which they are good. They want the best luxuries society can offer whether they deserve them or not. Therefore if they cannot get these luxurious objects the old-fashioned way, they see nothing wrong in selling drugs, stealing whatever and whenever they can; in other words, they would do whatever they can to obtain them. They also have problems with prostitution, use guns, kill people, drink alcohol, and at the same time they blame their sinful behavior on whites, who provoke them to behave this way on purpose in order to keep them in poverty and as a subclass of people.

If we add to this picture that blacks do not want to study and therefore are unable to get a good education and are scornful of those who do; insist that blacks with good educations, jobs, and decent living have sold their souls to whites, the question that remains is, what do blacks and whites have in common?

Now let me try to explicate some of these negatives on a one-by-one basis. I see no other way but to present them like situations that one might encounter in the real world.

Let's start with the characterization of a black man or woman as lazy and unwilling to work in the society in which he or she lives. First of all, it is not true. Not all blacks exhibit a lack of desire and willingness to work. But let's say we care only to ask why blacks do not want to work. Before I give you an example from real-life experience, let me give you my personal opinion on the many above-mentioned characteristics of blacks of which I became aware through many different contacts during many years I lived in the United States.

—

- Blacks are having a difficult time transforming their mentality after being forced to work through beatings, mistrust, inequality, and segregated occupations.
- They are still denied decent, well-paying jobs in the private sector, where there are no unions and where an employer can get away without consideration of affirmative action. At the same time, they are welcomed to the government positions at the level of clerks that rarely pay at the level of high-position jobs in the private sector.
- They have been misled by the so-called leaders of their communities who instill the mindset that blacks are foreign in white society.
- Finally, if some (I cannot give you statistics on that) might somewhat experience a feeling of laziness that possibly comes from their genes. Their recent ancestors came from Africa, where a constantly warm climate, along with an undemanding lifestyle, could help develop a type of people who are hereditarily relaxed (sleepy) and slow in motion. Shall we blame them for that? It probably would equal the characteristics of those who live in cold, wintry areas and who in the majority have somewhat excessive drinking problems that most people who live in warm climates do not have.

Anyway, besides this particular line of reasoning of why black people do not express a particular eagerness to work, let me bring here a few hypothetical situations that lead some few whites to form their negative opinions of blacks.

A private, medical, clinical group seeks a secretary for a front-desk job. A group of three doctors work in the region, where high-income residents mostly of Italian and Jewish descent live. The doctors, after interviewing a number of candidates for the job, must, in the end, make a choice between an experienced white female with excellent qualifications and a black woman with equally impressive credentials. The job goes to the white woman for one reason only: the Italian residents are somewhat prejudiced toward black people and the doctors unfairly, but in their mind reasonably, fear that hiring a black secretary might potentially jeopardize their patient base.

Another example: A black man drives a big Mercedes to an expensive restaurant. He exits it with his girlfriend; both of them are dressed very well and wearing expensive jewelry. In a contemptuous manner, he throws the keys to the attendant, who happens to be a white man. The attendant might equally think that the black man might be an athlete, musician, or celebrity, or a drug dealer.

From where does this mentality come? It is actually self-explanatory. Human nature is mostly cultured by specific relations of society. A professional black male who is a doctor or a successful lawyer will almost never appear in public with ostentatious jewelry and act disrespectfully to someone like an attendant.

Many negative stereotypes of African Americans—that they are looters, having no morals and responsibility, or that they are mainly angry people who are willing to rob, kill, and are prone to violence— served as justifications for the denial of a decent living to African Americans for generations. On the other hand, you may pose the question: Why should anyone care about their employment success? You and I haven't enslaved them. You and I have to fight for our own well-being. Why should either of us be forced to consider that the needs of a black person are somehow more important than yours and mine? Let them struggle, as each of us does in the same honest way without reference to their unfortunate past.

One thing to consider is that no one can dismiss a proven and therefore existing phenomenon of posttraumatic stress disorder. African Americans are burdened with obstacles most white people in contemporary America either have never experienced or didn't experience for as long time as African Americans did. While I am not trying to provide any justification for those African Americans who do succumb to violence or crime, their behavior might very well be caused by their long-lasting mistreatment. But by the same token, it is exactly the opposite picture when a contemporary black man states that the success the white man assumes comes not much from his credentials but from only having a white skin that offers him a success, deservingly or not.

Separately stands a topic of struggle many black people face in order to get an education. Again, as with each previous consideration, one cannot come to a possible understanding and solution of a problem from one side or one reason only.

—

We should realize that in order to study, one must have a good solid family. And by that, I do not only mean a father and mother presence in such a unit. Family in this sense means those two specific adults who can and are willing to provide nurture along with the wide meaning of this term. The overall mood of a learner must coincide with those in charge. But when a single mother with three or more children tries to cope with burdens in her life, at the same time demanding a good report of a child's achievements in school, only a child can realize how difficult it is to accomplish what is expected, or even worse, demanded of him or her. A child doesn't have to be a genius to recognize his mother's inability to struggle with the stress befalling her, which eventually affects all the family members. Yet despite these encumbrances, a child makes plans and sets goals that he sometimes sees only partially accomplished.

Does striving to succeed really count if a child cannot fulfill his cherished dream at the end? Who should have cared that a child had financial difficulties or a sound, decent home or caring parents or little peer pressure and overall warmth coming from society?

Of course, to rely only on this superficial reasoning may not reflect the whole picture. There are numerous factors encountered in each separate case, including the unwillingness of an individual to go all the way due to unforeseen and unexpected encumbrances. The rebellious years of adolescence would be another reason.

These problems might be encountered in any ethnic group, and I discuss them anywhere else in this book. Yet here I'm trying to explain specifically one conspicuous ethnic group that, for one reason or another, is often mistreated, rarely fairly appreciated, and, as a rule of thumb, dismissed and neglected.

Another two stereotypical features of African Americans that might or might not definitely characterize these people is that of music and sports, abilities which seem naturally present in them as noticeable talents. Musicality is usually connected to people's soul, expressed through emotional desire. Two types of music—sad or blue and rhythmically fiery or jazz like—say exactly that. Could these types of music reflect on people's historical past? It looks like it does in the case of the formerly enslaved race. When it comes to sports, for those blacks who rely on their athletic excellence, success comes much easier than for those less physically developed. So now that we have recognized many unpleasant features for which blacks were stereotyped, let's speak about why not all whites perceive blacks the same way.

First of all, whites are also different and need to be separated by their own qualities. There are whites who are sympathetic to the sufferings of blacks; there are whites who cannot tolerate injustice no matter who the oppressed class or group of people are. There are whites who don't care much about blacks and their problems; and there are whites who want blacks out of their lives once and for all.

The first group is usually represented by intelligent and educated people with good intentions and warm hearts, people who try to prove that all people are equal under the sun (or God).

The second group is mostly the rebellious type, revolutionaries actively seeking equal rights for people no matter what color or creed. These people fight any regime that suppresses the rights of its citizens. They are sometimes called terrorists and may act singlehandedly, but more often they are organized in special groups with a clear agenda, either successful or not.

The third group is filled with selfish, egotistical people who are not always prospering in life but who decisively think that they have enough problems on their own.

And the fourth is a group of people with limited abilities and qualities. These people see the world in two colors: black and white. They are angry with blacks, Jews, American Indians, foreigners, other minorities, rich people, successful people, and all those who either made it in society or are capable of making it. They are neo-Nazis, skinheads, white supremacists, and other such people.

If we try to evaluate African Americans from their own position, they will be easily seen sometimes as a group and sometimes as individuals. As a group, they are aware of a subtle separation and distancing from them by white society. They are aware of their acceptance by whites only on an individual basis. Being acutely sensitive of such an attitude toward them, they cling to each other, having no need to justify their differences, abilities to survive, or to overcome separate and individual obstacles in their lives.

But in general, all blacks are encircled as a minority who live among the majority of whites and who are forced to adjust to such a society. Whether they are successful or not depends on individual qualities, luck, and perseverance.

—

Let me now analyze the relationship or lack thereof between blacks and Jews. For one reason or another, these two minority groups are often mentioned together. Do they have anything in common?

"We have been deceived into thinking that the Jews have been our allies in our recent civil rights struggle," remarked Louis Farrakhan on Jews in a radio interview with WPFW-FM, a Washington DC radio station, on April 1, 2010. It is not hard to say who deceived blacks into such a thought process when it comes from the mouth of such people as Farrakhan, but to say these words in 2010 is to acknowledge that Jews and blacks do have things in common. Correct? Not quite.

Only a few months later, Minister Farrakhan gave this speech at Mosque Maryam in Chicago, Illinois, on March 14, 2010:

> *These people* [the Jews] *started apartheid in Africa. The same Jews are guilty of Jim Crow and the laws that segregated us* [blacks and whites] *and they are the same forces that are in Palestine right now telling Palestinians in their own land what roads they can travel on and what they're not free to travel on.*

Is it possible that these and other hateful speeches coming from Farrakhan are in fact nothing new and therefore do not need to be paid attention? Is this minister alone in his class? Are there other black leaders who might spew venomous propaganda against the Jews? I don't think that offering the reader a list of those who try to do "justice" by portraying the Jews as Satan or as the great manipulators or as the crooked deceivers will accomplish much. And that is not the reason I raise this dialogue anyway. The reason I bring up this topic is based on the historical facts of physical clashes, genocide, and the extermination of people in masses that were connected to ethnicity, religion, or political affiliation.

First of all, one needs to decide why among all the offenders against black people, the Jews are underscored as the most dangerous and vicious people. Somewhat surprisingly, the answers (and there are a few) are not only obvious but straightforward. Jews are the most picked-upon group of people when others need to find someone to blame for one's own problems. Jews are the easiest of all people to be chosen as a target, since they normally do not fire back. The Jews are the people who, to some degree, could always be portrayed as guilty. It has happened for many centuries. The Jews have gotten used to this. The rest of the world has gotten used to it.

It is not yet obvious to what degree the provocations Farrakhan has chosen are dangerous to the well-being of the whole nation. For ordinary folks burdened with everyday struggle to do well, such speeches might be that unexpected thirsty soil that people like Farrakhan enjoy poisoning. Why does he do it? The reasons might be a few, but those that are clearly connected to logical analysis are not tangible enough to prove. Still, at least one question comes to mind. Would people like Farrakhan have any other topic to rely on for their so-called long-term success?

For what kind of sins cannot Farrakhan and other similar black propagandists and instigators forgive the Jews? Let's see:

- "Jews killed Jesus Christ."
- "Jews lie that they were in slavery in Egypt. The real people who were in Egypt at that time were the Hebrews who are not the Jews."
- But if the Hebrews, according to this minister, were actually not the Jews, then there is no record pointing to this bondage in any Egyptian book either. The most extreme group, the Nation of Islam, claims that Hebrews are the blacks and that when the Bible speaks about the Hebrews, it actually speaks about black people.
- "Jews were often involved in usury as a method of exploiting the people of the Gentile world."
- "Jews persuaded innocent Gentiles to buy and sell Negroes for the purpose of using cheap force and for them get rich without the need to work."
- "Jews were slaughtered during the Holocaust because they angered German people to the point they had to kill them to get rid of them."
- "Jews have always used their money to influence people, countries, continents and, in fact, the whole world."

If this is not enough to remove the Jews from the surface of this earth, I don't know what is. The question that comes to mind then is, are Jewish people so much worse than the blacks that even blacks hate them so much?

RESPONSE 1: That the Jews killed Jesus Christ, any intelligent man knows is a lie. The Jews had their motives not to respect Jesus, who mocked them by claiming that he was their Messiah. He showed his disrespect of the old traditions they had followed faithfully. Would that not produce confusion among people of any religious nation?

RESPONSE 2: Were those Jews or Hebrews who were in bondage for four hundred years in Egypt as we read from the Hebrew Bible possibly black people? Was the Bible then written by blacks who called themselves Hebrews to confuse future generations? Were the ancient Egyptians also black? Was Jesus Christ a black person who appeared among the Jews to save them?

RESPONSE 3: Did Jews use usury to lend money among gentiles? From where did they get this money? Why were they allowed to get possession of such huge sums? These questions seem to be simple and straightforward and, in context, need to be answered in the same fashion. Charging interest on loans (usury), according to the book of Ezekiel, is a sin forbidden by Jewish law. Charging interest, however, would be an acceptable practice if the borrower were a non-Jew. Without going into the painful details about under which circumstances the Jews were allowed to make loans, let me, in fairness, mention that most ancient Jewish traditions prohibited usury in most cases.

Besides, the Jews did not invent this kind of trade, since it was practiced in many ancient societies including Egypt, Sumer, Phoenicia, and other Mesopotamian cultures. It was also known in a form of mortgage invented by Englishmen that provided shelter to money being lent while securing the loan. Jews, who were mostly known for getting involved in mercantile business, normally accumulated different sums of money that they could lend to needy people. The idea of profiting from lending money to someone was considered by the Christian church as a mortal sin that would unequivocally lead to eternal damnation in hell.

Why then are the Jews the only people pointed to for such exploitative means of suppressing needy people? For one, making loans was habitual for the Jews, as they were not allowed to pursue many other different fields of work. That does not mean that I am justifying Jews as profiteers. They have their own laws prohibiting this kind of practice. And as long as in today's contemporary world Jews are not restricted from most jobs, they should and possibly must abandon this type of exploitation of other people where it still exists. There should not be two opinions on this. And as a matter of fact, such practices were mostly abandoned a few centuries ago.

Is unjust or unlawful accumulation of money by Jews is still a factor in today's world? No more than a few people will doubt it. Who should we blame for that? Are there more than a few Jews who continue such behavior? Has any other nation completely rid itself of its bad apples? It is not such an easy task. As long as society cannot produce a paradise in which only righteous people can be found, it is an unfortunate fact that Jews also have their bad apples.

RESPONSE 4: Jews eagerly participated in the slavery of blacks. But to what degree did the Jews have influential power in the New World at the beginning of the seventeenth century anyway? They had just been expelled from Spain (1492) and Portugal (1497). When the newly formed Dutch province declared its independence from Catholic Spain and allowed the Jews to enter on religious grounds, Jews migrated most abundantly to Amsterdam. The relative success of Jews in the Netherlands for the next few decades was remarkable, but that does not mean that Jews were the most abundant in this kind of trade. It is true that those who got involved in this business were prominent and very successful. But isn't that a characteristic attribute of Jewish people that shows itself independently of profession? They definitely succeeded while actively participating in enslaving black people.

Did those Jews see the opportunity to make money by selling black people around the world? Probably no less than the other slave owners. Did they do it in a more arrogant, insulting manner? Possibly, yes. And it was done while shrewdly and with wit, yet it was done immodestly and therefore in an uncivilized manner, if one can speak of such business.

Did anything change in that regard concerning Jews? For one reason or another, the behavior of some Jews continues to be displayed so insolently and without regard to the opinion of surrounding public that people not only notice it, they often become disgusted with it. There is a common stereotype that Jews are famous for an excessive love of money, which we discussed in the section devoted to the Jewish paradox. Are all Jews like that? Do all whites think of themselves as superior?

RESPONSE 5: How successful was Hitler in his campaign to finalize the Jewish question? The Jews are still around. But did they learn any lessons? Hitler is long gone, Germany is relatively dormant, but many other smaller-caliber Hitlers sprout in different corners of the world. Would it be possible that Jews by their activity alone might produce feelings of estrangement toward them? Not all, for sure. But probably enough in numbers or, rather, by the way that some of these people do it in more than conspicuous way. Then a question comes to a rational mind: How could a group of people present themselves on one side of a coin as phenomenal Einsteins and on the other as unscrupulous greedy grabbers? How could a nation that produced a score of Nobel Prize winners simultaneously provide an equal, if not bigger, number of untidy profiteers? Was Hitler right all along? Was he sent by the Almighty to teach Jews a lesson? Did it help? Did Christians learn the lesson of the Passion of Jesus Christ? Did people eternally atone for their sins afterward?

RESPONSE 6: Jews used money to influence people in power. Even if that is true, isn't it characteristic of many people? Jews who know how to make money should know how to use it. Does that mean that Jews are seeking the world domination? Do they want or even need it? Haven't they had enough problems till now?

–

CHAPTER 19

Hispanics in the United States of America

Ethnically, these are the people who live in the United States but whose origins could be traced to Spain and other Spanish-speaking countries. While those who are called Hispanics (a term first adopted during Nixon administration) might still trace their roots to Spain, they are not necessarily directly descended from that country.

Spain, as the country found in the Iberian Peninsula, was under Roman domination known as Hispania even though the etymology of this name is unknown and presently disputed. Originally comprised of a few provinces under the Roman umbrella, starting from the fifth century CE, these provinces split into separate domains such as today's Portugal and Spain. With the development of maritime exploration in the middle of the fifteenth century and onward, Spain turned into the Spanish Empire, exploring and colonizing many different countries.

Portugal established a kingdom of its own in 1139, and with the last defeat of the Moorish government in 1492, the Iberian Peninsula was brought back to Christianity. This period known as *Reconquista*, or recapturing, marked the victory of Christianity over Muslim rule in that region. Portuguese and Spanish maritime exploration during that period tremendously advanced the countries as world powers. This led to not only an age of discoveries, it also helped these countries to reach global empire status.

Europe in the seventeenth century was going through an agrarian revolution that would require new labor for its large plantations. As the Portuguese continued to explore their neighbors, and in particular the African continent, Angola became their first colony. The original inhabitants of Angola were the Bantu-speaking people, who moved down there from Cameroon, Nigeria, and Congo, and who gave the country the name *Ngola*, meaning "the king."

The Portuguese had no problem acquiring slaves from this colony, as they were easily sold by their African chiefs in exchange for the wine and cloth that the Portuguese brought with them. Realizing the importance of slave trading, Portugal began to transport African slaves as far west and south as Brazil. Africans, who were much less vulnerable to tropical diseases, as well as a much cheaper labor force for the owners of sugar plantations when compared to the diminishing number of native indigenous people, suddenly provided a tremendous opportunity for the Portuguese to become a dominant power in the world.

The Spaniards, on the other hand, were the first people who came to North America's shores to stay. Spanish conquistadors, as they were called, were looking for gold and trading passages with China, at the time the finest market in the world. They landed in Florida in 1539, and from there they traveled west and north, passing what would become the South and North Carolinas and Texas, advancing as far as the West Coast.

They expanded their exploration and colonization through most of the Americas, including the Caribbean islands and Mexico, overpowering the indigenous people they encountered. The result of their expansion was in direct line with the reduction in the numbers of aborigines everywhere they went.

It was also another characteristic feature of that time that people began to experiment with intermarriages. Mixtures of different races became the norm. Thus the Creole people, whose ancestry consists of blacks and white French, and the mulattos, whose ancestry consists of blacks and European whites, as well as black Hispanics, Asians, and even Latino Hispanics, came into existence. Latinos were those people who could trace their ethnic roots to Cuba, Costa Rica, Nicaragua, Panama, Argentina, and, in fact, all the rest of the Spanish-speaking countries in South America.

–

These mixtures confused people, as they could not cling to any of the original isolated races. As a result, more and more cases began to appear where black people began to separate themselves from these mingled cultures, not recognizing them as equal. These blacks would not freely accept Hispanic blacks as their own. Those blacks who had skin sometimes so light that they might be easily taken for white were the least accepted.

Why does all this matter? It turned out that people in the majority needed to recognize their own kind based on external features. Ethnic groups, be they blacks, Hispanics, or whites, accept each other by these visible signs and often show animosity toward those they do not recognize as their own.

It is an unfortunate intolerance that continues until today and exists among most people. To combat it, such a religion as Baha'i became a positive role player that extended its religious hand to many different ethnic groups and disparate people. I discussed this in my chapter devoted to that religion.

CHAPTER 20

Non-African Blacks Outside of North America

Actually, the expression "non-African black" is somewhat misleading, in a sense that all people must be considered Africans if we follow the roots leading to our ancestors. But for the reason that we distinguish Africans from people who do not presently live on African continent, I will continue to call those blacks who were born outside of Africa as non-African blacks according to their ethnicity.

Let us consider two countries in the Caribbean, Haiti and the Dominican Republic, as examples. The reasons I have chosen these two countries are manifold. For one, these countries share the island of Hispaniola (little Spain). Second, these countries seldom have been at peace with each other. Third, there are blacks who are Hispanics by ethnicity, and this becomes a real problem in how they want to be identified. Dominicans see the people of Haiti as black and therefore African. Yet it is not completely true as many Haitians (by some statistics 25 percent) are the result of a mixture of French and African blacks and therefore are technically Creole.

Dominicans, on the other hand, think of themselves as white Europeans whose ancestry goes back to Spain. Yet the census record of 1514 shows that 40 percent of Spanish men had Taino (indigenous) wives. And what about those Dominicans that came from the mixture of white Dominicans and Haitian blacks? If they go by their skin color, they must claim themselves to be black. Still, depending on their parents or grandparents, they might be both black and white. In past times, they were called mulattos, although today that is considered an offensive term (?). Historically Haiti is a former French colony; France occupied the whole island until 1844 and, until fairly recently, tried to invade its geographical neighbor. This complex relationship inevitably produced racial tensions that continue to this day.

When considering these two countries together because they occupy one island, one can definitely ask the question: Why is Haiti so poor but the Dominican Republic is the second-richest country in the Caribbean Basin?

Under French authority, Haiti was the richest colony in the world. Indigo, tobacco, coffee, sugar, and cotton were all produced there, and Haiti successfully traded its produce with the international markets. If we were to look for the explanation of what brought this country down to the status of the poorest country in the Caribbean region, we might find several substantial causes. Yet we might also be impartial and ask why two countries occupying one island and therefore enjoying relatively similar fertility of soil and climate are so different in their success. Both countries experienced substantial external interference as well as internal problems, yet each recovered with different levels of success.

Today these two countries peacefully coexist, but the Dominicans are steadily progressing and the Haitians are steadily regressing. The Dominicans are not only reaching new heights in their economy, they allow workers from the neighboring country to come and live there. Out of roughly ten million people who live in the Dominican Republic, about eight hundred thousand to one million are people from Haiti who permanently moved to that country.

It is true that the poorest regions in the Dominican Republic are represented either by Haitians or Dominicans of Haitian ancestry, but then a conclusion might be drawn that the condition in which people live depends on their race and ethnicity. Those few different minorities (Lebanese, Syrians, Palestinians, Chinese, Japanese, Spanish, Italians, Germans, British, Dutch, Danes, and Hungarians) who live in the Dominican Republic, although far from rich, still are not poor in their majority, and the question that necessarily might arise is "why?"

—

As this question is touching a very sensitive subject, I would like to note that one cannot provide proof that blacks are unable to work and prosper on their own. But at the same time, while blacks barely showed in any place they live much progression to which most people became used, we might attempt to do justice to it based on historical facts and to draw a conclusion based upon those.

With a history of exploitation by colonialists in their past, including the colonial forces' ensnaring local leaders in corruption and encouraging their greediness and lack of sympathy toward their own people, many African countries unsurprisingly have experienced stagnation and regression.

AFRICAN BLACKS

Whether one has heard of Bushmen or the Khoisan people or the other many indigenous peoples of Africa, the unfortunate facts are that many African regions are stricken by hunger and diseases and, on top of it, are prone to corruption, violence, and tyranny.

Yet it is not my purpose to give you a thorough history lesson of how African countries developed in the last few thousand years. I am not going to justify the land's occupiers either. My goal is to persuade the reader that Africa is a part of our human endeavor, and we cannot neglect this part of the world if we want to achieve real harmony in the human world.

Having said that, a short excursion into the history of African countries is still due.

Whether tropical jungle or deserts with severe droughts, savannas or abandoned lands, none of Africa's physical conditions contributed to the advanced technological breakthroughs contemporary societies enjoy today. As if nature desired to emphasize this vicious circle, severe droughts forced people to drill boreholes so they could retrieve groundwater that is naturally scanty but essential for survival. As a result, Africa today is facing severe erosion in many places. Another problem, arising from the necessity to raise cattle and sheep, led to overgrazing of the green parts of the land. Increased livestock populations as a means for survival and income meant more grazing further jeopardized the African land.

With *desertification* or *degradation* used as another term to describe the land often encountered in Africa due to semi-arid areas and the expansion of the desert at an alarming pace, it is easy to see how the inhabitants of these lands have gradually moved down south and to the coast of the continent. This migration necessarily brought two features that are characteristic of African people: they intermarried, and, as a result of overpopulation, they had to fight for survival.

While some people think that Africa is represented by mostly related black people that together struggle for better living conditions, few are aware that Africa is represented by many different peoples and cultures.

The indigenous people of Africa who could be identified as such are those who were marginalized in the lands where other lifestyles were dominating. The indigenous people in Africa were known mostly as hunter-gatherers or pastoralists before the colonization of their lands that began in the fifteenth century and lasting through seventeenth. Today these people are recognized as those ethnic groups separate from the prevailing political and economic structure of any particular nation.

Out of the few indigenous languages used by Africans, the Bantu is the dominant language spoken by roughly six hundred ethnic groups of that continent. It is the oldest language in Africa, and some argue that it came from proto-Bantu more than four thousand years ago, originating in Nigeria. Nigeria is in fact the most populous country in Africa (more than 150 million people), inhabited by over 250 ethnic groups.

The recorded history of Nigeria, like most other parts of Africa, goes back to 1000 CE. Since that time, Nigerian culture was influenced by Islam, which accounts for two-thirds of the Muslim population. After the fall of the Muslim regime, Nigeria developed its own army (in the kingdom of Benin), established commodity trade, and between the seventeenth and nineteenth centuries became known to Europe for its artisans specializing in works containing ivory, wood, bronze, and brass. It also participated in traffic of slaves destined for the Americas.

It fell under the protectorate of Britain as its colony; this lasted until full independence was declared in 1960. Since that time, Nigeria has suffered a number of coups, civil war, and thousands of lost lives.

—

This brought the country into chaos, stemming from the inability of each new regime to govern, corruption at every level, and hundreds of unfulfilled promises leading to even more problems such as high maternal mortality and flourishing tuberculosis and HIV and AIDS co infections, to name just a few.

Kenya, with its forty-one million residents, is a country divided by forty-seven semiautonomous districts. It is known for its long and short rain seasons, variety of climate, and hottest months in February and March. It has considerable wildlife, and its first human habitat is believed to have been established as long as human history has existed. Its proximity to the Arabian Peninsula has dictated the appearance of Arabs as early as the first century CE. By the fifteenth century, Kenya became a colony of Portugal. It later became a protectorate of Great Britain, from which it received independence in 1963.

Since that time, Kenya has seen different endemic corruptions intimately connected to the KANU (Kenya African National Union) party rulings. The party was led by Kenyatta until 1978 and then by Daniel arap Moi until 2002. While both presidents were popular among Kenyans, both were involved in corruption scandals. The election of the third president, Mwai Kibaki, marked significant changes in governing the country. First of all, he ended thirty-nine years of KANU reign. Under Kibaki, the government began to function not as an authoritative ruler but as three branches, akin to Western governance. Strong macroeconomic management, substantial investments in infrastructure, the support of innovations, and integration spurred the country's economy to robust growth over the last two years. As a result of this, the general level of living has dramatically improved for the Kenyan people.

The Republic of Congo, a former French colony, is dominated by Bantu tribes. It became an independent country in 1960 and, from 1970 to 1991, it was ruled by the Marxist-Leninist single-party system. The idea of national unity that began with the attempt of the first leader of that party, Patrice Lumumba, to implement it could not be accomplished due to Lumumba's assassination a year after becoming prime minister. It is impossible to say today whether the ideas of a communist regime would work in that African country in the long run, but the civil unrest, lack of popular education, competing factions, and other multitude of factors affecting it from inside as well

–

as outside speak for themselves. After the collapse of the regime and the first democratic election held in 1992, the country held a few elections, each accompanied by a fierce fight for power.

Today Congo is a presidential republic, which means that the president is the head of state and head of government at the same time. With a new constitution accepted in January 2002 and the presidential term extended to seven years along with a new bilateral assembly as form of government, Congo is on its way to prospering.

The economy of this country is mainly based on oil, natural gas, timber, diamonds, and somewhat based on iron, phosphate, and gold. It has developed agriculture and recently the government signed an agreement to lease two hundred thousand hectares of its land to South African farmers. Congo is actively involved in trades with the United States, China, South Korea, Brazil, India, and a few other countries. With a relatively small population, the economy of Congo is overtaking many other larger African countries.

These are only three countries presented out of many more I picked for their contrast and different levels of success. To come to an objective conclusion based not only on those countries, but also on all of Africa given the divergences in culture, economy, and particular history between each country, seemed impossible. Nevertheless, I will attempt to do exactly that in the following improvised and very short summary.

First of all, we have to disregard a typical description of African countries as underdeveloped. There are between forty-seven and fifty-three countries in Africa, depending on which countries one includes, numbering about one billion people in population. They are all different, and if one wants to compare it, is fair to say that one country has either an advantage or disadvantage relative to a comparable country. If we consider African countries in comparison to the rest of the world, it will be almost the same picture.

The long history of exploitation of most African countries has resulted in the Africans having been long denied self-expression and the ability to achieve a modern level of civilization. Without trying to deny such existing problems and obstacles, I only wish to conclude that prejudice aside, only time will show what African people can or cannot do.

—

ON THE COEXISTENCE OF BLACKS AND WHITES

Without any doubt, blacks and whites might and must coexist. While *must* is quite a strong word in this context, this is the only such phrase I am going to use in this regard. The reason this will be the only suggestion of that sort is that I am not in the business of conducting propaganda. Here, as well as in many other places, I was trying to understand the psychology of different people. That, in my mind, is the most important attribute man must possess if he wishes to understand his fellow humans. Why do we need to understand each other? Isn't it the only practical and, actually, the most important step in peaceful coexistence if we want to coexist?

Our feelings come naturally to us. Our tension around, fear of, or hatred of a stranger who, besides being different from us, sometimes acts aggressively, rudely, or inconsiderately is elevated in such circumstances. We do not easily accept others' different habits, always weighing them against our own or those established in our community. But if people, while having some inherited differences, will start to pursue one goal to live in a friendly fashion and attempt to understand other people's needs, the task of mutual survival will be easily accomplished.

AT THE CLOSING

Until very recently, African Americans were denied complete freedom despite the fact that they were free from slavery. They would not, for the most part, feel either dignified or equal among other people and especially the white people. They did not have many friends on their side who would be able to help them in their recovery, and those who could were more sympathetic to their cause than being able to accomplish much.

The current has changed though in recent years, with whites going to another extreme by feeling overly guilty for the past times. To say that it does more good for blacks would be wrong, as now whites begin to feel somewhat of reverse discrimination and that cannot be an advantage for either whites or blacks.

Taking all this into consideration, one may do his own analysis of where each group stands and the benefits versus possible damages society may incur.

So while the most important thing is that the process of recovery is on the right track and a definite journey to a better future, it is not less important to find the middle ground. It is also very important not to dwell in the past, especially if this remembrance is accompanied by a direction backward, and not to success but to blame. So if we try to realize that those generations of slaves are gone and that connections to them are elicited mainly from our memories, it would be a much better and sounder approach for blacks in today's world to live without that load.

Calls to provide the descendants of former slaves with separate states, land, and reparation, no matter who said calls come from—the leaders of the Nation of Islam, the Old and New Panthers, or the clergy of African-American churches—do not reflect on beneficial accomplishments but contribute to postponing resolution of the problem.

A recovery process is seldom fast, yet it might be progressive. While the old generations are gradually phasing out, new generations have more and more chances to live in harmony with all other people. Such attributes of civilized society as morality, education, the helping hand of a neighbor—all these can be learned without referral to one privileged or special group or class of people.

To conclude, it is mostly up to the people whose interests are involved to solve their problems. Will it happen? It is hard to know, but it is certainly the right way to go.

PART FOUR

SOME MORE FEATURES

CHAPTER 21

Few More Thoughts on Some Other Dispositions of Humans

Here, I will continue to describe briefly human behavior, not in the conventional way but by pointing out at unusually short yet distinct pictures of *how* and *why*. This, in my mind, will explain our actions under a different angle, bringing clarity to what separates us as humans from the rest of the animal world. It will also help us understand the fundamentals of our nature in an unconventional way.

We are born with a number of basic features that when combined make us human. Such are striving for progress, general feelings that produce dissatisfaction with our accomplishments, insatiable curiosity for the unknown, and self-assertion as unique individuals. We all possess a set of emotions that, while being universal, are expressed with different intensities.

These human emotions were somehow implanted in us a long time ago, and we have been able to reproduce them from generation to generation. As humans, we are also able to evoke them on a regular basis, although it would be wrong to describe our feelings as simply black and white. It is not so, and here are a few examples that should illuminate some of the most conspicuous ones.

FIGHTING FOR ONE'S PLACE

As trivial as it sounds, we all fight for a place under the sun. Whether this fight is palpable and perceived as real and eliminating the enemy would mean your literal survival or the enemy, while not particularly specified and therefore invisible still exists, we always compete with different vigor at different circumstance and precise point of lifetime. Not fighting at all would simply mean our inability to survive. But as this though rarely occurs, it still may take a precedent. It does not matter what agency one may use. As long as it will be a vehicle to pull someone through, that is all that counts. Examples should be plenty but one in this case must be suffice:

Often we encounter a negative perception by a younger individual of an elderly person making remarks at him as not being able to perform per accepted standards; this young fellow seemingly thoughtlessly and without merit demeans or describes this elderly being as a good-for-nothing, formerly active creature.

One of the explanations for such an approach could come from the youngster's subconscious fear of the possibility of growing old. Another explanation might be that this young man should think that denying another fellow human his mere existence would provide an extra space with an increased opportunity to last.

Thus mockery and derision that can be often heard from the offender that seemingly comes unprovoked, in hidden reality makes sense, however, up to a point.

Clarification: the previously mentioned desire to eliminate unwanted competition. Even though it is a remote possibility that these two common people that are not connected by place of living or job positions would cross each other's roads, they still are not able to eliminate perception of being an obstacle in reaching a personal goal. However incomparable the position of both might be each has sense of hatred of the opposing party. The elder might feel being pushed and the desire of the youngster to eradicate his persona. On the less-emphasized position of the old guy, a colorful sequence of silent scathing words might transverse his brain, which would nevertheless be the result of slipped-away youthfulness and, along with it, vibrant energy.

Both parties have a point or rather the reason to behave this way. But both are doing it subconsciously not being concerned to explain why or to worry about people's opinion of them.

PITY

This is another feature that most humans possess.

If we refer to the expression coined by the nineteenth-century philosopher Herbert Spencer of "survival of the fittest," based on Charles Darwin's *On the Origin of Species*, humans should fairly easily understand that nature eliminates the weakest. One can endlessly philosophize about the possible reasons nature presents its inhabitants, but the main theme of it directs us to the plotted purge of all and any impurities encountered on earth.

If nature denies the survival of the weakest, then what should one expect from an organism in a higher taxonomic gradation? Yet we know of many examples of animals protecting their offspring as newborns, especially if they enter this world sick and therefore weak. This kind of protection is characteristic of many highly organized species, with obvious prevalence among humans, necessarily leading to personal attachment. This last feature of humans is built through many intricate considerations that normally are grown into a pattern of behavior and character.

On the other side of a spectrum, it might be linked to the subconscious desire to deny our inevitable deaths. Fighting nature helps us to contend with our own recalcitrance.

We might also question what humanity might gain by protecting the sick, the weak, or the severely handicapped as, for instance, those with severe Down syndrome or untreatable schizophrenia. Society spends a great deal of time and money nurturing such people without actual recompense. Some might wrongly conclude that humans are wasting their time and energy on taking care of people who are actually unproductive and generally are an impediment for society.

Before I ponder the positive motifs by which people might be guided, let me consider the negative type of reaction that is exhibited by some people and that displays enjoyment that the offender gets while hurting a defenseless person. This trend has historically surfaced again and again, especially during major calamities, such as wars. War, in fact, reveals many negative inclinations in humans that are otherwise hidden or not noticeable in less strenuous times. It may also show in quiescent, peaceful times. Such would be the case of taking advantage of the elderly in nursing homes or assisted living and the like. In situations like these, the behavioral impropriety of the offender might be related to many reasons, starting with falling into category III of my classification, up to stumbling upon a sick, uncontrollable mind with a no-less-sick agenda and idea. It is also connected to the need of survival through the competition, and we spoke about it previously.

We may see the deeper meaning than what just had been offered as well, however remote and hidden it might sound. People who are devoted to helping the sick and needy inadvertently develop a positive attitude toward each other. They learn endurance in their fighting for a better life. They feed themselves by positive emotions, spreading an aura of warmth and kindness.

Yet not being afraid to repeat myself in trying to explain negativity shown by abusers, this kind of behavior might tell us of their insecurity and inability to compete in society by other more acceptable means, instead of trying to suppress or eliminate possible competition.

All human emotions are produced by electrical charges stimulating neurons, but it is not my goal to investigate this physiological mechanism in the pages of this book. The questions I raise are the following: why does the body get so stimulated that it puts an individual on edge? How does the brain react to produce complicated feelings such as anger and hate?

Anger can be dictated by either rational explanation or irrational frustration, the inability to prove one's point, false pride, or a desire to prove one's superiority. No matter what provokes it or how suddenly it appears, it can become uncontrollable.

Still, both anger and hate are self-protective mechanisms that arise from a combination of events, perceived directly or indirectly, and pointed toward the recipient. These perceptions are tightly connected to an individual's ego and his ability to apply willpower. While ego is a necessary trait for survival, it is often mismanaged from early childhood.

—

Given this lack of education along with an improper use of willpower, an individual finds sublimation channels that will alleviate his struggle in order to achieve a specified goal by a progressively increased usage of anger and hate. This progression is explained not only by the mastery of its user, but added to by an unexplainable enjoyment and excitement evoked in the mind of an abuser. During times of duress, these feelings substitute for the noble features of man such as love and kindness, letting negative feelings overwhelm the mind that needs relaxation and pleasure.

Whether negative or positive, either emotion plays a treacherous role in the brain, in this case strangely relaxing it.

THE NATURE OF LIES

On the surface, a lie is used as a protective mechanism. It usually starts as an innocent action that helps one to avoid possible punishment, however benign it might be. With time, lying becomes an indispensable vehicle used to overcome many obstacles. The lie becomes a tool seen by its user only as a resource he or she needs for smoother navigation.

Whether it works or not often depends on circumstance, ability, and the experience of its user. We all know that lying is characteristic of many politicians. We get angry with them for it, and we demand to replace them with another candidate. But who could honestly say that truthful and sincere politicians would accomplish their routine jobs better than those who lie? Doesn't their job require some deviation from always telling the truth? Wouldn't an inflexible, straightforward, and outspoken politician do more harm than the complaisant type?

EXAGGERATION VERSUS CRITICISM

Another curious feature of man is to honor and to glorify people and events of the remote past while at the same time rigorously screening the events and people of the present. People from past times are often ascribed such qualities as nobility, wisdom, far-sighted vision of future events, and so on. This is due to man's tendency to

—

seek mystery where none exists, hoping to find the water of life and discover the source of eternity. Many events described in such sources as the Bible would be a perfect example, as discussed in the first part of this book.

THE ROOTS OF RAGE AND VIOLENCE

Before rage, there is always anger. By definition, rage is uncontrollable anger. If rage does not produce satisfaction, it may lead to violence. Violence, in the majority of events, is a conflict in which one party prevails as an aggressor and the other often becomes a victim.

Today, most scientists agree that rage and violence can be inherited. Episodes can be triggered by a breakdown in communication, particularly if the aggressor perceives that the other party is violating the aggressor's rights.

Violence is mostly the province of men. It has multiple causes. The violent behavior connected to the aggression of a parent or an adult against a child versus the aggression of a drug addict, while possibly displaying similar types of violence, have different underlying mechanisms.

To make this point more succinct, I would like to use a couple of examples under circumstances that most of us might have experienced and in which others were quick to judge someone's behavior expressed inadequately in a particular moment and thus could not be explained sufficiently.

EXAMPLE 1: A young woman receives a phone call while driving. Her boyfriend is breaking up with her. Her heart is aching. Her head is pounding. Her mind is preoccupied with their last unpleasant conversation. She slows down because she is afraid she will get into an accident. Suddenly, another driver passing her on the left side yells at her angrily to get off the road if she doesn't know how to drive. The young woman bursts into tears.

EXAMPLE 2: A young man receives a phone call from his household. His brother has been taken to the emergency room with stomach pains. His brother has a chronic ulcer and something is definitely wrong. The young man is in the middle of heavy traffic.

–

In order to get out of the jammed road quickly, he starts driving erratically, cutting in and out of lanes to get ahead. Other drivers start yelling at him with quite clearly expressed indignation. Yet the young man has no time to explain his driving behavior. He continues to push ahead.

How many of these or similar situations have any of us been in?

Are we rational creatures, or are we not? In the scenarios above, one acceptable answer might be that we often act irrationally, having no time and patience to see the rationale behind it. That is human nature. We act; we, from time to time, try to explain our acts, but no matter what or how many causes produce our emotions, they would not be elicited if we were not born with them.

Of course, there are some other factors such as hormones that play a role, but I am not going to consider here these medically proven facts since we mostly are trying to determine the psychological aspects of our routine conduct.

Why then are men the most vivid possessors of such demeanor? It would be superficial and insufficient to point to testosterone as the only reason. In reality, it is a combination of societal, masculine culture educating men to be strong; it is a learned desire to compete and win, along with the clear preference of a crowd to admire a physically stronger competitor. It is scornful and disdainful behavior toward the weak, unpractical, or maladjusted individual. These are the obvious reasons that lead to behavior as described above and that society often inadvertently receives.

While so-called education described above requires physical superiority, the word itself implies the impossibility of such an achievement. If under these circumstances, a man encounters a weaker though smarter version of himself, he tries to eliminate such an obstacle, conforming to the contemporary rules of the culture he lives in. The result is unevenly distributed levels of society where the stronger, whether physically or occupationally, prevails over the less powerful and strong.

There are many other features we humans possess that have not been mentioned here. As I might have commented on previously, this is not a detailed book about all occurrences in life. But as long as we started on the right track, we will most likely continue to move in the right direction.

—

THE ROOTS OF MISUNDERSTANDINGS

There are many causes that may lead to misunderstandings among people. Still, they can all be described with one or two mechanisms. One that I will not consider here is the ill-perceived action of a stranger that is mostly based on the lack of knowledge of one's cultural roots, language barrier, and, thus, the inability to fathom one's conduct. The other mechanism is based upon self-projected importance that is intimately confined within one's sense of ego.

The word *respect* is often heard, especially among men. It is tightly connected to such feelings as pride, self-assertion, the desire to be appreciated and to be reckoned with. It is also subconscious dissatisfaction with one's own life achievements that might have resulted from accumulated small and neglected and, therefore, slipped-away opportunities. Such baggage will necessarily produce negative appreciation of life in one's general understanding of it and self-deprecation and bad luck in a particular individual. Such individual often becomes an introverted outcast that cannot smoothly blend into a particular society. On the other hand, the display of this ill-conceived understanding of respect often expresses itself through a physical violence. Again, men are the culprit; they often find themselves in this kind of dispute, in situations that otherwise could many times theoretically should have ended benign.

Chapter 22

Phenomenon of Death

This will be the last chapter of my book.

Unfortunately, our inescapable journey always ends with remarkable predictability at the final step to our demise. Our lifespan, however long it lasts, will end at some day and hour. All the people surrounding us today will be completely gone in a historically brief period of one hundred years. None of those with whom you are familiar or with whom you correspond will be around in a short while.

People, by inventing calendars, globes, and cosmic maps, most likely had in mind softening the comprehension of our inevitable expiration. But if you think about it, what is the difference for a dead person if he or she lived 20 or 120 years? When someone is dead, that means he has ceased to exist and will never come back to life. Whether you believe in resurrection or in a life someplace else, those who lived have never come back here. This is a sad fact with or without religious belief.

So why did I decide to speak about death? What possible good, noble, or beautiful thing could it accomplish? Can death mean anything other than what it is? Could I suggest anything new or provide some kind of relief for this horrific blow that awaits us all?

It is my firm conclusion that not highlighting this phenomenon, this occurrence, this tragic finale, does not allow us to speak of any other problems occurring in our lives. With this statement, I will suggest that no matter what we do, our actions are invisibly led by

—

death. "What profit has a man from all his labor in which he toils under the sun? 2:22; 3:9 famously says the author of Ecclesiastes, beginning his sermon. What use is it to you if you are going to die anyway? This thought strikes us for the first time in early childhood, approximately at age eight or nine; being one of the most lasting diseases that afflict humans, it stays with us for the better part of our conscious lives. The tragedy that we must deal with comes forcefully and unconstrained. When compared with other emotions, I would say this is probably the most powerful one. While we are learning the rules on earth, showered by love, sexual pleasure, and other positive or negative feelings, we do not invite death, wondering if we could do away with it.

With such thought comes questioning God. Why did he make us mortal? Why did he make us suffer tragedy and happiness? Why did he make us full of senses if those senses instead of helping us overcome grief make us feel and suffer even more acutely? How can we justify it all when we are not in a position to keep what was provided to us?

From this barrage of questions comes a whole gamut of features molding us into a definite and often-peculiar character. We rarely speak of death, suffering in silence. We work, we love, and we join together in families. Yet our loneliness stays with us, forcing us to learn that we are in this world always singled out when death comes either sooner or later.

We might try to live our lives as we damn well wish to, without apologizing or following rules invented by someone else. Could that somehow be a wise decision?

Our experience has shown that it is not. So what do we do then? Before I try to answer this, let me speak a little further of death. Doctors have distinguished different causes of death:

- Physiological death is death that comes when a body becomes so old and weak that it cannot tolerate the environment.
- Sudden death is death that comes to a visibly healthy individual.
- Death brought about by disease is another type of death.
- An accidental death is obviously the result of an unfortunate circumstance.

Having that many reasons to die, a question arises almost involuntarily: Is it scary to die? Most human beings will agree that it is a terrifying phenomenon. There is, of course, a small group of people who are brave and aren't afraid of it. Whether they are supported by their faith or have their level of thinking according to my classification does not matter much as long as this is the case for them.

I will speak to the people who cannot avoid being scared.

The majority of us agree that death is horrifying, no matter what causes it. Therefore it is no wonder that faith has become a large part of our lives. Because of it, people are able to survive. They create means for living and overall develop a tolerance for their surroundings. Just think about the hypothetical ability to eliminate faith from people's consciousness. Such a move would mean disaster for all humanity. An army of frightened people would be creating havoc, destroying all around them, and that would mean the end of the world.

For these people, the invention of faith brought relaxation and relief; it allowed them to believe in the immaterial spirit, paradise, and life after death. It helps them to stay afloat, and even though they most likely suffer like unbelievers do, they receive a boost of energy to struggle, empowered by faith and hope. The invention of families, societies, and like communities was most likely the result of that primal fear dictated by exposure to the real, magnificently cold world.

Considering the ability of death to influence human minds, one can comprehend why people wish to settle down. They become conservative. They surround themselves with pretty things, build houses, and try to stick to one place. All this is done almost subconsciously, and so humans might feel that they could last, if not forever, then for an unforeseeably long time.

Moving away from philosophical explanations of why death had to become a necessary part of our existence, I wish to say a few words about how to oppose it.

We cannot predict our future by using science or miracles. We cannot say much in advance when someone will die. What we can say is that all kinds of death are terrible. To me, and I suspect for many others, sudden death is the best one to endure. It is easy to take because you should not think about it in advance. You also don't feel its approach, and that is very important, or at least rewarding.

—

A few years ago, as I was walking on a street, I suddenly heard a gunshot. At the same moment, a small object hit me in the back and ricocheted to the pavement. I picked it up and discovered that it was a finishing nail from a nail gun. Above my head, a worker repairing a building had lost the nail while using the nail gun on a concrete wall. At that moment, the first thought that came into my mind was how easily death could have claimed its toll. I remember my sigh of relief. And only later—not much later, but still later—I thought how wonderful it is to be alive. I appreciated a Supreme Power or possibly destiny ensuring that I could continue enjoying life. I looked around and asked myself a question: How many people enjoy their life? Really enjoy? How many and how often do people think that life is an ephemeral gift?

When dying from an incurable disease or suffering from tremendous pain, a human being calls death upon himself. Of course, death is a terrible event, but even more horrible is the loneliness that comes with it, as is the case with intimate friends or close relatives of the deceased. That's why when someone close to you dies, you are the one who is punished.

Seneca taught us that we have to be prepared for death and that preparation should continue all throughout our lives. With all due respect to the ancient philosopher, I cannot accept his version because, as I mentioned earlier, death is a moment of cutting us from life permanently. It is a moment of depriving us of our consciousness. So why should we poison our lives by depressing thoughts? What good does it bring you if you do not enjoy your life fully? Why do you need to prepare yourself all your life for that one moment? Would it be so important for you to know that you had been prepared?

Death is inevitable, no matter what. But to me, even though Seneca teaches that each moment something is dying in us, we may contradict it with the knowledge that each day something new is born. That novelty or its expectation keeps us on our feet and allows us to live, work, and enjoy our lives.

Afterword
and
Final Conclusion

We are born into this life without much ability to choose. We are born into this life without much ability to grasp the details of all the events that happen around us and all the phenomena that exist and most likely will exist with some few moderations here and there. We have definite limitations in that regard that are dictated by a reason or two. One such reason is connected to our physical confinement that is called a life span, in which we reside but in which we manage to collect a great deal of experience. Would that experience be usable in future endeavors, it might be somewhat justified. But we don't know that for sure. None of us does. Yet our limited ability might be for the best. If we had a chance to accumulate actually more knowledge, we might not last as sane humans, even those few decades that were given us so far. Our perception of events would overwhelm us to the point that they would become intolerable, and we would incinerate ourselves. That is because we are thoroughly equipped with emotions. Thank God (?) we have learned how to manage our emotions most of the time through a feature that we call willpower. We even learned to wisely adjust its application under certain circumstances. Thus, from time to time, we may allow ourselves to loosen up, and that is when we are mostly prone to "commit" sin. But even if we knew how to constantly control our emotions, we don't know how to use them in the most efficient and beneficial way. We are not rational beings in the sense that our emotions could be applied optimally and proportionally. At the same time, our quest for knowledge is unfading and looks like it is an everlasting feature ingrained in us.

So who are we indeed? And what we are here for anyway? There is no simple answer to these questions. Even if we were able to come up with one answer or two, in reality, we continue to simply dwell in the dark. We might try to explain things to the best of our accumulated knowledge, but while doing that, we inadvertently imagine things. Though when confronted, we try to analyze the concocted events and present them as we knew what is happening all along, still, no matter what we do, we are guessing at best, from time to time discarding our previous theories into the oblivion, bringing yet another bundle of hopes. Often beaten and bruised nonetheless, we find ourselves rarely knocked down and capitulated. Fortunately, however, what we've learned to do is to try to cope with our emotions. And that's what I have been trying to show you in the pages of this book. I also tried to show you my way of appreciation of life. I tried to share with you my experience and tried to persuade you to accept it or, better yet, to develop your own and possibly a much better one. I hope you've acquired some useful advice.

Why do I say that?

Let me answer this question in this way. Even if I doubt that my sermon will produce positive results right away, something will be planted in to your brain. To make this last sentence even more provocative, I will hit you with *Why* I say it this one last time.

We are mostly stubborn. We rarely use someone's experience as our own. We go in circles, making the same mistakes that our *predecessors*, unfortunate peers, or parents did. Even when we admire someone's success after that person, bruised and beaten, gets on his own feet, never again falling back to the bottom of his misery. We refuse to follow the existing roads, seeking our own and applying different levels of vigor. Our progress on the evolutionary tree is specific and often limited to scientific achievements, without which we would be barely distinguished from primitive man. Our addictions are as bad as they are real, and we destroy ourselves without much ability to correct our mistakes once we have made them on our own.

We usually are not satisfied with our achievements and possessions. Hence we start wars, dislike our neighbors, and enjoy finding out about someone's dirty laundry.

We are torn by controversy. We are vengeful, and our minds are not easy to be calmed down and to undergo objective thinking and logic. So we're better off if we believe someone deserves it.

There are many more negative features that we possess, some of which were described in this book.

But this book's goal was not to make us all feel bad. This book would not be justified if it didn't provide a positive message or two.

While I could not promise you an eternal rose garden (nor can anyone else for that matter), we might try to answer questions, such as how morality may play a positive role in our well-being, how could our weak features be diminished and overpowered instead of becoming detrimental to our lives, how do we find the secret to being really happy without jeopardizing ourselves and our fellow travelers in life, and, finally, how should we conduct our lives so we will not intentionally, or rather unknowingly, destroy ourselves.

If you don't know at least some answers by now, you didn't read this book carefully. If so, read it again. I cannot promise it will help you, not because you are stupid but because it is very difficult to change your opinion if it is already crystallized. That is the way we are—as I said, stubborn and opinioned.

To finish this book on a positive note, though, let me say this. The knowledge I have accumulated has always kept me on my toes with the appreciation that there are enough things in this world to produce a positive mood. Knowing this is very important, as it signifies the simple reality that we are not easy to exhaust ourselves. Therefore, we keep going, and while we find that there is more than one road, and more than one thing to discover, we may and will progress.

As far as to our possible continuation of life after death is considered, we might never know the truth to it. It might be real but a hidden fact from us, or it might be just our hope and wild imagination. We might transform into another form, or we might come as different species, although not the way we were told or assume it occurs. Our knowledge had been substituted by imagination. Beyond that, no one among us exists who can say how it is indeed.

And with such conclusion, I wish to say good-bye and Good Luck. Be fruitful and not detrimental. Be happy but not at the expense of others. And most of all, remember, this home is home for us all.

ACKNOWLEDGMENT

Writing this book has been tightly connected to the disparate episodes, multiple events, and overall spectacular journey of my life. I consider myself lucky in being able to live in two, so drastically opposed in their political agendas and atmosphere countries as the former USSR and the USA are. Owing to this luck I had been able to harvest knowledge of people's longing for better life no matter which background one comes from.

Owing to my curiosity and profession, I also had a chance to encounter many different personalities from many different professional and cultural levels that enabled me to understand human yearning and hopes.

Still, I would not thank anyone individually for two reasons:

1. There are too many unknown and "non-specific" authorities I had an ability to approach and discuss the issues raised in this book with.
2. As it would become clear right from the start (through the reading of the topics underlined in the contents), the issues discussed in this book could be neither indifferent nor would reflect in the minds of people uniformly.

Thus this would also mean that while seeking the truth, I had not once got involved in quite heated debate with people whose prejudice would come from their position and conviction on one or another topic.

As I gradually grew in my position on a subject as well, I cannot deny the fact that my opinion could not be completely flawless no matter how objective I tried to be.

Yet, in my point of view, I mostly attempted to maintain that mentioned flawless approach.

Whether I was successful or not is not for me to decide.

I wish to thank those people who helped me with an expressing my thoughts in not easy for me English language, who strived to make it distinctly clear for an American reader, and whom I will not mention by name to be consistent with my approach to the matter.

Not to sound controversial still, I wish to thank my wife, Isabelle who is not the only exception from my rule of non-disclosure, but who good-naturedly agreed to let me work on my project as much and as long as I needed without complaining and grumbling about my selfish reclusion, devoting most of available time to writing this book.

Glossary

AGE OF ENLIGHTENMENT
Sometimes called the Age of Reason, a cultural movement of intellectuals in eighteenth-century Europe that emphasized scientific reasoning and the "emancipation of human mind" versus superstition and ignorance.

AHURA MAZDA
Or Lord Wisdom, the supreme god who, according to the beliefs of ancient Persians, was a benevolent and just god and who created the heavens and the earth for a just man.

ANTINOMIANISM
Considered to be the heretical doctrine that taught that Christians, specifically the Protestants, were exempt from the obligations of moral law. Such assertion was based upon the Protestant belief in justification through faith alone, without having to keep the commandments of the Mosaic Law.

APOCRYPHAL
Of doubtful authorship or authenticity.

APOSTLE
Often a religious messenger who is entrusted with a particular mission.

ARK OF THE COVENANT
According to the Hebrew Bible, the ark was a special chest in which the tablets of stone inscribed with the Ten Commandments given by God to Moses on Mount Sinai at the time of Exodus are.

ATOMIST
This term was specifically applied to the ancient Greek scientists—such as Democritus, Epicurus, and Lucretius—who had proposed that all matter consists of simple, minute, indivisible, and indestructible particles that are the basic components of the entire universe.

AVATAR
In Hinduism, this word literally means "descent" and in spiritual understanding refers to the descent of a deity to earth in a form of incarnation.

BAHÁ'Í
A fairly new (less than two centuries old) religion that is today globally recognized and considered to be the fastest-growing religion in the world.

BAPTISM
According to the description of the *Catholic Encyclopedia*, "baptism is the first sacrament that when instituted confers upon men the very beginnings of the spiritual life to transfer them from the state of enemies of God to the state of adoption, as sons of God."

BHAGAVAD GITA
A seven-hundred-verse Hindu scripture that is part of the ancient Sanskrit.

BLACK CODES
A body of laws enacted by Southern states right after the Civil War, in order to keep control over the freed slaves.

CANONIZATION
The process by which a list of documents or books, as for instance those in the Bible, was accepted as the body of authoritative scripture.

CARVAKAS
An atheistic materialism in ancient India.

CIRCUMCISION
The surgical removal of the foreskin from the penis, usually a procedure performed on baby males. A practice used in some religions for the expression of loyalty and devotion to God and God's laws.

CONFISCATION ACT
In 1861, during the U.S. Civil War, Congress passed a law permitting authorities to confiscate any property, the main purpose of which was directed to lawfully free the slaves held by the Confederate forces in the South.

CONTINENTAL CONGRESS
The Continental Congress was a convention of delegates from the original thirteen colonies that became the governing body of the United States. The First Congress took place in Philadelphia in 1774, with twelve colonies being represented.

COVENANT
In Jewish scripture, a solemn contract between God and the children of Israel, under which the Jewish people agreed to follow the special demands of their God.

CREATIONISTS
Those who believe in the creation of the universe and all the matter in it by a Supreme Being.

DOMINICAN
A term applied to the members of a Catholic religious order founded by Saint Dominic in thirteenth century in France. The Dominicans were also known as Black Friars in England or Jacobins in France.

EBIONITES

A Jewish Christian sect that appeared in the first century AD.

ECCLESIASTICS

Those persons who in the hierarchical steps of the church assumed a role of preacher, acting as *qoheleth* (the Hebrew word for preacher), ministers, or priests.

GENTILE

A person of non-Jewish faith.

GOSPELS

A genre of early Christian literature (the four canonical gospels are widely known examples) describing the life and teachings of Jesus from Nazareth.

GULAG

The forced labor camp system that convicted mostly political prisoners, which the former Soviet regime often used to silence the free speech of citizens who disagreed with the regime.

HERETIC

A person who chooses different beliefs from those established and accepted by the religious dogma of the community.

JIHAD

The religious duty of a Muslim believer to build a good Muslim society, one that is virtuous and moral, and that implies the divine duty of worshiping God, as well as defending Islam with force if necessary.

JUDGMENT DAY

Also known as Final Judgment, a day believed by religious people of many major denominations to be God's final assessment of humanity, during which all people are placed in heaven, purgatory, or hell corresponding to their deeds.

KARMA

In Hinduism, the concept that every act, whether good or bad, will cause an entire cycle of cause and effect and will return to the doer with equal impact.

LINGA-DEHA

In Sanskrit, the same as an astral body; along with the migrating Soul, it is the subtle body that is made up of nineteen principles, five organs of action, five organs of knowledge, five *pranas*, mind, intellect, *chitta* (the subconscious), and *ahankara* (or egoism). This subtle body moves toward heaven, where it gathers for itself a new physical body after the fruits of good karmas have been exhausted. Then it reincarnates on this earth plane.

MAHAYANA BUDDHISM

A separate school of Buddhism that emerged in the first century BC as a "great vehicle" for the enlightenment of all beings. Mahayana teaches that beings and phenomena have no intrinsic existence of their own and take identity only in relation to other beings and phenomena.

MOKSHA

In Indian philosophy and religion, liberation from the cycle of death and rebirth through the process known as *samsara*.

NATION OF ISLAM

A religious movement founded in Detroit, Michigan, by Wallace D. Fard Muhammad in July 1930. Today, it is an extreme organization that exists under the leadership of Minister Louis Farrakhan, who expresses mostly anti-Semitic views as well as blaming white America for the ills of black people.

NIRVANA

A central concept in Indian philosophy directed toward teaching its followers to how to become free from human sufferings.

OEDIPUS COMPLEX

A psychoanalytical theory developed by Dr. Sigmund Freud describing an early childhood desire to be sexually involved in with

—

the parent of opposite sex, including jealousy and anger toward the other parent.

PROTESTANTS

Broadly, a Christian not of a Catholic or Eastern church, a member of any of several church denominations denying papal authority of the pope and ascribing to Reformation principles.

RESURRECTION

A religious belief in the literal coming back to life of the biologically dead body of Christ.

RIG-VEDA

An ancient collection of over a thousand Vedic hymns, dedicated to the Hindu gods, and one of the most important foundations of the Hindu religion.

SABBATH

The seventh day of each week, always observed on Saturday, which is worshiped by the Jews as a religious ritual and is celebrated as a time of rest from Friday evening to Saturday evening.

SAMHITAS

A Sanskrit collection of four mantras of sacred devotional hymns, constituting one of the four Vedas.

SANSKRIT

An ancient Indo-Aryan language used for over two thousand years among educated people and the primary liturgical language of Hinduism, Jainism, and Buddhism.

SHIA

The second largest group of followers of Islam, believing that after death of their prophet, Muhammad, the leader should come from his family tree, presently Imams.

SHINTO

In Japanese culture, a creative preaching of the sacred spirits as their gods. These spirits usually take the form of things such as winds, rain, or rivers and mountains. Traditionally, Shinto worship in natural shrines such as groves of trees, mountains, or waterfalls.

SHOCK BRIGADES

A movement that arose in the mid-1920s when groups of advanced workers at industrial enterprises went to the countryside to create a competitive enthusiasm among not-so-enthusiastic working peasants.

SOVIET JEWRY

The Jews who were living in the Soviet Union between 1963 and 1990 and who strived to emigrate from the country of the regime that persecuted Jews only on the bases of their ethnicity and/or religious beliefs.

SPIRITUALISM

A belief system that spirits of the dead have the ability to communicate with those who are alive, thus confirming their existence.

SUNNI

The largest religious group out of two major denominations in Islam. Sunni believe that the leader of the Muslim people must be elected from those capable to lead, as opposed to the Shi'a belief that they must be relatives of the Prophet Muhammad or imams appointed by Muhammad or God.

SURA/SURAS

The division of the Qur'an into 114 chapters of different lengths.

SYNAGOGUE OF THE FREEDMEN

A term that applies to a few different Jewish communities. Some sources refer to the released Roman slaves who had their synagogue in Jerusalem. Others point to a Jewish community in Africa who dwelled in Libertum and thus were called "Libertines." Another

Greek-speaking synagogue in Jerusalem had parishioners who were Cyrenians and Alexandrians.

SYNOPTIC (GOSPELS)

The gospels of Matthew, Mark, and Luke in the New Testament, so referred to because they include many of the same stories and are similar in description and structure of events.

TABERNACLE

According to the Hebrew Bible, a dwelling place that contained the Ark of the Covenant that was divinely provided by God to Moses at the mountain Sinai during the time of Exodus.

TATAR YOKE

Established in the thirteenth century as a result of the rule of the Mongol-Tatar lords who invaded Russian lands and who systematically exploited the conquered country, mainly through the obligatory tax system.

TIRTHANKARA

In Jainism, a savior who has succeeded in crossing over life's stream of rebirth and has made a path for others to follow. The last one, called Mahavira, to appear in the sixth century BC.

TRANSMIGRATION

The process of a soul passing at death from one being or body into another.

TRINITARIAN/ TRINITY

A Christian doctrine that defines God as three divine persons: the Father, the Son (Jesus Christ), and the Holy Spirit.

UPANISHADS

The philosophical texts in early Hindu religion that form the core of Hindu teaching.

VEDANTIC

In Vedanta (Hindu) philosophy, as in Upanishads that teach that man who is having naturally divine nature at his birth has to transform his human nature into that divine that is hidden within him.

VEDAS

In Sanskrit, it literally means "knowledge" and is a large body of texts containing sacred Hindu concepts.

ZARATHUSTRA, ZOROASTER

The founder of Zoroastrian faith, an Iranian prophet who presumably lived in 550 BC.

ZEN BUDDHISM

While the word *Zen* means meditation, Zen Buddhism refers to the enlightenment that comes through the profound realization of one being enlightened, which comes with proper meditation.

BIBLIOGRAPHY

Reference Texts

Abdu'l-Bahá. *Foundations of World Unity.* Wilmette, Illinois: Baháí Publishing Trust, 1945.

The American Heritage Dictionary. Second College Edition. Boston, Massachusetts: Houghton Mifflin, 1982.

Bahá ú Íláh. *Gleanings from the Writings of Bahá ú Íláh.* Wilmette, Illinois: Baháí Publishing Trust, 1976.

Bhagavad Gita. London, England: Penguin Books Ltd., 1962.

Buddhist Scriptures. London, England: Penguin Books Ltd., 1959.

Collier's Encyclopedia, vol. 19. New York: Crowell-Collier Educational Corporation, 1972.

Clark, Andrew G. "Human, Chimp DNA Differences." *Science* (December 12, 2003).

Cochran, Gregory. "Natural History of Ashkenazi Intelligence." *Journal of Biosocial Science* (2005).

Bukkyo Dendo Kyokai (Society for the Promotion of Buddhism). *The Teaching of Buddha.*
Tokyo: Kosaido, 2004.

Donahue, Phil. *The Human Animal.* New York: Simon and Schuster, 1986.

Entine, Jon. *Abraham's Children: Race, Identity, and the DNA of the Chosen People.* New York: Grand Central Publishing, 2007.

Ford, Henry. *The International Jew.* Published by the author, 1920s.

Freud, Sigmund. Collected Papers. The Theme Of The Three Caskets. (1913). *The Ego and the Id.* Page 250. Volume IV. Published by Hogarth Press, 1950.

Gish, Duane. *Evolution: The Challenge of the Fossil Record.* Creation-Life Publishers, 1985.

Gould, Stephen Jay. "Introduction." *Evolution: The Triumph of an Idea* by Carl Zimmer. New York: Harper, 2001.

Gottfredson, Linda et al. "Mainstream Science on Intelligence." Public statement in the *Wall Street Journal* (December 13, 1994).

Guth, Alan H. "Inflationary Universe: A Possible Solution to the Horizon and Flatness Problems." *Physical Review D* vol. 23, issue 2 (January 15, 1981).

Haeri, Shaykh. *The Elements of Islam.* Rockport, Massachusetts: Element Books Ltd., 1993.

Hawking, Stephen and Leonard Mlodinow. *A Briefer History of Time.* New York: Bantam, 2005.

Horney, Karen. *Feminine Psychology.* New York: Norton, 1922.

—

Jung, Carl. *Modern Man in Search of a Soul.* New York: Harvest/HBJ, 1933.

Lemaître, Georges. "Un Univers Homogène de Masse Constante et de Rayon Croissant Rendant Compte de la Vitesse Radiale des Nébuleuses Extragalactiques." *Annales de la Societe Scientifique de Bruxelles* (1927).

Linnaeus, Carolus. *Systema Naturae.* Published by the author, 1767.

Lovejoy, C. Owen. "Reexamining Human Origins in Light of *Ardipithecus Ramidus.*" *Science* vol. 326, no. 5949 (October 2, 2009): 64-86.

Mayr, Ernst Walter. "Introduction." *On the Origin of Species* by Charles Darwin. Cambridge, Massachusetts: Harvard University Press, 2003.
What Evolution Is. New York: Basic Books, 2001.

Momen, Moojan. *Hinduism and the Baha'i Faith.* Oxford: George Ronald Publisher Ltd., 1990.

Need, Anna C. and Dalian Kasperaviciute, Elizabeth T. Cirulli, and David B. Goldstein. "A Genome-Wide Genetic Signature of Jewish Ancestry Perfectly Separates Individuals with and without Full Jewish Ancestry in a Large Random Sample of European Americans." *Genome Biology* (Duke University Center for Human Genome Variation) vol. 10 (January 22, 2009).

Olson, Steve. *Mapping Human History.* New York: Mariner Books, 2003.

Poplawski, Nikodem. "Radial Motion into an Einstein-Rosen Bridge." *Physics Letters* vol. 687, issues 2-3 (April 2010): 110-113.

Rachkovsky, Pyotr Ivanovich. "The Protocols of the Elders of Zion." *Znamya* (1903).

Rig-Veda. Forgotten Books, 2008.

Segev, Tom. *One Palestine, Complete: Jews and Arabs Under the British Mandate*. Translated by Haim Watzman. New York: Metropolitan Books, 2000.

Stein, Joel. "How Jewish Is Hollywood?" *Los Angeles Times* (December 19, 2008).

Tsien, Joe. "Genetic Enhancement of Learning and Memory in Mice." *Nature* 401 (September 1999): 63-69.

The Upanishads. London, England: Penguin Books Ltd., 1965.

United States Equal Employment Opportunity Commission. Policy Guidance on Current Issues of Sexual Harassment 29 C.F.R. § 1604.11 (1980).

United States Office of Management and Budget and the United States Justice Department. "Standards for the Classification of Federal Data on Race and Ethnicity." *Federal Register* (August 28, 1995).

Webster's International Dictionary. Springfield, Massachusetts: Merriam-Webster, 1981.

White, Michael. "The Ambitious Ancestors of Whales." *Adaptive Complexity* (February 2009).

Zimmer, Carl. *Evolution: The Triumph of an Idea*. New York: Harper Perennial, 2002.

Online Sources

GodlessGeeks. http://www.godlessgeeks.com (accessed December 10, 2011).

Kean, M. "The Difference between Race and Culture." Progressive Scholar. http://progressivescholar.wordpress.com/2010/05/13/race-and-culture/ (accessed May 13, 2010).

Khan, Muhammad Muhsin and Muhammad Taqi-ud-Din Al-Hilali, translators. *The Noble Quran.* Online: Dar-us-salam Publications. http://www.dar-us-salam.com/TheNobleQuran/index.html.

Owen, James. "Did Discrimination Enhance Intelligence of Jews?" *National Geographic News.* http://isteve.blogspot.com/2005/07/national-geographic-on-iq-evolution.html (accessed July 18, 2005).

Roach, John. "New Proof Unknown 'Structures' Tug at Our Universe." *National Geographic News.* http://news.nationalgeographic.com/news/2010/03/100322-dark-flow-matter-outside-universe-multiverse/ (accessed March 22, 2010).

Sato, Rebecca. "Is Dark Matter and Dark Energy the Same Thing?" The Daily Galaxy—Great Discoveries Channel. http://www.dailygalaxy.com/my_weblog/2009/02/could-dark-matt.html (accessed February 5, 2009).

Segelen, Roger. "DNA Analysis Reveals Striking Differences between Humans and Chimps." Emptysuit. http://www.news.cornell.edu/Chronicle/04/2.12.04/human_chimp_DNA.html.

Than, Ker. "Every Black Hole Contains Another Universe?" *National Geographic News.* http://news.nationalgeographic.com/news/2010/04/100409-black-holes-alternate-universe-multiverse-einstein-wormholes (accessed April 9, 2010).

INDEX

A

Aaron, 114, 146

Abbasids, 161

Abd al-Malik, 164

Abdu'l-Bahá, 178-79

Abel, 98-99

Abijah, 146

abnormality, 336, 350, 371

abortion, 355-58

Abraham, 108, 111, 113, 137, 147-48, 156, 163, 168, 432-33, 472, 530

absorb, 20, 27, 255, 260

Abu Bakr, 160

Abu Lahab, 168

abuse, 359, 391-92, 472, 504-5

Abu Talib, 168

Abyssinia, 169

acellular structures, 202

acquaintances, 10, 16

acronym, 104

Acts of Paul, 121

Adam (first man), 97-100, 132-33, 158, 230, 325-26

adaptation, 43, 63, 67, 191, 209, 212-13, 215-16, 220, 223, 231, 292, 318, 323, 326

addiction, 394, 396, 398, 514

Aden, 440

adenine, 65, 226, 324

adenosine triphosphate (ATP), 66

Adoptionists, 34

advocacy, 13

affiliation, 16, 128, 339, 344, 348, 473, 482

affirmation, 40

Afghanistan, 332

Africa, 94, 159, 214-15, 217-18, 324-25, 345, 469, 473, 475, 478, 482, 490, 492-93, 495, 525

African, 157, 213, 218, 325, 342, 407, 438, 468, 470-71, 473-77, 479-81, 488, 490, 492-96

African Americans, 468, 473-77, 479-81, 496

African slaves, 342, 470-71, 488

afterlife, 36, 72, 105, 147

Age of Enlightenment, 335

agnostics, 11, 35, 51, 72, 153, 239, 398

agra mainyu, 91
agrarian development, 343
Ahriman, 91
Ahura Mazda, 17, 39, 90-91
airplane, 30
akarma, 80
Akkad, 110, 427
alcohol, 88, 303, 381, 390-91, 394,
    396, 411, 436
Alexander the Great, 91, 428
Alexandria, 122, 124, 126, 137, 265
Algeria, 449
Ali, 160-61
Allah, 17, 158-59, 161, 163, 166-68,
    171, 429, 431, 433, 435, 469
allegiance, 170, 432
allotted, 47, 443, 448
al-Sharif, Haram, 448
Amalekites, 109
ambiguity, 25, 309, 332
ambivalent entity, 238
America. *See* United States of America
American English, 13, 367
American Enterprise Institute (AEI),
    407
American Heritage Dictionary, 26, 81,
    220, 321, 331, 410, 412, 460, 529
American Revolutionary War, 340
Americans, 13-14, 159, 317, 344-46,
    349, 366, 371, 389, 406, 418,
    468, 473-77, 479-81, 496, 531
American society, 13, 144, 339,
    342-43, 351, 371
Americas, the, 159, 471, 488, 493
amino acids, 44, 67, 156, 188-89, 196,
    222-24
Anatolia, 428

ancestors, 10, 43, 94, 102, 111, 157,
    188, 190, 192, 194-95, 198-99,
    213, 326, 430, 443
Ancient Egypt, 156
ancient Egyptians, 157, 469, 484
ancient tribes, 155
Anderson, Carl, 245
angels, 58, 364
animals, 26, 72, 79, 92, 107, 192-93,
    195-96, 199-200, 206-7, 209-11,
    214-17, 221, 278-79, 322-23,
    359-60
  abuse of, 359
  domesticated, 28, 204, 207, 327, 359
  hoofed, 191-93
*Annales de la Societe Scientifique de
    Bruxelles*, 246, 531
anointed, 118-19, 130, 150
anthology, 75
antimatter, 241-45, 249, 252, 271
Antimatter (Close), 243
antinomianism, 34
antiparticles, 242-45, 271
antiprotons, 242-43
Antiquities of the Jews (Josephus), 126
anything about, 133, 139, 240
apocalypse, 152
apocryphal, 121, 127, 139
Apocryphal Acts, 121
apostles, 118, 120-21, 123, 127-28,
    136-37, 149, 421
Apostolic Fathers, 123
apostolic teachings, 123
Aquinas. *See* Thomas Aquinas, Saint
Arabian Peninsula, 154-56, 426, 430,
    432, 494
Arabized Arabs, 157
Arab Jews, 431

Arab League, 447

Arab Muslims, 92, 160, 164, 170, 426, 434

Arab-Palestinian community, 446

Arab people, 154, 156-58, 168, 426, 430, 440-41, 443

Arabs, 156-57, 159, 162-63, 165, 426-27, 429-30, 437-38, 440-48, 450-51, 494, 532

Aramaic, 111, 122, 159

Arameans, 156, 429

archaea, 188, 200-202

archaeological, 26, 72, 94, 102, 125, 156, 207, 212, 320, 430

documentation, 26

excavations, 72

findings, 94, 102, 156, 207, 320, 430

period, 94

site, 125

team, 212

Ardipithecus ramidus, 94, 212-13

Argentina, 332, 488

Aristarchus, 30

Aristotle, 39

Arius, 124-25

Arjuna, 73

Ark of the Covenant, 138, 163, 526

artifacts, 71, 115, 156

artificial, 15, 35, 206, 245, 317, 388, 391, 472

Aryan, 71, 414

Asia, 128, 159, 345, 465

Assyria, 402, 405, 428-29, 470

Assyrians, 427-30

Athanasius, Saint, 124

Atharva Veda, 75

atheists, 9-10, 35-37, 54, 88, 368-69

atman, 38, 73-74, 77-79, 84-86

atomist, 39

atoms, 41, 43-45, 59, 63, 68, 177, 189, 222, 239-45, 267-68, 271-72, 274-75

Australia, 61

Australian aborigines, 31

avatars, 72-73, 76, 82, 88, 90

awakened, 84

B

Babel, 101

Báb'í Faith, 173-74

Babylonia, 402, 405, 427-29

Babylonians, 164, 427, 429-30

bacteria, 61, 188, 199-202, 225-26, 326

Badasht, 173

bad luck, 80, 508

baggage, 46, 508

Bahá'í Faith, 17, 35, 92, 103, 115, 168, 173-74, 178

Bahá'u'lláh, 60, 168, 173-78, 180

baleen whales, 191

Balfour Declaration, 441-42

balsamic potion, 19

baptism, 122, 126, 132-33

Bar Kokhba revolt, 445

Battle of Badr, 432

Battle of Karbala, 161

Battle of Khaybar, 170

Battles of Lexington and Concord, 340

begotten, 34, 123, 125

behavior, human, 33, 210, 239, 297, 320, 501

Behe, Michael, 204

beliefs, 10, 15, 26-27, 32, 34-35, 40, 68, 73, 79, 104, 124-25, 130, 136, 419-20, 434-35 benevolence, 60, 91, 412

Bhagavad Gita, 38, 73, 77-78, 80, 84, 86, 254, 520, 529

Bible, 94-95, 98-100, 102-8, 110-17, 119-20, 125, 138-40, 149, 156-57, 163, 401-4, 421, 429-30, 483-84, 520-21

bicarbonate ion, 62

big bang theory, 247-48, 277

Big Crunch, 221, 256, 258, 260, 271

bilayer, 63

Bilhah, 109

biological clock, 47

bipedal, 44, 212, 215, 323

black holes, 240, 254-55, 260, 263, 273

blacks, 296, 344, 347, 407-8, 468-70, 472-78, 480-85, 488-90, 492, 496-97

Black Stone of the Kaaba, 161

blasphemy, 34

blended, 13

Bliss Body, 88

blood flows, 62

body, 38-46, 62, 64, 66-67, 73, 77-79, 90-91, 97, 119, 143, 204, 227, 394-95, 520-21, 523-24

  action, 73

  celestial, 135

  corruptible, 132, 134

  human, 73

  spiritual, 73, 135

  subtle, 78

Bohr, Niels, 246

Bolsheviks, 9, 440, 455-59

Bonaparte, Napoleon, 439

bone marrow, 63

bonobos, 43, 213-14

Book of Isaiah, 103, 150

Book of Revelation, 121

borders, 107, 237, 345, 440, 442, 447, 449-50, 462

Borochov, Ber, 445

bosons, 243, 271

Brahma, 76, 89, 254

Brahmin priests, 88

Brahmins, 72, 84

brain, human, 41, 300, 395, 471

branded, 34

bread, consecrated, 140

brethren, 135, 143, 145, 421

Britain, 197, 320, 340, 342, 416, 438-42, 493-94, 521, 529, 532

British Mandate, 165, 442-43, 446-48, 532

Brunet, Michel, 94

Buddha, 60, 74, 76, 82-85, 87-89, 126, 141, 180, 422, 530

Buddhi, 77

Buddhism, 35, 71, 74-75, 79, 83-86, 88-90, 523-24, 527, 530

Buffon, Georges, 196

building blocks, 41, 67, 188-89

Bureau of Labor Statistics, 347

C

Cain, 98-99

Caliphate, 437

Caliph Umar, 164

Canaan, 106-8, 112, 115, 403-5, 429, 443

Canaanites, 107, 429

capillaries, 63

carbohydrates, 63, 67, 189

carbon, 41, 63, 67, 189, 200-201, 223, 233, 241

carbonic anhydrase, 62
carnivores, 101
Carvaka, 74, 521
Cary, Phillip, 135
caste system, 72, 84
cataclysm, 100, 102, 230
catalyze, 62
Catholic Church, 40, 139
Catholic doctrines, 124, 139
Catholic Encyclopedia, 26, 139, 520
cells, 41, 61-66, 198, 200, 202, 211,
    224-26, 324, 326
  bacterial, 225
  germ, 226
  host, 202, 372
  sperm, 66-67, 226, 357
Celsius, 201
centralized worship, 35
Chaisson, Eric J., 261
Chambers, George, 203
charismatic leaders, 152
chemicals, 42, 59, 62, 291, 395
cherubim, 98
children of Lot, 109
chimpanzees, 43-44, 211, 213-14, 326
China, 332, 334, 339, 470, 488, 495
Chomsky, Noam, 336-37
chosen people, 104, 106, 109, 112,
    115, 530
Christakos, 118
Christendom, 125
Christian communion, 126
Christianity, 11, 17, 34-35, 115,
    118-20, 122-24, 128-29, 135,
    148-49, 151, 155, 158, 421-22,
    452, 487
Christians, 16-17, 34, 50, 118-22,
    124-27, 133, 148, 151, 153, 155,

164-66, 168, 170-71, 421-23,
    431-32
Christian scientists, 186
chromosomes, 43, 66-67, 211, 226,
    292, 318
churches, 11, 35, 54, 126, 135, 139,
    165, 358, 466, 522
Church Fathers, 34, 123-24, 136
circumcision, 123, 404, 421, 521
circumcision group, 34
clan, 83
Clark, Andrew G., 43
classical physics, 265
  law of gravity, 233, 265
  laws of electromagnetism, 265
  laws of motion, 265-66
  laws of thermodynamics, 265-66
classification, 306-7, 314, 532
Clement of Rome, 123
Clinton, Hillary Rodham, 302
Close, Frank, 243
cognition, 50, 389
coherent, 53
comets, 61
common ancestor, 43, 185, 187-88,
    191, 193, 195, 198, 232, 291,
    320, 322, 326
Common Era, 127, 157
communism, 9, 27
communist country, 27
competitiveness, 293-94, 413
conduct, 45, 61, 63, 77, 90, 119, 126,
    133, 158, 189, 232, 371, 407-9,
    452-53, 507-8
conflation, 13, 453
Confucianism, 35
Congo, 214, 471, 488, 494-95
conscience, 133, 308

Constantine (emperor), 124-25
Constantinople, 125, 431, 439-40
construes, 28
conundrums, 37, 199, 232
conversely, 31
converts, 34, 92, 223
Copernicus, Nicolaus, 30, 265
Coptic Gospel of Thomas, 121
copy, 19, 202, 226, 318-19
Corinthians, 130, 132-35
cosmic microwave background (CMB), 247-48, 261
cosmic rays, 240, 243-44, 272
cosmic structures, 31, 280
cosmos, 15, 30-31, 89, 196, 237-40, 251, 264, 279, 300, 376
Council of Nicaea, 122, 124-25
covenant, 56, 104, 117, 138, 163, 178-79, 404, 421, 425, 520-21, 526
    tangible, 178
creationists, 32, 186, 194, 220, 229-31, 521
Crick, Francis, 49, 324
crime, 110, 314, 372, 479
Cronin, James, 244
Crusades, 165, 171
cubits, 100
culprit, 258, 508
cultural roots, 452, 508
cultures, 29, 35, 126, 151, 159, 180, 191, 279, 317-20, 331, 337-38, 352, 424, 427, 434
Cuvier, Georges, 196, 232
cycles, 47, 77-78, 80, 82, 250, 254, 258, 260, 267, 523
cytoplasm, 62, 225
cytosine, 65, 226, 324

D

daily ritual bath, 126
damage, 97-98, 101, 201, 204
dampened, 15
Darius, 92
dark energy, 240, 252-54, 258-59, 272, 274, 533
dark matter, 240, 252-54, 259, 272, 275, 533
Darwin, Charles, 53, 195, 197, 203, 210, 291, 432, 503, 531
Darwin, Erasmus, 197
David (king), 137-38, 140, 151, 531
Dawkins, Richard, 36, 51, 238
Dayan, Moshe, 448
Dead Sea, 126
Dead Sea Scrolls, 125
death, 28, 34, 72-74, 76, 79-82, 84, 91, 125, 128, 132, 260, 279, 377, 509-12, 515
death phenomenon, 278, 509
Decalogue, 105
decoding, 49
decree, 34, 463
degree, 60, 124, 177, 189, 266, 303, 307, 310, 352, 360, 381-82, 388, 392, 394, 483
deha, 73
dehin, 73, 78, 80
dematerialize, 18
demigod, 17
demise, 34-35, 47, 140, 194, 278, 334, 337, 385, 427, 509
democracy, 331-32, 424, 436
demography, 35
denominations, 15, 40, 46, 118, 123-24, 134, 151, 422, 435

deoxyribonucleic acid (DNA), 43, 49, 65, 67, 157, 185, 190, 196, 202-3, 205, 222-26, 324, 327, 529-30, 533

Descartes, René, 39

Descent of Man, The (Darwin), 203

Deuteronomy, 104, 113-14

devas, 76

Dhammakaya Movement, 84

Dhimmi, 170

diametrically opposing approach, 334

Didymus, 121

Dinah, 109

Dirac, Paul, 242, 245

disciples, 83, 121, 124, 140-42, 145, 147-48

Discover, 187

disparate nature, 32

divine emanations, 116

divine intervention, 35

divine powers, 149

divinity, 17, 373, 375, 420, 423, 434

doctrines, 15, 34, 39-40, 72, 74, 81, 89, 119, 122, 135, 139, 151, 178, 279, 421

documentation, 26, 45, 155

dogma, 18, 29, 139, 179, 324

dogs, 192, 206-7, 291, 319, 359, 444

Dome of the Rock, 162-65, 448

Dominicans, 490-91, 521

Donahue, Phil, 300, 372, 388

Dostoyevsky, Dmitry, 414

drugs, 303, 381, 390, 394-98

Du Bois , W. E. B., 476

E

earthquakes, 219, 229

Eastern Europe, 402, 405-7, 453

Ebionites, 34, 122-23, 151

ecclesiastics, 104, 522

economy, 424, 458, 463, 491, 495

Edomites, 156

education, 9, 79, 166, 175-76, 286, 305, 307, 342, 345, 347, 358, 370, 380-81, 387-89, 391

ego, 78, 84, 304, 308, 310, 314, 356, 504, 508, 530

Egypt, 107-14, 121, 124, 128, 156, 405, 430, 439, 441, 447-50, 469-70, 483-84

Egyptian papyrus, 103

Egyptians, 107, 110-11, 157, 279, 439, 469, 484

Einstein, Albert, 246, 252, 265

Eisner, Michael, 418

Eldredge, Niles, 227, 322

electrolytes, 62

electrons, 222, 226, 241-43, 245, 260-61, 264, 267-68, 271-74

Elements of Islam, The (Haeri), 158-59, 530

Eliezer, 157

Elijah, 144-45, 149, 175

elucidation, 14, 27

eluded, 33

embracing, 11

emissaries, 27, 136

Emlen, Stephen, 209

emotions, 59, 87, 89, 180, 294-95, 300, 303, 306, 335, 375, 380, 410, 501, 505, 513-14

human, 306, 501, 504

empirically, 38, 40

Encyclopedia Judaica, 164

endurance, 175, 294, 335-36, 473, 476, 504

energy, 42, 47, 62, 66, 189, 224, 226, 243, 245, 250-51, 254, 262, 266-67, 272, 274

England. *See* Britain

enigma, 61, 188, 241, 402

Enki, 101

enlightenment, 74, 83-84, 88, 335, 519, 523, 527

Entente Powers, 440

Entine, Jon, 407

entities, 29, 38, 40, 44, 46, 57, 188, 245, 254, 281, 332

entropy, 64, 221, 260, 266-67

environment, 9, 44, 62-63, 67, 101, 191, 200-201, 211, 213-19, 292-94, 296-97, 318-20, 327, 332-33, 378-79

enzymes, 41, 44, 61-63, 66, 200, 222-23, 225

ephemeral, 74, 375-76, 512

Epic of Gilgamesh, 101

Epicurus, 39, 520

epistemology, 16

epistles, 120-21, 128, 130

epoch, 278, 462

Era of Judaism, 106

erythrocytes, 62

Esau, 108-9

eschatology, 126

esoteric, 116, 119

establishing society, 343

establishment, 19, 162, 231, 298, 304, 347, 406, 452, 454, 456

eternal torture, 48

ethnic groups, 138, 321, 327, 333, 347, 366, 399, 402, 406, 411, 413-14, 416, 480, 489, 493

ethnicity, 156, 320-21, 332-33, 347, 465, 482, 490-91, 525, 532

Eucharist, 122, 126

eukaryotes, 61, 200

Euler, Leonhard, 40

Eurasian, 157

Europe, 159, 335, 402, 405-8, 414, 438, 445, 452-53, 488, 493, 519

Eve (first woman), 98-99, 133, 188, 325-26

evil, 76, 79, 81, 83-84, 90-92, 96-97, 112, 131, 142, 318, 404, 469

evolution, 15, 40, 53, 58, 185-87, 189-92, 196-99, 201-5, 207-9, 213, 215-23, 230-32, 291-92, 322, 530-32

evolutionary bottom-up cell development, 63

evolutionary changes, 119, 187, 196-97, 202

evolutionists, 185, 187, 193, 202, 213, 227, 231, 281, 316, 326-27

Evolution: The Triumph of an Idea (Zimmer), 187, 190, 207, 530, 532

excuses for inaction, 348

Exodus, 105, 111, 114, 520, 526

experiments, 50, 186-87, 189, 197, 206, 232, 239, 241, 244-45, 252, 265-66, 278, 350, 356, 384

exploded, 238, 243, 249, 447

extrapolates, 40

extrapolating, 29, 347

Ezra, 404

F

faculty, 45, 61, 307, 387

Fahrenheit, 56

faith, 34, 36-37, 72-73, 92, 118,
   129-31, 135-36, 153-55, 158-59,
   166-67, 169-71, 420, 422,
   431-34, 511
  monotheistic, 432
false dichotomy, 60
Faravahar, 91
Farrakhan, Louis, 469, 476, 482, 523
father of mankind, 72
Federal Office of Management and
   Budget (FOMB), 321
Ferraro, Geraldine, 301
fertile offspring, 44
First Temple, 163
Fitch, Val, 244
flaming sword, 98
Flower, William, 193
Flugel, J. C., 297
Fossil, 530
fossil record, 190, 192, 194, 530
fossils, 61, 94, 192-93, 195, 207, 218,
   232
Four Noble Truths, 85
France, 320, 332, 340, 416, 438, 440,
   491, 521
freedom, 332, 340, 342-43, 346,
   348-49, 370-71, 389-90, 454,
   471-72
Freud, Anna, 303
Freud, Sigmund, 297, 309, 379, 523
fringe extremists, violent, 155
Fromm, Erich, 297
fungi, 196

G

Gabriel (angel), 169
Galapagos Island, 195, 231

Galatians, 34
galaxies, 29-31, 46, 230, 239-41, 246,
   248-50, 253-62, 264, 273, 280,
   369-70, 533
Gamow, George, 247
Garden of Eden, 96, 98
Gautama Buddha. *See* Buddha
Gaza Strip, 442, 448-50
Gebal, 103
Geisler, Jonathan, 195
generalization, 45, 299, 469, 476
general relativity, theory of, 246,
   251-52, 265, 273-74
generations, 75, 100, 105, 108-9,
   117, 137, 160, 198, 205-6, 208,
   213-14, 219, 324-25, 411, 501
genes, 9, 43-44, 65-67, 189, 214, 223,
   226, 291-93, 296, 304, 311,
   318-19, 324, 388, 412
genesis, 95-96, 98-103, 107-8, 185,
   197, 229-30
genetically determined diseases, 49
genetic drift, 186, 198, 323
genetic tools, 204
genome, 49, 205, 211, 407, 531
genotype, 61, 291-92, 294, 325
gentiles, 129, 135, 406, 408, 416, 418,
   421-24, 483
Germany, 325, 332, 405, 438-39,
   455-56, 471, 486
Gershom, 157
ghosts, 35
Gingerich, Philip D., 192
Ginzberg, Asher, 445
Gish, Duane, 194
glorified body, 135
gluons, 241, 271, 273, 275
Gnostic, 121-22

God
  great spirit of, 50
  kingdom of, 40, 133, 135, 141, 152
God, Manifestation of, 175
God Delusion, The (Dawkins), 36,
    51-54, 56
godlike attributes, 53
Godunov, Tsar Boris, 453
Gospel of Peter, 121, 125
Gospel of Philip, 121
gospels, 120-21, 125, 127, 129, 131,
    137-39, 141, 144, 146-48, 150,
    522, 526
Gould, Stephen Jay, 187, 190-91, 215,
    227, 322, 530
government, 164, 331-32, 334-35, 337,
    341, 343, 345-46, 349, 364, 370,
    411-12, 436, 456-58, 463-66,
    494-95
  federal, 341-43
grace, 100, 129, 131, 135, 419
Grand Unified Theory (GUT), 264, 268
grave, 10, 53, 131, 292, 360, 378, 423
gravitational pull, 250, 253, 257
gravity, 251-53, 255, 271, 273-75, 314,
    319, 323
Greater Iran, 93
Great Flood, 101
Great Spirit, 31
Greece, 39, 103, 375, 428, 452
Greenland, 61
Groves, Colin, 322
guanine, 65, 226, 324
Gujarat, 93
Guth, Alan, 250

H

Hadiths, 160-61, 433-35, 437
Haeri, Shaykh Fadhlalla, 158
Hagar, 156
hallucinations, 58
Ham, 101-2
Hamilton, Alexander, 342
Hanukah, 116
Haran, 106-8, 403
Harappa, 71
Harmsworth, Alfred Charles William,
    442
Harris, Sam, 36, 238
Hazor, 102
heaven, 39-40, 72, 78, 86, 90, 92,
    95, 129-31, 134, 142, 144, 163,
    176-77, 519, 522-23
Hebrew Bible, 95, 98, 102-6, 108,
    110-11, 116-17, 123, 154, 157,
    163, 401-2, 404, 421, 430, 443
Hebrews, 16, 34, 101-3, 105-6, 108-15,
    117, 120, 123, 130, 136, 150,
    401-2, 404-5, 421-22, 483-84
Hebrew tribes, 109, 111, 128
helix, 65, 224
Hellenic Jew, 128
hemoglobin, 62
hereditary traits, 65, 226
heredity, 66, 196, 203, 226, 297, 319,
    387-88
heretics, 34, 123, 522
Herod (king of Judea), 120, 139, 146
Herzl, Theodor, 445
heterodox, 75
heterosexuals, 351-54
hexadecimal, 101
hieroglyphic writings, 157

Hinduism, 35, 38, 71-77, 79, 81-82, 84, 86, 88, 90, 92, 117, 186, 520, 523-24, 531
Hindus, 17, 71-72, 76, 79-81, 279, 423
Hindu trinity, 76
history, 25, 52, 115, 117, 153-54, 156, 316-17, 401-2, 405, 422-23, 428, 460-61, 469-70, 492, 529-31
  evolutionary, 195, 214
Hitchens, Christopher, 36
holy cow, 72
Holy House, The, 163
Holy Spirit, 124, 137-39, 466, 526
homeostasis, 63
Homer, 39
hominid genus, 94
hominids, 95, 213, 215
homogeneity, 247, 249, 251, 333
homosexuality, 351
Horeb, Mount, 105, 114
Horney, Karen, 297
Hoyle, Fred, 247
Hubble, Edwin, 228, 247, 253
hubris, 32
human, 529-31
  body, 41-42, 50, 64, 67, 134, 202, 225, 280, 299, 395
  history, 94, 102, 316, 325, 494, 531
  nature, 35, 117, 156, 160, 168, 192, 283, 287-88, 332, 343, 371, 381, 434, 460, 479
Human Animal, The (Donahue), 300, 388
humankind, 76, 173, 176, 178-80, 410, 435, 473
humans, 16-18, 28, 33, 42-44, 199-203, 206-7, 210-12, 214-17, 286, 321-23, 334-35, 359-60, 381, 501, 503-4
hydrogen, 41, 63, 67, 189, 222-23, 233, 241, 272, 280
hydrophilic, 63
hydrophobic molecules, 63

I

ibn Ali, Hussein, 441
Iger, Robert, 418
Ignatius of Antioch, 123
ill-perceived actions, 508
Immaculate Conception, 139
immortal, 38, 40, 77-78
impetus, 44, 196, 375
inadvertently, 504, 507, 514
inanimate elements, 27, 75
incantations, 27, 75
incarnate, 134
incarnated, 50, 73, 90, 119-20, 186
inconceivable, 207
incongruent, 30, 145, 340
incorporeal, 31
incumbent, 26
India, 72, 75, 82, 92-93, 332, 339, 345, 470, 495, 521
indigenous people, 31, 301, 460, 488, 492-93
indisputable paradise, 27
Indus, 71-72
Indus River Valley, 71
infectious agent, 202
Inflationary universe, 530
inhabitants, 426, 429, 443, 446, 493, 503
inhibitory substances, 66
insurmountable, 17

intellect, 39, 44-45, 407, 418, 523
intelligence, 32, 65, 209, 222, 295-96,
        318, 407, 529-30, 533
    higher, 44, 209
intelligent design, 53, 57, 277
intelligent designer, 217
intelligentsia, 455-56, 465
intercourse, 17
interrelated systems, 29
intricate minutiae, 18
introverted outcast, 508
invigorated, 14
invokes, 53
Iran, 90, 92-93, 175, 428
Iraq, 106, 175, 427-28, 440
Iron Curtain, 461
Irreducible complexity, 56
irreducibly complex, 204-5
Isaac, 108-9, 113, 137, 147, 163, 233,
        245, 252, 265, 403
Isaiah, 103, 150
Ishmaelites, 157, 426
Islam, 35, 90-92, 103, 115, 154-56,
        158-59, 162, 164, 168-71, 173,
        186, 426, 430-31, 433-35, 524-25
Islamic traditions, 17, 157
Israel, 109-13, 140, 151, 164-65, 174,
        404-5, 415, 437, 445, 447-51, 521
Israelis, 165, 442, 447-51
Israelite nation, 108
Israelites, 109, 113, 149, 405, 443,
        447-48, 450
Italy, 39, 332, 443

J

Jabotinsky, Ze'ev, 445
Jackson, Jesse, 476

Jacob, 108-9, 113, 137, 149, 403-6
Jainism, 35, 71, 75, 82, 524, 526
Japan, 26-27
Japanese people, 27
Japheth, 102
Jehovah's Witnesses, 56
Jerusalem, 115, 126, 138, 163-65, 422,
        437, 444, 448-49, 451, 525-26
Jesus Christ, 118-19, 121, 124-26,
        128-31, 133, 136-37, 140, 142,
        144, 149, 152, 166, 414-15,
        419-21, 483-84
Jesus of Nazareth, 129, 149-50, 421
Jewish Bible, 102, 104, 149, 413
Jewish identity, 115, 406
Jewish laws, 34, 104-5
Jewish patriarchs, 56
Jewish tradition, 108, 157
Jews, 10-11, 115, 122-23, 139-40,
        152-53, 164-66, 170, 401-2,
        404-25, 430-32, 437-38, 441-48,
        465-66, 481-86, 524-25
    American, 10, 412, 416, 419
    Ashkenazi, 405, 407-8
    Conservative, 105
    Hassidic, 408
    Israeli, 406
    Karaite, 105
    Mizrahi, 406
    of Morocco, 406
    Reformist, 105
jigsaw puzzle, 58
jihad, 171, 439, 522
Jim Crow laws, 472, 474-75
John, 133, 135-37, 145, 147-48, 533
Johnson, Philip E., 205
Jones, Ernest, 303
Jordan, 108, 442-43, 446-50

Joseph (son of Jacob), 108-9
Josephus, Titus Flavius, 126
Judaism, 17, 35, 90, 92, 94, 103-6, 115,
	125, 155, 158, 164, 186, 405-6,
	422, 433
Judas Didymus Thomas, 121
Judgment Day, 116, 166, 437
Jung, Carl, 285, 297

K

Kaaba, 161, 164, 168, 171
Kabbalah, 109, 116
kami, 26
karma, 78, 80-82, 86, 523
Kibaki, Mwai, 494
King, Martin Luther, Jr., 476
King Sargon, 110
King Solomon, 163, 443
Kirkpatrick, Jeane J., 301
Klein, Melanie, 303
knowledge, 15-16, 18, 20, 26, 30,
	33, 35, 49, 65, 96-97, 177-78,
	277-78, 392, 404, 512-15
  body of, 18
  lack of, 76, 222, 307, 508
  levels of, 186, 269
  sources of, 30
  traditional methods of, 72
Krauss, Lawrence M., 238
Krishna, 38, 60, 72-73, 77-78, 80, 82,
	84-85, 280
Kuwait, 440, 449

L

Lamarck, Jean-Baptiste, 197, 204, 210
language barrier, 508

Latinos, 317, 347, 366, 488
Lebanon, 440, 442, 447, 450
Lemaître, Georges, 246
Lenin, Vladimir Ilyich, 460
leptons, 241, 273
Levites, 114
Levite tribe, 110
Libya, 447, 449
Linnaeus, Carolus, 285
lipids, 41, 63, 67, 200-202, 223
liturgical prescriptions, 105
Lord Jesus Christ, 129-30, 149
Lord of Death, 78
Lord Rama, 76
Lord Shiva, 72
Lot, 106, 108-9, 402
Luke, 127, 137, 141, 146-47, 150, 169,
	526
Lynton, Michael, 418
lysosomes, 61

M

Madison, James, 342
magic dot, 238
magnitude, 16, 56, 196, 309
Mahabharata, 72-73, 76
Mahavira, 82, 84, 526
Mahayana, 84-85, 88, 523
Mahayana Buddhism, 84-85
Malachi, 144
Malcolm X, 476
malicious, 19
mammals, 189, 193-94, 211, 323
manifests, 19, 44-45, 53, 131, 258, 332,
	381, 388
manipulated society, 334
Manu, 72, 180

manufactured culture, 27

Mapping Human History (Olson), 316, 325, 531

Mark, 122, 127, 137, 140-42, 144-47, 526

marriage, 108, 112, 176, 373-74, 377, 383-85, 403

Marx, Karl, 455

Marxist teachings, 27

Mary Magdalene, 121

Matthew, 137-40, 143, 145-47, 150-51, 422, 526

maya, 78

Mayr, Ernst Walter, 197, 316, 326

McMahon, Arthur Henry, 441

Mecca, 154, 161, 163-64, 168, 171, 431-33, 441

mechanism, 53, 198, 205, 219-20, 226, 252, 261, 323, 380, 396, 506, 508

medical education, 13

Medina, 170, 431-33

meditate, 47, 75

meditation, 83-84, 166, 527

Mediterranean, 103, 157, 345, 429, 439-40

Mediterranean basin, 157

Megiddo, 102

meiosis, 65

membranes, 61, 63, 200

Menorah, 116

Mesopotamia, 101, 106, 427-28

Messiah, 34, 92, 118, 120, 126, 129, 136-39, 150, 422, 484

messianic beliefs, 34

metabolize, 43

metaphorical, 98, 115, 135

metaphorically, 64

meteorites, 61, 202

Michelangelo, 54, 419

Middle Awash River, 94

Middle East, 159, 334, 429-30, 439-40

Midianite priests, 111

Midianites, 109, 111-12, 157

Milky Way, 30, 246

millennia, 30, 75, 105, 132, 229, 405

Miller, Stanley, 189

millisecond, 31

Mimamsa, 74

minorities, 287, 332, 347-48, 401, 481, 491

minority groups, 347-48, 469, 482

minuscule, 30

miracles, 20, 35-36, 49, 59, 147, 261, 269, 279-80, 397, 403, 423, 511

miraculously appeared, 238

Miriam, 114

mitochondria, 62, 66

mitochondrial Eve, 325-26

mitosis, 65

mnemonics, 75

Moab, 109

Moabites, 156

moksha, 38, 76, 79, 82, 86, 523

molecules, 59, 61, 189, 220, 239

Monastersky, Richard, 193

money, 80-81, 141-42, 376, 390, 416-17, 419, 442, 463-64, 471, 483-86

monotheism, 117

monotheistic, 91, 150

monotheistic religion, 76, 169

moral codes, 35

Morocco, 406, 449

morphological, 44, 188-89, 196, 198, 204

Moses, 60, 96, 105-6, 108, 110-14, 122, 128, 142, 157, 163, 166, 168, 174, 404, 422

mosques, 35, 397, 466

Mother Book, 161

Mount Hira, 166

Muhammad, 17, 60, 153-54, 158, 160-64, 166-71, 173-76, 180, 431-37, 469, 476, 523-25, 533

Muhammad, Elijah, 469, 476

multifaceted, 72

multiverse, 277

Muraviev, Nikita, 454

Murray, John, 203

Muslim community, 432, 436-37

Muslim faith, 17, 155, 157, 161, 163-64

Muslims, 17, 90, 92-93, 154-55, 157, 159-61, 163-66, 168-71, 175, 423, 425-26, 430-37, 439, 444, 448

mutations, 43, 67, 100, 186, 191, 198, 203-5, 212-13, 219-20, 223, 226-27, 292, 324, 327, 387

myriad, 10, 28, 379

mysterious atoms, 39

mystical, 27, 104, 116, 123, 309, 467

N

Nabateans, 156, 426

Nag Hammadi Library, 121

narration, 20, 95, 110, 170

National Geographic, 187, 254, 342, 533

nations, 102, 131, 139, 151, 332, 401, 405-6, 409-10, 414, 443, 445, 447, 450, 483, 485-86

naturalists, 196-97, 204, 231

natural selection, 53, 56-57, 63-65, 67, 185-87, 197-98, 203-4, 211, 213, 216, 219, 231, 292, 317, 327

nature in an unconventional way, 501

Nazarenes, 128

Nepal, 83

Netherlands, 438, 485

neurotransmitters, 41, 395-96

neutrons, 240-42, 249, 258, 260, 264, 267-68, 271-74

New Economic Policy (NEP), 458-59

New Testament, 16, 103, 120-28, 137, 139-40, 149, 154, 158, 169, 421, 435, 526

Newton, Isaac, 233, 245, 252, 265

Nicene Creed, 125

Nimrod, 101

nirvana, 88

Noah, 100-102, 230

Noble Eightfold Path, 85

nonbelievers, 15, 27, 36, 54, 140, 191, 238, 398

nonfiction, 20

North America, 341, 408, 470, 488, 490

Northern India, 93

North Korea, 334

North Vietnam, 334

nucleotides, 65, 224, 226

nucleus, 61, 65-66, 267-68, 271, 274-75, 333-34, 410

O

Obolensky, Eugene, 454

O'Connor, Sandra Day, 301

official doctrine, 40

—

Old Testament, 16, 103-4, 120, 123, 131, 139, 143-44, 148-51, 421, 469

Olson, Steve, 316, 325

omnipotent, 30, 52, 134, 155, 186, 277

omniscient, 30, 52, 155, 277-78

omnivores, 44

On the Origin of Species (Darwin), 197, 203, 216, 231, 503, 531

opiate, 9, 394

ordinary matter, 240, 243, 250, 257, 259, 272

organelles, 61-62, 200, 224

organisms, 43-45, 53, 62-64, 185, 188-90, 196-202, 204-5, 211, 213-14, 222-23, 225-27, 232, 291-93, 323-24, 326-27

organs, 39, 41, 63-64, 204, 232, 299, 523

Origen, 34

Orthodox Judaism, 105

orthodoxy, 34-35, 123-24

Ottoman Empire, 437, 439-41

Ottoman Turks, 437-40

ovum, 66

Oxford English Dictionary, 26

oxygen, 41, 62-63, 67, 101, 189, 218, 222-23, 272

P

Pahlavi dynasty, 91

Pakistan, 92, 194, 332, 449

Palestine, 115, 427, 438, 440-48, 482, 532

Palestinian Arabs, 165, 437, 441-42, 444-45, 447-48, 450-51

Palestinian Liberation Organization (PLO), 450

Pali collection, 88

pandemic disease, 33

pandemic killer diseases, 28

pangenesis, 197

papyrus scrolls, 103

paradoxically, 11

paranormal activities, 35

paraphernalia, 108

parishioners, 11, 526

Parsis, 93

particle physics, 245, 250, 265, 272-73, 275

particles, 43, 188, 224, 241-45, 253, 257, 260, 267, 271-75, 280

Partition Plan of Palestine, 446

Passion's Logic (Zimmer), 207

pathogens, 202

Paul, Saint, 34, 40, 118, 121, 127-37, 141, 168, 242, 245, 256, 421-22, 429
    vision of, 129

peasants, 458

pebble, 30, 237

pelvic bones, 190-91

Pentateuch, 104-5

pentose, 65, 223

peptide bond, 189

Persia, 90, 92, 173, 175, 429, 431

Pestel, Pavel, 454

Peter the Great, 453

Petra, 156

pharaoh, 107, 109, 111

Pharisees, 105-6, 126, 128-29, 140-42, 144, 146-47, 152

phenomena, 67, 81, 132, 229, 240, 254, 265, 267-68, 280, 332, 379, 513, 523

phenotype, 198, 291-92, 294, 324-25, 327
Philippi, Caesarea, 145
Philo of Alexandria, 126
philosophy, 54, 71, 74-76, 79, 84, 88, 128, 179, 527
Phoenician, 103
photons, 243, 252, 261, 271, 274
physical violence, 508
physics, 15, 29, 60, 228, 239, 241, 246-47, 250, 255, 264-67, 271, 274, 300, 418, 531
Pickthall, Marmaduke, 170
pilgrimage, 161, 164-65, 433
pineal gland, 39
Pinsker, Leon, 445
plague, 112, 414
planets, 18, 28, 30-31, 96, 99-100, 178, 228, 230, 240, 249, 253, 257-59, 263, 267-68, 279-80
Plato, 39
Pliny the Elder, 126
PLOS One, 195
Poland, 332
politics, 171, 302, 411, 424, 428, 435, 458, 460, 463, 475
Polycarp of Smyrna, 123
population, 139, 206, 317, 322-23, 326, 331, 337, 341, 366, 446, 454, 458, 495
Portugal, 339-40, 485, 487-88, 494
Portuguese, 471, 487-88
positrons, 241-45, 260, 271, 274
preacher, 11, 522
prebiotic synthesis, 188
precarious, 16
predators, 180, 207, 210-11, 215, 217, 219, 323, 327, 371

priesthood, 35, 72
primordial earth, 189
primordial soup, 189
Prince Rama, 76
pronouncements, 29
propaganda, 457, 460, 462-63, 496
proteins, 41, 62-63, 66-67, 189, 196, 201-2, 219, 222-25, 324
protists, 61
protons, 222, 226, 240-43, 249, 258, 260, 264, 267-68, 271-74
Ptolemy of Alexandria, 265
punctuated equilibrium, 322
puppets, 33, 461, 466
Putin, Vladimir, 467
pyramids, 157

Q

Qahtan, 156
Qahtani culture, 156
Qahtani tribe, 156
Qedarites, 426, 429
quantum mechanics, 246, 264-65, 274-75
quarks, 241, 245, 261, 271, 273-75
query, 14, 38, 241
Qumran, 125-26
Qur'an, 17, 30, 68, 154, 158, 160-62, 166-67, 169-70, 429, 431-36, 525
Quraysh, 168-71, 431-32

R

rabbinical discourses, 104
rabbis, 104, 106, 130, 406
radiance, 116, 176
Rama, 72, 76

Ramadan, 161
Ramayana, 72, 76
Rebecca, 108, 533
receptors, 41, 43-44, 296, 379-80, 396
reciprocal relationships, 28
recycled, 28
red blood cells, 62-63
redeemer of humanity, 125
reflection, 46, 278, 362, 368, 434
rehabilitated, 48, 313
reincarnated, 28
reincarnation, 46, 77, 79-81, 85
religio, 27
religion, 9-10, 25-28, 35, 71-72, 90, 92,
        155, 158, 170-71, 177-79, 334,
        420, 422-23, 433-36, 489
    role of, 334
religious adherents, 40
religious advocates, 369
remorse, 78, 81, 314
replicates, 65, 202
repressions, 460, 462, 465
reproducible experimentation, 59
respect, 27, 34, 52, 72, 84, 88, 92,
        98, 112, 123, 136, 158-59, 164,
        424-25, 508
resurrection, 40
Revelation of Saint John, 135
revelations, 60, 105, 121, 128, 135,
        154, 158, 161-63, 167-69, 177,
        179
ribonucleic acid (RNA), 188, 196,
        223-25, 324
rigorous, 17, 25, 65, 82, 120, 128, 130,
        160, 217, 220, 232, 505
Rise of Islam, The (Haeri), 158
Rishabhadeva, 82
rishis, 76

ritual purification, 126
rituals, 75, 84, 92, 114, 117, 126, 422
River Nile, 110
Roman Empire, 115, 128, 145, 171,
        405, 429, 431
Roman military machine, 115
Romanov, Tsar Peter. *See* Peter the
        Great
Romans, 106, 127, 129-32, 165, 441,
        443
ruminating, 37
Rushton, Philippe, 408
Russia, 389, 406, 440, 452-56, 460-62,
        465, 467
Russians, 419, 452-53, 461, 466

S

Sabbath, 140
sacred container, 163
sacred cow, 72
Sadducees, 105-6, 126, 136, 140, 152
sages, 16, 76, 100, 103, 110, 116, 163
Sal tree, 82
Sama Veda, 75
Samhitas, 75
Samkhya, 74
Samyaksambuddha, 84
Sanatana Dharma, 71
Sanhedrin, 116, 128, 136, 140
Sanskrit hymns, 38
Saudi Arabia, 447, 449
Saul of Tarsus, 127-28, 421
schism, 35, 135, 436
schizophrenia, 350
scholars, 71, 86, 90, 92, 104, 115, 122,
        127-28, 130, 141, 158-59, 164,
        448

Schopf, J. William, 61

science, 18, 36-37, 47, 50, 58, 60, 81,
    154, 177, 179, 189, 193, 206,
    212, 529-31

Science, 187

scientists, 48-50, 60-61, 64-68, 188-89,
    193-96, 211-12, 215, 237-44,
    247, 249, 253, 260-62, 277-78,
    280-81, 299-300

Scientologists, 60

scriptural record, 27

scriptures, 29, 33, 60, 72, 75, 87, 91,
    103-4, 117, 139, 281, 529

scroll, 103, 125-26

Second Temple, 106, 127, 164, 404

sectarian, 17, 103-4, 106, 115, 119

secular, 35, 40, 435-36

seers, 76, 114

Segev, Tom, 442

selected genes, 43

Selection in Relation to Sex (Darwin),
    203

self-deprecation, 508

self-projected importance, 508

sentient, 45, 90, 180-81, 278

sermon, 46, 56, 112, 150, 510, 514

seventh heaven, 163

sex, 199, 207-8, 311-12, 379-82, 390
    evolution of, 199, 209

sexual activity, 373, 381-82

sexuality, 312, 353, 379, 381

sexual reproduction, 66, 198, 200

Shem, 102

Shepherd of Hermas, 121

Shias, 156, 160-62

Shinar, 101

Shinto, 26, 35, 525

Shiva, 72, 76

Siddhartha. *See* Buddha

Sikhism, 35, 90

Sinai, Mount, 105, 112, 114, 404, 520

singularity, 248-50, 255, 262-63

sins, 40, 79, 81, 96, 98, 113, 115, 125,
    131-32, 138, 140, 142-43, 148,
    151-53, 483-84

Sistine Chapel, 54

slackening, 31

"Slaughter of the Innocents," 139

slavery, 109-10, 432, 468-73, 483, 496
    in Egypt, 110, 469, 483

slaves, 33, 109, 343, 374, 454, 468,
    470-72, 488, 493, 497, 521

socialism, 141, 455

society, 56, 212, 331, 339, 358-59, 368,
    371, 454, 503, 530

Soloviev, Vladimir, 378

Son of God, 34, 119, 130-31, 136-37,
    146-49, 152, 421

soul, 28-29, 38-40, 42-46, 48, 73-74,
    77-82, 85, 88-89, 91-92, 113,
    125, 177, 180, 280, 377

Soviets, 456, 462

Soviet Union, 13, 444, 449, 457, 525

Spain, 339-40, 405, 416, 485, 487, 490

specialized living organisms, 63

spermatozoa, 66

spermatozoon, 66-67

Spielberg, Stephen, 418

spirits, 38

Spiritual Assemblies, 178

spiritualism, 35, 279, 473, 525

spiritual way, 31

sponged skeleton, 56

Stalin, Josef, 457

Stanford Linear Accelerator Center
    (SLAC), 244

stars, 260, 271
Stein, Joel, 419
Steinschneider, Moritz, 414
stemming, 32, 494
Stephen, martyred, 129
subatomic particles, 59, 251-52, 267, 272, 274-75
subconscious dissatisfaction, 508
subcultures, 74
subspecies, 196, 198, 206
succinctly, 14, 45, 76, 199, 292, 301
Sufi schools, 163
Sumerians, 101-2, 279, 427, 430
sun, 30, 72, 95, 215, 228, 230, 265, 267-68, 273, 280, 293, 385, 481, 502, 510
Sunnis, 156, 161-62, 175
supernatural, 88
superstition, 35, 519
Supreme Reality, 88
Supreme Spirit, 17, 76
supreme Unknown, 27
Sutcliffe, Peter, 55
symmetrical body, 97
Synagogue of the Freedmen, 128
synagogues, 10, 35, 128, 144, 150, 164, 397, 525
synapses, 41, 43-44
Syria, 427-29, 440, 443, 447-50

T

Tabernacle, 138, 177
Talmud, 104-6
Tanakh, 104, 111, 116, 120
Taoism, 35
Teacher of Righteousness, 126
telepathic ability, 36

televangelists, 11
Temple Mount, 163-64, 448
Temple of the Lord, 165
temples, 101, 157, 466
Ten Commandments, 105, 114, 142, 163, 520
tenets, 90, 103, 162, 180
Thailand, 84, 207
in their majority, 53, 346, 491
these topics demand, 51
thirteen years, 13
thirty-three years, 13
thoracic skeleton, 97
thymine, 65, 226, 324
tiny gods, 28
Tipler, Frank J., 256
Titus (general), 164
Tolstoy, Leo, 414
tombs, 157
Torah, 104-6, 108, 131, 134, 138, 159, 169, 401
Tower of Babylon, 102
transactions, 10
transcendent, 116, 434
transcendent spiritual world, 116
transcribe, 202
transcription, 200
transformed, 26, 42, 119, 136, 144, 188, 190, 243, 251, 319, 379, 426
transient, 74, 360
transitional forms, 185, 188, 193-95, 199, 205-7, 211, 232
translate, 42, 71, 110, 115, 122-24, 135, 158-59, 162, 200, 202, 375, 378, 414, 426
translations, 122, 124, 162, 200, 375, 378
transmembrane, 63

transmigrates, 73
transmigration, 78-79, 85, 526
transmutation of species, 204
tree of the knowledge of good and evil, 96, 404
Trubetskoy, Sergey, 454
truth, 19, 29, 51, 68, 72-73, 76, 84-85, 130-31, 148, 166, 177, 179, 187, 192, 461
Tsien, Joe Z., 296
twelfth imam, 175, 437
twenty-five years, 13

U

Umayyad Muslims, 93
Unidentified Massive Objects (UMOBs), 257-61
Union of Soviet Socialist Republics. *See* USSR
United Kingdom. *See* Britain
United Nations (UN), 443, 446-47, 449-50, 463
United States of America, 31, 294, 298, 338-47, 366-67, 369, 408, 411, 416-17, 419, 463, 470, 472, 474, 487-88
Universal House of Justice, 178
universe, 38, 238, 255, 262, 272, 530, 533
inflationary, 250-51, 530
A Universe from Nothing (Krauss), 238
University of California, Los Angeles (UCLA), 61
unusually short, 501
Upanishads, 75, 527, 532
Ur, 102, 106-7, 402
Urban II (pope), 165

Urey, Harold, 189
Uthman, 160-61

V

vacuum, 251-52, 398
false, 250-51
true, 250-51
vague, 15, 18, 28, 116, 190, 371, 429
vastness, 30, 240, 248, 280
Vedangas, 75
Vedanta, 75, 527
Vedantic Hinduism, 84
Vedas, 68, 71, 75-76, 78-79, 84, 117, 524
Vedic sacrificial rituals, 75
Vedic Sanskrit corpus, 75
veered, 19
versatile, 17, 48, 205
vessels, 62, 439
vestigial, 39, 190, 212
vestigial legs, 191
Vietnam, 207, 332, 334
Vignaud, Patrick, 94
vigor, 36, 67, 502, 514
vikarma, 80
violence, 214, 388, 390, 392, 444, 446-47, 467, 479, 492, 506
Vishnu, 76, 82

W

Watchtower, 56-57
Watson, James, 49
Watt, William Montgomery, 170
wealth, 141, 180, 337
Wegener, Alfred, 229
Weizmann, Chaim Azriel, 441, 445

West Bank, 125, 442, 448-50
whales, 190-92, 194-95, 532
What Evolution Is (Mayr), 316
White, Michael, 194
White, Tim, 94, 212
whites, 296, 347-48, 468-69, 474,
    476-77, 481-82, 486, 489, 496
Why is this happening? 346
Williams, George C., 292
willpower, 306, 394
World War I, 455-56
World War II, 344, 461-62
wormhole, 255, 260-61, 275
wrathful god, 123

Z

Zacharias, 146
Zarathustra, 39, 91
Zen Buddhism, 84, 86, 527
Zhao, Hong Sheng, 254
ziggurats, 101
Zilpah, 109
Zimmer, Carl, 187, 207, 530
Zionists, 443, 445, 448
Zoroaster, 39, 91-92, 174, 180
Zoroastrianism, 35, 71, 90-92, 115
Zoroastrians, 17, 90, 92
Zurvanism, 91

Y

Yahya, Mirza, 175
Yajur Veda, 75
Yemen, 430, 447
Yoga, 76-77
Yogic philosophy, 76
yogis, 75
Yorkshire Ripper, 55

Edwards Brothers Malloy
Ann Arbor MI. USA
August 3, 2017